Understanding Reading Problems

Understanding Reading Problems
Assessment and Instruction

Jean Wallace Gillet
University of Virginia

Charles Temple
University of Houston — Victoria Campus

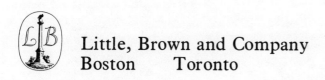

Little, Brown and Company
Boston   Toronto

Library of Congress Catalog Card No. 81-82649

ISBN 0-316-313521

9 8 7 6 5 4 3 2 1

MV

Published simultaneously in Canada
by Little, Brown & Company (Canada) Limited
Printed in the United States of America

Acknowledgments

The authors gratefully acknowledge permission to use excerpts from the following works:

Bellugi-Klima, Ursula. Modified from "Some Language Comprehension Tests," in Celia S. Lavatelli, ed., *Language Training in Early Childhood.* © 1971 by The Board of Trustees of the University of Illinois. Reprinted by permission.

Ekwall, Eldon. *Diagnosis and Remediation of the Disabled Reader*, pp. 226–227. Copyright © 1976 by Allyn and Bacon, Inc. Reprinted by permission.

McConaughy, Stephanie H. "Using Story Structure in the Classroom," *Language Arts,* Vol. 57, no. 2 (February 1980), p. 158. Reprinted by permission.

Preface

Understanding Reading Problems: Assessment and Instruction is intended as a primary text for preservice and in-service teachers in reading diagnosis and diagnostic-prescriptive reading courses. Moreover, it can be used as a guide or reference book for those who have already completed such a course and who are now working with children. Our purpose is to help teachers develop diagnostic insights and strategies so they can better meet their students' needs in reading.

Helping students become competent, effective readers is one of the challenges facing teachers. In addition to knowing how to use commercial reading programs and administer standardized tests, today's teachers must understand how reading skills normally develop and how reading problems can occur. They must also be able to carry out their own diagnostic procedures in the classroom, determine students' strengths and needs, and implement corrective instruction while maintaining responsibility for ongoing instruction and evaluation. To do this, teachers need diagnostic strategies and devices that yield qualitative information about students' reading performance and can be used during regular teaching activities. They need diagnostic tools that are flexible and practical, tapping the kinds of everyday reading tasks students must accomplish in and out of school. Such strategies and devices are the heart of this book.

Diagnosis is not the result of giving tests or compiling test scores. Rather, it is a kind of detective work requiring insight, imagination, and judgment. Since one cannot use a cookbook to develop these skills, this book presents no recipes for diagnosis. We have offered many suggestions, ideas and models, but no step-by-step formula. While conceptualizing and writing this book, we have proceeded from our belief that understanding why is as important as knowing how. Theory and practice are woven together as are diagnostic implications and suggestions for corrective instruction.

This book not only examines traditional topics, but also features in-depth discussions of a number of topics that are often treated superficially or omitted from reading diagnosis texts. In Chapter One we describe the reading process from a primarily psycholinguistic perspective and outline important principles of diagnosis. In Chapter Two we detail prereading competencies and concepts

v

which are prerequisite to learning to read, regardless of the learner's age. Chapter Three is devoted to the assessment of these prereading competencies, including suggestions for developing them at home and school. In Chapter Four we describe and model informal procedures for assessing students' abilities after they have learned to read, including assessment of word recognition, word analysis, reading comprehension, and listening comprehension. Chapter Five extends these discussions with the use of non-test procedures that are primarily instructional but that yield important diagnostic information at the same time. The development of spelling ability and the teaching of spelling are the topics of Chapter Six. In Chapter Seven we describe methods of reading assessment and instruction in both elementary and secondary content areas. Chapter Eight describes formal measures of assessment, including test and measurement concepts, descriptive statistics, and generic types of norm-referenced and criterion-referenced reading tests. In Chapter Nine we deal with topics related to reading: intellectual, physical, and emotional factors including intelligence, learning disabilities, vision and hearing problems, self-concept, and attitudes about reading. In Chapter Ten we describe the assessment of the classroom and school as environments for reading growth and present strategies for improving their effectiveness.

Several features have been included as aids in using the text. One is the inclusion of case studies in several chapters. These case studies feature a "wraparound" format. At the beginning of the chapter children are introduced and their day-to-day reading described. The body of the chapter details the assessment procedures, and the chapter closes with an extended description of how the procedures were implemented with the children and how the results were used to provide corrective instruction.

Additional features include extension activities, suggested readings, and illustrations. Each chapter is accompanied by extension activities that can be used as projects by both preservice and in-service teachers to practice using new procedures, create assessment materials, and develop diagnostic decision-making skills. Annotated suggested reading lists provide direction for teachers interested in further reading and study. Illustrations and photographs are used to show particular methods and materials in actual use.

This book could not have been written and produced without the help and encouragement of many people. We cannot name them all, but we wish to thank our students and colleagues at the University of Virginia and the University of Houston-Victoria Campus who read and critiqued our material and tried out ideas, and our friends at other universities who encouraged us and offered their suggestions. We also wish to acknowledge those who taught us and helped us grow professionally, especially Edmund Henderson, Tom Estes, Ronald Cramer, and Dorsey Hammond.

We also thank Mylan Jaixen and the staff of Little, Brown and our reviewers: Donald O'Brien, State University College at Buffalo; Leo D. Geoffrion,

State University of New York at Albany; Zelda R. Maggart, University of New Mexico; Janell Klesius, University of South Florida; Gary Anderson, Arizona State University; and David W. Moore, The University of Connecticut. We are especially grateful to Helen Collier and Brenda Kelley for their careful typing of our manuscript, and to our families for their patience, humor, and understanding.

Brief Contents

Contents

Chapter One

Introduction to Reading Diagnosis

The Reading Process

There are many methods used to teach children to read: basal reader approaches, phonics, language experience, whole-word, linguistic methods, and others that are explained in any reading methods textbook. Although there are considerable differences among them, virtually all reading instruction methods work with most students, provided the method used is applied consistently and it is expected that the child will learn to read.

By the same token, none of the reading methods will work well with some students. Even those methods that are specifically designed to teach poor readers will not help unless they are adapted to the child's specific needs.

How to deal effectively with those children who do not profit readily from the instructional methods that work with the majority of children is not a simple topic. Poor readers read poorly for many different reasons, and a different procedure may be required for each child. The task of reading assessment or diagnosis is to find out what a given child can do or can do only with difficulty, as well as what that child cannot yet do. The task of correction is to teach the child appropriately. Both assessment and instruction are the main topics of this book.

What is reading? We asked children, some young, some older, that question and here is what we heard:

> Something older people do all the time. It's very important. It's good for spelling and homework. I like the stories reading tells. (four-and-one-half-year-old prereader)

> Looking at the pictures and telling a story about them. (five-year-old prereader)

> Saying the words — all kinds of words in a book. (six-year-old prereader)

> Looking at words and saying them, especially the words I don't know. Some words, I just look at them and I know them. (eighteen-year-old remedial reader)

> Listening to the letters say their sounds. (six-year-old beginning reader)

> Looking at words someone has written down and understanding what he means. (fifteen-year-old developmental reader)

> It's like figuring out words and sentences and stuff, figuring out what they say. (ten-year-old developmental reader)

> Getting the letters. (four-year-old prereader)

It is interesting how often the younger children claim that they use the sounds of the letters to sound out the words. Learning letter sounds and sounding out are perhaps the most conscious reading activities beginners perform, but it would be wrong to conclude that they are the only activities necessary in order to read. When we observe beginning readers, we often see them become quite skillful at sounding out, demonstrating a surprising amount of knowledge of how letters sound, before they can read a sentence. Then suddenly something happens. There is a click, a light, an "aha!" when they discover how to integrate what they know about letter sounds into words that mean something. Reading becomes a unified act of getting meaning from print.

It is also interesting to note how many older poor readers are still good at sounding, still steeped in letter-to-sound correspondence rules, and still unable to read sentences with confidence. Clearly, knowing the letters and their sounds is not all there is to reading, as often as we may hear that suggestion in one form or another.

Reading and Perception

What more there is to reading has been revealed in a number of experiments throughout this century. Before the turn of the century, Erdman and Dodge, in an experiment reported by Huey (1908/1968), investigated what the eyes do in reading. They noted that as their subjects' eyes traversed a line of print they made little jumps (called *saccades*) and pauses (called *fixations*). Erdman and Dodge demonstrated this by means of a procedure in which light-weight styluses were attached to their subjects' eyeballs and a small electric charge fired through these styluses at rapid, timed intervals. When the styluses were directed against a piece of smoked glass they made a record of the direction and rate of eye movements across a page. You can get an impression of what they found, however, simply by closely observing the eye movements of someone who is reading.

Further experiments demonstrated that it is during the fixation that visual information is taken in; during the saccade the eyes register nothing. You can demonstrate this to yourself in this way: Make a small circle with your thumb and fingers, close one eye, and look through the circle with the other eye so as to restrict your field of vision. Now as you sight though the circle of your fingers, move a page back and forth across your field of vision and try to read it. Why does this result in a blur, when normal eye movement in reading gives us no blurring and little sensation of motion? The answer is that in reading we only have the sensation of seeing during the fixations, when the eyes are stationary. When the eyes move during a saccade, the brain ignores the blur.

Why the brain ignores the motion touches on a basic process of perception. In visual perception, that is, when we see things and are aware that we have seen them, it is as if our eye-brain system sees a series of individual pictures rather than one continuous picture. More specifically, during an act of perception the eyes take in information for about 50 milliseconds (a millisecond, abbreviated *msec.*, is one one-thousandth of a second). After this the eye

*E*very reader approaches reading for different purposes and with different ideas of what it is about. Readers bring to reading the sum of all their prior experiences and expectations about print.

ceases to take in more information, and what was taken in during the first 50 msec. is conveyed to a temporary storage capacity called short-term memory. From there it is either transferred into long-term memory (this seems to happen if some use is found for the information or if it is rehearsed) or it is forgotten within seconds. The process of analyzing the information in short-term memory and sorting it out takes an additional 200 msec. During this time the eyes are effectively blind, although we have the illusion of seeing whatever we saw when the eye was fixating. In fact, in experiments where new images were flashed before subjects who had just fixated on a previous set, the subjects were not aware of the new images.

All human beings can make about four fixations per second: 50 msec. of visual intake, and 200 msec. of processing the intake. All human beings are subject to another basic limitation, too. During the intake, they can attend to only five to seven items, give or take a couple (Smith, 1978, 1979).

To understand what we mean, consider the items in Figure 1.1.

We sometimes perform a demonstration with an overhead projector in which we flash these items briefly on a screen, one line at a time. We ask our students to write down as much as they can remember after each line has been flashed. They can usually remember four to six of the squiggles in the first line, four to six letters from the second line, most of the letters in the nonsense word in line three, all of the letters in the real word, four to six words from the line of random words, and most of the words from the sentence.

In each case, the limit of about five to seven items per fixation is in force, but from line to line the nature of the items changes. The first line contains squiggles that are not immediately recognizable. But in the second line the same squiggles occur, only this time they are combined to form letters. Hence in line one the students might remember five squiggles, and in line two, five letters. By recalling five letters, however, the student has recalled perhaps ten to twelve squiggles. Similarly, in recalling the nonsense word *larmorkle*, as many as nine letters are recalled. In recalling a meaningful sentence many more than five words may be remembered.

FIGURE 1.1. Visual arrays.

1. ⟋ɔᶜ⟍⟍⎮ ⁷⊥ ᴸ⟋ ᶜ⎮ᴸ⟍⎮
2. pnsrvntcb
3. larmorkle
4. Washington
5. cranked squirm call rash sugar do
6. the boy was hungry because he hadn't eaten

Thus we see that this limitation of five to seven items per fixation is a variable one. An item may be a single unit or a group of several other units that have been combined in some meaningful way. Meaningfully combining units in perception is referred to as *chunking* (Smith, 1978).

Chunking enables perceivers to take bigger "bites" when they make a fixation. Whether or not chunking occurs depends as much on the perceiver as it does on what is perceived. In Figure 1.1, if line 1 were parts of Chinese or Sanskrit characters and line 2 the complete characters, few of us could recall more marks from line 2 than from line 1. This is because few of us are familiar with these characters. However, when the squiggles and letters are familiar elements of our alphabet or other familiar marks, they are more easily recalled. Similarly, in Figure 1.1 we needed a sense of English word formation patterns to recall more letters when they were presented in the nonsense word than when they appeared individually. We needed to know how words are ordered in sentences to remember more words from the sentence than from the unrelated string of words. In every case the basis for chunking, the meaningful relation between the items, existed in the display. But there also had to be corresponding knowledge in the mind of the perceiver before the relation could be exploited and chunking could occur. Thus we can see why it is often said that perception is a thoughtful act. We don't perceive first, then think. Either we perceive and think at the same time, or we perceive much less.

Given the nature of our faculties of perception, we can read letter by letter, word by word, phrase by phrase, or perhaps in even larger units. But the rate at which we perceive is fixed, so if we read letter by letter we will cover far less text in a given amount of time than if we read by larger units. In fact, if we read letter by letter or even word by word our progress will be so slow that we will have difficulty remembering what was said at the beginning of a paragraph by the time we reach the end of it.

Efficient readers chunk together many words at a time and thereby take in far more information with each fixation. In order to accomplish this, they bring prior knowledge to the reading encounter and actively use it. They use the grammar or syntax of the sentence to relate words together and the meaning of the text to relate groups of words meaningfully. They even use the structure of the text, whether it is written in a story format, as a sequence of events, or as comparison and contrast, to take in more information and read more efficiently.

Reading and Prediction

Not all of this efficiency can be explained by chunking alone. Efficient readers also use the strategy of *predicting* the words and ideas that will follow what they have already read. Instead of reading word by word, readers who predict form a hypothesis about what the text is likely to say in the next few words or sentences, and then read on to see if their predictions are correct. If the predictions are confirmed they make more hypotheses and proceed. If their hypotheses are not confirmed they read more carefully to see what the author does say, perhaps modify the thrust of their predicting in light of this new information, and then proceed.

All efficient readers predict, though not all may be conscious of doing so. Goodman (1967, 1969) has shown that predicting strategies may be detected by analyzing a reader's oral miscues, or oral reading divergences from the written text. He has pointed out that even good readers routinely make word substitutions as they read, substitutions that do not violate the meaning of what they are reading. Nearly 80 years ago Huey wrote,

> It is not indeed necessary that the child should be able to pronounce correctly or pronounce at all, at first, the new words that appear in his reading. . . . If he grasps, approximately, the total meaning of the sentence in which the new word stands, he has read the sentence. . . . And even if the child substitutes words of his own for some that are on the page, provided that they express the meaning, it is an encouraging sign that the reading has been real, and recognition of details will come as needed. (1908/1968, pp. 348–349)

Readers make predictions using the same bases as they use in chunking: grammatical cues, meaning cues, and the structure of the text. Readers who fail to predict usually rely heavily on letter-to-sound patterns or phonics to help them identify words.

By allowing readers to read faster, predicting and chunking are important to comprehension. Comprehension requires relating new information to old information already in our heads and implies several things about what we should do when we read. First, we should have some background knowledge that pertains to whatever we read about. Second, we should actively relate what we read to what we already know. Readers use their knowledge of grammar, of the topic, of text structure, and related prior knowledge to chunk and to predict, as described above. As readers chunk text in the course of perceiving it and make predictions in the course of reading it, they are comprehending.

Readers vary in the extent to which they chunk and predict, and they use different bases, favoring different sorts of information, in chunking and predicting. Those who do too little of either become enmeshed in letters and sounds and read slowly and uncomprehendingly.

Such differences have inspired some researchers to speak of two basic processes that may occur with different emphasis during an act of reading. The two processes, intake of visual information from the page (the perception of letters, words and punctuation) and the use of prior information (bringing knowledge of sentence structure or grammar, knowledge of the topic, and knowledge of the structures in which writing is typically organized), are both important to successful reading. As those who teach young children know, the recognition of alphabet letters and of written words represent important milestones in children's learning. But it is also important for children to be freed-up from the page, to trust in their abilities to take in more text at a glance, to predict what follows, and to make sense of it.

In the task of getting meaning from print, individual children develop different strategies and approaches to both processes. As we shall see, how they develop these strategies probably depends as much upon their own powers of discovery as it does on the method by which they are taught. Hence, even within the same classroom individual children do very different things as they read. Most of them are successful eventually; but some are not, and the job of the teacher is then to find out what each nonproductive reader is doing, what strategies he or she is using, and to direct the child toward a path that leads to efficient reading. The remainder of this text will provide information and assessment and teaching strategies to help accomplish this.

Principles of Diagnosis

The range of techniques available for reading assessment is wide. While we have attempted to be comprehensive in our coverage of them, we have nevertheless proceeded from certain assumptions and beliefs about how assessment should be approached.

1. Diagnosis is more than a testing and measuring process. Testing is a contrived activity. Children respond differently in testing than in their other school work. Measurement assumes that there are arbitrary standards for performance in whatever is being measured. Placing a child in an inherently artificial learning situation and applying arbitrary standards to the performance yield a very restricted view of the child's behavior.

Diagnosis is a process of *becoming informed* about a child. This requires that we observe the child's responses and behavior in the course of natural everyday learning. We have to keep an open mind while observing so that we can be aware of and respond to unexpected behaviors and insights.

Any hypotheses made about a child should remain tentative until they are tested during actual instruction. Becoming informed means that we must reserve judgment until we have seen the student exhibit the same types of behavior in a number of instances rather than forming judgments on the limited sample of behavior that tests represent.

To assume that "diagnosis equals testing" implies that instruments can be selected that will provide answers to our questions on the basis of the test results. This is a very narrow view. We believe that diagnosis is a process requiring decision-making by people, not instruments. It requires gathering many types of information, synthesizing this information, and creating informed hypotheses. Tests of certain kinds can provide some data for analysis, but the analysis and synthesis must be done by the human mind. Ransom (1978) wrote, "Measurement gives us numbers, but human judgment and interpretation turn those numbers into evaluations" (p. 152). In our view, diagnosis is more a process of judgment and interpretation than of deriving numbers, and this book reflects that belief.

2. *No single set of diagnostic procedures or tools can be used in every case.* If diagnosis is viewed as a process of becoming informed about a child's reading, no single set of procedures would be sufficient unless: (a) all children learned in the same ways; (b) all children read by applying the same strategies; (c) all children read under the same conditions or for the same purposes; and (d) all teachers shared the same standards, biases, and teaching experiences. None of these four conditions is ever the case.

We know of practitioners who have a "kit bag" of tests they give every pupil they diagnose. Every time they test, such examiners analyze these same aspects of reading — but no other aspects. In effect, they ask the same questions in every case. Not surprisingly, they tend to come up with the same types of answers every time, and diagnosis then becomes the systematic compilation of largely the same data in every instance. This, of course, makes diagnosis a fairly simple process: ask these predetermined questions, get these answers, and form these judgments. After a while, the process can almost be done by rote.

If one were trying to figure out what was wrong with a set of mechanical devices, each the same as the other, this process would work; but students and diagnosticians are not like clocks or car engines. A nearly infinite set of variables is at work in each case, for each person is unique. Therefore, no single set of procedures or criteria is sufficient to analyze every individual.

This does not mean that there are no procedures or criteria that we can depend on for reliable information. If that were so, diagnosis textbooks would not be written. The point is that although procedures for diagnosis may not be infinitely variable, they certainly cannot be neatly set forth and adhered to in a set formula. The process of diagnosis must always be flexible, and practitioners must be able to apply different strategies "on the fly." In this book we have not only described many procedures that will help you gather information in most cases but also have supplemented these basic strategies with suggestions for additional strategies that may be helpful in other cases. This is not always a neat, precise process, and our task would certainly have been easier if we could have set forth step-by-step procedures in a "manual" format. Diagnosing children's reading, however, is not like diagnosing broken clocks, and we are glad for that because we like working with children better than clocks.

3. *Diagnosis means looking for strengths and competence as well as needs and difficulties.* Many diagnosticians use their assessment procedures to determine

all the things a student cannot do or does incorrectly. Remediation, then, becomes a "repair job," fixing up all those weaknesses and errors.

When viewed in this way, diagnosis is a dismally *negative* process. It is negative for the reader, who is faced with task after task ending in failure. Such testing soon reaches the point where the student can no longer continue to work because the procedures dwell only on errors and weaknesses. No wonder many students who have been tested once have a fear of going through it again. The examiner is also affected negatively. Faced with a growing list of the things a student cannot do or does poorly, the examiner develops a view that is sharply skewed toward failure, and if the reading problem is a serious one, the teacher may feel overwhelmed by all the myriad weaknesses brought to light. Both student and examiner are left with the bitter taste of failure.

Diagnosis must be as much a process of locating *strengths* as of detailing weaknesses. It is only by knowing what the student already can do that we can begin to know how to attack the weaknesses instructionally. By learning what the child's strengths are, we can base remedial instruction on success rather than on failure. We can build instruction on the solid foundation of already acquired skills rather than on the sand of those yet to be mastered.

By looking first for strengths, then for problems, we can also make the diagnostic process a more positive one for everyone involved. When students are shown what they have done well, they approach other aspects of assessment with enthusiasm and persistence instead of fear and avoidance. The teacher, too, develops a picture of the student as a person who can do some things well and some things poorly, a more balanced and realistic view of the learner than that yielded by listing weaknesses alone. Those responsible for carrying out the remediation are also aided by knowing the areas of strength from which to teach, and they are reassured by knowing that the student is a person with recognized *abilities* as well as *disabilities*.

This tenet also implies that not all reading problems lie within the learner. Aspects of home and school life beyond the student's control can impinge on the ability to read. These must be explored as rigorously as those aspects of the student's reading that are more easily assessed. Unfortunately, classroom instruction and background influences are often ignored in diagnosis, yet the student exists as a reader within both spheres.

In this book we have attempted to show teachers how to look systematically for areas of strength and competence and to approach remediation as a way of building on these positive aspects. We have also included assessment of ways in which the home and school influence the student's reading, such as language development, experiential background, development of attitudes toward reading, and the profound influence of instructional programs. We have included an entire chapter on assessing classroom and school environments and their impact on reading success. We have done so because students do not learn to read, or fail to do so, in a vacuum. Diagnosis of the "whole child" means examining the reading environment as well as the reader.

4. *Diagnosis should result in instructional change rather than solely in the classification of disabilities.* To have value, diagnosis should result in more than labeling or categorizing of problems. To know a problem is not to solve it. Diagnosis must point the way for instructional change and, through instructional change, to progress in learning. Diagnosis that results in labeling rather than in concrete direction for instruction is merely an academic exercise as well as a waste of time and resources.

Many teachers have experienced the frustration of requesting special testing for a student, waiting patiently for the results, and finally receiving a report that merely places the student in some category of disability. We have personally read numerous diagnostic reports from different sources that simply label the child's disability. Terms like "dyslexic," "learning disabled," "emotionally disabled," "culturally disadvantaged," "perceptually or neurologically impaired," "reading-retarded," and "motivationally dysfuctional" buzz around like flies at a picnic. All serve only to categorize the student, all imply specific meanings when few actually exist, and none serve to point the way for better instruction. Pedagogically they do little if any good and many even scare off the teacher because they imply grave disabilities or disturbances that the average teacher may feel unequipped to handle. Such labels have the same negative effect as the detailing of weaknesses described in the previous section. They can effectively hinder, rather than promote, the process of corrective teaching.

Unfortunately more time is often spent delving into the students' history for the precise cause of a disability than is spent determining what their present functioning levels are. Searching a child's past can be fruitful if it induces a present-day change that will help overcome the problem. Sometimes, however, nothing can be done to mitigate the effect of past events. Although factors such as a head injury, childhood illness, or frequent changing of schools may be interesting to uncover, they do nothing to determine where we should go today. Causative factors are often heralded as though they had some intrinsic value, but since we cannot undo the past, such findings are helpful only if they point the way to present-day change.

It is sometimes assumed that diagnosis results in final answers. This assumption could be true if children developed to some point and never changed thereafter, but teachers know that students of every age change and grow daily. Diagnosis, therefore, is a *continuous* process of asking, Where is the student *today* in his or her development, and where should we go at this time? There is no final answer to this question, for tomorrow each student will be different than today. Diagnosis can never be a once-and-for-all event.

5. *Informal procedures and instruments can be the most useful source of infor-*

mation about the student's reading. Standardized tests are administered under controlled conditions and yield numerical results that allow comparison of one pupil or group to others. These devices are widely used to assess achievement and to diagnose difficulties. They are adequate for the former purpose but have relatively little diagnostic usefulness. Numerical scores do not yield specific information about what the student can or cannot do. Test reading is not like reading for information or pleasure in the classroom or at home. It is usually the reading of single sentences or short passages under timed conditions and constructed so as to test the recall of information rather than to inform or arouse interest. A student's reading tastes, interests, and purposes are relatively unimportant in test situations, although they are of great importance instructionally.

In contrast, informal assessment devices and procedures more closely resemble natural reading in the classroom and outside of school. Informal assessment means observing the student reading meaningful material for a variety of purposes and takes place during regular instruction or in an assessment setting that simulates the instructional environment. The informal approach to diagnosis looks at reading behaviors *qualitatively* rather than only *quantitatively*. Informal procedures are basically exploratory in nature since they allow the examiner to determine what a reader does and does not do during reading based on an in-depth, personal perspective. In informal diagnosis we are more concerned with determining what readers do during natural reading than in how their reading compares with someone else's reading. The rationale for this is our belief that in order to provide more effective instruction it is necessary to know with some precision what the individual can and cannot do in reading.

We have a definite bias in favor of informal assessment because we have found that such procedures yield the most useful information for direct teaching applications. Moreover, these procedures can be carried out during regular teaching activities with groups of students as well as with individual students. Other informal assessment procedures, even though they are more "testlike," also make use of typical classroom reading materials and simulate everyday reading and writing tasks. All such devices and procedures consider the whole child as he or she operates within the instructional setting. We prefer these means of assessment to more traditional standardized tests because they help us form a more realistic, accurate view of the way the reader functions.

In this book we have demonstrated how informal measures can be developed and used in the regular classroom as supplements to, or even in place of, standardized reading measures. We have consistently attempted to relate diagnostic findings to corrective teaching procedures and to illustrate the use of such methods in our case studies and examples. We are also aware, however, that standardized testing is a fact of life in every classroom, and we have analyzed and described the major types of norm-referenced and criterion-referenced tests in a separate chapter. We hope that as a result teachers will be able to make qualitative judgments about students' reading by using informal classroom methods and that they will be able to evaluate and interpret more clearly the standardized measures they use.

We have placed the focus of diagnostic and corrective efforts within the regular classroom because we firmly believe that the teacher, not the outside specialist, has the greatest need for diagnostic information and data. Diagnosis of reading problems has often been invested with a false sense of mystery and complexity, which serves only to make teachers feel uncertain and ill-prepared. This need not be the case. The person with the fullest and clearest perception of the students is the one who works with them daily, not the specially trained expert who comes in to do the testing. In the final analysis it is the teacher, not the specialist, who will be responsible for the student's instruction. Diagnosis and corrective teaching are inextricably related, and both should be done within the regular classroom with the active involvement of the regular teacher.

Summary

There are many approaches to teaching reading and to diagnosing the problems of poor readers. Most instructional methods work well with most children, but none is successful with all. Both diagnosis and instruction require an understanding of the reading process.

One general description of reading is that it is the sum of a number of discrete subskills learned and used automatically. Without attention to thinking and knowing, such a definition is incomplete. Visual perception studies have shown that the amount of information perceived in a single fixation depends largely on the perceiver's familiarity with the visual array. The more familiar and meaningful are the items, the more visual information can be perceived. When items are perceived in meaningful, rather than random, units they are more easily stored in memory and recalled. Combining many items in meaningful units, such as letters in words and words in phrases, is called chunking.

Chunking allows more information to be perceived and processed and allows perception and recall of idea units rather than letters or single words. By chunking units of several words at a time, the reader can form hypotheses about what words and ideas may occur next. Readers use their prior information about word order and word meanings to predict, and by predicting they actively comprehend what they read, even though they may substitute similar words for words in the text. In chunking and predicting readers bring different prior information and strategies to the act of reading. Diagnosis of reading problems must take these differences into account. Such diagnosis is based on these diagnostic principles:

1. Diagnosis is more than testing and measurement. It requires interpretation and judgment based on observation of reading ability for real purposes in a natural setting.
2. No single set of diagnostic procedures or devices can suffice to diagnose all reading problems. The process of diagnosis must be flexible and suited to the individual reader's abilities and needs.
3. Diagnosis means looking for strengths and competence as well as weaknesses and needs. Only by determining what the reader knows and can do well can we determine what should be taught.
4. Diagnosis should result in instructional change rather than in the labeling or categorizing of disabilities. Diagnosis is undertaken in order to solve problems rather than just to describe them.
5. Informal procedures can provide more practical, relevant information about a student's reading than formal measures yielding quantitative results. Informal assessment yields qualitative information about a student's reading that can be directly applied to instructional decisions.

Suggested Readings

Ashton-Warner, Sylvia. **Teacher.** *N.Y.: Simon & Schuster, 1963.* Account of a New Zealand teacher's work with young Maori and white children and her development of a method similar to the language experience approach.

Burns, Paul C. and Roe, Betty D. **Teaching Reading in Today's Elementary Schools, 2nd ed.** *Chicago: Rand McNally, 1980.* (Ch. 1). An excellent overview of the reading process, broad theoretical models and basic principles of teaching reading.

Hittleman, Daniel R. **Developmental Reading: A Psycholinguistic Perspective.** *Chicago: Rand McNally, 1978.* (Chs. 1–3). Scholarly overviews of societal views of reading, the nature of language, and human cognition in readable, well-illustrated text.

Huey, Edmund Burke. **The Psychology and Pedagogy of Reading.** *Cambridge, Mass.: MIT Press, 1968.* (Originally published, 1908.) Seminal work on the reading process. Huey's speculations on the work of the mind during reading predated modern cognitive psychologists by over fifty years.

Kohl, Herbert. **Reading: How To.** *N.Y.: Dutton, 1973.* A radical humanistic approach to literacy, the nature of teaching and how schools and society create reading failure.

Smith, Frank. **Reading Without Nonsense.** *N.Y.: Teachers College Press, Columbia University, 1979.* An absorbing, largely nontechnical description of the reading process, learning and teaching from a psycholinguistic perspective.

References

Goodman, Kenneth S. "Reading: A Psycholinguistic Guessing Game." *Journal of the Reading Specialist* 6 (1967): 126–135.

Goodman, Kenneth S. "Analysis of Oral Reading Miscues: Applied Psycholinguistics." *Reading Research Quarterly* 5, no. 1 (1969): 9–30.

Huey, Edmund Burke. *The Psychology and Ped-*

agogy of Reading. Cambridge, Mass.: MIT Press, 1968. (Originally published, 1908.)

Ransom, Grayce A. *Preparing to Teach Reading.* Boston: Little, Brown, 1978.

Smith, Frank. *Understanding Reading, 2nd ed.* N.Y.: Holt, Rinehart & Winston, 1978.

Smith, Frank. *Reading Without Nonsense.* N.Y.: Teachers College Press, 1979.

Chapter Two

Fundamental Aspects
of Learning to Read

In order to discern where and when things go wrong in reading, it is necessary to understand how reading normally develops and matures. To use a medical metaphor, we must understand health before we can diagnose illness. In this chapter we consider factors involved in normal reading success, whether the reader is a child or an older learner.

In literate societies most children learn to read between the ages of five and nine. They generally do not begin reading before five or six, because most of them lack the mental maturity and linguistic experience necessary. Some children do learn to read without much coaching before entering school (Durkin, 1966), but others resist many months, and even years, of efforts to teach them to read once they've arrived in school — and some don't learn to read until they reach adolescence or adulthood.

The rather dated concept of reading readiness implies a "magic moment" when the learner is ready to be taught to read. Readiness has traditionally been thought of as something that happened to children in kindergarten and first grade. If the children were truly lucky, it came when they completed their readiness workbooks and began working in a preprimer-level reader. Thus standardized readiness tests, purported to predict success in beginning reading, have long been routinely administered at the end of kindergarten and the beginning of first grade to determine who had reached that momentous milestone and who, sadly, had not.

The concept of readiness, however, has never been applied to older nonreaders or adult illiterates. No one would dream of administering a readiness test to illiterate twelve-year-olds to see if they had acquired the prerequisite experiences or concepts to learn to read.

Why not? Are there prerequisites that six-year-olds must have acquired to learn to read but that are unnecessary to the adolescent prereader? Not really. Learning to read and developing as a reader demand certain preliterate concepts and experiences, whether the prereader is a young child, a teen, or an adult. Apparently there is a certain degree of mental maturity that people must attain before they can efficiently acquire these preliterate concepts and experiences. Thus maturity is a factor in the development of youngsters, but it is important only because it enables them to develop the prereading concepts. The concepts are the critical aspect here, not maturity itself. We should be assessing the development of prereading competencies and experiences in nonreaders at whatever age they are.

In this chapter we discuss the more important factors that underlie the acquisition of reading ability. Although these factors most often relate to children, we should keep in mind that people learn to read at all ages, not just as young children. A child who has not experienced and internalized these concepts will have great difficulty. That same child may not really begin to read until years later, if these factors have not been present in his or her experience. Our aim in this chapter is to expand the rather narrow concept of reading readiness to include not only young children, but all learners who learn to read effectively, no matter what their ages.

The factors we will explore are:

- competence as a language user
- sense of story structures
- concepts of written language
- the ability to match speech and print units
- recognition of written words

Competence as a Language User

We often hear that language ability is involved in learning to read, but exactly what this means is not always clear. Most children learn to talk before they learn to read.[1] Adults speakers of English cannot read German, for example, unless they have been taught to speak the language, which is not surprising since any writing system is a representation of a spoken language (some important qualifications of this point are given below). We would not expect to understand a representation of a language we did not understand any more than we would expect to recognize a picture of someone we didn't know.

The assertion that knowing how to speak a language is prerequisite to reading it is too broadly stated to be helpful, however. It is necessary to identify some more specific and manageable aspects of knowing a language before we can relate this factor to reading. Two such aspects are the development of *syntax* and the *expressive use of language*.

Syntactic Development

When we study a foreign language, we have to memorize hundreds of new words for the concepts we want to talk about. We usually buy a dictionary and spend hours looking up and memorizing words, but words alone do not make a language. We also need to know how to combine these words into sentences. We must be able to combine a given group of words into a statement, a question, or a command, as our intended messages require. This ability develops from the rules of syntax, that is, *the arrangement of words for different types of sentences and the way the words should be changed to show changes in meaning*. Sometimes these rules are explicit statements that we memorize. Sometimes they are relationships we figure out for ourselves without stating them consciously. We still call them rules, however.

Children acquire rules of syntax step by step. The rules that enable them

---

[1] This is not always the case. Children with severe speech or learning handicaps may learn to read before they learn to talk. They know the language before learning to read it, although this knowledge is not manifested in speech as with most children.

to produce and understand simple sentences are learned early; those governing more complex sentences come later. In normally developing children, rules for some kinds of complicated sentences are still being acquired during the early school years. Youngsters who lag behind the norm in language development may not have acquired comparatively simpler forms until well after reading instruction has begun.

What are some syntactic forms that children may be acquiring as they approach and enter their school years? The following sentence forms are arranged in order of their difficulty to children. These examples are adapted from Bellugi-Klima (1971) and Chomsky (1969), who have studied syntactic development extensively (see Table 2.1).

The syntactic structures numbered 1 through 9 have developed in most children by the time they enter first grade. The last two do not usually develop before the ages of nine or ten. Occasionally children are either well ahead or well behind their peers in syntactic development. Those who are behind usually have difficulty in listening and following directions, in class discussions, and in reading.

The difficulty is especially pronounced in learning to read. If sentences like these were encountered in everyday speech, there would usually be other nonverbal cues, like gestures, facial expressions, and the physical context of the conversation itself available to help the listener understand the meaning without puzzling over the syntax. When these forms are encountered in print, however, other cues are not available.

How many nonverbal cues are available to written language? We must eliminate situational context, tone of voice, facial expressions, and gestures, as none of these transfer into writing. Except for the relatively minor effects of punctuation, bold-face print, and the like, we are left with only vocabulary and syntax. Because writers use words and syntactic arrangements almost exclusively to convey meaning, readers must have a receptive control of syntactic structures approximately equal to the syntactic structures in the material they read. In other words, there should be a rough match between their syntax and the author's.

When children have limited syntactic development, however, it is hard for them to find meaningful material written in sentences they can completely understand. Learners with an underdeveloped control of syntax may have some trouble comprehending speech, but much difficulty in understanding what they read.

Expressive Use of Language

Although a limited command of syntax can translate into a limited potential for reading comprehension, there is more to language development than syntax. Two learners may have a roughly equal command of syntactic forms, yet one may be decidedly better equipped linguistically to read.

TABLE 2.1. Syntactic forms acquired in early and middle childhood.

1. SUBJECT/VERB/OBJECT ORDER
John hit Bill.
Bill hit John.

Does the child understand that the first boy is the doer and the second the receiver of the action?

2. PLURALS OF NOUNS
Show me the monkey.
Show me the monkeys.

Does the child understand that the s on the noun means "more than one"?

3. POSSESSIVES OF NOUNS
Show me the child's daddy.
Show me the daddy's child.

Does the child understand the relationship of possession denoted by the 's?

4. NEGATIVE AND AFFIRMATIVE STATEMENTS
The boy is sitting.
The boy is not sitting.

Does the child understand the significance of not?

5. SINGULAR AND PLURAL VERBS
The girl walks.
The girls walk.

Does the child understand that the s on the verb indicates the number of the subject?

6. MODIFICATION OF NOUNS
The little boy has a big ball.
The big boy has a little ball.

Does the child correctly match the attribute with the object modified by the order of the words?

7. NEGATIVE AFFIXES
The blocks are stacked.
The blocks are unstacked.

Does the child understand the meaning of the negative affix, un, and how it works?

8. REFLEXIVE PRONOUNS
John hated him.
John hated himself.

Does the child understand who is referred to by each pronoun?

9. PASSIVE SENTENCES
The boy has more marbles than the girl.
The boy has less clay than the girl.

Does the child understand who has more and who has less?

10. SELF-EMBEDDED SENTENCES
The boy that the girl hit fell down.
The cat that chased the dog was out of breath.

Does the child know who hit and who chased?

11. COMPLEX VERBS
Suzie promised Mary to bake cookies.
Suzie asked Mary what to wear.

Does the child know who will do the baking? Does the child know who will do the wearing?

The difference lies not only in the forms of language the learner has mastered but also in the degree of elaboration used. Syntactic development and verbal elaboration can be thought of as vertical and horizontal dimensions of language development. When, for example, we are in a familiar situation with someone we know intimately, talking about something well known to both of us, then the verbal part of the messages that goes back and forth between us may be quite reduced.

Imagine a husband offering his wife coffee at the breakfast table:

HUSBAND: Want some?
WIFE: Lovely.
HUSBAND: Enough?
WIFE: Um hm.
HUSBAND: Sugar?
WIFE: Unh unh.

Five words and two grunts are adequate for the messages intended.

Notice what happens, however, when someone not familiar with the topic is involved in the conversation. Imagine that the wife recounts this scene later to a friend:

WIFE: My husband is so sweet.
FRIEND: Why?
WIFE: Well, since he got this new job, he doesn't have to go to work until an hour after I do.
FRIEND: So?
WIFE: Well, now he's the one who gets up and fixes the coffee.
FRIEND: That's nice.
WIFE: Yeah, you should see the old bear. Bumping around the kitchen in his ratty blue bathrobe, eyes half shut. But he makes good strong coffee.
FRIEND: I like it that way.
WIFE: Funny thing, though. We've been married five years and he still can't remember I don't take sugar!

In this example, scores of words were required for adequate communication. The language used in the two scenes represents two very different styles of talking that have been termed *restricted* and *elaborated codes* (Bernstein, 1966). The restricted code is used by all of us when we and the people we are talking with both presume that there is no need to "spell things out." The restricted code is telegraphic; we use gestures, grunts, and a lot of unspecific references like "it," "that," "this thing," and "here." The restricted code is used when we talk about concrete things in the here-and-now: we are more likely to use it when serving each other breakfast than when speculating on the nature of the lost continent of Atlantis.

The elaborated code, on the other hand, is what we use when we do have to spell things out, when the topic or the audience requires it. We might be forced to use the elaborated code if we were serving coffee to a Buddhist monk who had never had coffee before; we certainly would use it to explain photosynthesis to a class of children. Language in the elaborated code is less dependent on the setting of the communication or the shared understandings of the communicators to get the message across. It takes few short cuts. It is richer in explanations, more complete, more precise.

Most adults shift back and forth between restricted and elaborated codes many times a day, depending on their perception of the information needs of the people they are talking to. Children begin to develop the ability to differentiate their speech for different audiences before school age, though they continue to develop this ability in the elementary years (Ervin-Tripp and Mitchell-Kernan, 1977; Ochs and Schiefelin, 1979).

Bernstein (1966), however, has found that social background may determine the extent to which learners can use restricted or elaborated codes. According to Bernstein's research, some social groups in England predominantly use the restricted code. Their form of speech may be well suited to their communicative needs within their social environment, but the lack of facility with the elaborated code puts these children at a clear disadvantage in school.

Bernstein's finding has been a controversial one since it seems to support views based on class or racial prejudice that one group's language could be "better" or "worse" than another's, which was never his intention when he advanced this theory. Rather, he was trying to deduce why working-class children with apparently normal intelligence performed less well in school as a group than other children. He was also trying to point to a solution: by identifying school failure as a language problem, he was making the way clear for others to develop remedies for the school failure (Halliday, 1980).

More recent approaches to this problem have avoided attributing restricted or elaborated codes to particular social groups. One such approach is Halliday's (1975) description of language as a collection of *functions*. Halliday has suggested that children learn language for its functions or uses. They develop proficiency in language for each function as their experiences provide the necessity and opportunity to practice each one. Because Halliday lists functions, finding a relationship between specific home and school experiences and language growth is somewhat easier with Halliday's than with Bernstein's terminology. Note that Halliday uses the term *model* for language function. Here are his seven models and our descriptions for each.

1. "Gimme!" (the instrumental model) Language is used as a tool to get something for the speaker.
2. "Stop that!" (the regulatory model) Language is used to control another's behavior but not for the direct benefit of the speaker.

3. "What's that?" (the heuristic model) Language is used to find things out: to ask questions, assess answers, and form new questions.
4. "How are you doing?" (the interactional model) Language is used to build a "we-ness" between speaker and listener.
5. "I'm scared." (the personal model) Language is used to explore and communicate the speaker's feelings and his or her point of view.
6. "Twinkle, twinkle little star." (the imaginative model) Language is used purely for the fun of it, for the "feel" of sounds and for the fun of combining words and ideas, or repeating old ones to amuse or entertain.
7. "It's snowing!" (the representational model) Language is used to represent reality and convey information to others.

According to Halliday, it is quite possible that a child could undergo uneven development in the ability to use these models of language. The process of growth is related to the kinds of experiences a child has. To explore this point, Tough (1973) visited children at home to see what sort of language was encouraged there. Then she observed the same children at school to see how well matched their language was to school tasks. One four-year-old boy's mother subtly but effectively discouraged his use of heuristic and representational language. When he came home with a frog, she rebuffed his efforts to explain what he discovered and ask questions about it; instead she told him to get rid of it. What she did encourage was his use of instrumental and regulatory language. She gave him frequent commands and was more responsive to his own language when he made requests or demands for things. Even at that, the quantity and elaborateness of the language instructions, even the instrumental and regulatory ones, were few and restricted.

In a preschool class, the same boy could not collaborate successfully with others of his age in discussions about why certain plants grew and others didn't. He rarely volunteered observations about things. He responded only to the most directly stated commands from the teacher. Hearing "Those who have finished cleaning up their work areas may come have some cake," he immediately sprinted for the cake. When told to clean up his work area, however, he would do so. Tough reflected that what might therefore have been interpreted as a behavior problem was in fact a linguistic one.

The child in Tough's example was a year or more away from reading instruction, but his case illustrates the potential problem of this mismatch between the language used at home and at school. For some children, reading difficulties are a part of this problem.

Reading uses written language that, in Bernstein's terms, is elaborated and, in Halliday's terms, follows usually the representational or imaginative model. It is elaborated because it has to be. Writers rarely know their readers personally or know precisely the environment in which the reading will be done. Thus they cannot take linguistic short cuts such as referring to what

*O*ral language fluency is a stepping stone to reading for most children. A puppet theater provides a stimulus for much oral language development as children make up stories, act them out, and discuss each others' productions.

they assume the reader already knows or gesturing to things and events in the environment. They have to spell things out and elaborate. Likewise most writing, at least that encountered in school, serves no function between writer and reader as persons who know each other. Since texts are written largely to inform or to entertain, they employ the representational and imaginative models.

For children to become readers, a match must be made between their language and the language of writing. Sometimes the writing can be adjusted to suit the children's language, which is a prime advantage of using the language experience approach (Chapter Three) wherein we record their own speech in writing and use it as reading material. At the same time, however, children's language must be drawn out. They must be encouraged to talk about things, to use detail, and to move beyond simple interpersonal exchanges. Therefore, language experience teaching begins with an interesting experience, usually a concrete one that generates discussion and inquiry.

In order to ensure that every child has a language base of sufficient elaboration to prepare him or her for future reading the classroom must provide stimulating experiences, opportunities to discuss them, and models of elaborated language. These provisions can be made through discussions with concerned adults and other children or through the experience of being read to from interesting books.

From a reading diagnosis perspective, the teacher must be sure that children have a command of language sufficiently elaborate to match the language found in their books. They should be fluent in the use of the representational, heuristic, and imaginative models of language as well as the more familiar interpersonal exchanges.

A final point should be made regarding English dialects, those variations of English that are spoken by certain geographical, ethnic, or social groups. Like Bernstein's British subjects, some Americans who speak nonstandard English dialects use a restricted oral code almost exclusively while others who speak the same dialect do not. Thus teachers may confuse the restricted code with the dialect itself. They may sometimes attribute these students' difficulty in learning to read "book English" to their dialect and bend every effort to get them to speak in standard English. Such an approach is rarely effective. In fact, it may convince students to stop talking to the teacher altogether.

The predictable grammatical forms of nonstandard English dialects and a restricted oral code should not be confused. Speakers of both standard and nonstandard English may use an elaborated code, rich in description and precise in vocabulary. Whether they speak in standard English or not, they will find the language of print, which is largely elaborated *and* standard, easier to understand than speakers of restricted English, standard or not.

With students of any age, the issue is not whether we should attempt to change their dialectic forms. Whether this can even be accomplished without doing violence to their desire to express themselves is uncertain. Attempts to do so have certainly met with little success. What we must do with all speakers of a restricted code is to help them expand and elaborate their oral language, while preserving their self-confidence as communicators.

Bilingualism

Teachers in the southwestern United States, southern Florida, and the larger urban areas have long been finding children in their classrooms who were more proficient in another language than in English. The "boatlifts" of the late 1970s and early 1980s have brought hundreds of thousands of non-English-speaking people into the United States. Large numbers of people from Viet Nam, Cambodia, Cuba, and Haiti settled in areas that did not previously have bilingual populations or bilingual education programs.

Before this influx of new immigrants, bilingual education in America was concerned mostly with students who spoke Spanish and English. Spanish-English bilingual education has been promoted with special success in those areas of the United States where Spanish was the original language, such as Texas, Arizona, New Mexico, and Southern California.

Many Hispanics are bilingual when they enter school, and bilingual programs seek not only to give them access to English but also to maintain their use of Spanish so they can maintain contact with their linguistic heritage. Furthermore, since language and culture are closely related, maintaining fluency in Spanish helps to make Hispanic families feel welcome in the school. When Spanish is not promoted at school, many Hispanics feel that their culture is not welcome either. This feeling is not merely an idle concern. As a group, Hispanics have a high dropout rate and low achievement patterns. These findings provide a powerful rationale for bilingual education, which can make such children feel comfortable in school as they sense that the school values their native culture.

Not all bilingual programs for speakers of Spanish focus on developing fluency in Spanish. In Texas, a state with a large Hispanic population, the state education agency has through its actions defined bilingual education as an instrument for remedial English. Thus many bilingual programs in Texas and other border states can be described as ESL (English as a second language) programs.

What bilingual education programs should be like is not our concern here. We believe that most teachers are primarily concerned about how to teach reading to children who speak English as a second language.

What can the teacher who speaks only English do to help bilingual children learn to read? For many children, learning to read is a difficult task anyway, and accomplishing it at the same time they are learning another language is nearly impossible, especially for those from homes where reading is not a regular part of family life. Therefore, it is often recommended that children first be taught to read in their *dominant* language, the one they speak more fluently, and begin reading in their second language only when their spoken proficiency is established. In many programs they are taught to read in their first language and simultaneously given oral language instruction in English. They do not begin reading instruction in English until their spoken English approximates the level of English in their first readers.

Because of the shortage of bilingual teachers, however, this often doesn't work out. What usually happens is that they never learn to read their native language at all. They are given instruction only in spoken English and then in reading written English.

Children who come to school already knowing how to read another language form a different group. For these students, it is still important for them to develop oral proficiency in English before they can read it successfully. Nevertheless, reading can be a helpful adjunct if the teacher uses devices such as written labels on classroom objects, picture dictionaries, and labeled wall posters to teach English vocabulary. Also, seeing familiar English sentences in written form gives newcomers to the language an indication of what the word units are. Knowing where the written words are separated is a necessary starting point in language learning, and writing provides a far better indication of this than speech.

Children who can read fluently in one language can usually learn to pronounce written words in another language well before they know what the words mean. Teachers of children who speak and read Spanish sometimes report that they can read English aloud with surprising fluency but understand little or nothing of what they are pronouncing. This situation can be especially misleading to teachers who consciously or unconsciously consider oral reading fluency a measure of reading skill.

Here are some recommendations for teaching bilingual students who do not read any language:

1. *Make sure their fluency in oral English matches the level of language in the material they are to read.* Children should be able to discuss and respond to others' ideas orally with about the same degree of complexity that the reading material has so that they will be able to comprehend what they read as well as pronounce the words.

2. *Provide oral language practice in English until their oral English matches that of their textbooks.* Such practice should not be solely of the "repeat-after-me" variety, for this does not encourage true language learning. Rather, children should manipulate and describe concrete objects, listen to material read aloud to them, have interesting concrete activities in the classroom to discuss and dictate for experience stories, and practice manipulating sentence patterns aloud by substituting different nouns, verbs, and pronouns to change the meaning. It may be necessary to maintain such oral language practice for several months or a year in order for students to gain enough English fluency to begin to read written English.

3. *Help them associate spoken and written forms of words by using labels.* It is helpful to label the objects in the students' environment so that they can

practice naming objects and matching objects with their written labels. Teaching them the names of letters, labeling things in the room, and helping them make picture dictionaries will support their desire to learn to read while at the same time providing them with necessary vocabulary. Teachers should be careful, however, not to overwhelm them with the double tasks of learning to speak a language and learning to read it at the same time. Oral fluency must come first.

Here are some suggestions for teaching bilingual students who can read their native language but not English:

1. *Help them with oral English fluency.* Their listening comprehension in English should approximate the level of the language in the books they have to read.

2. *Use the written form as an aid to learning the spoken forms of English.* Label objects and use picture dictionaries, dictated experience stories, illustrated wall posters, and simply written books (even with older students at first).

3. *Be careful not to confuse oral pronunciation with comprehension.* The ability to pronounce written words can be transferred from one language to another, even when the student does not understand what the words in the second language mean. It is better to emphasize the silent reading of English followed by discussion to check comprehension, rather than to give out a steady diet of oral reading in English.

There are two points that should be made regarding the teaching of bilingual students in general:

1. *Be aware that language is intimately involved with the children's culture and with the things that are familiar and important to their lives.* If school instruction ignores their own first language in favor of the language of the school, they may feel lost and alienated.

2. *Be prepared to make an asset of the language diversity that non-English speakers bring to your classroom.* Use this opportunity to learn some of the non-English speakers' language, to learn about their holidays, national customs, history, and literature. Such an approach puts cultural and linguistic differences in a positive light and helps bilingual or non-English-speaking students to become an integral part of classroom life. It can also make the classroom more interesting for your other students.

The Sense of Story Structures

We often hear it said that children who are read to at home will learn to read more easily than children who lack this experience. Why should being read to make such a difference? Many answers to that question are possible. Being read to creates pleasurable associations with reading for children. It gives them a chance to see adults reading, and they will later be inclined to model the adults' behavior. It demonstrates for children that books tell stories. It helps them experience the world vicariously through language.

But one advantage in being read to stands out from the others. Being read stories helps children understand the way written narratives are organized by developing a sense of story structure. Children who have a rich sense of story structure have a useful means of predicting what comes next in a reading passage, reducing the need for word recognition and the interpretation of syntax. They will also have a ready means of organizing the information in the text to make that information easier to understand and remember.

What exactly is story structure? Consider the following lines:

> It happened that a fox was ambling along a country lane when he spied a bunch of ripe grapes hanging from a vine high above his head. Hungry as he was, the fox determined to have those grapes for his dinner. He stood tall on his hind legs, but could not reach the grapes. He leapt high in the air, but missed the grapes and fell painfully onto his back. He was too sore to make a further attempt at the grapes, so he sighed and turned away down the road. "Well," he said to himself. "The grapes were probably sour anyway."

The reader will immediately recognize the above group of sentences as a story. If you compare the number of lines of the story with the same number of preceding lines in this book, you will discern that the story has a pattern of organization or structure that is quite distinct from the other lines of writing. How would you describe the structure of the story? What are its parts? What are the relationships between the parts?

The answers different readers bring to those questions may vary. However, most would probably include a *character*, a *setting*, a *problem*, an *attempt* to overcome the problem, and a *conclusion*. Some would add a *motive*, a *cause and effect* relationship, a *theme*, and perhaps other elements. Researchers on story structure have found that virtually all stories told in Western culture share these elements in some combination (Greimas, 1971; Propp, 1968). There have been several interesting attempts to describe the essential components and structures that stories have in common. Notably, Rumelhart (1975), Mandler and Johnson (1977), Thorndyke (1977), and others have each developed *story grammars*, elaborate sets of rewrite rules modeled after transformational grammar or computer programs. These grammars can account for the structures of a variety of different types of stories, and they impress us with the complex nature of the knowledge children must have in their minds that enables them to understand and to create stories.

Below we give a much simplified account of some key elements that most story grammars employ. For each element an illustrative passage is supplied from *The Fox and the Grapes*.

1. *A setting* — the protagonist is introduced in some place and time.
   It happened that a fox was ambling along a country lane. . . .

2. *An initiating event* — either an action or an idea that strikes someone and sets further events in motion.

  . . . *when he spied a bunch of ripe grapes hanging from a vine high above his head.*

3. *An internal response* — the protagonist's inner reaction to the initiating event, as a part of which he sets a *goal*, a desired state of affairs.

  Hungry as he was, the fox determined to have those grapes for his dinner.

4.* *An attempt* — the protagonist makes an effort to achieve his goal.

  He stood tall on his hind legs. . . .

  He leapt high in the air. . . .

5.* *An outcome* — an event or new state of affairs that directly results from a given attempt.

  . . . *but could not reach the grapes.*

  . . . *but missed the grapes and fell painfully onto his back.*

6. *A consequence* — an action or state of affairs that follows from the protagonist's success or failure to achieve the goal.

  He was too sore to make a further attempt at the grapes, so he sighed and turned away down the road.

7. *A reaction* — an emotion, an idea or a further event which may express the protagonist's feelings about his success or failure to achieve the goal, or relate the events in the story to some broader set of concerns.

  "Well," he said to himself. "The grapes were probably sour anyway."

Theorists of story structures (Applebee, 1978, 1980; Stein, 1978) claim that ideally the story structure resides both in the story itself and in the mind of the listener. People who can comprehend stories have some sort of internalized idea of story structures in their minds, and they use these structures to comprehend and remember stories (Bartlett, 1932). Because of the internalized structures, actual stories may lack one or more elements of structure and still be comprehended, because listeners or readers are able to supply the missing element or the missing relationship.

How Do Children Learn Story Structures?

Children's use of story structures is a deep-seated psychological process and not something they can readily talk about. Terms like *initiating event* and *internal response* mean nothing to a six-year-old child and little to most adults. Yet it is clear that learners do develop a sense of story structure from their early experiences in listening to stories.

Consider pupils who hear stories read aloud or told again and again. Although the stories differ in particulars, such as who the characters are and what specific events take place, they are similar in their structure. They all

---

*Note that *attempts* and *outcomes* may come in groups, as they do in *The Fox and the Grapes.*

have some kind of setting, initiating event, a goal, attempts at the goal, and so forth. More often than not, stories present these elements in the same sequence. Slowly but surely, students' expectations are shaped by encounters with these stories. When they hear a new story, they will be ready to assign someone to the role of character and an incident in the story to the role of initiating event, and they will comprehend the character's attempts to achieve a goal. Thus they can use story structures to understand a story, even though they may not be able to talk about the structures explicitly.

Children may have a well-developed sense of story structures, yet be unable to describe directly what these structures are or how they are used. We can *infer* their use of such structures, though, by observing some of their interactions with stories.

Making Predictions

One way that we can see the use of story structures demonstrated is to ask students to predict events as yet unheard or unread, on the basis of the parts of the story that have already been revealed. Suppose, for example, we were reading the story "The Dog and His Shadow" to a class.

THE DOG AND HIS SHADOW

Once there was a big brown dog named Sam. One day, Sam found a piece of meat and was carrying it home in his mouth to eat. Now on his way home, he had to cross a brook. He looked down and saw his own shadow reflected in the water beneath. He thought it was another dog with another piece of meat, and he made up his mind to have that piece also. So he made a snap at the shadow, but as he opened his mouth, the piece of meat fell out. The meat dropped into the water and floated away. Sam never saw the meat again. (McConaughy, 1980, p. 158)

When we read the sentence "He thought it was another dog with another piece of meat . . ." we would stop and ask the class, "What do you think Sam the dog might do now?" Here are some responses we might get:

1. "I don't know."
2. "Jump in after the other dog."
3. "Keep on walking."
4. "Go sit and eat the meat."

Which of the responses reveals a better sense of story structure? With *1.* we cannot be sure what the student thinks, except that he or she may not have realized that predicting what might come next is an important part of understanding a story; *3.* seems to be based on everyday reality, as does *4.*; but neither recognized the initiating event that will shape succeeding events in the story. Only 2. does this. Even though it is not a correct prediction, 2. reveals a better sense of story structure than the other three predictions.

Remembering Stories

Another indication of the use of story structure lies in the way students *retell* a story they have heard or read. When asked to retell a story, the student should pick out several of its important elements for inclusion in the retelling.

Here are different versions of "The Dog and His Shadow" as recounted by two fifth-grade children:

1. "There was a dog that found a piece of meat and he went to some water and he saw another piece of meat and he opened his mouth and the piece fell out and he never saw it again."
2. "A dog tried to get another piece of meat and lost his." (McConaughy, 1980, p. 158)

Both accounts include the setting, the character, the initiating event, and the reaction. The first account includes attempts and outcomes but omits the internal response and the goal. The second includes the goal but omits attempts and outcomes. Both retellings are skeletal versions of the original. Not all the information is retold, but the parts included are important ones. The first retelling is more elaborate and explanatory than the second; it also demonstrates more awareness of story structure than the second.

Another aspect of remembering stories can be demonstrated by using a deliberately "scrambled" story. By changing the logical order of story parts and asking students to retell the story, we can see whether they use a logical sequence in the retelling. Two interesting things usually happen, depending on how distorted the story sequence is.

When events in a story are only slightly out of order, say by placing an attempt before an initiating event that sets the stage for the attempt, even young children will correct the order. Although the story was originally told with the order of events violated, their retellings will usually conform to the normal structure of stories.

If, however, the structure is seriously violated, with several key aspects out of order, the retellings suffer. The amount of information included is seriously reduced compared with the retellings of normally ordered stories (Stein, 1978). These findings give considerable weight to the contention that story structures help learners remember the stories they hear or read.

While story structure is an important cue to meaning and a valuable basis for making predictions about what one is likely to encounter in written text, it is possible to read without making use of story structure. Some beginning reading materials limit the writing to simple phonogram patterns without any

*R*eaders develop a sense of story structures by listening to stories told and read aloud. A sense of how stories are structured helps readers to predict what comes next and remember story events.

real story structure, as shown by this "story" from the Merrill Linguistic Reading Program, 1975:

> A cat sat on a mat.
> Pat the cat.
> Is the cat Nat?
> The cat is fat Nat.
> Pat Nat on the mat.
>   (*I Can*, p. 10)

In sentences like these there is no story structure to employ, and real comprehension is necessarily minimal since there is little to comprehend.

The use of meaning cues such as story structure varies from learner to learner, as their individual reading strategies differ. Some students read clearly structured stories without relying on the structure to organize their comprehension. Many beginning readers do rely on story structure to guide their comprehension, and probably all efficient mature readers do (Marshall and Glock, 1978–1979). Those who develop early reading strategies without building in higher order meaning cues like story structure often show up later in a special reading class with comprehension problems.

In summary, the use of story structures in reading depends on:

1. assimilating a sense of story structure from encounters with stories learners have heard read aloud to them
2. recognizing that it is important and beneficial to use story structures to predict what is coming next in a story
3. having access to reading materials that are written around perceivable story structures rather than those that are written solely to conform to readability formulas or phonic patterns

Concepts of Written Language

The Purposes of Reading and Writing

We learn to do things more easily when we know what we're trying to get done. If we want to teach someone a new game, the first thing we usually do is to tell the player what the object of the game is. Look at the instructions for any commercial board or card game. The first information given is the object of the game, with the plays and sequences following. If we know the overall goal, the components of play begin to make sense, and we can learn these components more efficiently because we know how they fit together in an overall strategy.

A few years ago a teacher in Scotland (Reid, 1966) wanted to see if her first graders knew the object of the "game" of reading. "What are we trying to get done when we read?" she asked. The children weren't sure. Since then, that question has been raised again and again with children in other parts of the world. The rather startling answer has often been "We don't know."

Downing and Oliver (1974) investigated children's understanding of the reasons for reading and also of the "parts": what a letter is, what a word is, what "sounding out" means, and so on. They found that those who knew the most about what reading was for, and what the terms meant that we use in reading instruction, were performing more proficiently than other children when their reading was measured some months later. Downing and Oliver called the concepts of these higher achievers *cognitive clarity*. Students who have cognitive clarity about reading take to beginning reading instruction more successfully than those who do not have it.

What sort of confusion arises in early reading? Many students are not convinced that reading is for finding things out, whether it is finding out what happens in a story, how a lima bean grows, or how to make tacos. Such confusion is found not only in young children, who have not yet had much experience with print, but also in older nonreaders who have had little experience learning anything positive or interesting from print.

Many students think the end product of reading is to render print out loud. It is easy to see how children with this conception of reading might develop superficial strategies for reading while ignoring story structure, syntax, and even meaning as they render print into sound. Beginning readers whose experience with reading has been entirely oral frequently do this. They quickly figure out that "reading" must mean "saying," and they concentrate on pronouncing letter sounds correctly rather than on understanding what the words mean.

Many young prereaders are confused about the respective roles of print and pictures in text. Kita (1979) showed that they thought the pictures in storybooks told the story and that printed words were added to embellish the pages. Many prereaders do not know precisely what we mean when we say "word," or "letter," or "sentence." Some do not know that words are written from left to right or that the beginning of a written word is the part on the left and the end of the word is the part on the right.

Some prereading youngsters have had little contact with print outside of school, have heard few stories read aloud, and have not observed adults reading very often. Such students rarely have an adequate idea of why one would want to read. If they have not explored storybooks and other print with someone who can already read, asking questions about print and trying (or pretending) to produce print themselves, they rarely have much of a concept for the terms we use frequently in beginning reading instruction: *word, letter, sound, sentence,* and *line*. Clay (1975) has written an incisive account of how a group of beginning readers try to follow the teacher as she leads a reading lesson:

Suppose a teacher has placed an attractive picture on the wall and has asked her children for a story which she will record under it. They offer the text "Mother is cooking" which the teacher alters slightly to introduce some features she wishes to teach. She writes:

Mother said,
"I am baking."

If she says, "Now look at our *story*," 30 percent of a new entrant group will attend to the *picture*.

If she says "Look at the words and find some you know," between 50 and 90 percent will be looking for *letters*. If she says, "Can you see Mother?" most will agree that they can, but some *see* her in the picture, some can locate M and others will locate the word "Mother."

Perhaps the children read in unison "Mother is . . ." and the teacher tries to sort this out. Pointing to *said* she asks, "Does this say *is?*" Half agree that it does because it has "s" in it. "What letter does it start with?" Now the teacher is really in trouble. She assumes that the children *know* that a word is built out of letters but 50 percent of children still confuse the verbal labels "word" and "letter" after six months of instruction. She also assumes that the children know that the left-hand letter following a space is the "start" of a word. Often they do not. (Clay, 1975, pp. 3–4)

Since the percentages used by Clay derive from her research with children in New Zealand, they may not translate exactly to the case of American children, but clearly the trend is the same with our own children. Just like the adult learning to play a game for the first time, the child approaching reading instruction without an idea of the overall goal or outcome is apt to experience difficulty in mastering the process.

Ability to Match Speech and Print Units

Preschoolers with a favorite book they have heard read many times often surprise their parents by "reading" the book spontaneously. They turn the pages, reciting the story line as they go, although they put in many deviations from what may be written in the book, and may even be turning the pages from back to front!

When do children start to match the story line in their heads with the print on the page? This event, which we will call the *speech-to-print match*, is a critical prereading competence. Before they can truly read, children must be able to make the speech-to-print match, literally "finding" the word on the page. To do this they must realize that a word in the head corresponds to a set of marks on the page. A word in the head may be difficult, even impossible, to separate from the stream of speech, but on the printed page each word is a *bound configuration*. A bound configuration is simply a group of letters clustered together with space on either side, and until children grasp this concept they won't be able to recognize the word because they literally won't be able to locate it in a line of print.

Here is an example: Suppose two children have memorized and can recite the nursery jingle, "Fuzzy Wuzzy was a bear. Fuzzy Wuzzy had no hair. Fuzzy Wuzzy wasn't fuzzy, was he?" Now they are shown the jingle in print:

Fuzzy Wuzzy was a bear.
Fuzzy Wuzzy had no hair.
Fuzzy Wuzzy wasn't fuzzy, was he?

If you asked them to point to each word in print as they recited the jingle from memory, could they do it? Many young children could not. One might point to the *F* in the first word and say "Fuzzy," point to the *U* and say "Wuzzy." The other child might point to *Fuzzy* and say "Fuzz," then point to *Wuzzy* and say "zy", point to *was* and say "Wuzz," point to *a* and say "zy", and so on. Neither child has realized that each word in the head or on the tongue, and each unit of print with a white space on either side of it, correspond in a one-to-one relationship. Such children will not progress very far in beginning word recognition until they learn where each printed word begins and ends, which is part of *the concept of the word in print.*

This difficulty is not peculiar to young children, although it is more common with them. Older nonreaders also may have a good deal of difficulty matching the spoken word and its printed counterpart when they recite a memorized segment of text. Older learners, even the illiterate, have probably had more experience looking at letters and words than young children, so the older student generally avoids pointing to an individual letter when saying an entire word. Matching a multisyllabic spoken word to a single written configuration, however, can cause confusion. And just as in the case of the young child, an older nonreader who cannot locate the written counterpart of a spoken word in a memorized utterance will have trouble learning to recognize the written word.

How does one develop this concept? Not by direct teaching; it is almost impossible to explain to those who don't already have the idea. Principally, the concept is developed by hearing stories read aloud over and over and looking at each page as someone says the words, with the reader running a hand along the line being read or indicating even in a quick passing way where the reader's eyes are as the words are read. Whether the student is a young child or an older nonreader, the concept is learned by such indirect demonstration. By using written material that has been memorized the recitation is automatic. Reciting memorized written text and learning to point to the individual written words as the spoken counterparts are uttered is a basic activity leading to the concept of the word in print.

Recognition of Written Words

As the ability to match spoken and printed words develops, the person learning to read comes to locate printed units quickly and confidently as the corresponding words are spoken and eventually begins to recognize written words as individual entities. Words located over and over begin to look different from all others, and characteristics of the appearance of individual words begin to appear obvious. When the same words occur frequently and in a context that gives them meaning, they become recognizable with very little examination needed. Only a glance suffices to recognize a familiar word, just as only a glimpse is necessary to let us identify a very familiar face in a crowd. The learner has begun to recognize written words, a basic competency underlying the ability to read. Recognizing a word automatically, as soon as it is seen, is called *sight recognition*. A word so familiar that it is recognized instantly is called a *sight word*. Sight words are necessary for all reading. When nonreaders have sufficient experience with print that they begin to develop sight recognition of some words spontaneously, they are learning to read.

Sight words serve as stepping stones in a line of print. If readers recognize a few of the words in the line as sight words, they can often make an educated guess about what the other words are; they can begin to use syntax, picture clues, letter-sound clues, and any other means they can to make sense of the text.

Sight words also serve as anchors for the neophyte reader who practices making the speech-to-print match. Let's suppose, for example, that Becky knows what the following line says, as she would if she had dictated it or heard someone read it aloud:

Becky brought her rabbit to school today.

If Becky recognizes her own name and *school* as sight words, then she will discover a mismatch if she reads *rabbit* as *rab* and *to* as *bit*. By this strategy, *school* should be read *to;* but Becky knows this is not right, because she recognizes *school* as a sight word. Then she will be led to reexamine the print to the left of *school* to find a better fit for her words.

Until a child has accumulated enough sight words to encounter two, three, or more in each line of print, smooth reading will not be achieved. Without sight words the child has no basis on which to activate meaning cues, and is thus dependent on phonic decoding, but decoding every word is far too burdensome for anyone, especially a beginner. Besides, the speech-to-print match is not likely to be fully developed before some sight words are learned, so the reader may not be able to apply decoding strategies to the right units of print! The acquisition of some sight words precedes real reading, whatever methods of instruction one undertakes.

Let us clarify a point that is sometimes confusing. The term *sight word* is used by different authors to refer to somewhat different concepts. In its broadest sense, the term means any printed word a person can immediately recognize with no analysis or aid needed. Some authors, however, use the term *basic sight words* to refer to a special collection of words a reader should recognize at sight. Numerous lists of this kind have been compiled, such as the Dolch Word List (Dolch, 1955). Most lists contain the same 100–200 words.

The basis for such lists is quite logical. Numerous studies have been undertaken to determine how frequently different English words normally occur in print. These studies have shown that some words are used frequently and some infrequently. Durr (1973) analyzed 80 juvenile trade books and found that 10 words occurred so frequently that the reader encountered one of the 10 in every 4 or 5 words, on the average. Durr further found that 188 words accounted for only 6 percent of the different words used in the 80 books he studied, but those same 188 words occurred so frequently that they made up almost 70 percent of the running text. Ekwall (1976) cited studies showing that 200 words accounted for nearly 70 percent of the words in easy reading materials. Thorndike and Lorge (1944) assessed and classified the frequency of 30,000 words in adult reading material, and their frequency ratings are still used to construct school materials.

There is clear justification for the development of these basic sight word lists: beginning readers who could quickly and accurately recognize such words would find a number of handy stepping stones to help them get across any line of print. Most commercial lists feature largely the same words, so it doesn't matter much which list is mastered. The words are frequently taught *in isolation*, however, so their meanings can't be used as a recognition clue, which is a very poor instructional practice.

Selected lists of basic sight words and the groups of words children actually acquire on their own usually overlap (Henderson, Estes, and Stonecash, 1972), but they don't overlap entirely, and for a good reason. Basic sight word lists are mostly composed of the grammatically necessary but nondescript words such as articles, conjunctions, pronouns, and prepositions that bind together the real information-bearing words in a sentence. The lists sometimes include a few nouns, adjectives, and verbs in their ranks, but these are used so generally that their meanings are not precise, and the words are not very memorable.

A child could know all the basic sight words in a sentence, however, and still not approach the meaning. As an example, here is a passage with only the basic sight words left in. We took out all the words that Ekwall (1976, p. 70) did not designate as basic for preprimer, primer, and first grade levels:

_____ _____ and his _____ _____ _____ in the _____ . They _____ in green. They _____ the _____ for _____ with their _____ and _____ .

Could you make any sense of this passage? All the meaningful and memorable words have been left out. There is not much left to carry the meaning of the sentences.

Now here is the same sentence with the basic sight words left out and the less frequently encountered words restored:

Robin Hood _____ _____ Merry Men lived _____ _____ forest. _____ dressed _____ _____ . _____ shot _____ deer _____ food _____ _____ bows _____ arrows. (Manning-Sanders, 1977, p. 1)

It is easier to guess the basic sight words if we know the low-frequency words than it is to infer the low-frequency words when we know the basic sight words

Words like *Robin Hood, Merry Men, shot, bow,* and *arrow* become sight words more readily than the basic sight words simply because they are more vivid and interesting. The less memorable words must be recognized too, but they are most easily learned and recognized when taught in the context of sentences rather than in isolation.

Summary

Diagnostic judgment is built on an understanding of how reading normally begins and develops, and this chapter has examined some competencies underlying the ability to read, regardless of the age of the learner.

Before students can learn to read a language they must be competent users of that language in oral form. Two language aspects important to reading are *syntactic development* and the *expressive use* of oral language. *Syntax* is the system of explicit and tacit rules of word order and sentence structure. Normally developing children acquire simple syntactic forms earlier and complex forms later in their language development, and by their early school years they have mastered most of the sentence forms that adults use. Students whose syntactic development lags significantly behind the norm may have difficulty understanding more complex sentence structures in print, but they can often understand complex speech because oral language uses vocal and facial expressions, gestures, and situational context as well as syntax and vocabulary to convey meaning. Written language, however, uses only words and their arrangement to convey meaning, and students with underdeveloped syntactic comprehension may have trouble understanding written sentences that they could ordinarily comprehend in speech.

Elaborateness of oral language is another important aspect. Two students may have similar syntactic competence but vary in verbal elaboration. Most speakers use both *restricted* and *elaborated oral codes* depending on the situational context of the speech and the listener's informational needs. A restricted code is telegraphic, featuring much use of unspecific references, gestures, and vocal inflection. It is used when both speaker and listener share very similar understandings and there is little need to spell things out. Much informal communication between intimates occurs in a restricted code. An elaborated code is much richer in description and detail, uses extended utterances and more precise vocabulary, and does not rely so heavily on devices like gestures and vocal inflection. Elaborated codes are used when speaker and listener do not necessarily share the same informational background, which is the case with written language. In order to understand the elaborated code in writing, the student must be familiar with it in speech.

Some speakers use the restricted code habitually, or have not developed the use of language forms that correspond to the language of books. Such people have difficulty understanding written language. Restricted codes, like elaborated codes, are used by speakers of standard as well as nonstandard English. Students who speak in restricted codes should be encouraged and guided to expand and elaborate their own language, while preserving the integrity of their natural language pattern. *Bilingual* students may or may not be able to read their first language. In either case, oral fluency in English is a prerequisite in reading English. For those who can read another language, written and oral forms can be used to facilitate their mastery of English.

Listening to stories told and read aloud gives children a *sense of story structures*, which is necessary for understanding and remembering stories. Story structures include such elements as a setting, characters, an initiating event, a goal, attempts at the goal, episodes, and consequences. Knowledge of story structures is usually tacit knowledge, but it helps in organizing story events and recalling them. Story structures are inferred, as are rules of syntax, from hearing stories read and told many times rather than by direct instruction.

Many prereaders, especially young children, lack sufficient experience with print to know why writing and reading exist. If they have been exposed to stories, directions, informational nonfiction, and other forms of printed material before reading begins, it will help them realize that print has a *communicative purpose*. Children who have inferred that print tells you something and that reading helps you learn more about it have an easier time learning to read than those who have little prereading print experience and few ideas of what reading and writing are used for.

The ability to *match speech and print units* is a basic prereading competence. When students memorize a short piece of written material and can point to individual words as they are recited, their *concept of a word in print* is established. Youngsters often demonstrate this speech-to-print matching when they pretend to "read" their favorite storybooks by reciting the story and pointing to the words. As this matching ability develops, the child comes to recognize that printed words are *bound configurations*, groups of letters separated by spaces on either side of the groups. Recognizing the boundaries of words underlies the acquisition of word recognition abilities.

As the prereader becomes facile with the process of matching printed and spoken words, individual words begin to look different from one another. When certain individual words are seen frequently and in a meaningful context they come to be recognized quickly and accurately as wholes. Immediate recognition of words without analysis, or *sight recognition*, is necessary for effective reading to begin. Words recognized in this way are *sight words*, which enable the reader to read smoothly and to focus on the meaning the words convey. There are various lists of basic sight words, words that occur very frequently in all written material. Since these high-frequency words are often articles, prepositions, and pronouns they are imprecise in meaning and thus may be difficult to recognize in print. Specific nouns, verbs, and adjectives are often learned as sight words more easily because they are more memorable. They also convey more of the meaning of text than the basic sight words. Reading is difficult without rapid recognition of the high-frequency words, but they are difficult to learn and easily confused if they are taught in isolation rather than in their meaningful context.

Extension Activities

1. Discuss with a nursery school or kindergarten teacher the role of oral language development in learning to read. How do average children differ in their syntactic development and elaborateness of oral language? How does the teacher aid children who lag behind in these abilities?
2. Discuss the same issues with a teacher of nonreaders who are older students or adults. Are there particular characteristics of the oral language of older nonreaders? What role does the teacher believe oral language facility plays in reading improvement? How does the teacher improve a student's oral language?
3. Talk to some young children who have not yet begun to read and then to some older nonreaders. What do they believe reading and writing are for? If they could read (or read more easily), what could they do that they cannot do now? How are the responses similar or different, in respect to the respondent's age?
4. Find a simple story with an obvious structure, like a short fairy tale, folk tale, or fable. Revise it so that one or two events are slightly out of sequence. Read or tell the story to some young children individually and ask each to retell the story. Do they correct the order of events? Do they realize that anything was wrong with your version? What aspects of story structures does each include in the retelling?
5. Teach a young prereading child a jingle, nursery rhyme, or short poem. Recite it with him or her until the jingle has been memorized. Then show the rhyme in print and ask the child to recite the words and point to the written words at the same time. Observe the pointing: can the student do the task easily? If not, what units does the child point to while reciting? Where does the process seem to break down? If you show the student how to do it, can he or she then do the task correctly?

Suggested Readings

Clay, Marie M. **Reading: The Patterning of Complex Behavior, 2nd Ed.** *Exeter, N.H.: Heinemann Educational Books, 1980.* An unusually detailed account of what a young child must perceive, comprehend and do in order to become a reader, along with suggestions for helpful teaching.

DeVilliers, Peter and DeVilliers, Jill.

Early Language. *Cambridge, Mass.: Harvard University Press, 1978.* A short but well-informed description of children's language and how they learn it.

Downing, John and Thackray, Derek. **Reading Readiness, 2nd Ed.** *London: Hodder and Stoughton, 1975.* Downing and Thackray condense decades of research on reading readiness, and add some commonsense approaches that are new.

Mandler, Jean M. and Johnson, Nancy S. **"Remembrance of Things Parsed: Story Structure and Recall."** *Cognitive Psychology, 9 (1977): 111–151.* An influential treatment of the topic of story grammars.

References

Applebee, Arthur N. *The Child's Concept of Story: Ages 2 to 17.* Chicago: University of Chicago Press, 1978.

Applebee, Arthur N. "Children's Narratives: New Directions." *The Reading Teacher* 34, no. 2 (Nov. 1980): 137–142.

Bartlett, Frederic C. *Remembering: A Study in Experimental and Social Psychology.* Cambridge, England: Cambridge University Press, 1932.

Bellugi-Klima, Ursula. "Some Language Comprehension Tests," in Celia S. Lavatelli, ed. *Language Training in Early Childhood Education.* Urbana, Ill.: University of Illinois Press, 1971.

Bernstein, Basil. "Elaborated and Restricted Codes: Their Social Origins and Some Consequences." In George Smith, ed. *Communication and Culture.* N.Y.: Holt, Rinehart & Winston, 1966, pp. 427–441.

Chomsky, Carol. *Acquisition of Syntax in Children from 5 to 10.* Cambridge, Mass.: MIT Press, 1969.

Clay, Marie. *What Did I Write?* Auckland, New Zealand: Heinemann Educational Books, 1975.

Dolch, Edward. *Methods in Reading.* Champaign, Ill.: Garrard, 1955.

Downing, John and Oliver, Peter. "The Child's Conception of 'A Word.' " *Reading Research Quarterly* IX, no. 4 (1974): 575–590.

Durkin, Deloris. *Children Who Read Early.* N.Y.: Teachers College Press, 1966.

Durr, William K. "Computer Study of High Frequency Words in Popular Trade Juveniles." *The Reading Teacher* 27, no. 1 (Oct. 1973): 37–42.

Ekwall, Eldon. *Diagnosis and Remediation of the Disabled Reader.* Boston: Allyn and Bacon, 1976.

Ervin-Tripp, Susan and Mitchell-Kernan, Claudia, ed. *Child Discourse.* N.Y.: Academic Press, 1977.

Greimas, A. J. "Narrative Grammar: Units and Levels." *Modern Language Notes* 86, no. 6 (1971): 793–806.

Halliday, Michael A. K. "Learning How to Mean," in *Foundations of Language Development: A Multidisciplinary Approach,* vol. 1. Eric Lenneberg and Elizabeth Lenneberg, eds. New York: Academic Press, 1975.

Halliday, Michael A. K. Personal Communication, 1980.

Henderson, Edmund; Estes, Thomas; and Stonecash, Susan. "An Exploratory Study of Word Acquisition Among First Graders at Mid-Year in a Language Experience Approach." *Journal of Reading Behavior* 4, no. 3 (Summer 1972): 21–31.

I Can. Merrill Linguistic Reading Program, Level A. Columbus, Ohio: Charles Merrill, 1975.

Kita, M. Jane. "Children's Concepts of Reading and Writing." Paper presented at the annual meeting of the National Reading Conference, San Antonio, November 1979.

Mandler, Jean M. & Johnson, Nancy S. "Remembrance of Things Parsed: Story Structure and Recall." *Cognitive Psychology* 9 (1977): 111–151.

Manning-Sanders, Ruth. *Robin Hood and Little John*. London: Metheun, 1977.

Marshall, Nancy and Glock, Marvin. "Comprehension of Connected Discourse: A Study into the Relationship Between the Structure of Text and Information Recalled." *Reading Research Quarterly* XIV, no. 1 (1978–1979): 10–55.

McConaughy, Stephanie. "Using Story Structure in the Classroom." *Language Arts* 57, no. 2 (February 1980): 157–165.

Ochs, Elinor and Schieffelin, Bambi, ed. *Developmental Pragmatics*. N.Y.: Academic Press, 1979.

Propp, Vladimir. *Morphology of the Folktale*. Austin: University of Texas Press, 1968.

Reid, Jesse. "Learning to Think About Reading." *Educational Research* 9, no. 1 (1966): 56–62.

Rumelhart, David E. "Notes on a Schema for Stories." In D. G. Dobrow and A. Collins, eds. *Representation and Understanding*. N.Y.: Academic Press, 1975.

Stein, Nancy. *How Children Understand Stories*. Urbana, Ill.: University of Illinois Center for the Study of Reading, Technical Report #69, March 1978 (ERIC: ED 153 205).

Thorndike, Edward and Lorge, Irving. *The Teacher's Word Book of 30,000 Words*. N.Y.: Teachers College Press, 1944.

Thorndyke, Perry. "Cognitive Structures in Comprehension and Memory of Narrative Discourse." *Cognitive Psychology* 9 (Jan. 1977): 77–110.

Tough, Joan. *Focus on Meaning: Talking to Children to Some Purpose*. London: Allen & Unwin, 1973.

Chapter Three

Assessment of Prereading Competencies (Readiness)

Two six-year-old girls sit beside each other in a first-grade reading group. One of them matches each point of the teacher's instruction with two leaps forward of her own. The other is taught and retaught with much practice and encouragement but makes little progress. By November of the first-grade year, the first child is reading fluently but the second is not.

Teachers of young children are aware that their young students differ considerably in their *readiness* for reading instruction. The little bit of encouragement that is necessary to start one youngster reading seemingly has no effect on another. It is now standard procedure in schools to assess children to determine which ones are ready to read and which ones are not.

Recently, however, the concept of readiness has been criticized because the term carries the connotation that children become ready for reading in the same mysterious way that flowers become ready to bloom. This concept implies that readiness is more dependent on biological maturation than on experience. In contrast to this view, recent studies have shown that reading readiness may consist of several prereading competencies, such as familiarity with story structure, concepts about print, the concept of what a word is, or about what reading is and what it is for. Children must reach a certain level of maturity before they can acquire these competencies effectively, but maturity alone is not the issue. Many reading experts prefer the term prereading to reading readiness because prereading and the competencies that it consists of suggest a more active agenda for teachers than the term readiness. Whether children profit from beginning reading instruction may not be so much a matter of whether they have become somehow ready to read but rather whether they have had the requisite prereading experiences. And if we look at the problem this way, then it is easier to see a course of action for the teacher whose students need to develop prereading competencies.

In Chapter Two of this book we discussed in detail the factors we think are most necessary for learning to read. In this chapter we discuss ways of assessing the prereading competencies we consider to be essential:

- oral language fluency
- sense of story structures
- the speech-to-print match
- print orientation concepts
- sight word recognition
- letter recognition

The main part of this chapter is devoted to techniques for assessing prereading competencies, or readiness for reading, and the assessment techniques described here should be acceptable to those who prefer either term. The emphasis in this chapter is on *informal* assessment techniques. (Standardized readiness tests are discussed in Chapter Eight along with other standardized tests.) Why the emphasis on informal procedures?

The range of prereading assessment techniques is very wide. It extends from sitting down and telling a child a story to lengthy machine-scored commercial tests. Which assessment procedure is best? Obviously no single type is best for all situations, and in deciding which approach to use it is wise to consider the following three factors:

1. Does the assessment technique examine aspects of prereading that can be productively taught, or does it only attempt to predict future reading success?
2. Can the assessment technique be integrated with ongoing instruction, or does it require strict test conditions?
3. Does the assessment technique work in a large group setting, is it best done with one child, or can it be done with a small group of children?

For immediate application in the classroom, especially when guidance is sought for planning instruction, teachers need assessment devices that tap the competencies the child must develop in order to read. Most of these techniques are informal measures; that is, they yield qualitative information about each child rather than quantitative scores. They are also patterned closely after teaching and learning processes, since it is in these processes where children's strengths and weaknesses most related to real acts of reading are revealed.

Informal prereading assessment taps a wide range of competencies at once because reading is itself a very complex activity, and a child who is reading is doing many things at once. Informal prereading assessment is patterned closely after real reading tasks — which is an advantage because the artificial atmosphere formal testing engenders is frightening to many children and because testing that teaches is time better spent than testing that does not.

In the two case studies that follow, you will meet Lisa and Katie, who are each having trouble learning to read. In the first parts of the studies you will see how they interact with print and with others in their classrooms. After we have presented the various assessment procedures discussed in this chapter, we will come back to Lisa and Katie, and see how their teachers used these diagnostic procedures. There you will find out how the diagnostic findings were implemented in classroom teaching practices. We hope the case studies in this and subsequent chapters will help clarify procedures and applications for you.

Case Studies

LISA

Lisa entered first grade at the age of five years, eight months, one of the youngest in her class. She attended kindergarten the previous year where she did not experience noticeable difficulty, although she was somewhat shy and often played alone. When she began first grade Lisa was tiny, spoke softly, and was somewhat timid about joining in group activities. She rarely volunteered a response in discussions and at times seemed overwhelmed by the activity around her.

As the first weeks of school went by, Lisa made very little progress in learning to read, and her teacher, Betty Decker, was puzzled by her erratic performance. She seemed to learn something one day only to forget it the next. Or, she would have two or three "good days," when she was able to remember the letters and words in her lessons and could apply what she had learned, but then she would forget it all again. At times she would stare at a letter she'd known for days just as though she'd never seen it before. It was as though every time Lisa learned something new, she'd forget something that had come before.

Ms. Decker paced the lessons in the basal series more slowly for Lisa's reading group and took advantage of every practice activity in the manual as well as making up her own. The other children in Lisa's group benefited from all the additional practice, but the teacher suspected they could move forward a bit more quickly. Lisa, however, needed enormous amounts of practice and still was not very successful. Ms. Decker hesitated to remove her from the reading group because she felt that the group interaction would be helpful in drawing shy Lisa out of her shell. After six or seven weeks of instruction, however, Lisa was becoming discouraged. She seemed more withdrawn than ever, was easily discouraged, rarely finished her independent seatwork, and several times had broken into tears after minor mishaps. Ms. Decker knew that these were behavioral signs of Lisa's frustration and unhappiness, but *why* was she having such difficulty learning to read?

KATIE

Betty Decker often sought advice from her friend Myra Whittier, who taught second grade next door. As Ms. Decker described some of Lisa's problems, Myra Whittier's thoughts turned to Katie.

Katie was almost nine years old in October of second grade; she had been retained in first grade the year before. Katie was a tall, athletic girl with a sunny nature and sweet personality. She gloried in the responsibility of running small errands and helping the teacher and could always be depended on in this role. She took an almost maternal interest in the welfare of her younger classmates and would ignore her own work to help others if allowed to. Ms. Whittier often thought fondly of Katie as her "mother hen."

Katie's sweetness and helpfulness could not hide her slow academic progress, however. After two years in first grade she could just barely read at a primer level and was always in the lowest reading group. Although her work was always done with painstaking care, it could take her all morning to complete a workbook page or dittoed exercise. She worked diligently and never got discouraged, but her progress was painfully slow. It seemed so unfair, mused Ms. Whittier, that a child so industrious, responsible, and motivated should have so little success in reading. Katie tried so hard and yet moved forward so slowly. What would happen if she lost that enthusiasm and began to give up? How could her progress be enhanced?

Assessing Oral Language Fluency

As discussed in Chapter One, reading is a language act. The development of reading ability demands that children be able to name things, associate thoughts with words, and string together ideas in grammatical units of sentences and groups of sentences. As we have also seen, it is important that children be fluent language users. In this section we describe two procedures that allow the teacher to assess the oral language fluency of children in the context of activities that also serve as valuable teaching strategies. The first of these procedures is the *dictated experience story*, an activity to which we will return throughout this chapter, because it offers the teacher other diagnostic insights beyond the assessment of language fluency. The second procedure is *echo reading*.

Dictated Experience Stories

Dictated stories are accounts that are told aloud by a child and printed, exactly as spoken, by another person. One child can dictate a complete account, or a group can collaborate with several children or each child contributing individual sentences.

Dictated experience stories are a part of the language experience approach to beginning reading (Stauffer, 1980). Language experience is usually thought of as an instructional method, but dictations and rereadings have considerable value as a diagnostic technique for a small group or an individual child.

MATERIALS

1. Individual story
   a. a stimulus (a hamster, arrowhead collection, picture book, or other concrete object or actual experience the child has just had)
   b. paper and pencil
2. Group story
   a. a stimulus (concrete object or event the group has just experienced together)
   b. an experience chart (a pad of large newsprint)
   c. a felt pen or crayon

*D*ictated experience stories are an aspect of the language-experience approach to beginning reading. They can be useful in assessing children's oral language fluency.

PROCEDURES

Whether with an individual or group, the dictated experience story starts
with a concrete stimulus, which the children experience directly. The stimulus
should be out of the ordinary enough to (a) give the children an urge to talk
about it and (b) enable them to remember it two or three days later when the
dictation is reread.

After the experience has been enjoyed and discussed, sit down with the
students and explain that together you are going to write a story on what has
happened. You can begin by having the children talk about the stimulus and
writing down some key words they use. Then ask each child to tell something
about the experience and write down each one's contribution, including the
child's name, like this:

THE STRIP MINE

John said, "We went and saw a strip mine."
Avery said, "It was real deep."

Sheila said, "I was scared we would fall in."
Bobby said, "They dig up coal with big machines."
Sue said, "My daddy works on a strip mine."

Be careful to write down exactly what the children say, regardless of whether the sentences are complete or have errors in syntax, so as to preserve the integrity of their language. When it is all written up, read the whole story aloud two or three times, rapidly pointing to each word or line as it is read. Then ask the children to chorally read the story with you. The idea is to have them memorize it so that the sentences become firmly anchored in their minds. When they have choral-read it twice or more, and seem confident, ask for volunteers to come forward and read a sentence, or the whole story, if they can do so. As they recite the sentences, they should point to or underline individual words they know.

You can then make up a duplicating master of the group story and reproduce a copy for each child. These can be illustrated, reread many times, and as additional single words are recognized they should be underlined. Many children collect these stories in booklets.

The dictated experience story can be done with one child, a small group of children, or a whole class. For diagnostic purposes it is best used with an individual or small group.

The activity can be spread over a number of days: the dictation one day, the choral and individual reading on the second day, and the distribution of copies to the children for individual reading on the third day.

What to Look for in Dictated Experience Stories.   When a child dictates an experience story or account, the teacher can get an indication of the child's fluency as a language user. Some aspects to consider are:

- ☐ Does the child speak in sentences, or in single words and word clusters?
- ☐ Does the child use descriptive names for objects and events or many ambiguous terms like "it," "that," "this thing"?
- ☐ Does the child speak slowly and distinctly and repeat as necessary for the teacher to take the dictation or blurt out or mumble sentences and then forget what was said?
- ☐ Does the child provide information that a reader who had not experienced the stimulus would need in order to reconstruct the event or assume that everyone has the same information about the event?

The more precise their terms are, the more inclusive their sentences, the more their speech takes into account the listener's informational needs, then the more we would say that they are speaking in an elaborated code. As we learned in Chapter Two, this is the speech style that is closest to the language of books. Children who speak in an elaborated code will learn to read that language more easily than children who speak in a less elaborated code. Perhaps the best summary of the expressive use of language is this: a dictated experience story is "talk written down" (Allen, 1976); nevertheless, the more children's talk sounds like book language, the better their oral language prepares them for learning to read.

Echo Reading

In Chapter Two we noted that language fluency has two aspects that are especially important. One, expressive use of language, can be informally examined by using the dictated story. The other aspect, development of syntax, can be examined by using an *echo-reading* procedure.

We are not speaking here of a reading activity in the traditional sense, for of course we are assessing *prereaders!* In echo reading, the teacher reads a sentence aloud and the child repeats or *echoes* the teacher's words, verbatim if possible, while looking at the line of print. The reading is not independently done but is accomplished in a highly supportive setting. What we are interested in is the precision with which the child can echo the teacher's words.

Syntax, you will recall, is a system of ordering and inflecting words within sentences and ordering sentences within utterances. The intuitive understanding of syntax helps in constructing and understanding sentences with many components. Syntax is a complicated topic, but in the present context of reading diagnosis we are concerned with only a minor aspect of it — namely, that syntactic development can limit the number of words a child can speak in a single sentence, which in turn can hinder the child's reading and discussion of written language, so it is a matter of concern in diagnosis.

Ordinarily by the time children are about five years old, their utterances are complex and lengthy, and counting the number of words in their sentences has ceased to be a worthwhile enterprise, as it was when they began talking. Some children, however, are still limited in the number of words they can comfortably handle in one sentence when they reach first or second grade. When this is the case it is sometimes hard to spot, since the paucity of speech may be mistaken for shyness. If the teacher does have a child who is a reluctant speaker, using echo reading is a fairly straightforward means of deciding if there is a lack of syntax.

The procedure for echo reading is as follows:

MATERIALS

Select an eight-line passage from a book written at approximately a first-grade level. To record the echo reading, make a copy of the lines. To keep records on several students, type the lines, triple spaced, and duplicate a copy for each student.

PROCEDURE

1. Sit down with one student at a time in a place that is relatively free of distractions.
2. Explain that you will read the lines aloud and that as you do so you want the student to repeat the words you just read, exactly as you read them.
3. Read a line clearly, stop, and have the student echo it.
4. Repeat for each of the eight lines.
5. As the student echoes, record his or her words on your copy. You may find it convenient to tape record these sessions and score the echo reading later.

Code the echo reading as follows:

1. Place a check mark (√) over each word repeated correctly.
2. Circle words, word parts, or phrases that are omitted.
3. Write in words substituted for those in the line and draw a line through the words that were not repeated.
4. Write in words inserted in the line; use a caret (ʌ) to indicate where the insertion was made.

Here are some example sentences.

My new red wagon has (four shiny) red wheels. (correct and omission)

My ~~brother~~ friend and I pull lots of things in it. (correct, substitution, and insertion)

Why is the ability to repeat sentences important? It is a curious fact of language development that children cannot accurately repeat a sentence that is more syntactically advanced than one they can produce spontaneously.

If you ask children to repeat a sentence more complicated than one they can produce themselves, they will normally simplify the sentence in the repeated version (Slobin and Welsh, 1971). Here, for example, are some sentence repetitions by young children between two and four years.

1. Adult: Look at the doggy.
   Child: Doggy.
2. Adult: This boy is all wet.
   Child: Boy all wet.
3. Adult: The new bikes and roller skates are over there.
   Child: A new bikes are there and a skates are over there.

The link between children's ability to imitate sentences and the limits of their syntactic ability is fortuitous for language assessment. It enables us to get an idea of the limits of the complexity of their sentences by asking them to repeat sentences we read to them. Thus the method of echo reading can indicate whether a child's syntax is sufficiently developed to encompass the sentence patterns encountered in reading books written on a given level. Experience tells us that if the language patterns of a book do not lie within the children's control, they will be at a disadvantage in reading that book. And occasionally, reading teachers encounter children whose syntax is not adequate enough for any but the simplest books.

What to Look for in Echo Reading. One or two words deleted or substituted per sentence are not a cause for alarm, especially if the child substituted a familiar for a less familiar word such as *store* for *shop*. Similarly, if the child leaves off grammatical endings, plural markers on nouns, or tense markers on verbs, it is considered normal if he or she belongs to a dialect group that usually omits these endings. If, however, the child regularly leaves out important words or rewords whole phrases, it is more serious. In the examples above, *1* and *2* show important elements omitted.

If children have a great deal of trouble with a basal reader, it is helpful to find out what they *can* successfully echo-read. It is easier to echo-read material written with predictable patterns of language, such as nursery rhymes and simple poems and jingles. If the children are still having trouble even with this kind of material, you should observe whether or not they are taking advantage of the rhythm of the sentences. Do they repeat the sentences rhythmically? If not, make them tap their hands on the table along with you as they recite. Getting into the rhythm of the language will often help them repeat longer sentence patterns.

The important thing here is to find out what the children *can* do once the limits of their syntactic development have been found — that is, the length and type of sentence where their repetition falls below about 80 percent of the words, dialectical variances excluded. In these cases, their language in response to books will have to be drawn out before reading instruction can successfully proceed. Songs, poems, rhythm games and chants, and dictated experience stories should all be used lavishly, as well as any simple books with a pattern (a rhyming or rhythmic element, as many books for young children have).

Assessing the Sense of Story Structures

A sense of story structures is an important aspect of prereading competence. Children should recognize a main character when one appears, sense a complication when one arises, and actively wonder how the main character will overcome the problems of the story. Children with a sense of story structure can make the most of the information that a story presents them. Those without this sense will not be able to tell an important event from a minor detail and may have little comprehension of a story even after hearing and understanding all of the words.

We suggest two procedures for assessing a sense of story. The first is a predictive questioning procedure known as the *directed listening-thinking activity*. The second is the *oral retelling of stories*.

The Directed Listening-Thinking Activity

This procedure, developed by Russell Stauffer (1980), is another assessment activity that also teaches, and the predictive questioning it employs fits well into the classroom instructional routine.

MATERIALS

You need a storybook or picture book that has a good, strong plot with the elements of story structure described in the preceding chapter.

PROCEDURE

The teacher reads the story aloud in parts, pausing several times just before some important event to ask the students to predict or guess what they think might happen next in the story, to summarize what they have found out in previous sections, and to determine what they still need to know. The aim is to get them to hypothesize about what *might* occur and what seems *most likely*. All predictions are accepted noncommittally regardless of whether they turn out to be correct.

The directed listening-thinking activity may be done with an individual, small group, or whole class. The spirit of friendly give-and-take and the proliferation of ideas the children generate make a group session preferable to an individual session.

Here is an account of a directed listening-thinking activity carried out in a first-grade classroom. A teacher was reading the story "Roscoe Reese's Car Won't Start."

A group of ten children were seated in a circle in front of the teacher, who displayed the cover of the book and said, "Look at the picture on the cover. What do you see?"

"A race car!" shouted two boys at once.
"It's broken — they're working on it," pointed out another child.
"He's gonna roll over in that grease," said another.
"Who is?" asked the teacher.
"That guy under the car," the boy clarified.
"OK," said the teacher. "What do you think this story will be about?"
"A car race," said one.

*I*n a directed listening-thinking activity, children listen to a story read aloud and predict what might happen next at critical points in the story. This helps them develop listening comprehension and the sense of story structures.

"There was this man, and he built this race car, and it won a race," said another.

"Let's see," said the teacher. "The title of the story is 'Roscoe Reese's Car Won't Start.' "

"I told you the car was broken!" said one.

"Now what do you think it will be about?" asked the teacher.

"He was gonna be in a race, but he couldn't get his car started and he lost the race," blurted one little girl.

"No, I think he's gonna win the race. He'll fix his car and win the race," said another girl.

"Let's listen and see," said the teacher.

The teacher read:

Roscoe Reese drove a race car, faster than anyone else in the country. At the most important sports car races, men and women, boys and girls watched him roar around the race track in his bright red Portuguese Goman-go. The car had the number 57 painted on both doors, though it went by so fast you couldn't read it. When the judges waved the checkered flag for the end of the race, and the announcer's voice crackled over the loudspeaker to announce the winner, the winner was usually Roscoe Reese.

Today was the biggest race of the year, the Indianola Grand Prix. The fastest cars and drivers came from all around to race for the National Championship. Flyboy Flippin brought his ram-induction Wazzaroozy. It was coal black and had wings. Farrah Faretheewell was there in her yellow Italian Eatmyduster. It was rumored to have a jet engine. Ludwig Lightstreak brought a bright orange Onyamarkgettsett all the way from Germany. It had fifteen forward gears and three reverses.

"Well," said the teacher. "Now what do you think is going to happen?"

"There's going to be a big race," said one of the children.

"Who will win?" asked the teacher.

"Maybe the one with the jet engine," said one.

"No — it will be Roger what's-his-name. He's the one the story's about," said another.

"But what about the title?" asked the teacher. "It was 'Roscoe Reese's Car Won't Start.' What does that make you think of?"

"His car won't start, so the one with the jet engine will win," said one.

"It'll look like he won't get to go in the race, then at the last minute his car will start, and he'll go tearing around the track and win," said another.

"Let's see," said the teacher. And then she read:

But the driver to watch was Roscoe Reese. Everybody expected him to win the Indianola Grand Prix and sew up the National Championship for the third straight year.

But right now Roscoe didn't think he was going to win any race. In the long red shed with the number 57 on the side, Roscoe Reese paced back and forth across the floor. Three mechanics bent over the motor of his red Goman-go. They looked like the car was trying to swallow them. The legs of two more mechanics stuck out from underneath. Something was wrong.

"What could be wrong?" asked the teacher.

"His car won't start!" chorused several of the children.

"Let's see," said the teacher. And she read on:

The chief mechanic slowly stood up straight, rubbed his back, and shook his head.

"It's no use, Roscoe," he said. "We've checked the valves, changed the oil, watered the battery, and filled the gas tank. Your car just won't start." Roscoe Reese scratched the top of his head. "Put more water in the radiator," he said.

"More water in the radiator!" said the chief mechanic. The four other mechanics scrambled, hoses were fetched, and more water gurgled into the radiator.

"Do you think it's going to start?" asked the teacher. Some said yes, and some said no. She continued reading:

When they tried again, the motor whirred and groaned but did not start.

"Sorry, Roscoe," said the chief mechanic. "It's still no good." Roscoe Reese scratched his right ear. "Change the tires," he said.

"Four new tires!" shouted the chief mechanic. The four mechanics scrambled, tires rolled, and wrenches clattered.

"What's going to happen?" asked the teacher. This time most of the children predicted the car would not start. The teacher went on reading:

But when they tried the motor, it coughed and wheezed, and then was quiet.

"Sorry, Roscoe," said the chief mechanic, "No luck."

Nobody noticed a little girl standing in the door of the red shed, watching the mechanics. In her hand she held a bird cage, and it was empty. She tiptoed up behind Roscoe Reese and tugged on his sleeve.

"Excuse me, sir," she said. "I think I can help."

Roscoe turned around slowly and looked surprised when he saw the little girl. "You?" he said. "What would you know about race cars? Oh, this is terrible, terrible! The race is only an hour from now and this car refuses to start!" Then to his chief mechanic he said, "Paint the car blue!"

"The blue paint, quick!" shouted the chief mechanic. There was a flurry of brushes. Paint spattered everywhere, and in two minutes Roscoe Reese's bright red race car had turned a dull blue.

"What's going to happen?" asked the teacher.

"It still won't start," said several.

"I think the little girl will figure out some way to start it," said another.

"Let's see," said the teacher, and she read on:

But when they tried to start the engine, it went "gronk, gronk, gronk, kaphooey!" and then was quiet.

"Sorry, Roscoe," said the chief mechanic. "That engine is dead as a doornail."

Again the little girl tugged on Roscoe Reese's sleeve. "Excuse me, sir, but I'm sure I can help." The empty bird cage was still in her hand.

"There's no time! No time!" said Roscoe as he pulled on his left ear. Then to his chief mechanic he said, "Change the piston rings."

"Quick! The piston rings," shouted the chief mechanic. Eight elbows flew as the four mechanics loosened nuts, tightened bolts, and put in new piston rings. When they tried to start the car it went, "Kawunga, kawunga, kawunga, wonk, wonk, wonk, pooooosh." A tiny puff of blue smoke rose from the engine, and that was all.

"Sorry, Roscoe," said the chief mechanic. "Maybe we ought to go fishing instead."

Again the little girl tugged on Roscoe's sleeve. The empty bird cage was still in her hand. "Excuse me, sir," she said. "Now may I help?"

"Go ahead," said Roscoe, with a sigh. "I don't suppose you can make it any worse."

"What do you think will happen now?" asked the teacher again.

"She'll fix it somehow," said one of the children.

"The bird cage . . . It's something about the bird cage! Maybe she'll stick the bird cage in the motor and make the car run," said another child.

"Or maybe there was a bird . . ." said another child, but she suddenly looked puzzled, and said no more. The teacher continued:

> The little girl got down onto her hands and knees. Holding her empty bird cage in one hand, she crawled around the sports car. The chief mechanic and the other four mechanics watched her. If they wondered what she was doing, they were too tired to say anything. Then the girl began to whistle.
>
> "Tweet, tweet, tweet," whistled the girl.

"There *is* a bird!" exclaimed one of the children.

"The bird must be in the car somewhere," said another child.

"But how would it keep the car from starting, though?" wondered another child.

"It must be in the motor somewhere. Besides, it's only a story," said another.

"Let's see," said the teacher, and she read on:

> From deep inside the car came an answering chirp. "Tweet, tweet," it said faintly.

"There *is* a bird in the motor somewhere," shouted the children. The teacher continued:

> The girl whistled louder. "TWEET! TWEET! TWEET!"
>
> The answering chirp grew louder. "TWEET! TWEET!" Just then a little head appeared at the end of the sports car's tailpipe. It had a sharp beak, and two little beady eyes that looked this way and that. Then a tiny bird flew out of the tailpipe. It looped once around the shed, swooped into the cage in the little girl's hand, and lighted on the perch.
>
> "There you are, you dirty bird!" said the girl, slamming the cage door. And indeed, the yellow bird *was* smudged with soot and grease.
>
> "Well I'll be!" said one of the mechanics.
>
> "Start the car," said Roscoe Reese.
>
> "Start her up!" shouted the chief mechanic. Four mechanics crowded inside the car. Pedals were pushed and the key was turned.
>
> "VARROOOOM!" went the engine.
>
> "Hooray!" shouted the mechanics.
>
> Roscoe Reese jumped into one side of the car and the four mechanics crowded out of the other side. Then with a roar the Goman-go shot out of the shed and onto the race track.
>
> "Drivers, start your engines!" shouted the judge, just as Roscoe pulled up to the starting line.
>
> "And they're off!" crackled the announcer, and Roscoe was with them! Round and round the track they raced. Roscoe's Goman-go was blue instead of bright red, but at the end of the afternoon he had won the race all the same.

"And the winner is . . . ROSCOE REESE!" crackled the announcer.

"Let's go home," said the girl.

"Tweet!" said the bird, from his perch in the cage as the two of them made their way through the crowd away from the track.

"Which ideas were right?" asked the teacher. The children summarized the story's events and the closest predictions. One child recalled that there was a bird in the picture on the cover of the book, but no one noticed it when they were talking about the picture. The children agreed that you could guess what would happen by looking at the pictures, hearing the title, "and just thinking about it," as one child put it.

What to Look for in the Directed Listening-Thinking Activity. Reading a story with the predictive questions of a directed listening-thinking activity demonstrates two aspects of children's orientation to stories. First is their attitude toward them; second is their sense of story structure.

1. When you announce the activity, which children come quickly and enthusiastically to the circle? Which ones do not? Over a number of trials, this is an indicator of expectations and attitudes toward books and reading.
2. When shown the cover or illustration of a book, do the children expect the cover to contain clues to the story? Do they expect the title to contain clues? Do they expect the pictures to give information? Their comments and predictions will reveal whether they have such expectations.
3. After a part of the story has been read and they are asked to make predictions:
   a. Do they make any predictions at all?
   b. If so, are their predictions:
      1. wild and random?
      2. based on what might happen in real life?
      3. based on story logic and story structures?
   c. Can they give a reason or justification for their predictions?

These questions reveal their ability to sense the structure of a story and use it to predict upcoming events. As we have seen, this is an important component of prereading.

Oral Retelling of Stories

Another probe of children's awareness of story structure is to ask them to retell the story in their own words. Their retellings can be compared with the original for completeness and also analyzed for their story structure.

We can expect a youngster's retelling to have many of the structural elements of the original story: the setting, the initiating event, the goal, one or more attempts, or the resolution.

Consider these retellings of "Roscoe Reese's Car Won't Start":

"There was this man and he wanted to be in this race only he couldn't get his car started. There was this whole bunch of mechanics and they kept doing all of these things to the car, like they put new tires on it and painted it blue but the car kept making real funny noises and didn't start. So finally this girl came and they didn't want her to help but finally she whistled and a bird flew out of the tailpipe. And then they started the car. And, oh yeah, the man won the race."

So said one six-year-old. Another said this:

"They changed the tires. They painted the car over. The girl whistled. She crawled around and this bird came out. The end."

Which of the two children had a better grasp of the story structure? Which gave the more complete and elaborated retelling?

One retelling, however, is not an accurate measure of sensitivity to story structure. A child may not like a certain story or feel like saying much on a given day. On the other hand, if a child on two or more occasions leaves out most of the structural elements in the retelling and does not venture good story-based predictions in the predictive questioning activity, it indicates that this child has not yet learned to function well with stories.

Happily, the solution follows the same process as the assessment: read and talk about lots more stories! It is through rich exposure to stories read aloud that youngsters abstract these structures and develop expectations about stories. Nothing can substitute for being read to daily. The predictive questioning group activity just described is an excellent vehicle for bringing children and stories together and helping them to develop a sense of story structure and language.

Assessing the Speech-to-Print Match

As described in Chapter Two, the speech-to-print match refers to one's ability to match spoken words with the same words as they appear in print. Children gain this ability only after they have acquired the following concepts about written language: (a) words are separable units; (b) printed words have spaces on either side that separate them from other words; and (c) words and syllables are not necessarily the same things. Therefore, dividing a line of writing up into its audible syllables or "beats" will not necessarily be an accurate way to separate the line into words (Morris, 1979).

The speech-to-print match can be assessed by informal means, either in a special *voice-pointing* procedure or as a follow-up to a dictated experience story.

The Voice-Pointing Procedure

This technique is best carried out by the teacher with one child at a time, although good results can be obtained with two or even three children at once.

MATERIALS

You will need a short poem or a very memorable story, four lines long. A nursery rhyme, jingle, verse from a simple song, or similar material is perfect. Print or type the lines on paper or tagboard and triple space the lines. If large type is available, use that because it helps the children to locate the printed words.

We have found that rhythmic children's stories like Martin and Brogan's (1971) *Instant Readers* work well with prereaders. These little books come in sets that include titles like *Brown Bear, Brown Bear, What Do You See?* and *Whistle, Mary, Whistle,* which have just the right elements of rhythmic, re-petitious language and strong picture clues to make the lines easy to memorize and repeat. It is necessary for the child to learn to recite the lines confidently before the procedure begins, so choose some easily memorized text. Be sure that within the four lines you choose there are at least two words of more than one syllable.

Make a set of eight word cards, which you can use to see if the child already knows how to read any of these words from the text. For the word cards, choose two words from the beginnings of lines, two words from the ends of lines, and four words from the middles of lines. Two of the eight words chosen should be longer than one syllable. For example:

> *Twinkle,* twinkle little *star,*
> How *I* wonder *what* you are.
> *Up* above the *world* so high,
> Like a *diamond* in the *sky*.

PROCEDURE

1. Use the word cards to pretest recognition of the words.
2. Recite the lines until the child has memorized them but has *not yet* seen them in print.
3. Read the lines aloud, pointing to each word as you read.
4. Have the child recite the lines and point to the words while doing so.
5. Read selected words aloud and ask the child to point them out.
6. Use the word cards to posttest recognition of those words; the child may now recognize some or all of them as a result of the activity.

The first and sixth steps, using the word cards, are intended to show if the child already knew any of the words before the exercise and if any of those selected were learned during the exercise. You should take note of the number of words recognized, if any, during steps one and six.

The second step, memorizing the lines, is not timed or scored. It is important not to show the child the printed lines until after this stage is completed. Later on you will want to see how easily he or she can form associations between spoken words and printed ones, so it is important not to teach these associations inadvertently at this stage. Make sure that the child knows the lines before going on inasmuch as children differ in how many repetitions they need to memorize the lines.

In the third step, you model the voice-pointing procedure. Read each line at a normal speed and point to each word as you read but make sure that the child is watching your finger. Then, in step four ask the child to do the same thing, one line at a time. As each line is recited and pointed to, observe how accurately the child matches the spoken and printed words.

It is easier to keep track of the child's performance in step five. This time you should call out the eight words that you put on the word cards, one at a time, and ask the child to point to them. It is to be expected that children will have to recite the entire line to themselves while searching for each word, so do not show them the word card but just pronounce the word and see if they can "count" across or between lines to find it. Keep track of how successful each child was in this search.

In the last step, scramble the order of the word cards and see if any of the words are now recognizable in isolation. Keep track of the child's performance on this posttest step.

At the conclusion of this activity, you should have:

☐ pre- and posttest scores of the child's recognition of words from the text in isolation
☐ observations of the child's voice-pointing performance
☐ a score of the number of spoken words he or she could identify in the context of the printed lines

What to Look for in the Voice-Pointing Procedure. This procedure directly tests three important components of beginning reading:

1. the concept of the word as a written unit in print
2. the ability to recognize words in a meaningful context
3. the ability to learn new words from a supported reading activity

Research with this procedure by Morris (1979), who developed it, has indicated that children tend to fall into three groups by their responses:

1. One group of children perform poorly on word recognition and on the voice-pointing procedure. Their posttest scores show little or no improvement over their pretest scores. They cannot yet reliably match speech to memorized print, and they are not able to learn to recognize words even in a repetitious and highly supportive learning context like this activity.

Until they develop a concept of words through more exposure to and experience with print, they will probably not profit from beginning reading instruction. The best program for these children is to read to them a great deal, to do choral rereading of dictated stories, and to use role-playing reading by having them memorize rhymes and poems and practice the read-and-point routine.

2. Another group knows some words in isolation. These children can eventually identify words in context after they have learned to count through the line to the target word, reciting as they go. Their posttest score on word recognition in context is higher than their pretest score.

These children show some proficiency at pointing to words in a line, but two-syllable words usually throw them, which indicates an unstable word concept. Their word recognition in isolation posttest shows some improvement over the pretest, but they do not get more than half the words right.

This performance indicates that these children are making progress toward developing a concept of a word in print but that they need more practice at tasks similar to the testing procedure to help them develop this concept. You can accomplish this with any easily memorized text: dictated stories, poems, jingles, nursery rhymes, and songs.

3. A third group of children may miss the words from the story on the pretest of word recognition in isolation. Their voice pointing will be nearly perfect, however, and they will be able to correct any errors in voice pointing very quickly and confidently. Their posttest recognition of words in isolation is nearly perfect, which shows that they have learned several new words from this brief reading activity.

The children in this group are ready to begin formal reading instruction. The practice of reading new material with the support of a meaningful context produces new words for these children and rapidly expands their vocabulary in each new encounter with print. As they begin reading simple basal stories, they should have frequent experience with dictated stories and simple poems in order to reinforce their expectation that print matches speech and is predictable.

Using Voice Pointing with a Dictated Experience Story. Dictated experience stories provide excellent opportunities for teachers to test and develop a child's speech-to-print match. Earlier in this chapter we introduced the dictated story of "The Strip Mine" in which John dictates a sentence and the teacher reads the passage twice and then chorally reads it with the children. There is a good probability that John will remember his sentence, because he just said it: "John said, 'We went and saw a strip mine.' " He probably can recognize his own name, too. If the teacher asks him to read the sentence aloud he will be able to do so, perhaps even with his eyes closed! If the teacher asks him to point to his name, *John,* he should be able to do it. If she asks him to point to each word in the sentence as he says it, he probably will do so even though he may be a little hesitant. Now the question is: Can he point to a single word like *mine* or *saw*? If he can, he is showing signs of the speech-to-print match. He can recognize that bound configurations on the page correspond to spoken words in his head. This is how the sixth word, for example, in his spoken sentence comes to match the sixth word in his written sentence.

Assessing Print Orientation Concepts

Marie Clay's *Concepts About Print Test* (1972) assesses a number of aspects of a child's orientation to books and to written language that are not dealt with elsewhere. This test is highly recommended for kindergarten and primary grade teachers as well as for reading clinics. It comes with one of two reusable books and is available from Heinemann Educational Books, Front Street, Exeter, New Hampshire.

The aspects of the Concepts About Print Test that are especially relevant to the present discussion of prereading competencies are:

- □ book orientation knowledge
- □ principles involving the directional arrangement of print on the page
- □ the knowledge that print, not the picture, contains the story
- □ understanding of important reading terminology like *word, letter, beginning of the sentence, top of the page,* and so on
- □ understanding of simple punctuation marks

The assessment of orientation concepts about written language can be carried out by using a simple illustrated children's book, one that the child being tested has not seen before. The Concepts About Print Test has two specially made books (*Sand* and *Stones*) but teachers can get much of the flavor of the procedure with a book of their own choosing. The following are some concepts that can be tested and the procedures for them:

1. Knowledge of the layout of books. Hand the child the book, with the spine facing the child, and say, "Show me the *front* of the book." Make a note as to whether the child correctly identifies the front.

2. Knowledge that print, not pictures, are what we read. Open the book directly to a place where print is on one page and a picture is on the other (you should make sure beforehand that the book has such a pair of pages, and have it bookmarked for easy location). Then say: "Show me where I begin reading." Observe carefully to see whether the child points to the print or the picture. If the pointing gesture is vague, say, "Where, exactly?" If the child points to the print, note whether or not the child points to the upper left-hand corner of the page.

*T*he Concepts About Print Test helps reveal young readers' ideas about books and print. Above, *Jessica points out the bottom of the printed page of a book with elements such as upside-down prints and pictures and scrambled* words. Below, *she frames two words between cards.*

3. Directional orientation of print on the page. Stay on the same set of pages and after the child points at some spot on the printed page, say, "Show me with your finger where I go next." Then observe whether the child sweeps his or her finger across the printed line from left to right or moves it in some other direction.

Then ask, "Where do I go from there?" and observe whether the child correctly makes the return sweep to the left, and drops down one line.

Note that a correct directional pattern is like this:
If the child indicates some other directional pattern, make a note of it.

4. Knowledge of the concepts of beginning and end. Turning now to a new page, say, "Point to the beginning of the story on this page," and then "Point to the end of the story on this page." Observe whether the child interprets both requests properly.

5. Knowledge of the terms top and bottom. Turning to another pair of pages that have print on one and a picture on the other, point to the *middle* of the printed page and say, "Show me the bottom of the page," and then "Show me the top of the page." Then point to the *middle* of the picture and say, "Show me the top of the picture," and then "Show me the bottom of the picture." Note whether or not the child responds accurately to all four requests.

6. Knowledge of the terms word and letter. Now hand the child two blank index cards and say, "Put these cards on the page so that just *one word* shows between them," and then "Now move them so that *two words* show between them." "Now move them again so that *one letter* shows between them," and then "Now move them so that *two letters* show between them." Make note of the child's response to all four requests.

7. Knowledge of upper- and lower-case letters. On the same page, point to a capital letter with your pencil and say, "Show me a little letter that is the same as this one." (Beforehand, make sure that there is a corresponding lower-case letter on the page.) Next point to a lower-case letter and say, "Now point to a capital letter that is the same as this one." (Again, make sure that there *is* one.) You may repeat this procedure with other pairs of letters if the child's response seems uncertain.

8. Knowledge of punctuation. Turn to a page that has a period, an exclamation point, a question mark, a comma, and a set of quotation marks. Pointing to each one in turn, ask, "What is this? What is it for?" Note whether or not the child answers correctly for each of the five punctuation marks.

In order to follow the above assessment procedure efficiently, you will have to choose a book carefully and practice using the assessment questions enough times to become proficient. The procedure is easily carried out with Marie Clay's own test booklet, which is well worth the nominal cost.

The Concepts About Print Test was extensively reviewed by Yetta Goodman (1981), who has long been interested in what young children know about print and who has suggested several perceptive adaptations to the test. She recommended using a trade book relevant to the experience of the children rather than using Clay's *Sand* or *Stones*, which accompany the test. Goodman felt that the particular children pictured and their particular activities might not be culturally relevant to all. She also urged that teachers read the entire book to the children before asking the orientation questions because she found that some of the children she worked with became impatient with the interruptions of the story for the questioning.

It is also advisable to make up a record sheet that provides for the quick recording of information yielded by the assessment. Clay's own test is matched with a scoring system. We believe, however, that it is sufficient simply to make a list of those print orientation competencies the children do or do not have. Then, as you work with them in simple trade books and basals, with dictated stories and by reading aloud to them, you can begin to draw their attention to the concepts they have not yet mastered: the direction of print, capital and lower-case letters, periods, and the like.

Sight Word Recognition

Before children can read independently (that is, before they can make sense of text they have not dictated or heard read aloud), they must accumulate a number of sight words. Words that children recognize immediately are stepping stones that help them get through text that contains unknown words. Without sight words, reading is reduced to word-by-word decoding, and while this resembles reading in some superficial ways, it is not reading in a meaningful sense.

It is therefore important to see if children have begun to acquire some sight words. We cannot productively ask them to name all the words they can recognize in print, however. We must instead construct a sample list of words they are likely to encounter in beginning reading, test them on those, and estimate from their performance what proportion of typical words they are apt to recognize as sight words in other contexts.

A *sight word inventory* can be made up by the teacher from early reading material. Here are the steps:

1. Get a copy of the earliest reading books that have simple sentences. These are usually preprimers and primers. You probably can omit the commercial readiness books, as they usually feature only single words.

2. Open the first book to a page approximately a third of the way through.
3. Select the fifth word on that page and every fifth word thereafter until ten words have been selected.
4. Eliminate any repetitions of words already selected and replace them by the sampling method in step 3.
5. Select ten words from each of the next readers, using the process outlined in steps 2 through 4.
6. Type or print (in large letters) each group of ten words together on a piece of tagboard, arranging them in columns like this:

| dog |
| sat |
| the |
| cake |
| boy |

Don't label the lists according to the reading level; just arrange the lists in order, beginning with the easiest.
7. Make a ditto master of the word list and run off a copy for every child to be tested.

PROCEDURES

This procedure is used with one child at a time. If you are right-handed, sit with the child on your left. Put the tagboard with the word list in front of the child and a duplicated copy of the list by your right hand. (If you are left-handed, the placement is reversed.) Using two index cards, frame one word at a time to the child, asking, "What is this word?" "How about this one?" Put a check mark ($\checkmark$) on your sheet next to every word the child recognizes. You can put an X next to any word the child did not know at sight but was able to figure out after studying it awhile. Continue until all the words have been exposed unless the student becomes frustrated or unhappy with this experience, which may happen if the child knows only a few sight words. Use your judgment and stop if the child gets discouraged.

Record the percentage of correct identifications for each list on the score sheet, along with the date and child's name, and keep the paper for later reference. As sight vocabulary grows, so will reading proficiency.

Basal readers differ quite widely in the number of new words introduced at each level, the number of times they are repeated, the syntactic complexity of the sentences, and the degree to which the sentences sound like natural language. Some primers use forty or fewer words arranged in short, repetitious sentences; others have fewer vocabulary controls and feature a hundred or more different words and fairly lengthy sentences. Some basal series teach a core of ten to twenty basic words at the end of the readiness level so that children using preprimers have a few sight words established; in other series, the first words are introduced in the preprimers. Consequently, what constitutes an adequate score on the sight word inventory depends on what program you are using and where in the program the child is. We're not hedging; hard-and-fast criteria for everyone just cannot be established.

The best procedure is to look at your own students and their books. Try out the inventory with a number of children from all ability levels. Include some children you are sure can already read a little and compare their performance with the nonreaders. Using other informal assessments as well, determine what range of scores on the sight words is associated with each group of children: those who have begun to read, those who seem to be about ready to begin, and those who are not ready to read at all even with help. Normally, children who have begun to read and are comfortable in preprimers and primers will recognize about 90 percent of the words in these books; those just beginning to read with help will identify about 70 percent of the words; and those who are not yet ready will identify fewer than 50 percent even at the earliest levels.

Letter Recognition

Everything in reading education is controversial, even the teaching of the alphabet. Most educators, however, believe that children who do not know the letters of the alphabet are usually at a disadvantage when it comes to learning to read. If your students do not have the ability to read, it is a good idea to verify with an alphabet inventory whether or not they can identify all the letters, both upper and lower case.

There are two reasons to go to the trouble of making up a special assessment device for the letters of the alphabet. The first is to test their recognition out of the order in which they are usually recited. The *abcdefg* . . . routine is strong enough to cue an unknown letter by a known letter occurring before or after it. The *a-b-c* order, however, isn't very helpful when the letters are in words, and if a true test of letter recognition is to be made, the letters must be presented out of the normal order.

The second reason for preparing a special letter recognition inventory is to test children's ability to recognize different type faces. The lower-case letters a and g have alternate forms ɑ and ɡ, respectively, and children will sometimes fail to recognize both forms. Also, delayed readers have trouble associating handwritten letter forms with their printed counterparts. If this is suspected, then the teacher can prepare a different version of a letter recognition inventory that mixes handwritten and typed forms of the same letters.

MATERIALS

To prepare a letter recognition inventory, type a set of letters on sturdy paper with a triple space above and below each letter. Then prepare a duplicator master of the same list. Score sheets can be run off from the master. (These could be combined with the sight word inventory to make up a single test.)

Here is a randomly ordered list of letters that can be used for testing:

d	f	t	g	n	b	e	h	l	v	o	y	m
a	r	c	q	z	u	s	j	p	i	x	k	w

F	W	D	T	N	R	A	C	G	Z	B	Q	E
V	J	O	I	Y	P	M	X	K	H	L	S	U

PROCEDURES

As you proceed from left to right across the line, point to each letter and ask the child what it is. You may wish to enter on the record sheet only a notation of what letters were misidentified or unnamed.

Many beginning readers will have difficulty recognizing Z, Q, V, and perhaps one or two other letters encountered out of sequence. Difficulty with *b*, *d*, *p*, *q*, and *g* is also common because of directional confusion. Children who confuse these letters in isolation may still read them correctly in words, though they will be more uncertain than those who do not confuse them. Children who have difficulty identifying letters other than these are not likely to begin reading soon. They will need more experience with print and letters before reading instruction can begin.

Case Studies

LISA

Lisa was the small, shy first grader who was having little success learning to read in Ms. Decker's first-grade class. Her performance was erratic, she was unable to remember new material, and after six weeks of instruction she grew discouraged. Her cohorts in the low reading group were capable of making faster progress than Lisa, but Ms. Decker didn't want her to miss out on the group interaction.

Ms. Decker discussed with her supervisor the possibility that Lisa was unready for first-grade work. Several things pointed to this immediately: she was still only five when she began first grade; she was somewhat undersized; she was shy and timid; and she seemed overwhelmed at times by the demands of first grade. A meeting with Lisa's kindergarten teacher confirmed that she had been a pleasant, compliant child in kindergarten but that she had been shy and made few friends that year. The kindergarten teacher's judgment, however, was that Lisa would probably "grow out of her shyness" in first grade and that there seemed to be no reason for holding her in kindergarten.

Ms. Decker had been gathering various kinds of informal information about Lisa's abilities since the first weeks of school. She summarized it as follows:

1. Oral language. Lisa was adequately developed in this respect, but she rarely spoke spontaneously and sometimes had to be "really pulled" to get her to talk.

Lisa had dictated a number of group and individual experience stories, and although her language was complete and well formed, it was "terse"; one or two sentences were all she would produce. She always had great trouble memorizing dictated stories, and she rarely remembered one for more than a few days. She could echo-read a dictated story with little difficulty but had trouble repeating the longer sentences found in library books. After echoing a few sentences she usually wanted to stop.

2. Sense of story structures. This ability was somewhat hard to judge. In a directed listening-thinking activity, Lisa would rarely offer a prediction. She enjoyed listening to stories but never volunteered a prediction and usually said "I don't know" if asked directly. When Ms. Decker tried this activity individually with Lisa, she did offer a few simple predictions, but her guesses were very tentative and didn't always make sense. Her retellings of stories she had heard were always very brief and lacked main events as well as supporting detail.

3. Speech-to-print match. In dictated stories, Lisa had much difficulty with voice pointing even after many repetitions. She would get off the track when she came to words of more than one syllable, and she would reach the end of a sentence in print before she had said all the words in the sentence. She also had trouble remembering the sentences and often stumbled in reciting them. After much practice, Lisa did learn to recite and voice-point in two very simple repetitious trade books. She enjoyed rereading these books to herself and pointing to the words, but she preferred to practice reading these two books rather than trying new stories.

4. Print orientation concepts. Lisa was fairly well developed in this capacity. She knew which way print went, what letters and words were, and how books were laid out. She could discriminate between capital and lower-case letters but when she wrote she produced both a random.

5. Word and letter recognition. Lisa had a lot of trouble remembering the names of all the letters and more trouble remembering their sounds. She learned to recognize only her own name in print, which she often wrote as LIAS or LIA. In spite of much practice, she was unable to remember for very long the letters or the sounds she had been taught and was nowhere near learning to decode words yet.

When all the evidence was weighed, Ms. Decker and her supervisor could see that in almost every important way, Lisa was not ready for beginning reading instruction. She had just barely acquired but had not yet mastered the basic prereading competencies. She needed a great deal more experience with books and print, as well as greater socialization and oral language fluency, before beginning reading instruction could be a successful venture.

It was recommended that Lisa be returned to kindergarten for the rest of the school year and begin first grade the next fall. Her parents were uncertain at first, but they had noticed her growing unhappiness, and they reported that she had asked several times if she could just stay at home and not go to school anymore. They needed little convincing to see that Lisa was unready for the demands that had been placed on her and that she needed another year of growing up.

Certain other recommendations were made to ensure that Lisa got the experiences she needed:

1. Parents and teachers should read stories to her several times daily, sometimes asking her to guess about upcoming events. Some stories should be read uninterrupted, just for enjoyment so that she would be encouraged to retell stories as fully as possible.
2. Oral language should be developed as fully as possible by encouraging Lisa to tell stories, give descriptions and explanations, and recount stories for dictation. Her kindergarten teacher was encouraged to make use of a commercial self-awareness program for young children and to make sure that Lisa was included in it.
3. Several times weekly, Lisa should dictate a story at home or school, practice voice pointing, retell the story in other words, and identify letters and words within the story. Not much emphasis should be placed on her learning new words, but the dictation should be used to build her experience base with print.

After a few weeks in kindergarten, Lisa's parents reported that she seemed to be much happier and more relaxed now that she had less tension, and she began to make progress again.

KATIE

Katie was the second grader who had been retained in first grade and was now almost nine. She was a sweet, cheerful child who enjoyed helping her teacher and the other students. She never got discouraged in spite of her slow progress, but in October of second grade she was barely holding her own in a primer.

Given Katie's age and her retention the year before, Ms. Whittier knew that transfer to a lower grade was not a good alternative. The school psychologist gave Katie an intelligence test, and since she scored at the low end of the average range, it was recommended that she stay in the regular classroom rather than going into a special education class. Ms. Whittier knew it was up to her to help Katie learn to read successfully that year.

Myra Whittier reviewed with her supervisor what was known of Katie's ability and background. She was the oldest of the girls in her family and several of her older brothers had also experienced reading problems. Little reading was done at home and school achievement was not emphasized. Her hours after school were usually spent caring for the younger children.

In both her years in first grade Katie was well liked by teachers and peers but made little academic progress. She had almost no prereading experience with books or print and was slow to learn letters, sounds, and words. Although her oral language was underdeveloped at first, much work had been done in this area in the past two years, and now her oral language was normally developed and she expressed herself freely and fully.

By fall of second grade Katie was operating with print much like a normally developing first grader. Her oral language was adequate. She had now heard enough stories read to have some sense of story, and she made enthusiastic and logical predictions in directed listening-thinking activities, which she loved. She was particularly apt at remembering and retelling stories and often told these stories to her young charges at home to entertain them. Katie knew all the letters, upper and lower case, and had all her print orientation concepts mastered. She knew a lot of letter sounds and could recognize about forty to fifty different words in print. She could read simple sentences using high-frequency words if there were picture clues to follow, and she could do some rudimentary decoding of simple words.

Myra Whittier and her supervisor agreed that Katie was a normal child who had reached a level of prereading competence later than many other children. Coming to school with very little preliterate experience with print, it had taken her the last two years to acquire the necessary competencies and experiential background to begin reading. The fact that she could read some material and was acquiring sight words indicated that she had acquired sufficient experience for reading to commence.

Her best assets were her persistence, diligence, and optimistic nature. Ms. Whittier felt that these personal qualities should be nurtured by giving Katie every possible success and many opportunities to gain status in the eyes of others.

Katie's most serious problem was that everything came to her so slowly. In the immediate future her reading progress would probably remain slow and would have to be accompanied by much practice. Most important, she needed to be in a language-rich environment where she would be constantly surrounded by print and oral language.

Ms. Whittier and the supervisor agreed on a two-part plan to enrich Katie's experience with print and provide active support and encouragement. In the classroom, her primer-level instruction was extended to daily use of dictated experience stories. She began compiling and illustrating a collection of stories, mostly retellings of stories she heard read in class, which she could read to her little siblings at home. She worked assiduously at memorizing and learning to reread her dictated stories for this purpose. Without much ado, Ms. Whittier began focusing on helping Katie to recognize individual words from these stories so that she could expand her sight vocabulary. She also did echo reading from a storybook Katie chose until Katie could read it smoothly on her own. Then she arranged for Katie to visit the kindergarten and share her story. Katie was delighted at this responsibility, and it became a regular part of her program.

At home, Katie was encouraged to read to the other children. Ms. Whittier also helped her to make up some simple card games with the alphabet letters and some simple letter sounds to entertain her younger siblings. Ms. Whittier knew that these activities would provide needed practice for Katie without her really noticing it.

Through these procedures, Ms. Whittier tried to enrich Katie's experience with print, increase the amount of contact she had with print, support her emotional need to feel competent and responsible, and make productive use of her after-school hours.

Katie responded well to these efforts. As she worked at polishing her reading for the younger children, she began to recognize more words in other contexts. Since the younger children gave her positive reinforcement for being able to read, she worked even harder and began to feel more confident. The more time she spent in contact with print, the more she gained. Although reading never came easily to Katie, and she was still reading below grade level at the end of second grade, she was getting the extended print experience she needed, and for Katie that made all the difference.

Summary

Six aspects of prereading competency were discussed in this chapter:

- □ oral language fluency
- □ sense of story structures
- □ the speech-to-print match
- □ print orientation concepts
- □ sight word recognition
- □ letter recognition

Two of the important aspects of oral language fluency discussed in Chapter Two were syntactic development and the expressive use of language. In this chapter *dictated experience stories* were used as a means of informally assessing both aspects. Dictated stories are accounts written down exactly as the child tells them, reread chorally until the story is memorized by the child. Aspects of the dictated story that can be assessed are grammatical completeness of utterances, precision of vocabulary, awareness of the listener's informational needs, and the degree of speech elaboration. *Echo reading*, the child's repetition of sentences read aloud by the teacher, gives an indication of the degree of complexity of the child's syntax. *Sentence repetition* is used because children generally cannot imitate sentences that are too complex for them to produce on their own.

A child's *sense of story structures* can be inferred in at least two ways. One method is the *directed listening-thinking activity* in which children listen to a portion of a story and are asked to predict what might happen next. The predictions and comments can reveal whether the child has certain expectations about the structure of stories. Another method is to ask children to *retell stories* they have heard read aloud. Retellings can be analyzed to see if critical story structures were included in the retellings.

The child's ability to make the *speech-to-print match* in a memorized written sequence can be assessed by using the dictated experience story or some other easily memorized material. The *voice-pointing procedure* is used with either type of material to determine if children can match spoken and written words in a familiar portion of text and if a supported rereading activity helps them to recognize new words in print.

Print orientation concepts can be assessed by using the *Concepts About Print Test* or by adapting this procedure in minor ways, such as varying the questions asked and the text used. The *Concepts About Print Test* represents a real reading experience with young prereaders. It helps the teacher learn what a child knows about book orientation, directionality of print and pages, concepts of letters, words, spaces, and punctuation marks, and the communicative nature of print and pictures.

The *acquisition of sight words* can be informally assessed by using a *sight word inventory* made up of frequently occurring words in beginning reading materials. Words are presented in isolation, but the presentation is untimed. A similar inventory can be used to assess *recognition of letters*, upper and lower case. The letter inventory can also be used along with the word inventory if desired.

Extension Activities

1. Using the procedures described on pages 70–72 of this chapter, make up a sight word inventory from the preprimer through first-reader levels of a recent basal series. Then try out the inventory with several children from first or second grade. From the results, determine which level would

contain material that could be read comfortably by each child. Compare your estimate with the basal level in which each child is currently placed.

2. Conduct a directed listening-thinking activity (see pages 57–62) with a small group of young children. (Try to get at least two and not more than ten children.) Choose a well-illustrated children's book appropriate to their age level. Plan two or three "stops" for predicting and place them just before some critical event happens. Accept all predictions as possible, but ask children to tell why they guessed as they did. (Review the procedures described in this chapter beforehand.)

   A little later, read the same story to a group of children of the same age but omit the predicting. Just read the story straight through. Which group seemed more interested in and curious about the story? Why do you think this was so?

3. Make up an alphabet inventory or a simple game involving matching and naming of letters on cards. Visit a kindergarten, assess the letter recognition of a number of children, and rank-order them according to their letter recognition. Then ask their teacher to tell you which children he or she thinks are at or closest to readiness, and why. Does your ordering roughly correspond to the teacher's? Why or why not? What factors does the teacher believe are more important in judging readiness?

4. Try a dictated experience story (see pages 51–54) with a kindergarten or a first-grade child. Using a concrete stimulus, elicit four or five sentences and print them exactly as spoken. Choral-read the story completely several times until the child can recite it confidently.

   Now try the voice-pointing procedure (see pages 64–67) by modeling how to read and point for each line and see if the child can successfully make the speech-to-print match. If he or she can do this easily, use a simple primer or very easy book to see if the child has begun to read yet. If there is difficulty with the voice pointing, where does the trouble occur? Can the first and last word in the story be located? As the child recites, what elements are pointed to? Letters? Whole words for single syllables? After a number of tries, can the child do it correctly or is the process still too difficult? Make a judgment about the child's state of readiness and compare your judgment with that of the child's teacher.

5. Take the story "Roscoe Reese's Car Won't Start" on pages 57–62 and read it to a kindergarten or first-grade student. When you have finished, ask the child to retell the story and tape record the retelling.

   Examine the retelling according to the story grammar we outlined in Chapter Two. What elements were left out?

   For more extensive practice, pick a different story, a short one with a clear plot structure and one the children have not heard before (don't use well-known fairy tales, for example). Analyze its story grammar components and proceed as above.

6. With three kindergarteners and three first graders, try the echo-reading procedure found on pages 54–56. Work with the children one at a time. Were there more differences among children within a single grade or between the two grades? If you rank-order their performances within each grade, do your orderings match the teacher's judgment?

Suggested Readings

Allen, R. Van and Allen, Claryce. **Language Experiences in Early Childhood.** *Chicago: Encyclopedia Brittanica, 1969.* A wealth of ideas and techniques, most of which are relevant to prereaders.

Clay, Marie M. **The Early Detection of Reading Difficulties, 2nd ed.** *Exeter, N.H.: Heinemann Educational Books, 1979.* An excellent guide for screening and helping young problem readers.

Pflaum, Susannah. **The Development of Reading and Language in Young Children,** **2nd ed.** *Columbus: Charles Merrill, 1978.* Summarizes a number of important concerns as well as useful procedures for dealing with prereaders and beginning readers.

Tough, Joan. **Focus on Meaning: Talking to Children to Some Purpose.** *London: Unwin Educational Books, 1973.* Applies Halliday's and Bernstein's research to preschool and primary grades and describes techniques for helping those who most need to develop oral fluency.

References

Allen, R. Van. *Language Experiences in Communication.* Boston: Houghton Mifflin, 1976.

Clay, Marie. *Concepts About Print Test, Sand, and Stones.* Exeter, N.H.: Heinemann Educational Books, 1972.

Goodman, Yetta M. "Test Review: Concepts About Print Test." *The Reading Teacher* 34, No. 4 (Jan. 1981): 445–448.

Martin, Bill Jr. and Brogan, Peggy. *Bill Martin's Instant Readers.* N.Y.: Holt, Rinehart & Winston, 1971.

Morris, R. Darrell. "Beginning Readers' Concept of Word and Its Relationship to Phoneme Segmentation Ability." Paper presented at the National Reading Conference, San Antonio, Nov. 1979.

Slobin, Daniel I. and Welsh, Charles A. "Elicited Imitation as a Research Tool in Developmental Psycholinguistics," in Celia J. Lavatelli, ed. *Language Training in Early Childhood Education.* Urbana, Ill.: University of Illinois Press, 1971, pp. 170–185.

Stauffer, Russell G. *The Language Experience Approach to the Teaching of Reading,* Revised ed. N.Y.: Harper & Row, 1980.

Chapter 4

Informal Measures of Word Recognition and Comprehension

In this chapter our focus shifts from prereading students to those who have already begun to read or who have been reading for some time. The main questions we address are the following:

1. What sorts of things can go wrong in basic reading and how can we tell when they do?
2. How do we judge the level of reading materials in which a child should be placed?
3. How do we "get inside" children's reading and determine what strategies they used?
4. How can we tell if children are reading as well as their potential indicates they should?

In order to answer these questions, we need assessment devices and techniques that will help us to observe students reading real text in a natural situation. We want to be able to analyze aspects of their sight vocabulary, word analysis strategies, skill in understanding and remembering main ideas, details, and vocabulary items, and the ability to make inferences and judgments about what they read. We don't want to get bogged down, however, in giving separate tests for every possible reading skill, which would take more time than the average teacher has.

Moreover, it would break up or "partition" the reading process to the point where the wholeness of the process would be lost. If we wanted to study the architecture of a building, we would not knock it down and study each separate brick and board. Something would definitely be missing from such an analysis! Likewise, our aim is to study aspects of reading within the context of real reading, not as isolated components of a complex process. Therefore, we need assessment devices that will have students read the kind of text they must read in school and at home. Only then can we draw meaningful conclusions about various important reading skills.

We also want assessment devices that will yield more than just numerical scores. In order to provide just the right materials and instruction we need to learn more than just the reading levels of our students. We also have to know what they do well and what needs improvement so that we can discern patterns of strength and weakness. Therefore, we want reading tests that will give us *qualitative* information as well as *quantitative* information.

A reading assessment procedure that combines all these features is the *informal reading inventory* (IRI), which has been around for many years. There are numerous commercial IRIs, and many basal series also supply their own. Some of them, however, are flawed by poor questions or overly short, dull passages, and some teachers prefer to construct their own IRIs, drawing material from their basal readers or content area texts. Many IRIs are also coupled with an informal *word recognition inventory* (WRI). This device, which also may be teacher-made, examines both of the aspects of word recognition previously discussed: recognizing words immediately and figuring them out from their letters and parts. The WRI tests are constructed for many different levels of difficulty.

In the following pages, we will discuss the IRI and the WRI in detail. Specifically, we will explain:

- □ how to construct your own IRI and WRI or adapt a commercial one to improve passages or questions
- □ how to administer each instrument effectively
- □ how to score the instruments and determine the levels on which the child is reading
- □ how to use quantitative and qualitative analyses to determine what strategies the reader has used and where strengths and weaknesses lie in silent and oral reading and word recognition

Case Studies

JERRY

Jerry, a twelve-year-old fifth grader, took little interest in school and moved passively through each school day. He was a quiet boy who avoided contact with adults when he could and never drew attention to himself. He did little real work, just enough to get by, and much of what he produced was poorly done. He never volunteered a remark in discussions and although he never overtly refused to do his work, he was adept at stalling and other strategies to avoid reading and writing tasks.

Jerry was a year older than his classmates because he had been retained in second grade. His reading and general school achievement were low, and he never had a really successful school year. Each year he did just enough to be promoted but was always in the lowest reading group and his school record showed consistently low achievement. Since his retention in second grade, he had received remedial reading instruction in addition to language arts in his regular classroom, but the remedial work never did much to help him improve in reading.

As the end of Jerry's fifth-grade year approached, his teachers were faced with the dilemma of making recommendations for the next year. If he were promoted to sixth grade, he would go to the middle school where he would have five academic subjects and a different teacher for every class. Should he go on to middle school, they wondered? Could he handle the work? Was he too old for another retention? If he were to go on, what support would be available to him?

Jerry's teachers knew that his passivity and disinterest were the usual cover of a student who reads very poorly. At the end of fifth grade he was able to read comfortably at only an early second-grade level. For her lowest readers, Jerry's teacher used a supplementary basal series written for older poor readers, and Jerry's reading group was working in a book of second-grade difficulty. In remedial reading Jerry worked with "high-interest, low-vocabulary" books for teen readers and did individual work from skills kits.

Other than these materials, he read very little. His math, social studies, and science textbooks for fifth grade were much too hard for him to read himself. His reading teacher let him listen to tapes of these books, so he did learn something about these subjects, and sometimes his mother read his homework assignment aloud to him. He never read library books, however, or even comics. When his class did sustained silent reading he sometimes fell asleep, and when his teacher pressed him to read something he would idly flip through a magazine. It was apparent that print had little importance in his life. His teachers knew his unwillingness to read and his slow progress in reading were related, but they just couldn't spark any interest on Jerry's part.

His teachers were gravely worried about his academic future. How does a twelve-year-old student with a second-grade reading level cope with the many social and academic demands of middle school? At the middle school Jerry would attend, the reading teachers faced the common dilemma of having large numbers of students in need of special reading help, many with severe reading problems and chronic school failure. Reading classes of less than ten students were an impossible luxury.

Because of Jerry's age and social development, the decision was finally made to promote him to sixth grade and try to provide as much specific information about his reading as possible. His teachers began drawing up a descriptive profile of his strengths and weaknesses in reading and an accurate assessment of his reading level so that they could make recommendations for support at home and instruction at his new school.

BRIAN

Brian, a small wiry boy who was a fine athlete, entered fourth grade with a record of excellent school achievement and high standardized achievement test scores. Because of his "late birthday," Brian was only five when he began first grade. Although he was usually the youngest child in his classes, he was always described as "mature." In many ways, he was a model student: a diligent worker whose work, if not always correct, was always neatly and promptly completed. He was a conforming student who observed the rules and valued his teacher's praise very highly. He was popular with his classmates, a leader in group discussions, and a fierce competitor on the playing field.

Brian's parents were highly educated professionals who closely supervised his school achievement, urged him to participate in a number of group sports, and rewarded him for good grades with money, toys, and privileges.

His fourth-grade teacher expected that he would experience the same pattern of achievement as in earlier grades, so she was surprised when, as the autumn wore on, he began to have more and more difficulty with his work. His oral reading was rapid and highly accurate, although he did not read with much expression. In activities dealing with word analysis skills and vocabulary, he was a star. In discussions of what was read, however, Brian often could not recall important events or ideas, and in comprehension activities he made what his teacher thought were "careless mistakes." She frequently had to caution him to be more careful and think harder.

Brian's conformity gradually gave way to a growing tension. His teacher noticed that he was becoming restless, bit his nails, hummed and whispered to himself, and began to ask if he were right more and more often. He became almost obsessively neat in his written work, often erasing over and over again before he was satisfied. Eventually he refused to turn in written work, saying he'd "messed it up."

By late winter of fourth grade, Brian's achievement had reached a plateau. He was falling behind in his work, he showed more anxiety and restlessness, and his achievement test scores plummeted. Faced with these problems, his parents realized that they had to confront his difficulty and arranged a school conference. His teacher, unable to understand why such a capable and willing student could begin to fail so rapidly, sought the help of a reading specialist and an elementary school counselor to determine the causes of his decline.

Levels of Reading Ability

Parents, teachers, and students alike are concerned about reading levels, which are often linked to issues of retention, promotion, and graduation. Usually the statements and questions we hear about reading levels assume that a reader has one single reading level, but this is an oversimplification. Most readers who have progressed beyond beginning reading have three reading levels, each appropriate for reading of different kinds of text for different purposes:

1. Independent reading level. At this level of difficulty the student can read text *easily*, without help. Comprehension of what is read is generally excellent, and silent reading at this level is rapid because almost all the words are recognized and understood at sight. The student has to stop rarely, if at all, to analyze a new word. Oral reading is generally fluent, and occasional divergences from the written text rarely interfere with comprehension.

2. Instructional reading level. At this level the material is not really easy but is still *comfortable*. Here the student is challenged and will benefit most from instruction. Comprehension is good, but help is needed to understand some concepts. The silent reading rate is fairly rapid, although usually slower than at the independent level. Some word analysis is necessary, but the majority of the words are recognized at sight. Oral reading is fairly smooth and accurate, and oral divergences from the written text usually make sense in the context and do not cause a loss of meaning.

3. Frustration reading level. Here the material is *too difficult* in vocabulary or concepts to be read successfully. Comprehension is poor, with major ideas forgotten or misunderstood. Both oral and silent reading are usually slow and labored, with frequent stops to analyze unknown words. Oral reading divergences are frequent and often cause the reader to lose the sense of what was read. Because of this difficulty, it is frustrating for students to attempt to read such material for sustained periods of time, and their efforts often fail. This level is to be avoided in instruction.

Table 4.1 shows the characteristics of each level and some typical kinds of reading a student might do at each level.

The instructional level, where the student is comfortable yet challenged and will benefit most from instruction, is the level we usually mean when we refer to a student's reading level. The other two levels, however, are also very important. At the independent level we want students to read for pleasure, information, and enrichment. Reading assignments such as homework, tests, and seatwork should also be at the independent level so that they can complete it alone.

TABLE 4.1. Functional reading levels.

	CHARACTERISTICS	TYPICAL READING
INDEPENDENT LEVEL Easy	Excellent comprehension Excellent accuracy in word recognition Few words need analysis Rapid, smooth rate Very few errors of any kind	All pleasure reading All self-selected reading for information Homework, tests, seatwork, learning centers, and all other assigned work to be done alone
INSTRUCTIONAL LEVEL Comfortable	Good comprehension Good accuracy in word recognition Fairly rapid rate Some word analysis needed	School textbooks and basal reader Guided classroom reading assignments Study guides and other work done with guidance Forms and applications
FRUSTRATION LEVEL Too hard	Poor comprehension Slow, stumbling rate Much word analysis necessary	No assigned material Reading for diagnostic purposes Self-selected material where student's interest is very high in spite of difficulty

We want to be able to place a student at the instructional level with regard to materials for direct instruction, such as basal readers, other textbooks, study guides, workbooks, skills activities, and worksheets that are to be read in class where the teacher can provide help and guidance.

It is necessary to determine what material represents the frustration level even though trying to read these passages on an informal reading inventory is difficult for the student. Unless we explore the outer limits of the student's reading ability, we will not know how far he or she can go. The teacher has to see what strategies students can use when pushed and what strategies continue to serve them well. After the frustration level has been determined, a reader should *never be assigned* to read material that difficult.

The Informal Reading Inventory

An informal reading inventory consists of a set of passages for oral and silent reading, followed by comprehension questions the teacher reads orally. Some basal series provide an IRI to be used for diagnosis. There are also complete commercial IRIs, such as those by Burns and Roe (1980), Ekwall (1979), Johns (1981), Silvaroli (1976), and Woods and Moe (1981). Because these commercial tests do not always fit an individual teacher's diagnostic needs, many teachers prefer to construct their own IRIs.

Teacher-made IRI passages are selected from basal readers or other school texts while commercial IRIs have passages that are selected from many types of trade books or that are specially written for the test. Usually they are only 50 to 250 words long and can be comfortably read in a few minutes. An IRI consists of a student's booklet of the reading passages and an examiner's copy of the instrument. The examiner's copy contains the reading passages and the corresponding comprehension questions with their correct answers.

So that an examiner can assess oral and silent reading separately, a good IRI should have two or more different passages at each grade level. The passages should be from different stories but comparable in difficulty. To be most useful in testing children of various abilities and ages, the grade levels represented should range from preprimer or primer through at least sixth-grade text, preferably through ninth- or even twelfth-grade material.

Figures 4.1 and 4.2 show a student page and corresponding examiner's page from a commercial IRI (Woods and Moe, 1981).

Commercial IRIs have both advantages and disadvantages. They offer the teacher a complete set of word lists, passages, and questions already compiled and ready to reproduce and use. They feature multiple forms at each grade level, which allow the teacher to assess oral and silent reading or to retest later with new material. They are inexpensive and widely available.

FIGURE 4.1. Commercial IRI pupil page.

Joe sat down on the sidewalk in front of the trading post with his buckskin jacket thrown over his shoulder. He felt worried because it was difficult to know what to do.

"Grandfather told me never to sell these blue beads. He said they would bring me good fortune and good health. Grandfather is a wise and understanding man. He is proud to be an American Indian. He remembers when his grandfather gave him these same beads. He has often told me many interesting stories of how his grandfather rode horses and hunted buffalo on the plains."

Joe held the string of beads high into the air toward the sunlight. "These are perfectly beautiful beads," he said out loud. "I can't sell them because I too am proud of my great past. Yes, I will keep the beads!"

SOURCE: Mary Lynn Woods and Alden J. Moe, *Analytical Reading Inventory*, 2nd ed. Copyright © 1981, 1977 by Bell & Howell Co. Reprinted by permission.

They do have shortcomings, however. IRIs that accompany a basal reading series are made up of passages from that series, and the students being tested may have previously read one or more of the stories from which the passages came. Therefore, their comprehension scores on those passages may be falsely inflated. Other commercial IRIs have passages that are specially written to conform to readability levels or passages selected from sources other than basal readers, but the quality of such passages varies widely. Also, some tests use short passages, which severely limit the number of ideas available to the reader and the number of questions that can be asked.

In addition to the above disadvantages there are several others: some passages are written in short stilted sentences, particularly at the lower levels, which don't sound much like real language. Some portray males and females in very stereotyped ways or contain derogatory comments about females. Some carry on the same story from passage to passage, making it difficult to omit the lower levels or move from a higher to a lower level during administration. Some are taken from the middle of a story, but no introduction is provided to help the reader understand what preceded the passage. Some have fairly interesting passages but use factual recall questions almost exclusively while ignoring other aspects of comprehension.

For these reasons, many teachers still prefer to make up their own IRIs. Directions for constructing an IRI are given in the next section. If you prefer to use a commercial IRI, read the passages and questions carefully. The passages should be interesting, around 100 words long, complete in themselves, and should be followed by a sensible balance of types of questions. (A discussion of question types also follows in the next section.)

FIGURE 4.2. Commercial IRI examiner's page.

Level 3 (138 words 12 sent.)

Examiner's Introduction (Student Booklet page 66):

Joe wanted more than anything in the world to buy the electric train set in the trading post window. But should he do this? Please read the following story.

Joe sat down on the sidewalk in front of the trading post with his buckskin jacket thrown over his shoulder. He felt worried because it was difficult to know what to do.

"Grandfather told me never to sell these blue beads. He said they would bring me good fortune and good health. Grandfather is a wise and understanding man. He is proud to be an American Indian. He remembers when his grandfather gave him these same beads. He has often told me many interesting stories of how his grandfather rode horses and hunted buffalo on the plains."

Joe held the string of beads high into the air toward the sunlight. "These are perfectly beautiful beads," he said out loud. "I can't sell them because I too am proud of my great past. Yes, I will keep the beads!"

Comprehension Questions and Possible Answers

(mi) 1. What is Joe's difficult decision?
      (whether to sell the beads his grandfather had given him)

(f) 2. Where was Joe sitting?
      (on the sidewalk in front of the trading post)

(f) 3. What did Joe's grandfather say the beads would do for Joe?
      (bring him good fortune and good health)

(t) 4. What is meant by the word *remembers*?
      (to recall from the past)

(f) 5. Who had given the beads to Joe's grandfather?
      (Joe's great-great grandfather)

(t) 6. What is meant by the phrase "on the plains"?
      (western great plains)

(ce) 7. Why did Joe finally decide he couldn't sell the beads?
      (He was proud of his past.)

(con) 8. What is said in the story that makes you think Joe has respect for his grandfather?
      (Stated: Grandfather is a wise and understanding man; he couldn't sell the beads.)

Miscue Count:

O____I____S____A____REP____REV____

Scoring Guide		
Word Rec.		Comp.
IND	1–2	IND	0–1
INST	7	INST	2
FRUST	14+	FRUST	4+

Form B / Teacher Record / Graded Paragraphs

SOURCE: Mary Lynn Woods and Alden J. Moe, *Analytical Reading Inventory*, 2nd ed. Copyright © 1981, 1977 by Bell & Howell Co. Reprinted by permission.

Constructing an IRI

1. *Select passages for oral and silent reading for each grade level, preprimer or primer through ninth (or above).* You may choose to select passages from the basal reader series you use every day, although some authorities advocate using a different series so that none of the stories will be familiar to the students. Many teachers, however, don't have an available alternate that is current and similar to their regular basal. Whatever the source, prepare two (or more) different passages for each grade level. If you try to use one long story and split it into two parts, whatever is understood (or misunderstood) from the first passage will necessarily affect comprehension of the second.

   Passages should be roughly 100 to 200 words long. Preprimer and primer passages can be as short as 50 words long. Beyond sixth or seventh grade you may need passages of 250 to 300 words in order to provide enough text to really probe the reader's comprehension. Double check the difficulty level of the passages by using a simple readability formula (see Chapter Seven for directions). Select passages that seem to be "typical" in subject matter and content. Avoid those with many unusual proper names, words in another language, or very unusual or technical topics. Both fiction and nonfiction selections can be used.

2. *Write comprehension questions for each passage.* Usually five questions are sufficient for preprimer, primer, and first-grade levels, and ten questions are usually enough thereafter. Using ten questions for the somewhat longer passages ensures greater accuracy in assessing comprehension.

   The questions should call for interpretation and evaluation as well as literal understanding. Main ideas, supporting details, sequence, inferences, cause-effect relations, and understanding of vocabulary are all factors in reading comprehension. Figure 4.3 shows sample questions that call upon various comprehension abilities.

   Here are a few guidelines that may be helpful in writing comprehension questions:

   a. Make sure every question can be answered or inferred from the selected passage.
   b. Do not make all the questions literal comprehension questions; about half is sufficient.
   c. Formulate questions for each passage that require interpretation and judgment as well as literal comprehension (see Figure 4.3); however, you need not include every type of question for every passage.
   d. Frame questions that call for understanding the most important events or concepts in the passage. Ask yourself, "What is the student most likely to remember after reading this passage?" Don't ask for unimportant details.

FIGURE 4.3. Sample comprehension questions.

Literal Comprehension
(Answers to questions explicitly stated in passage)
Main idea: What event was this story about?
            What might make a good title for this story?
Important detail: What kind of animal was Nitwit?
            What did Bob do as soon as he got home?
Sequence: What happened after Jill heard the window break?
            Where did the children go first?
Characterization: What did Ms. Willis do that showed she was angry?
            How did Bruce act when he saw Jamie again?

Interpretation and Judgment
(Answers to questions not explicitly stated in passage)
Inference: Why do you think Jim spoke roughly to the dog?
            What makes you believe Cathy might enjoy flying?
Vocabulary: What did Rita mean when she said "I'm simply green"?
            What is a "chopper" in this story?
Prediction: What might happen if the delivery boy loses the package?
            If Shana runs away, where might she go?

---

  e. Keep the wording simple. A long, involved question can preclude a
     correct response.
  f. Avoid yes-no and either-or questions. They can be answered correctly
     50 percent of the time by guessing. "Did Bob go to the zoo?" or "Did
     Bob go to the zoo or to the park?" are poor questions. A better ques-
     tion would be "Where did Bob go?"
  g. Avoid questions that require only one-word answers; encourage the
     reader to respond and explain in natural language.
  h. Ask the questions in the order in which the information appeared in
     the story. If you don't, one question can give away the answer to a
     subsequent one.
For additional aid in writing comprehension questions consult Johnson
and Kress (1965), Pearson and Johnson (1978), Stauffer, Abrams, and
Pikulski (1978), and Valmont (1972).
  3. *Make up scoring sheets.* The examiner will need a copy of the IRI passages
     to record the responses and scores. These sheets provide a detailed record
     of what the student said and did during the assessment and make possible
     the detailed analysis of strengths and weaknesses.
         Reading passages. Each reading passage should be typed, double or
     triple spaced, to allow the examiner to write in the student's words during
     oral reading. The passage should have the title, page number, and series

of the book from which it came. At the top of the page, the exact number of words in the passage should be shown along with a decimal number called the *word recognition deduction*. Thus you can see the percentage that one single word from the passage represents out of the total number of words. These figures will be used to calculate the percentage of accuracy the student achieves in word recognition during oral reading.

To illustrate the word recognition deduction, imagine a passage consisting of exactly 100 words. If the student recognized 99 words accurately and had one uncorrected error, the reading would be 99 percent accurate, because each word in the passage represented 1/100 of the whole. Few passages, however, are exactly 100 words long.

Use this formula to compute the word recognition deduction:

$$100.0 \div \text{total number of words in passage} =$$
word recognition deduction (round off
to nearest tenth)
Example: for a 158-word passage,
$$\underline{.63} \text{ (rounded to .6)}$$
$$158\overline{)100.00}$$

Each uncorrected error is counted as .6 percent wrong, or about one-half of 1 percent for each error.

Compute the word recognition deduction for each passage and include it on the examiner's copy. (We will return to the use of this figure when we score the IRI.)

Each comprehension question is followed by a space to jot down the gist of the student's answers, and each question is coded to show what is being asked for: fact, inference, main idea, and vocabulary are the major types of questions, and these can be coded by using first letters. A question preceded by (MI) is a main idea question, one preceded by (V) is a vocabulary or context clue question, and so forth.

Score summary sheet. A form on which scores from all the parts and levels of the assessment are summarized allows the examiner to quickly compare performance across and within grade levels and form judgments about the performance. Figure 4.4 is a sample that can be adapted to include other information. (On this form we have included space for scores on the word recognition inventory, which will be discussed later in this chapter.)

Using an arrangement like that in Figure 4.4, it is easy to scan across any grade level and see the percentages achieved in each aspect of reading, which will help the teacher determine reading levels and patterns of achievement.

FIGURE 4.4. Informal reading inventory record sheet.

Student _____

Age _____ Grade _____

Date tested _____

Tested by _____

GRADE	WORD RECOGNITION INVENTORY		ORAL READING (IN CONTEXT)	COMPREHENSION		
	FLASHED	UNTIMED		ORAL	SILENT	LISTENING
PP						
P						
1st						
2nd						
3rd						
4th						
5th						
6th						
7th						
8th						
9th						

READING LEVELS   Strengths: _____

Independent _____   _____

Instructional _____   _____

Frustration _____   Weaknesses: _____

Hearing capacity _____   _____

Recommendations: _____

4. *Make up the student's copies of the reading passages.* Separate passages should be very carefully typed, double spaced, on durable paper or light-weight tagboard cards. For primary grade children use the larger primer type since they are more accustomed to larger type. For older students have these passages retyped in regular type, as they may find the large print babyish.

Administering the IRI

Giving an IRI takes about thirty to fifty minutes, depending on the student's reading ability, and it does not all have to be done in one sitting. You will need a student copy of the passages or the appropriate books, an examiner's copy for recording, and pencils.

It is not necessary to begin with the lowest level passages. If you are testing to see whether a particular book or other material would be comfortable reading, begin there. If the student is successful you may proceed to higher levels or stop. If he or she is unsuccessful you should drop down to an easier level.

A *teacher using an informal reading inventory to assess reading comprehension. The student reads story passages aloud or silently and answers comprehension questions about the passages.*

If your diagnostic purpose is more general, begin two or three grade levels below the student's present grade. For primary graders, begin at primer or first grade. If the student is not reading easily and experiencing immediate success at that level, drop back. If the first passage seems easy, go on to higher levels.

Here are the steps in administering an IRI:

1. Start where you think the student will be able to read easily. (If you overestimated you can drop back to lower levels.)
2. Give the oral reading passage at that level first. Show the student where to begin reading and where to stop and say, "Please read this passage out loud to me. When you are finished close the book, and I will ask you some questions about what you have read."
3. Follow the reading on your copy and carefully mark down the responses that diverge from the text. These divergent responses, which happen naturally when we read aloud, have been termed *miscues* by researchers who have studied oral reading behaviors systematically (Goodman, 1970; Goodman and Burke, 1972). These miscues will be analyzed later in order to provide detailed information about the reader's use of phonic and structural analysis, syntax, and word meanings during oral reading.

   Here is a simple coding system that will allow you to record all miscues accurately:

Substitution of a word or phrase: the student's word written over a word in text

dog
The doll fell from the shelf.

Insertion of a word not in text: a word written in over a caret or small arrow

down
The doll fell from the shelf.
      ∧

Omission of a word, word part, or phrase: the omitted element circled

The (big) dog ran away.

A word given by the examiner: parentheses placed around that word

The climbers were assisted by (Sherpa) tribesmen.

These marks will be used to calculate the student's *quantitative* accuracy in oral reading when the IRI is scored. We will later analyze the miscues to determine the reader's word recognition strategies. There are a few other miscues the reader may make that will not be included in the accuracy score but will provide additional *qualitative* information about the oral reading:

Miscue spontaneously corrected: check mark next to original coding

doll ✓
The big dog ran away.

Repetition of word or phrase: wavy line under repeated element

Once upon a time a wizard . . .

Reversal of order or words: proofreader's symbol for inversion used

"Let's go," shouted Sally.

Pauses longer than normal: slashes to indicate long pauses (one per second)

The // controversial theory was discussed. . . .

Figure 4.5 shows a sample passage with miscues coded.

4. When oral reading is completed and the passage is removed, ask the comprehension questions. Jot down key words or phrases from the student's answers. Don't hesitate to prove for more information or ask a student to explain or justify an answer.

5. Give the silent reading passage for that level. Show the student where to begin and stop reading. Tell him or her to read silently and close the book (or turn over the card) when finished. Then ask questions after the reading is completed.

6. If the student answered 60 percent or more of the comprehension questions correctly, proceed to the next level. (The scores may rise again at the next level.) If oral comprehension scores are low but silent comprehension is still above 60 percent, discontinue the oral reading but continue silent reading at higher levels until these scores also drop below 60 percent and remain there. The same is true if the student shows poor silent comprehension but oral comprehension scores are still above 60 percent.

Assessing Listening Comprehension. When the student reaches a level of 60 percent or lower comprehension, functional reading has broken down. One very important aspect remains to be tested, however: the student's *listening comprehension,* sometimes referred to as *hearing capacity.* The hearing capacity level, the highest level of text a reader can comprehend when listening to another read aloud, provides a rough estimate of one's potential for reading improvement. It is of great help in forming reasonable expectations for growth in reading and is quite easy to determine.

FIGURE 4.5. Miscue coding.

(158 words, .63 percent per word)

FIRST, ORAL

Each and All, p. 94

the

Sheep dogs work hard on a farm. They must learn to take the sheep from place to

don't

place. They must see that the sheep do not run away. And they must see that the sheep

do   get

are not ˄ lost or killed.

Sometimes these dogs are // trained to do other kinds of farm work. They

// (earn) the right to be called good helpers, too.

another   sheep

Can you think of one other kind of work dog? He does not need a coat or strong

legs like the sheep dog's. He does not learn to work with a sled in the (deep, /cold)

snow. He does not learn to be a (farm) worker.

king

He learns to help the man who cannot see. This dog must be kind and wise. He

to

must help the man ˄ do many things. He must stay right beside the man day and night.

He must learn to see for the man. Sometimes he must learn for the man, too.

SOURCE: *Each and All* [Level E] p. 94, READ Series, American Book Company, © 1971. Reprinted by permission of D. C. Heath & Co.

When reading comprehension scores indicate that the reader has become frustrated (scores of 60 percent or less), read either of the next level passages aloud to the student and then ask the comprehension questions. Before you read, say: "You've worked hard and the last story was difficult. This time I want you to listen carefully while I read the story. Afterward I'll ask you questions as I did before." Read normally rather than too slowly or with exaggerated expression. If the student gets more than 60 percent of the questions correct, read a passage from the next level. Proceed until you reach a level where the student gets 60 percent or fewer of the questions correct, and then stop.

To summarize, the steps in administering an IRI are as follows:

1. Begin the IRI two or three levels below present grade or at a level you think the student can read comfortably.
2. Administer the first oral reading passage and code the miscues. Tape record oral reading, if you wish, for greater accuracy. Ask comprehension questions and record the gist of the answers.
3. Administer the first silent reading passage. Ask comprehension questions and record the gist of the answers.
4. When silent and oral comprehension scores drop to 60 percent or less, read one of the next level passages aloud and ask questions as before.
5. When listening comprehension drops lower than 60 percent, stop the IRI.

Scoring an IRI

Scoring procedures for an IRI are quite simple. Accuracy in oral reading and comprehension is scored by percentages, which help the teacher determine the student's independent, instructional, and frustration levels.

Because IRIs are often used to determine a student's independent and instructional levels, the criteria for setting these levels are very important. IRIs have been widely used since the 1940s when Betts (1941, 1957) and others popularized their use and the criteria for setting levels were derived largely from clinical experience (Beldin, 1970). For many years the minimum instructional level criteria attributed to Betts (95 percent oral reading accuracy and 75 percent comprehension) were widely accepted.

Today many authorities still use the Betts criteria, although 70 percent comprehension is most often used. The oral reading accuracy criteria, however, have been recently challenged as too stringent (Powell, 1970, 1971; Powell and Dunkeld, 1971). Powell (1970) presented convincing evidence that primary grade readers can read effectively at the instructional level with about 85 percent or better accuracy, and third to sixth graders with 90 percent or better accuracy. He later (1971) stated that in easier material a higher level of miscues could be tolerated than in more difficult materials. From our experience we concur that 95 percent is too high, and we use 90 percent as the lower end of the instructional range for oral reading accuracy.

Oral Reading Accuracy. For each oral passage of the IRI used, score the oral reading by counting the number of uncorrected substitutions, omissions, insertions, and words provided by the examiner. (Review the types of scorable miscues listed on pages 95–96; see also Figure 4.6, page 104. Use the word recognition deduction (see page 92) to calculate the percentage of oral reading accuracy:

1. Multiply the number of uncorrected omissions, substitutions, and insertions by the word recognition deduction figure.
2. Subtract the product from 100 percent.

The resulting number is the percentage of oral reading accuracy or word recognition in context.

Refer again to Figure 4.5, which showed a sample IRI page with coded miscues. In this passage the reader made nine uncorrected miscues: five substitutions, two insertions, one omission, and one word given by the examiner. The reader made two corrections, which are not included in the score. The two regressions, one reversal of word order and two long pauses are marked but are not counted in scoring.

In this 158-word passage, the deduction for each scorable miscue was .63 percent. Nine scorable miscues were coded:

$$9 \times .63\% = 5.7 \text{ (rounded to 6)}$$
$$100\% - 6\% = 94\% \text{ oral reading accuracy}$$

(When you are calculating word recognition in context, round off decimal numbers to the nearest whole. Franctional numbers suggest a level of certainty that is not possible to achieve in an informal assessment of this kind.)

The score criteria for oral reading accuracy are:

> Independent level: 97% or higher
> Instructional level: 90–96%
> Frustration level: below 90%

These criteria may still seem very high, but remember that the context of a sentence provides a powerful word recognition aid. In sentences, words are constrained by their grammatical usage and meaning. An unknown word in a sentence does not appear there arbitrarily, as in a list, but because it fits grammatically and semantically. The number of alternatives for any individual word is therefore small, and it is easier to recognize words in context than in isolation.

Reading and Listening Comprehension. Score the silent and oral reading comprehension questions separately for each passage and determine the percentage of questions answered correctly. Enter the scores on the record sheet. Repeat the same procedure for all passages read to the student. The generally accepted criteria for reading and listening comprehension scores are:

> Independent level: 90% or higher
> Instructional level: 70–90%
> Frustration level: below 70%

(In our discussion of administering IRIs, you were told to continue testing until 60 percent or less was attained. By doing so we can be sure that the frustration level has been reached.)

Interpreting the IRI

As with all assessment procedures, the IRI scores are not an end in themselves. They should be interpreted and then applied in instructional planning. To do so, the student's functional reading levels must be determined.

Establishing Reading Levels. The scores derived from the oral reading and comprehension measures are used to determine overall levels. Scores for both oral reading and comprehension areas should meet the criteria for the instructional level in order to be sure the reader will be comfortable at that level. The necessary scores are:

	ORAL READING	COMPREHENSION
Independent level:	97%	90%
Instructional level:	90%	70%
Frustration level:	below 90%	below 70%
Hearing capacity level:	—	above 70%

The child in Example 1 is reading comfortably at the preprimer (PP) level with accurate word recognition, excellent comprehension, and scores at the independent level.

At the primer (P) level, her oral reading accuracy is still good although she made more miscues, and comprehension is good in both oral and silent reading. Primer level is a good instructional level for this youngster, but beyond primer, both word recognition and comprehension break down. The first-grade level represents her frustration level.

The listening comprehension score of 80 percent at second grade shows that this youngster's hearing capacity level is second grade, which corresponds with her grade placement. She has the potential, represented by her hearing capacity, to read at second-grade level but presently is able to read only primer level material, about two levels below her potential at this time.

EXAMPLE 1. Scores for eight-year-old student, second grader (in percentages).

GRADE	ORAL READING	COMPREHENSION		
		ORAL	SILENT	LISTENING
PP	97	100	100	—
P	94	75	80	—
1	88	60	50	—
2	—	—	—	80
3	—	—	—	60

EXAMPLE 2. Scores for eleven-year-old student, fifth grader (in percentages).

GRADE	ORAL READING	COMPREHENSION		
		ORAL	SILENT	LISTENING
PP	—	—	—	—
P	—	—	—	—
1	—	—	—	—
2	99	100	90	—
3	94	85	80	—
4	91	70	70	—
5	86	50	55	—
6	—	—	—	90

The student in Example 2 read the IRI passages at second-grade level because of his age. If his performance at second grade had not been good, we could have moved back to lower levels. His scores at second grade on oral reading and both oral and silent comprehension show that he can read material through the second grade independently. His scores on all measures at the third and fourth grades fall within the instructional range, and consequently we can say that fourth grade represents his highest instructional level. His instructional reading level includes both third- and fourth-grade material.

With all fifth-grade scores falling in the frustration range, we can conclude that fifth-grade material is too difficult for this youngster to read, but the 90 percent hearing capacity score at sixth grade shows his ability to deal successfully on an auditory basis with material above his present grade. A fifth grader with a fourth-grade instructional level is probably not experiencing serious difficulty in his present grade, but this youngster's hearing capacity score shows that he has the ability to read at least sixth-grade material. Thus he is not functioning at his full potential.

Deriving percentages of correct responses and using these scores to determine reading levels is called *quantitative analysis*. It shows *how many* correct and incorrect responses the reader has made. Although this analysis is useful, it is incomplete because it lacks the essential element of in-depth analysis of the student's responses. In order to determine what the reader knows and where help is needed, we must determine the strategies underlying the correct and incorrect responses. We have to look for patterns of strengths and weaknesses. From this perspective it is not so important *how many* correct responses the student made but rather *which* responses were right and *why*. This assessment is termed *qualitative analysis* because it focuses on the quality of responses and the strategies the reader demonstrated. Quantitative analysis will aid us in determining the levels of difficulty of text the reader can deal with successfully. Qualitative analysis aids us in determining what the student has mastered and what skills and processes are lacking. Only when both kinds of analyses are accomplished can we develop a prescriptive program for a reader.

Analyzing Oral Reading. The context in which a word appears is a powerful aid to word recognition, but context is provided only by connected text. When we code the responses during the oral reading of IRI passages, we can analyze word recognition within the real act of reading. Thus accurate coding and analysis are important.

In oral reading, even the most fluent adult reader will occasionally say something a bit different from the precise words on the page. Any well-read adult who has made minor slip-of-the-tongue errors while reading aloud knows this, and we are usually unaware that what we said was not precisely what was written. These divergences can hardly be called errors. In fact, they are not even noticed when the syntax and meaning are perfectly preserved. While some miscues change the meaning very little, if at all, other miscues can change the author's message and interfere with comprehension. Consider the following examples.

Two young readers encounter this sentence in print:

My father and I went fishing.

One reader says, "My daddy and I went fishing." The other reader says, "My fatter and I went fishing." Each youngster made one divergent oral reading response, both on the same intended word. Are the young readers alike in their reading strategies? Not at all! The first reader shows much the better reading power because this miscue preserved the author's intended meaning. "Daddy" is an acceptable synonym for "father," particularly in some widely used Southern and Western dialects.

The second reader's miscue, however, did not preserve the author's meaning. "Father" and "fatter" do not have the same meaning, nor do the two words function similarly in text; they are different parts of speech — one is a noun and the other is a comparative adjective. Therefore, both meaning and syntactic continuity are broken. What has the second reader used to produce this miscue? Apparently, letter sounds. The initial and final sounds in "father" and "fatter" are alike, although the first-syllable vowel sound and medial digraph are not; also, both words have two syllables and look very similar. While the printed word and the miscue look and sound somewhat alike, the miscue violates both syntax and meaning within the sentence. The first reader's miscue was not serious, but the second reader's miscue was a serious error.

We can ask ourselves three basic questions about any oral reading miscue that involves the substitution, insertion, or omission of a word or phrase in text:

1. Does the miscue *mean* about the same as the word(s) in the text? Is the message radically altered?
2. Does the miscue *function* syntactically in nearly the same way as the word(s) in the text? Is the miscue the same kind of word (part of speech)?
3. Does the miscue *look* or *sound* much like the word(s) in the text? Are the number of syllables, general configuration, or letter sounds largely preserved?

A reader can use meaning, syntax, and letter sounds to identify unknown words without radically changing the author's message or the syntax. In the foregoing example, the substitution of "daddy" for "father" preserves both meaning and syntax. This is qualitatively the "best" kind of miscue, for there is little or no loss of comprehension. Because meaning and syntactic function are so closely related in language, qualitatively "good" miscues often reflect both semantic and syntactic similarity to the author's usage. However, syntax can be changed somewhat without necessarily changing the meaning. A reader might change the tense of a verb or change an adverb to an adjective and still preserve the author's intended message. Thus a qualitatively "good" miscue can preserve the meaning even if the syntax is altered.

The least productive strategy, exemplified by the miscue "My fatter and I . . . ," is the use of letter and letter-sound cues exclusively, without regard for the word's meaning or function. When a student tries to read words letter-by-letter or syllable-by-syllable, the meaning is frequently lost because a letter-by-letter or part-by-part strategy slows down the reading of the text too much for comprehension. It also fragments meaningful units to the point where their meaning is lost. A reader who uses both letter sounds and context clues to analyze an unknown word has the best chance of producing a miscue that will not interfere with comprehension.

Let's review the more common types of miscues and how they are coded on the IRI. (Figure 4.6 summarizes the miscue types and the coding system we introduced earlier in this chapter.)

Our previous example of miscue coding, Figure 4.5, illustrates how miscues would be analyzed qualitatively. Some of the miscues in Figure 4.5 occur singly, some in phrases. We will consider those that occur in phrases and meaningful units together, because here we are not concerned with how many miscues there are but whether there is a change in meaning as a result of them.

First, let's compile a list of the miscues, showing what the text said on one side and what a young boy said on the other. Our list would look like Table 4.2.

Included in this list are the two spontaneously corrected miscues, which are marked "optional." Some practitioners analyze corrected miscues, others do not. What is important is the fact that the reader did correct them. When meaning was being interfered with, the meaning loss was caught and cor-

FIGURE 4.6. Miscue types and miscue coding system.

Substitution of a word or phrase: student's word written over word in text

dog

The doll fell from the shelf.

Insertion of a word not in text: Word written in over a caret or small arrow

down

The doll fell ∧ from the shelf.

Omission of a word, word part, or phrase: Omitted element circled

The (big) dog ran away.

Examiner aid given to student: Parentheses placed around word

The climbers were assisted by (Sherpa) tribesmen.

Spontaneous correction: Check mark next to original coding

The (big) dog ran away.

Repetition of word or phrase: Wavy line under repeated element

Once upon a time a wizard . . .

Reversal of order of words: Proofreader's symbol for inversion used

"Let's go," (shouted ⌐Sally.

Pauses longer than normal: Slashes indicate long pauses (one per second)

The // controversial theory was discussed . . .

---

rected. For analysis we will look at corrected and uncorrected substitutions, insertions, and omissions, but we will not analyze regressions or words the examiner supplied. Table 4.3 shows eight uncorrected and two corrected language units involving one or more miscues. How many, and which ones, changed the author's meaning significantly?

Let's look at each miscue, compare it with the author's construction, and place a check next to each miscue that significantly alters the author's message.

It may be argued that the author's message *is* altered by such changes as "*a* farm" to "*the* farm" or "*one* other kind" to "*another* kind," but such alteration is exceedingly small, and it is doubtful that the overall facts or tone of

TABLE 4.2. List of miscues.

TEXT	READER
. . . on a farm.	. . . on the farm.
. . . sheep do not run away.	. . . sheep don't run away.
And they must . . .	They must . . .
. . . sheep are not lost . . .	. . . sheep do not get lost . . .
. . . one other kind . . .	. . . another kind . . .
. . . kind of work dog?	. . . kind of sheep dog?
. . . in the deep, cold snow.	. . . in the cold, deep snow.
optional: . . . a farm worker.	. . . a worker. (corrected)
optional: . . . dog must be kind . . .	. . . dog must be king . . . (corrected)
. . . help the man do many things.	. . . help the man to do many things.

the passage are at all modified by such minor semantic adjustments. It is very interesting to note that in this passage only one meaning-change miscue occurred that was not corrected. The correction on the other two meaning-change miscues indicates that although this reader's oral rendition does not precisely match what appears on the page, he was sensitive to and was monitoring his own comprehension and in two of three cases was aware of his more serious miscues and reread to correct himself. The other miscues, which preserved the author's message, were ignored (uncorrected). In spite of the inaccuracies, this reading was qualitatively good because there was only one uncorrected meaning-change miscue.

Recall that in the section "Scoring an IRI," when we counted the gross number of uncorrected miscues in the passage to determine the quantitative

TABLE 4.3. Miscues and original text phrases.

TEXT	READER	MEANING CHANGE?
on a farm	on the farm	
sheep do not run away	sheep don't run away	
And they must	They must	
sheep are not lost	sheep do not get lost	
one other kind	another kind	
kind of work dog	kind of sheep dog	✔
deep, cold snow	cold, deep snow	
a farm worker	a worker (corrected)	✔
must be kind	must be king (corrected)	✔
help the man do	help the man to do	

percentage of accurate word recognition in context, we counted nine scorable miscues: five substitutions, two insertions, one omission, and one word given by the examiner. In our qualitative analysis we did not include the "examiner aid" but did include the two-word reversal of word order. If we simply count the number of miscues, the student had 94 percent accuracy in the oral reading. When we look at the quality of each miscue, however, the 94 percent figure is somewhat misleading because only the substitution of "sheep dog" for "work dog" changed the meaning of the sentence.

We could carry our analysis one step further. Since we have calculated a *gross* oral reading accuracy score for all uncorrected miscues and evaluated each miscue for its degree of meaning change, we could now score the word recognition in context by including in the count only the uncorrected miscues that caused a meaning change. In this way we could derive a *net* oral reading accuracy score. In the "sheep dog" example (Figure 4.5, page 97) the reader's gross accuracy was 94 percent and the net oral reading accuracy about 99 percent, since for each uncorrected miscue we deducted .63 percent. The difference in these two scores, according to the criteria for independent and instructional levels, means that this material is appropriate for this student's instructional level if great oral reading accuracy is required. It is appropriate for independent level reading if the teacher tolerates a number of miscues or if the material is to be read silently.

Few teachers today require nearly perfect oral reading at sight, which is a demand few, if any, readers can fulfill. Miscue research has repeatedly shown that no one consistently reads aloud without miscuing, and most teachers tolerate miscues that do not change the author's meaning. In such a miscue-tolerant setting, the student could be given this material or comparable material to read independently for pleasure and information, homework, extended direct instruction, or a research project. Although the oral reading was not perfect, the miscues were qualitatively good and rarely caused his comprehension to suffer. The miscues indicate that this reader understands more than his oral reading accuracy suggests.

Informal analysis of the miscues in an oral reading passage sometimes reveals that, unlike this student, a reader's miscues do contribute to comprehension loss. These miscues are easily spotted when a meaning-loss checklist is made, like the list in Table 4.3. In this case, both the gross and net oral reading accuracy percentages will be similar. If most miscues involve meaning loss, it is evident that (a) the material is too difficult for the reader and (b) the reader is not effectively using meaning in context as a word recognition cue. The student should be simultaneously placed in easier material and systematically taught to consider context before attempting to sound out or otherwise decode the word. When students come upon an unrecognized word, they should be informally encouraged to consider the meaning of the words read previously and guess what would make sense. They can be told to try going back to the beginning of the phrase or sentence, reread up to the unknown word, and ask themselves, what would make sense here? A more systematic instructional procedure, which they should experience at the same time, involves replacing nonsense words in paragraphs with real words and also completing sentences and paragraphs in which words have been replaced by blanks. The nonsense-word procedure can be illustrated by Lewis Carroll's poem "Jabberwocky." The lines "T'was *brillig*, and the *slithy toves* did *gyre* and *gimbel* in the *wabe*" might be rewritten: "T'was springtime, and the laughing children ran and tumbled in the park," or "T'was midnight, and the slimy snakes hissed and snapped in the cave," or a like variation. The procedure of filling blanks in text, called a *cloze* procedure, is fully described (along with its somewhat easier cousin, the *maze* technique) in Chapter Five. The cloze, maze, and nonsense-word techniques all help sensitize readers to the importance of context as an aid to word recognition.

Analyzing Comprehension. By looking at oral and silent reading comprehension scores across several grade levels we can determine if the reader has a marked strength or weakness in comprehension during either oral or silent reading and whether this pattern is consistent with what others of the same age do. We can also spot a pattern by looking at responses to the different types of comprehension questions within a grade level and across levels that tell us whether the student has particular strengths or weaknesses in recalling main ideas or details, forming inferences, and other comprehension skills required by the questions.

Oral versus silent comprehension. If readers consistently show better comprehension performance with oral reading and lower comprehension scores with silent reading, we can conclude that they have to hear themselves say the words aloud in order to understand. Such readers process print as though they were processing speech. They translate or recode print into speech sounds and derive meaning from the spoken words. Ken Goodman (1970) has proposed the following model to describe this kind of oral reading dependence:

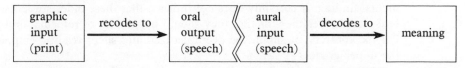

In this model, readers must hear themselves say the words in order to understand what is being read, which is quite typical of beginning readers, especially those whose initial reading instruction has been primarily oral. Often these beginning readers literally cannot read silently; they mumble, whisper, or hunch over their books and continue reading aloud, but softly. When forced to read silently, they sometimes lose their places because they do not have their voices to help "anchor" them in the print. It is not surprising when they read aloud and show consistently better oral than silent comprehension, since oral reading is still so widely used in primary classrooms. If, however, we see a student older than about eight or nine reading this way it is a matter of great concern. Reading aloud, even softly, is not mature, adult reading — silent reading is. Beyond the primary grades, emphasis quickly shifts to rapid, silent reading for meaning. An older student who has to read audibly may have much trouble reading the volume of material required in upper grades.

Also, silent reading is much faster than oral since it has almost no maximum limit. Speed readers can often read 1000 words a minute, and most fluent-reading adults can zoom through interesting material for pleasure at 400–600 words a minute. Speed is certainly not everything, in reading as in most of life's pleasurable pursuits, but it is important because of the limits of short-term memory. Poor readers who must claw their way across a line of text, suffering from Smith's metaphorical "tunnel vision" (1978), may find it virtually impossible to grasp the meaning of what is in front of them. Most fluent-reading adults can read popular adult materials silently at roughly 300–500 words a minute, perhaps faster when interest is high. On the other hand, oral reading, even when it is rapid, is limited to the normal speed of speech. Because of our articulatory limitations, we can be clearly understood only if we read no faster than 200–300 words a minute. In oral reading, even when the eyes are leaping ahead, the mouth must necessarily lag behind. Thus the speed factor is another reason why mature reading is silent rather than oral.

Most experts agree that oral reading is somewhat more difficult than silent, except perhaps for the very beginning reader. For everyone who already knows how to read, oral reading is a two-step process (getting meaning plus proper pronunciation with expression) while silent reading omits the pronunciation step.

It is therefore a common finding that as children approach the end of the primary grades, somewhere between the second and the fourth grade, they begin to shift toward more silent reading and characteristically show better comprehension after silent than after oral reading. This is a normal developmental finding; it certainly does not indicate that these older students show an oral reading weakness or that they should begin a lot of remedial oral reading! On the contrary, it should be deemphasized and silent reading emphasized in the upper grades.

Comprehension skill patterns. If we go back to the comprehension questions following the IRI passages, and if we included a notation of *what kind* of question each one was, we can discern whether there was a particular type that gave a student consistent difficulty. Now we can see the great usefulness of notations like (V), (F), and (MI) next to each comprehension question. By systematically looking from one grade level to another, we can see what, if any, pattern emerges. Was there a kind of question, for example, inference questions, that repeatedly gave the student difficulty at different levels? Was there a type of question which the student consistently answered correctly across several grade levels? A typical pattern might be one where they always got the main idea questions correct but had great difficulty with recall of important details; another might be that they showed much ability to remember factual, explicitly stated information but had difficulty arriving at conclusions or forming inferences based on implied information. Looking for individual patterns in comprehension responses allows us to design appropriate comprehension activities for students according to their individual needs.

Students who have difficulty remembering supporting detail from a story can be helped by problem-solving exercises where clues (details) must be noted and remembered in order to solve a mystery. Main idea weaknesses, on the other hand, can be reduced by the familiar "write a good title for this story," as well as by exercises where students have to restate the main idea in as few words as possible. Writing "telegrams" to communicate with a distant "newspaper editor" about news stories or composing "headlines" for news articles can be vehicles for this exercise. Vocabulary can be improved by teaching students how word meanings or clues can be found in context, or by having them write and exchange riddles in which clues to a nonsense word's meaning are hidden in the context, or by using materials that have context clues located in the text. This third activity can be particularly helpful to older pupils in reading science, social studies, and other nonfiction material that is often heavily salted with technical vocabulary and where definitions have to be inferred from context clues.

Patterns in listening comprehension. If students achieve 70 percent or better on the comprehension questions after listening to a passage read aloud by the examiner, we assume that they can deal successfully with similar concepts and vocabulary on an auditory basis, although they cannot read that level of material for themselves. We refer to the highest grade level at which the student had 70 percent or better as the student's listening comprehension level, or hearing capacity level. This level is important because it helps us determine what we can *expect* this student to achieve and thus makes it possible to set reasonable instructional goals.

Most students who are not fluent, mature readers can listen to someone else reading aloud and understand material they cannot yet read successfully because most of them, especially the younger ones, are still learning and developing as readers while they have been competent listeners and language users for a lot longer. Most students who are still developing as readers can grasp the meaning from oral language (including print read aloud) more easily and efficiently than from written language. Therefore, their hearing capacity levels are somewhat above their instructional reading levels, which is predictable, for it shows that they are not yet able to read as well as they can think.

Some youngsters will have instructional reading and listening capacity levels that are the same. Material too difficult for them to read is also too difficult for them to understand on an auditory basis. This is fine. What it shows is that they are reading just as well as they can and that at the present time there is not much room for improvement. These pupils are reading right at their potential, using all their ability to read as well as they do. They need support and further instruction, but if they are poor readers, they will probably make steady, but not spectacular, gains in reading. The hearing capacity level represents a sort of overall goal in reading improvement. If all conditions were ideal (which they never are, of course) readers might be expected to be able to raise their instructional levels up to their hearing capacity levels. If these levels already match, then for the present time they are doing as well as we could expect.

The capacity level is dynamic, not fixed or static. As children grow older and their experiences burgeon, they can understand more and more difficult material. The average seven-year-old can listen to and understand stories appropriate for second or third graders and understand them, but ninth-grade material would be too difficult conceptually. By the time the child is twelve or thirteen, however, ninth-grade material may well be comprehensible because vocabulary, store of concepts, and experiences have grown in those five years. The hearing capacity level represents an estimate of *present* functioning. Just as we would expect a child's instructional level in June to be somewhat higher than in the previous September, we would expect his or her listening capacity level to have advanced somewhat through a school year. Establishing a student's capacity level once and using it as an ongoing standard, however, is no more appropriate than expecting last year's instructional level to be the same next year.

The hearing capacity level should never be equated with or confused with I.Q., but it does give us some rough indication of whether a child's verbal intelligence is about average, or somewhat above, or somewhat below. Children with average verbal intelligence will usually have hearing capacity levels at or very near their present grade placement. Here are three examples, all second graders.

Jenny's hearing capacity level is late second grade. Since she is in second grade, we infer that her verbal intelligence is roughly average for her age and that she has the necessary concepts and vocabulary to learn to read second-grade material successfully, although at the present time she has a first-grade instructional level. Although her instructional level is low, she can improve her reading with appropriate instruction and support.

Matt has a hearing capacity level of sixth grade. He has the concepts and vocabulary to listen to and understand very advanced material, and he is obviously very bright. In spite of his potential, he is achieving at grade level, and has an instructional level of late second grade. Thus his achievement is average for his grade, although he has the potential for higher achievement. The finding that Matt is not performing at his full potential is not necessarily negative.

If he is comfortable, motivated, and interested, there is no need for concern. If he appears apathetic, bored, or frustrated then he certainly needs greater intellectual challenge.

Sandy has an instructional level of first grade, and his hearing capacity level is also first grade. Although Sandy's achievement is below grade level, it is in line with his present potential. Sandy may be a slow learner or of below-average verbal intelligence; he may have learned to read later than others, or may be disinterested in high achievement or in the materials he works in. At any rate, his performance and potential appear to be in line at the present. Sandy needs much support and instruction, and as he becomes a more proficient reader his hearing capacity level will increase. This in turn will make greater reading improvement possible.

The Informal Word Recognition Inventory

This instrument, consisting of graded lists of individual words, is used to assess sight vocabulary and some aspects of phonic and structural analysis. It also can be used to help in determining on what level to begin administering the IRI.

Commercially available IRIs include a word recognition inventory with the reading passages. Usually two to four word lists for each grade level are included, which makes retesting convenient.

You can use word lists from a commercial IRI or other graded lists, such as the Slosson Oral Reading Test (Slosson, 1963). If you construct your own IRI, you can select words for your word recognition inventory from the same books you took the IRI passages from.

Constructing a Word Recognition Inventory

The directions for developing a word list for prereading assessment (Chapter Three) can also be used to make up this instrument. Select at random twenty or twenty-five words from each basal grade level, beginning with pre-primer or primer. Continue forming word lists for each grade through at least sixth grade. The words should be numbered and carefully typed in triple-spaced columns with no indication of grade level. They can be stapled into a booklet or mounted on sturdy tagboard for repeated use. Table 4.4 shows a set of sample word lists.

The teacher's copy of this form consists of the words, spaces for the student responses, and columns labeled as to grade level (the student copy is unlabeled). Table 4.5 shows a sample page from such a form. Each word is followed by two blank spaces, one column marked "flashed" and the other "untimed," which represent the manner in which the words will be shown to

TABLE 4.4. Sample graded word lists.

PRIMER	GRADE LEVEL SECOND (LATE)	FIFTH
be	baby	digging
one	land	flashed
they	follow	reporter
house	does	strut
good	could	thicket
what	make	panic
the	has	interfere
red	large	vacant
know	girl	leaves
you	friend	contents
wait	ago	mustard
fish	enough	refer
yes	country	squirrel
help	hunt	jolly
but	color	dreamed
did	leave	luncheon
on	forest	caravan
this	carry	bundle
tree	train	approving
more	flower	strengthen

SOURCE: *Footprints, Tapestry,* and *Keystone,* Houghton Mifflin Reading Series, 1976.

the student. Word lists can be kept separate or stapled in packets right along with your IRIs.

Administering the Word Recognition Inventory

The word recognition inventory (WRI) is easy to give and score and usually takes only a few minutes to administer. It can be helpful in determining the approximate size of a reader's sight vocabulary as well as strengths and weaknesses in phonic and structural analysis. Here are the steps in administering this test:

1. Seat the student next to you at a table. If you are right-handed, the student should sit on your left; if you are left-handed, on your right. Place the word list in front of the student, face down, along with two 3-by-5-inch file cards. Place the examiner's copy, and a pencil, on the side away from the student.

2. Explain: "I'm going to show you some single words in between these two cards. You'll only see the word for a very short time, so watch closely.

TABLE 4.5. Sample page from the word recognition inventory.

WORD RECOGNITION — ISOLATION

SECOND GRADE

	FLASHED (%)	UNTIMED (%)
baby		
land		
follow		
does		
could		
make		
has		
large		
girl		
friend		
ago		
enough		
country		
hunt		
color		
leave		
forest		
carry		
train		
flower		
Recognition accuracy		

SOURCE: *Tapestry*, Houghton Mifflin Reading Series, 1976.

Tell me the word as soon as you see it. If you don't know it I'll give you more time to look at it again. Ready?"

3. Turn the word list face up. With one file card in each hand, cover the first word with one card and line up the bottom of the card with the bottom of the number in the margin. Place the top edge of the second card flush against the bottom of the first card. Now, moving only the *top* card, expose the entire word for a very short exposure — less than half a second. (This is the flashed presentation, and it shows whether or not the reader recognizes the word at sight.) Move the top card smoothly up, then smoothly down to meet the bottom card and hide the word. Move both cards down to line up with the number of the next word.

4. If the student incorrectly identifies the word, or does not identify it within about three or four seconds, move the top card up and hold it there to

*A*n informal word recognition inventory is useful in estimating sight word recognition and some important aspects of word analysis. The teacher shows individual words in a brief, flashed exposure.

reexpose the word for as long as needed (thus allowing the student to use word analysis to figure out the word). After about ten seconds go on to the next word, even if the word is not correctly identified on this untimed exposure.

5. If the student does not identify the word correctly, write down what the student says in the appropriate blank on the examiner's copy. If the error was made when the word was flashed, jot down what was said in the flashed column next to the word while you expose the word for the untimed presentation. For both flashed and untimed columns, use this simple system of notation:

> 0 = student does not attempt word
> ✔ = student corrects own error
> Substitution = write in word or sounds student substitutes for list word

If the word is correctly identified, there is no need to mark anything.

6. Continue down each column of words, giving the flashed presentation for each word and the untimed presentation for miscalled words or when no response is given. When the student fails to recognize about 60 percent of the flashed words, you should stop the procedure.

Score the flashed and untimed columns separately. Give the student credit for spontaneously corrected errors. Record the percentage on the record sheet.

Necessary criteria for the instructional level in word recognition vary somewhat from one expert to another. Some writers of commercial IRIs require 80 percent accuracy on the untimed presentation (Burns and Roe, 1980; Ekwall, 1979), but most authorities use 70 percent as the lower limit (Johnson and Kress, 1965). The point is really academic, since we are not interested in setting an instructional level with the WRI but rather in observing the student's word recognition strategies. Betts himself advocated using the WRI only for such observation (1957), but the following criteria (used mostly for untimed presentations) can be used to categorize the WRI performance:

> Independent level: 90% or higher
> Instructional level: 70–88%
> Frustration level: less than 70%

Analyzing Word Recognition in Isolation. The WRI can be helpful in assessing sight vocabulary and the use of phonic and structural analysis, but isolated words lack that most powerful word analysis cue: a meaningful context of other words. When words are read from a list rather than in sentences, there are no syntactic or meaning cues to the word's identity, and the reader can only use phonic and structural analysis to figure out unknown words. Thus the WRI gives us information only about those two aspects of word analysis. We must look at actual oral reading for clues to the use of context as a word identification strategy. Within these limitations the WRI can provide valuable information.

Analyzing sight vocabulary. The student's performance on the flashed portion of the instrument gives us information about the general size and strength of the sight vocabulary. We have already shown that sight recognition of a large number of words is necessary to grasp meaning because the need to analyze numerous words in running text is detrimental to comprehension. As discussed in Chapter Two, a large and stable sight vocabulary forms the very basis of fluent reading, and we can gain valuable insight by looking at the student's performance on the word recognition test.

In basal readers, the first few grade levels generally introduce and focus on the mastery of words that occur frequently in text (Chapter Two). In general, the more common a word is, the earlier the grade level in which it will appear. Preprimer, primer, and first-grade word lists are usually comprised of common words like *is, the, was, on, I,* and frequently occurring nouns and verbs.

An important aspect to consider, then, is the individual student's performance on the flashed words through the first-grade level. A reader with a large, well-established sight vocabulary will score between 90 and 100 percent on sight recognition of these common words. A reader with a small sight vocabulary, regardless of age, will generally do less well on these first few levels. Scores below the independent range (less than 90 percent) on the first three levels (preprimer, primer, and first grade) of flashed words is an indication that the student's sight recognition of basic high-frequency words needs development.

Analyzing word analysis strategies. The responses on the *untimed portion* of the instrument give us information about the use of phonic and structural analysis. We can tell whether readers are able to make use of word analysis to figure out new words by looking at the difference in scores between the flashed and untimed presentations. Do they consistently correct some of their errors in identifying words on the flashed presentation? If so, the untimed scores will be consistently higher than the corresponding flashed scores, which indicates that they are able to use some word analysis strategies to correct those initial errors. Thus a quick scan of the scores on the untimed presentations compared with the flashed tells us that they have some word analysis skills and understand how to use them.

Knowing whether a youngster can decode is not enough, however. To provide appropriate word analysis instruction, we also need to know *what* skills have been mastered. To learn this, we must look at the individual responses, correct and incorrect, that were made.

We look for patterns of strengths and weaknesses, not isolated incidents, by comparing the elements of the stimulus word to the elements of the responses. We do this by looking across the columns of the word recognition test and comparing the test word with what the examiner has written in the blanks wherever an error was made. What parts of the test word did the student get right when an error was made? Let's consider some samples:

	FLASHED	UNTIMED
trip	*O*	*trap*

In this example Mike got both the initial blend sound and the final consonant sound correct but was wrong in the vowel sound in the middle of the word. If Mike used the same strategy a number of times, it would show that he has a grasp of consonant sounds but has some difficulty with medial (middle-position) vowel sounds.

Jim made the following error:

	FLASHED	UNTIMED
trip	*flap*	*flip*

Jim's two attempts show that he preserved the final consonant sound, and he corrected his vowel error on the second attempt. He was unable to produce the correct initial blend, however. Repeated a number of times, this strategy would show a strength in final sounds and some mastery of vowels but difficulty with initial blend sounds.

Here is Becky's attempt:

	FLASHED	UNTIMED
trip	*O*	*tire*

Becky was able to use only the initial consonant sound of *t* to help her. She was not able to decode the blend sound of *tr* and got both the vowel and final consonant sounds wrong. On a number of attempts, this would show that Becky had few word analysis strategies other than beginning consonant sounds and that she needs instruction in all areas of word analysis including a review of initial sounds.

The Reading Miscue Inventory

Goodman and Burke have developed a commercially available, individually administered instrument for the detailed analysis of oral reading called the *Reading Miscue Inventory* (RMI). The RMI provides an in-depth analysis of the oral reading of a single story or passage. Using the RMI, a teacher can consider the student's miscues as evidence of interaction with the written text as well as comprehension of what was read and the ability to retell the story.

The RMI can be used following the administration of any commercial or teacher-made IRI.

After the IRI has been used to determine the student's instructional level, a story or fairly complete portion of a story that represents the reader's instructional level is selected to be read during the administration of the RMI. Selecting a story at the student's instructional level is important. If the story were at the independent level, there probably would not be enough miscues to analyze. At the frustration level the miscues would reflect the reader's overwhelming difficulty and would probably not show what strategies the student could use when reading comfortably. Also, we want to learn about the reader's interaction with text that would be appropriate for instructional use, not with very easy or very difficult material.

In general terms, the procedures for using the RMI are as follows:

1. *The teacher selects material to be read,* usually a basal story or trade book. A typewritten facsimile of the story is made for the teacher's use.
2. *The student reads the story aloud* and the teacher tape records it for greater accuracy in coding the miscues. After the reading, the student retells the story and the teacher probes for all details of plot, characterization, and description that the student can recall.

3. *The teacher evaluates the retelling,* calculates a retelling (comprehension) score, and analyzes the information recalled to show comprehension strengths and weaknesses.

4. *Each of twenty-five miscues is analyzed* according to the degree of correction or dialect involvement, graphic and phonological features, syntactic function and grammatical acceptability, and the degree to which the author's original meaning was preserved. Nine questions are asked about each miscue, which help to reveal the patterns of graphic, phonological, syntactic, and semantic awareness and use.

5. *The teacher prepares a profile* that shows on a bar graph the patterns of strategies used and the strengths and weaknesses in using letter sounds, syntax, and meaning. These patterns are used to plan appropriate instruction.

The Reading Miscue Inventory is a highly detailed device that takes about as long as an informal reading inventory to administer, score, and interpret. The reading and retelling takes twenty to forty-five minutes (somewhat less than the administration time for an IRI). Marking, coding, and scoring of miscues, computation, preparation of reader profiles, and recommendations take considerably longer — at least an hour, even for those experienced in using the instrument. Many classroom teachers find the instrument cumbersome and time-consuming and therefore use it only for particularly challenging cases. The RMI is most often used by reading specialists and clinicians, but classroom teachers may also find it of value since it provides a most in-depth analysis of natural reading behavior. The RMI has the following advantages, especially when used to supplement an IRI:

1. It takes the reader's dialect into account as well as successful correction attempts. (Commercial IRIs do not always state that dialect miscues should not be considered as errors. Thus the issue of interpreting dialect usage is left up to the examiner, and if dialect miscues *are* counted as oral reading errors, the dialect speaker's oral reading scores can be artificially depressed.)

2. It makes the evaluation of the quality of miscues more objective and less subject to examiner opinion than informal miscue analysis.

3. It takes account of the oral reading and comprehension of a whole story or a passage that is fairly complete in itself rather than only a portion of a story as in an IRI.

4. Comprehension of the story (the retelling) can be included in the analysis rather than being considered a separate matter, as is often the case in an IRI.

The RMI, however, also has a few disadvantages:

1. It takes at least an hour to complete the instrument and to draw conclusions.

2. Many of the grammatical and semantic forms are complex and confusing.
3. The manual provides few strategies for corrective teaching, so the teacher may not know where to go next when the RMI is completed.

With these limitations in mind, the RMI provides a valuable diagnostic tool that can greatly enhance the assessment of reading skills and strategies. The Reading Miscue Inventory extends the concept and process of informal evaluation of oral miscues by allowing detailed and objective weighing of the results of the miscues and the strategies they represent. Many teachers find that using the RMI greatly extends their understanding of a particular reader's strengths and weaknesses and provides a vehicle for in-depth analysis and comparison of strategies over time.

Some teachers, however, find that considering miscues within the context of the IRI is sufficient. If evaluated with care and judgment, informal analysis provides much insight into the reading process and makes possible the formulation of teaching strategies just as the RMI does. You should try both and decide for yourself what satisfies your diagnostic needs.

Case Studies

JERRY

Jerry was the passive, disinterested fifth grader with an instructional level of second grade. Because of his age and social development, Jerry was not retained in fifth grade despite his poor reading. Since his teachers were concerned that when he went to middle school the next year he would make even less progress, they prepared a detailed analysis of his strengths and weaknesses to send on to his next teachers.

Jerry's reading teacher wanted to include a detailed IRI with the information that would be sent on to the middle school, so she administered an IRI and computed the following scores (Table 4.6).

These scores demonstrated that Jerry had an instructional reading level of second grade. His flashed word recognition was not very good and his oral reading scores fell somewhat below the 90 percent criterion, but his reading comprehension scores were solidly in the instructional range. In addition, his teacher confirmed that he was working comfortably in a supplementary basal of second-grade difficulty. Third-grade material was clearly too difficult for him, and primer level material appeared to be closest to his independent level. His listening comprehension level was fourth grade. However, Jerry's teachers knew that his passivity tended to depress his scores somewhat, and they agreed that he could understand fifth-grade material auditorily if he were interested in it.

These scores showed that Jerry's major weakness was in word recognition. His sight recognition of isolated words and words in context was lower than

TABLE 4.6. Jerry's scores computed from the IRI.

	WORD RECOGNITION (%)			COMPREHENSION (%)		
LEVELS	FLASHED	UNTIMED	ORAL READING	ORAL	SILENT	LISTENING
PP	85	95	—	—	—	—
P	80	90	96	100	100	—
1	65	85	92	85	80	—
2	60	70	88	70	75	—
3	—	45	82	50	40	—
4	—	—	—	—	—	70
5	—	—	—	—	—	60
6	—	—	—	—	—	—

his comprehension at each level, but he could decode some words adequately through second-grade level, if he had time to study them. Analysis of his WRI showed that he was consistently able to decode consonants and blends, had difficulty with some digraphs, and often confused vowel sounds. He had particular trouble with polysyllabic words.

Jerry's biggest problem was sight recognition of words. His flashed scores of 85 percent, 80 percent, and 65 percent at preprimer, primer, and first grade showed that he did not have mastery of the high-frequency words at these levels. Consequently he stumbled over common words in everything he tried to read and lost the meaning of the words because it took him so long to identify them.

Jerry's oral reading scores bore this out. Although he could adequately understand second-grade material, his numerous miscues made his oral reading slow and laborious. Miscue analysis of the first- and second-grade passages revealed that he made many miscues that caused him to lose meaning.

His comprehension responses were generally poor and showed no particularly marked pattern. He had equal difficulty answering any type of question, and if he was at all unsure of an answer he would quickly say "I don't know." Also, his reading was slow and halting, even with first-grade material, in both oral and silent reading. He simply didn't recognize enough words at sight to really get going.

To accompany this analysis, Jerry's teachers developed a set of recommendations to send to his middle school reading teacher:

1. *Develop large sight vocabulary.* Jerry needs intensive work in sight vocabulary development, especially simple high-frequency words like *these, those, where, what,* and the like. We have used dictated experience stories and rereading of easy material to help him learn these, and he enjoys word

hunts where he searches magazines and books for words that he has in his word bank.

2. *Develop use of context in word recognition.* Jerry depends on phonics to figure out unknown words. (In phonics he has a lot of trouble with vowel sounds, especially variant vowels like *ei, au, ou,* and working with syllab-ication.) He usually tries to "sound out" rather than using context. We have used stories with words omitted so that he had to guess what would make sense in the blank, and he enjoyed these. He is beginning to under-stand that he should try to figure out words in this way as well as by sounding them out.

3. *Improve silent reading rate by repeated reading and other rate-building meth-ods.* Jerry reads very slowly because he recognizes so few words at sight. We have tried repeated reading, where he practiced reading the same story aloud over and over and kept a chart showing his rate. This technique is slowly improving his rate of reading new material and also gives him a feeling of accomplishment.

4. *Develop reading attitudes and interest.* Because he does it so poorly Jerry is very disinterested in reading, but he is interested in sports, cars, motor-cycles, and outdoor life, and these can be used to help get him started. He won't read "just to read." He has to see a concrete outcome from his reading, and he works cooperatively on projects that have a real goal.

5. *Read to him.* Jerry enjoys being read to and will sometimes try to read a book he's been read, if it is easy enough. Try this to get him started on a book and read aloud to him very often.

6. *Emphasize silent reading.* We have deemphasized oral reading and worked hard on silent reading for meaning. If Jerry *must* read aloud, we hope you will be tolerant of his miscues and let him rehearse by reading silently before he reads aloud. His oral reading is much better this way.

7. *Use appropriate material at second-grade readability level.* We have contin-ued to work in second-grade level materials appropriate for young teens, as well as magazines, newspapers, and any trade books that Jerry will use. He seems comfortable and challenged at this level of difficulty.

BRIAN

Brian, a nine-year-old who had always showed adequate reading achieve-ment, began exhibiting tension and stress in fourth grade. His test scores and daily work suffered and he was unable to deal with fourth-grade reading.

The reading teacher gave Brian an informal reading inventory and word recognition test. Because she was particularly interested in his performance at fourth-grade level, she began the IRI there. As in class, his oral reading was rapid and highly accurate although monotonous in tone. His silent reading of the fourth-grade passage was also quickly completed, at a rapid rate of about 170 words a minute, but his comprehension of both passages was surprisingly poor. He did somewhat better on the oral than on the silent comprehension and had more trouble with inferential and vocabulary questions than with questions of direct recall. The teacher noted that when he was unsure of an answer, he often said something like "I don't remember that" or "The story didn't tell that." After the fourth-grade level administration, she dropped back to third grade, then second-grade passages. At all levels, his reading was rapid and fluent but without expression, and he had difficulty with a number of comprehension questions. Only in second-grade material was he truly comfortable in both word recognition and comprehension. Brian's teacher then administered the hearing capacity test at grade five, where his listening comprehension was adequate. Following the IRI, she gave him the informal word recognition inventory, levels three through six. His performance, which was excellent through sixth grade, revealed a very large sight vocabulary and well-developed word analysis (Table 4.7).

These scores and test observations indicated that Brian was a *word caller*, a term used for those who recognize words fluently but have problems understanding what they read. Brian's difficulty lay in making sense of print; his comprehension scores showed that he had to read aloud, to hear himself say the words, in order to make much sense of it. Although his silent reading was fluent, it was lacking in meaning. His word recognition scores showed well-polished skills in recognizing and decoding words in isolation and in context. His sight vocabulary was adequate for reading even sixth-grade material, but, for Brian, *saying* the words had somehow become the goal of reading rather than *understanding* them. Third grade appeared to be his instructional level for oral reading, but with silent reading for meaning he would be better off in material of second-grade difficulty.

When his teacher went over these findings with the reading specialist, many of Brian's behaviors began to make sense to her. Because in fourth grade there is more emphasis on silent reading for meaning, especially in subject area texts, Brian was forced to do more and more of what he did least well.

TABLE 4.7. Brian's scores computed from the IRI.

	WORD RECOGNITION (%)			COMPREHENSION (%)		
LEVELS	FLASHED	UNTIMED	ORAL READING	ORAL	SILENT	LISTENING
2	—	—	100	90	80	—
3	100	—	97	70	60	—
4	90	100	94	65	50	—
5	85	95	—	—	—	70
6	80	95	—	—	—	—

His teacher could now see that many of his careless errors, apparent forgetfulness in discussions, and poor test scores were the inevitable result of his comprehension problems. She realized that when she had assumed he was a "good reader" because of his fluent oral reading, she had overlooked a major aspect of real reading ability. She suspected that Brian's word calling had hidden his basic reading problem for some time, and that his zeal to do well and win approval obscured the fact that he didn't understand what he read.

Brian's comprehension ability was underdeveloped, and when he was exposed to more challenging, complex materials where comprehension was critical, Brian was poorly equipped. As things got harder for him, his anxiety grew. The more tense he became, the harder it was for him to do well, and a failure cycle began. He started to manifest behaviors we associate with stress: shortened attention span, nail biting, talking to himself, and constant seeking of reassurance. Brian was rapidly becoming a nervous wreck.

It was apparent that Brian's achievement and emotional distress were closely related, and the teachers agreed that remedial action must take place on both fronts in order to relieve Brian's anxiety and improve his reading. They drew up a list of problems to be dealt with:

1. Reading comprehension poor compared with word recognition.
2. Weak silent reading for meaning; needs to hear himself read aloud.
3. Problems with inferential thinking and word meanings.
4. Growing tension and fear of failure.

Then they made a list of recommendations to attack the problems:

1. Work on reading for meaning only, deemphasizing word analysis.
2. Do silent reading only, to deemphasize word calling.
3. Use easier materials, third- or even second-grade difficulty.
4. Discuss retention in fourth grade so that he can catch up with peers.
5. Encourage him to stop reading at a certain point in a story and predict what might happen next; deemphasize being right; use open-ended writing activities, for example. Encourage him to take the risk of being wrong.
6. In written work and creative writing, deemphasize neatness and correctness; instead, reward creativeness and originality.
7. Read to him daily, just for enjoyment, from fine quality literature, especially themes of success and failure.
8. Give him extra encouragement and praise, especially when he takes a risk, as in predicting how a story might turn out or other use of divergent thinking.
9. Confer with his parents to discuss ways of taking the pressure off him; suggest a physical examination because of the many physical symptoms of anxiety and stress that may be affecting his learning (poor appetite, insomnia, etc.).

His parents agreed to have their pediatrician examine him and together with the teachers discussed ways they could deemphasize achievement and help Brian relax. At school, his teacher concentrated her efforts on comprehension and silent reading. With much encouragement and some of the academic pressure removed, he was able to concentrate on understanding what he had read and began to enjoy reading more.

Summary

This chapter has focused on informal means of assessing word recognition and comprehension in typical school reading materials. The procedures stressed *qualitative* analysis of reading behaviors as well as use of *quantitative* scores.

Informal measures are often used to determine a student's *independent, instructional,* and *frustration reading levels.* Independent level material is easy for the reader; no help is needed and comprehension is excellent. Instructional level material is comfortable yet challenging; new concepts and vocabulary are introduced and comprehension is good. This is the most appropriate level of difficulty for classroom instruction. Frustration level material is too difficult because comprehension is poor and little is gained from the reading.

An *informal reading inventory (IRI)* can be used to determine reading levels and analyze strengths and weaknesses. Both *commercial and teacher-made IRIs* consist of passages for oral and silent reading at many levels of difficulty, with a variety of comprehension questions on each passage. Most IRIs begin with preprimer or primer level passages and increase in difficulty through high school level material.

Because commercial IRIs vary in passage and question quality, some teachers prefer to construct their own IRIs from basal reader materials. Two (or more) different passages per level are selected and comprehension questions that call on a variety of comprehension skills are developed. The forms are such that the student reads each passage without questions or grade level designations, and the examiner reads the comprehension questions aloud to the student.

IRIs are *individually administered* and take about thirty to fifty minutes to give, depending on the reader's ability. During the oral reading the examiner observes accuracy by recording the student's divergences from the written text. Uncorrected *oral reading divergences,* or *miscues,* are counted to provide an accuracy score and are also analyzed to determine the word recognition strategies that were used during oral reading. Following the oral and silent readings at each level, comprehension questions are asked by the examiner. Responses are briefly recorded and later analyzed to provide insight into the reader's *comprehension skills.* After the frustration reading level has been determined, passages are read aloud to the student and questions are asked to determine the student's *listening comprehension* (or *hearing capacity*) levels. Hearing capacity levels represent an informal means of determining a student's *reading potential* at the time of the assessment. This potential is not static or fixed, and as students improve their reading ability, their potential for further improvement usually increases as well.

Scoring procedures for the IRI include an analysis of oral reading miscues to determine the degree to which each one changed the author's meaning, and also an analysis of patterns in answering different types of comprehension questions. These types of analyses, which provide *qualitative* information about the student's strengths and weaknesses, are combined with *quantitative* scores (percentages of accuracy or correct response) in determining reading levels and developing prescriptive teaching activities.

IRIs are often used together with an *informal word recognition inventory* (*WRI*), which is used to assess the recognition of words in isolation. WRIs consist of graded lists of single words taken from materials from preprimer or primer through at least sixth-grade levels. They can be helpful in assessing a student's sight vocabulary and phonic and structural analysis skills, and they can be given before an IRI to indicate on what level to begin testing.

Sight recognition of words is tested by *flashing*, or exposing, individual words for a very brief time, less than a second. Unrecognized words are reexposed in an *untimed* presentation so that the student can analyze the word using phonic and/or structural analysis skills. When words are presented individually, context is unavailable as a word recognition clue. The ability to use context is assessed during the oral reading of connected text by analyzing the miscues. The student's use of phonic and structural aspects can be determined by analysis of the word recognition errors on the WRI.

A commercially available informal device for analysis of oral reading miscues and oral reading comprehension is the *Reading Miscue Inventory*. This instrument extends and quantifies the analysis of miscues and can be helpful in detailed diagnoses, although the instrument is time-consuming and cumbersome for classroom use. The RMI can provide a highly detailed, in-depth analysis of real reading strategies.

Extension Activities

1. Choose two consecutive grade levels of a basal reader, first-grade level or above. From each level, select two passages of approximagely 250 words each to use for oral and silent reading. Construct a set of ten comprehension questions for each passage according to the guidelines presented in this chapter. If you can arrange it, have three different children read the passages and answer the questions.

2. Get a copy of a commercial informal reading inventory, or see if your basal reading series provides an IRI. Read several passages and their comprehension questions critically. Analyze the questions according to the

guidelines on page 90. Mark the questions you think are poor. Why are they poor? How could they be improved? What questions do you think should have been included that were not?

3. Administer one (or more) oral reading passage(s) to a student and record the miscues, using the coding system on pages 95–96. Compute the word recognition deduction and determine the gross accuracy for the passage.

4. Using the same passage as in number 3 above, analyze the miscues according to the degree of meaning change involved. (Review the section "Analyzing Oral Reading," page 102–107.) Considering only the meaning-change miscues, rescore the passage and compute the net accuracy. How are the two estimates different? Does the passage represent the reader's instructional level in either case?

5. Construct several levels of a word recognition inventory, or use the word lists from a commercial IRI. Administer the lists to several students using the flashed and untimed presentations. Analyze their responses as demonstrated in the section "Analyzing Word Recognition in Isolation," pages 115–117. What strengths and weaknesses does each student show in phonic/structural analysis?

Suggested Readings

Johns, Jerry; Garton, Sharon; Schoenfelder, Paula; and Skriba, Patricia. **Assessing Reading Behavior: Informal Reading Inventories.** *Newark, Del.: International Reading Association, 1977.* A thorough, nontechnical description of commercial IRIs and their use.

Johnson, Marjorie S. and Kress, Roy A. **Informal Reading Inventories.** *Newark, Del.: International Reading Association, 1965.* Practical description of construction and use of IRIs.

Jongsma, Kathleen S. and Jongsma, Eugene A. "Test Review: Commerical Informal Reading Inventories." *Reading Teacher 34, no. 6 (March 1981): 697–705.* Concise critical review of commercially available IRIs.

Goodman, Yetta M. and Burke, Carolyn. **Reading Stategies: Focus on Comprehension.** *N.Y.: Holt, Rinehart & Winston, 1980.* Practical handbook of classroom activities to help students develop reading comprehension.

Goodman, Yetta M. and Burke, Carolyn **Reading Miscue Inventory Manual.** *N.Y.: Macmillan, 1972.* Detailed description of miscue analysis with some general corrective strategies.

Stauffer, Russell G.; Abrams, Jules C.; and Pikulski, John J. **Diagnosis, Correction and Prevention of Reading Disabilities.** *N.Y.: Harper & Row, 1978.* (Chs. 1–6) Thorough discussion of informal methods of diagnosis.

References

Beldin, H. O. "Informal Reading Testing: Historical Review and Review of the Research." In William K. Durr, ed. *Reading Difficulties: Diagnosis, Correction and Remediation.* Newark, Del.: International Reading Association, 1970.

Betts, Emmett A. "Reading Problems at the Intermediate Grade Level." *Elementary School Journal* 40 (June 1941): 737–746.

Betts, Emmett A. *Foundations of Reading Instruction*. N.Y.: American Book, 1957.

Burns, Paul C. and Roe, Betty D. *Informal Reading Assessment*. Chicago: Rand McNally, 1980.

Carroll, Lewis, "Jabberwocky." In Helen Gardner, ed. *The New Oxford Book of English Verse*. N.Y.: Oxford University Press, 1972, pp. 730–731.

Ekwall, Eldon E. *Ekwall Reading Inventory*. Boston: Allyn and Bacon, 1979.

Goodman, Kenneth S. "Behind the Eye: What Happens in Reading." In Olive S. Niles, ed. *Reading: Process and Program*. Urbana, Ill.: National Council of Teachers of English, 1970, pp. 3–38.

Goodman, Yetta and Burke, Carolyn. *Reading Miscue Inventory Manual*. N.Y.: Macmillan, 1972.

Johns, Jerry L. *Basic Reading Inventory*, 2nd ed. Dubuque, Iowa: Kendall-Hunt, 1981.

Johnson, Marjorie S. and Kress, Roy A. *Informal Reading Inventories*. Newark, Del.: International Reading Associates 1965.

Pearson, P. David and Johnson, Dale L. *Teaching Reading Comprehension*. N.Y.: Holt, Rinehart & Winston, 1978.

Powell, William R. "Reappraising the Criteria for Interpreting Informal Reading Inventories." In Dorothy DeBoer, ed. *Reading Diagnosis and Evaluation*. Newark, Del.: International Reading Associates, 1970.

Powell, William R. "The Validity of the Instructional Reading Level." In Robert E. Liebert, ed. *Diagnostic Viewpoints in Reading*. Newark, Del.: International Reading Associates, 1971.

Powell, William R. and Dunkeld, Colin G. "Validity of the IRI Reading Levels." *Elementary English* 48, no. 6 (Oct. 1971): 637–642.

Silvaroli, Nicholas J. *Classroom Reading Inventory*, 3rd ed. Dubuque, Iowa: William C. Brown, 1976.

Slosson, Richard L. *Slosson Oral Reading Test*. E. Aurora, N.Y.: Slosson Educational Publications, 1963.

Smith, Frank. *Understanding Reading*, rev. ed. N.Y.: Holt, Rinehart & Winston, 1978.

Stauffer, Russell G.; Abrams, Jules C.; and Pikulski, John J. *Diagnosis, Correction, and Prevention of Reading Disabilities*. N.Y.: Harper & Row, 1978.

Valmont, William. "Creating Questions for Informal Reading Inventories," *The Reading Teacher* 25, no. 6 (March 1972): 509–512.

Woods, Mary Lynn and Moe, Alden J. *Analytical Reading Inventory*, 2nd ed. Columbus, Ohio: Charles C. Merrill, 1981.

Chapter Five

Diagnostic-Instructional Procedures

In Chapter Four we discussed several common informal assessment devices: the informal reading inventory, the informal word recognition inventory, and the Reading Miscue Inventory. These informal devices yield important diagnostic information of various kinds, although the teacher using them has to take time out from ongoing instruction to administer them.

There are times, however, when a teacher would like to gather informal diagnostic information without having to give a test, even if the test takes only a few minutes to administer. It is economical in terms of time and allows naturalistic observation of the student's reading when teaching activities have a diagnostic purpose as well. In Chapter Three we discussed such activities for use with prereaders or beginning readers, like the directed listening-thinking activity, the voice-pointing procedures, and the dictated experience story. Each of these activities has instruction as its primary purpose and use, yet each can yield a wealth of diagnostic information about the child.

In this chapter we discuss procedures for gathering informal diagnostic information about students who have already learned to read. Such procedures can be used repeatedly during a school year so that diagnostic information is kept current. We have selected four diagnostic-instructional procedures that we believe are most useful because they are appropriate for students of almost every age, grade, and subject. They can be used repeatedly without losing their appeal or usefulness; they require only typical reading or content area materials that students deal with on a daily basis; they are not time-consuming in construction or use; and they can be used for group or individual instruction. The procedures we have selected to describe and demonstrate are the *cloze* and *maze procedures*, *word sorting*, and *directed reading-thinking* or *listening-thinking activities*.

The Cloze Procedure

Figure 5.1 shows a portion of a cloze procedure. After the first sentence, you will find blanks in the text. Can you figure out what might make sense in each blank? (Only *one* word has been deleted each time.)

The cloze procedure (Taylor, 1953) has students read material from which words have been systematically deleted; that is, every *nth* word has been left out. Frequently, every *fifth* word after the first complete sentence is replaced with a blank, as in our example. Our aim is to see how accurately students can predict or infer the words that should fill the blanks, thus creating *closure*, or wholeness, in the passage.

A completely accurate prediction of every deleted word is usually impossible unless the material is extremely simple in content and vocabulary, but it is not necessary to fill in each deletion with total accuracy. If an adequate proportion of words to blanks is supplied, readers can usually employ their

FIGURE 5.1. Portion of a cloze procedure.

"When Emily Johnson came home one evening to her furnished room and found three of her best handkerchiefs missing from the dresser drawer, she was sure who had taken them and what to do. She had lived in _____ furnished room for about _____ weeks and for the _____ two weeks she had _____ missing small things occasionally. _____ had been several handkerchiefs _____, and an initial pin _____ Emily rarely wore and _____ had come from the _____-and-ten. And once _____ had missed a small _____ of perfume and one _____ a set of china _____. Emily had known for _____ time who was taking _____ things, but it was _____ tonight that she had _____ what to do."

SOURCE: Shirley Jackson, "Trial by Combat," in *The Lottery* (New York: Farrar, Straus, 1949), p. 35.

sense of what is going on in the passage to supply words that will complete the author's text. Can you give a "good guess" for each of the deleted words in Figure 5.1? You probably could fill in more than half of the blanks accurately but not every one. For some of the deletions, there are only one or two words that could possibly fit while for others there are more alternatives. The ninth blank, for example, occurs in the phrase, ". . . had come from the _____ -and-ten." You probably recognized almost immediately the expression "five-and-ten" and would have trouble thinking of a better alternative. On the other hand, what about ". . . a set of china _____"? You could probably think of several good alternatives for that blank: plates, figurines, animals, and the like. In spite of some uncertainty, the whole passage is not too frustrating or difficult to complete.

The cloze procedure indicates the extent to which readers are able to follow the sense of a reading passage. In fact, studies have shown that the percentages of correct words readers are able to supply in a cloze passage constitute as reliable a measure of general comprehension as much more elaborate devices (Bormuth, 1966; Jones and Pikulski, 1974; Rankin and Culhane, 1969).

Purposes of the Cloze Procedure

There are two common purposes for using a cloze procedure:

1. to determine whether a particular piece of written text represents an individual's independent, instructional, or frustration reading level (placement purposes)

2. to assess the quality of an individual reader's use of context as a strategy for understanding what is read (diagnostic purposes)

Using a Cloze for Placement

A cloze placement test is a fast and accurate device for determining whether an individual, group, or whole class can comfortably read a given book or other material. In classes where everyone must read the same required textbooks, cloze results can help the teacher form groups for differential instruction.

When constructing a cloze passage omit every fifth word systematically, that is, 20 percent of the words. Leaving 80 percent intact gives sufficient context for the reader to supply the remaining words. Deleting every fifth word in order ensures that words of all grammatical classes and levels of difficulty are sampled, not just all nouns or all long words, for example.

Constructing the Cloze for Placement. Here are the steps for constructing a cloze passage for placement purposes (Estes and Vaughan, 1978):

1. Select a passage the students have not read before, about 300 words long.
2. Leave the first sentence intact, to get the readers started. Then begin counting words, replacing every fifth word with a blank fifteen spaces long. If any word to be deleted is a proper noun, leave it in and delete the next word. (Proper nouns are harder to predict from context than other words.) Continue counting until you have fifty blanks.
3. Finish the sentence in which the last deletion occurs. Type one more sentence intact.

Administering and Scoring the Cloze. Administering and scoring a cloze are simple:

1. At the blackboard, show the students how to complete the passage. Give example sentences and discuss how to use context clues. Let students work together on short passages for practice. This step is important because even good readers will do poorly if they are unfamiliar with the demands of the task.
2. Direct the students to use only one word for each blank and to try to use the precise word the author would have used.
3. Explain that no one will get each word correct and that about 50 percent correct is a good score. If the students don't know this in advance, anxiety can affect their performance.
4. Give ample time for completing the passage without rushing. The students should not use their books because we want to see if they can read and understand the material without aid.

In scoring, accept only the *exact replacement*. Studies (Bormuth, 1966; Miller and Coleman, 1967; Ruddell, 1964) have shown this to be the most valid scoring system for placement purposes. When you use this activity instructionally to teach the use of context clues or work on vocabulary you may choose to accept synonyms or make other changes. The rank order of scores changes little, if at all, if synonyms are accepted, but interpreting the results can be difficult. Also, you may drive yourself crazy deciding what is "close enough."

Determine the percentage of correct responses, adding 2 percent for each correct word. (Don't count incorrect *spellings* as errors on the cloze.) You can judge more accurately by averaging each student's scores on two or more passages from the same text.

A score of 60 percent correct or higher indicates that the material is easy for these students and that the material can be used for *independent* reading. A score between 40 percent and 60 percent indicates that these students can comfortably read the material and that it is suitable for direct instruction because it represents their *instructional* reading level. A score of below 40 percent correct indicates that the material is too difficult and that it represents the readers' *frustration* level (Bormuth, 1968a, 1968b; Rankin and Culhane, 1969).

The cloze procedure can be very useful in classes where a single text or set of materials is required, as is typical of many secondary level classes and some upper-elementary content area classes. It enables the teacher to determine quickly and accurately which students will find that particular material too difficult (Jones and Pikulski, 1974). It is an effective procedure for gathering information about students' reading ability in the first days of school, before their teachers get to know them, especially when a teacher has more than one class. If the same text or material is used year after year, the initial cloze can be used again and again, or shared by several teachers who use the same textbooks.

Using the Cloze Diagnostically

The cloze procedure can be used diagnostically to find out what students know, to help them focus on context clues, and to read critically.

For diagostic purposes, it is not necessary to delete words systematically. Instead, *key words* can be deleted, words that convey much of the information. When used *after* a reading assignment the cloze can show a good deal about the concepts and vocabulary that students have gained from the assignment. Used *before* the assignment, the cloze can show their need for vocabulary and concept development prior to the reading.

A reader's tacit grasp of syntactic structures can be explored by deleting words of a particular grammatical class, that is, verbs, prepositions, or adjectives. If used on a regular basis, the cloze can help students focus on grammatical forms, learn concepts of parts of speech, become aware of context clues, and infer the meaning of new words (Hall, Ribovich, and Ramig, 1979; Jongsma, 1971; Spache, 1976). Cloze activities can be made up from students' dictated experiences stories and their own written productions. This approach will help reinforce recognition of sight words and can be especially helpful for youngsters having trouble recognizing those troublesome structure words (*the, is, there, at,* and so forth). The *oral cloze,* in which selected words are left out and suggestions solicited while the teacher reads aloud to students, can be very useful in encouraging critical listening and comprehension (Blachowicz, 1977).

Cloze activities are particularly worthwhile for students who have relatively good word recognition but poor comprehension. Because they aid students to focus on the meaning and sense of the material these activities can be invaluable in helping the word caller improve reading and listening comprehension (Bortnick and Lopardo, 1973, 1976).

The Maze: A Cloze Alternative

An alternative to the cloze technique of leaving out words altogether is the use of multiple-choice alternatives. This technique, called the *maze,* was proposed by Guthrie et al. (1974). The maze is a little easier than the cloze and thus is a good alternative for young students or any readers for whom the blank spaces are intimidating. Easily discouraged students and poor readers usually don't do well on a cloze because there is too much that is unknown and too many words to be filled in. With appropriate changes in the criteria for grouping, the maze can be more helpful for these students.

In a maze, the teacher provides three alternatives instead of leaving blanks. The choices are: (a) the correct word; (b) an incorrect word from the same grammatical class (i.e., another noun); and (c) an incorrect word from another grammatical class. The order of the choices should be random so that the correct choice does not always occupy the same position. Figure 5.2 shows a portion of a maze procedure.

Though we have used only the first three sentences from a longer selection here, you can see that a maze is constructed much like a cloze, with the first sentence intact and every fifth word altered. More information is available than in a cloze, however, and correct answers can be circled or underlined. At least twenty items should be used for placement purposes.

Readers with scores of 85 percent or better will find that the material is at their independent level. Scores between 50 percent and 85 percent indicate the instructional level. For students scoring less than 50 percent correct, the text is too difficult for them to read (Guthrie et al., 1974).

FIGURE 5.2. Portion of a maze procedure.

There was a person called Nana who ruled the nursery.

	envelope		about
Sometimes she took no	notice	of the playthings lying	under,
	none		table

	rabbit	
and sometimes, for no	rely	whatever, she went swooping
	reason	

afraid		and		coming
about	like a great wind	or	hustled them away in	cupboards.
over		ankle		cardboard

	also		it
She called this "tidying	out,"	and the playthings hated	at,
	up		them

especially the tin ones.

SOURCE: Margery Williams, *The Velveteen Rabbit* (New York: Doubleday, 1926), p. 20.

Word Sorting

Just as the cloze helps us learn important information on the use of context in reading, a set of categorizing activities called *word sorts* can be used to let students demonstrate what they know about individual words and what aspects of words they can use to analyze new words.

Word Features

Imagine a teacher working with a group of young beginning readers who have small collections of words printed on cards, words they recognize at sight that have been gleaned from dictated stories, familiar trade books and basal stories, signs, and lables. Such a collection of sight words is called a *word bank,* and today when the children come to the reading circle they bring their word banks along and sit on the floor.

The teacher tells the children to go through their word banks and group some of the words together on the floor in front of them. The words all have to go together in some way, and each child will have to tell *how* they go together. The teacher watches carefully as the students go through their words and sort them.

The first word in Tammy's word bank is *but*. After studying it for a moment, she shuffles through her cards and pulls out several more, arranges them in a line, and sits back with a satisfied smile. The words are:

| but | ball | boy | brown | bananas |

Chris studies his words intently after spreading them all out before him. With a good deal of muttering to himself he makes this group:

| butterfly | tomorrow | potatoes | Christopher |

Alicia also spreads her cards out and makes several false starts as she tentatively puts words together, then changes her mind. Finally she appears to be satisfied with this grouping:

| puppy | grass | Mother | flower | hamster |

Each child in the group has made a unique sort, because each child has somewhat different words in his or her word bank and because each has looked for a different sorting criterion. When told to "put together words that go together in some way," each has looked for certain *word features*.

What feature has Tammy used to categorize *but, ball, boy, brown,* and *bananas*? Obviously, they share the same beginning letter *b*. Tammy has also grouped her words by the same beginning sound feature, too, which she hears when she reads each word card aloud to the teacher. Tammy has attended to both letter and sound features in this sort.

Chris's words (*butterfly, tomorrow, potatoes, Christopher*) do not share the same letter or sound features. They do not start alike or have a similar vowel sound; two have a double consonant, but not all four. What feature do they share? They are all three-syllable words; Chris checked himself on this feature by pronouncing each word aloud. He attended to features of word parts, in this case the number of syllables in each word.

Alicia has apparently not used the same features as Chris or Tammy, for *puppy, grass, hamster, flower,* and *Mother* do not share the same number of syllables or a common affix, nor do they have a sound or letter feature in common. On what basis, then, has Alicia grouped them? She calls them all "living things," and we can see that she has used word meaning as the shared feature.

There are other word features the children might have used, such as grammatical features — the ways words function in sentences — what we know as parts of speech: for example, *car, mouse, tacos,* and *sea* are all nouns; *run, table, shoe,* and *light* can all be either nouns or verbs depending on how they are used; *happy, run-down,* and *fat* are all descriptive words. There are also spelling pattern features. *Mail, boat, shoes,* and *hear* all share the spelling feature of double vowels (precisely, vowel digraphs) as do *feet, sheep,* and *beer.*

Although there is no clear-cut, definitive sequence in which every child learns to recognize these word features, there are aspects that beginning readers seem to recognize first. Other word features appear later in the child's development. This approximate sequence is described in more detail later on.

The Importance of Classifying

In our example, the children were *word sorting.* To do this, they must study and compare words and determine the features several words have in common. The word sorting activity is based on principles of induction and discovery learning. The act of classifying stimuli into classes according to their common properties is one of the most basic and powerful operations of human thinking and is responsible for much of a child's natural learning ability, particularly the acquisition of linguistic concepts (Anglin, 1977).

From the first weeks of life, children demonstrate their powerful, autonomous drive to explore, experience, and make sense of their world. They do this by developing cognitive categories of objects and events that are similar in some ways. These categories become apparent to adults when young children begin talking, for then they can provide labels for their categories and assign new experiences to the appropriate classes. Most parents have patiently explained over and over to a toddler, "No, that's not a doggy, that's a squirrel. No, that's not a horsie, that's a sheep." Children usually overgeneralize their categories, calling every four-legged animal "doggy" or, for a short time, calling every adult man "Dadda," before they develop more numerous, sharply defined cognitive categories. Developing new cognitive categories and making old ones more specific are the bases for all cognitive growth and learning. Categorizing and classifying remain one of the most powerful natural learning processes we have throughout our lives (Ginsberg and Opper, 1969; Piaget and Inhelder, 1969).

This process can be used productively in school to help children develop strategies for recognizing words in print and analyzing unrecognized words. We often forget that children come to school with five or six years of solid experience in looking for similarities in things, categorizing them, and drawing

*I*n word sorting, students categorize
written words in groups according to
shared features and form generalizations about how words work. In closed sorts,
words are grouped on the basis of a prestated
feature, such as the initial letters w and wh.
When groups do sorting activities, students
share each other's insights about words. Simple board and card games can be adapted for
group sorting activities.

generalizations about how they work, but they have to be shown how to apply these thinking operations to the study of words in print.

Words for Sorting

Since word sorts are done with words on cards, students need a collection of word cards with which to work. Their word banks are particularly good for this purpose because they contain words they recognize at sight. The word bank is a traditional outgrowth of the language experience approach (Stauffer, 1980) wherein children learn to read dictated experience stories and learn to recognize at sight the words in those stories. They collect their newly mastered sight words on cards and then supplement them with words from other sources (basals, trade books, labels, student writing, etc.) as additional words are mastered. This growing collection of known words is perfect for use in word sorts, because the words must be quickly recognized before their components can successfully be analyzed.

A very quick way of helping children begin a word bank without using dictation is to give them a short story or passage that they can read fairly easily, have them underline each new word they can immediately recognize, and tell them to copy each word onto a small card. Then, working in pairs, they can run through each other's cards to weed out any words that are not quickly recognized. In this way they can develop collections of words they recognize and also accomplish the task of making the cards themselves, which is a time-consuming and tedious task for the teacher.

Using Word Sorts Diagnostically

There are two basic kinds of word sorts: those that call on *convergent* thinking and those that call on *divergent* thinking. In a *closed sort*, the feature that all words in a group must share is stated in advance. For example, the students are directed to search for words beginning like *stop*, having the same vowel sounds as *bake* and *sheep*, the same number of syllables as *feather*, or words that might be associated with a party. Students then search for words that fit the pattern. A closed sort helps them use convergent thinking.

In an *open sort*, which encourages divergent thinking, no sorting criteria are stated in advance. Instead, word cards are examined and categories formed as relationships suggest themselves spontaneously. In closed sorts, students search for instances of particular shared features; in open sorts they consider a number of features simultaneously, searching for those shared by other words. In both types of sorts, children are guided toward *discovering* similarities in words rather than being *told* or *shown* how they are alike in contrast to some of the more traditional word study activities.

As instructional procedures, both open and closed word sorts are very useful in helping youngsters form generalizations about how known words work, which they can fruitfully apply when they encounter a new word. Word sorts are also a powerful diagnostic tool through which we can learn a good deal about what features of words children can perceive and how they go about learning new word analysis strategies. An additional attractive feature is that word sorting is easily done in a group setting, which enables the teacher to gather diagnostic information about an individual child without separating him or her from the natural learning environment or taking precious teaching time away from the others in the group.

Closed Sorts. When teachers want to determine if children in the group can recognize certain features of words, they can use the closed sort in which they specify what the children are to look for and illustrate the salient feature with word or picture cards as examples. The children then search their word banks and word card collections for one or more words with the same feature. Each child then holds up or lays down the cards simultaneously. A quick look around the circle at each child's offering will show the teacher which children have recognized that feature.

Let's say, for example, that a teacher of beginning readers wants to find out quickly what each child in a reading group knows about certain initial consonant sounds, but the teacher doesn't want to give the group a test. Using a diagnostic sort, the teacher uses the regular reading-circle time to determine this information. First, if the children do not have word banks to begin with, each child makes a collection of several dozen words taken from basals and other books, as described above. This can be done as seatwork the day before the group sorting activity. The teacher spot checks to see that the children are including only known words, which takes only a few minutes because children are usually quite stringent with one another if given the responsibility of checking somone else's words.

The next day the children come to the circle with their *word* cards while the teacher brings a set of *picture* cards, commercial or homemade from magazine pictures. The teacher shows them one or more pictures of objects that illustrate the initial sound they will explore — for example, pictures of a *fox* and a *fire* to get at the initial consonant sound of *f,* or one picture for each of several sounds, like a *box,* a *mouse,* a *cake,* and a *hat,* to work on recognition of all four of those initial sounds. The teacher tells the children to find one or more words from their word banks that start with the same sound as these objects. The child names each pictured object, and the teacher observes the words given as a match. (It is easier if the children sit on the floor so they can place their cards on the floor in front of them.) In this activity, pictures, not printed words, are used as exemplars so that the children must rely on an internalization of the sound feature rather than just matching initial letters visually (Gillet and Kita, 1979). The teacher can provide immediate feedback to each child, and time is used efficiently because all the children are involved simultaneously in the task rather than one child performing and the rest watching or waiting their turns. Any letter-sound feature can be assessed as well as any other feature of words. Number of syllables, meaning relationships, parts of speech, and structural elements like affixes are examples of categories that could be formed.

Open Sorts. A related assessment activity, a little more open-ended, is the open word sort. A convenient format for this is a game in which students must "read each other's minds" by deducing the criterion another has used to form a group. In this game, each student begins with the same number of word cards; a dozen is an adequate number. Working individually, each child forms at least one category of words. Others must try to "read minds" by either stating the shared feature or, more abstractly, by finding words of their own to add to the category. During each phase of the activity, the teacher discovers what students know about words and what they still need to learn by observing the word groups formed and their attempts to "break" another's category.

Individual Sorts. Word sorts can also be used with one child individually, to plumb that child's word knowledge and see how well he or she is able to generalize from known words to similar unknown words. The student's word bank can be used or the teacher can make up a set of word cards.

First, the teacher makes up a set of cards from the words on the word recognition inventory being used (Chapter Four). Then the teacher administers the inventory and preselects from the deck all the words the student recognized at sight. Highly similar words can be added from the same word family to supplement the selected words. Now the teacher can conduct a number of sorts using words the student recognizes at sight.

Any closed or open sort format can be used. The teacher and student can also play the "read my mind" open sort game, in which the teacher forms a group and the student must find another word to fit it, then they reverse roles. This game demonstrates recognition of the shared feature.

The student's ability to generalize can be assessed in this way: the teacher groups several highly similar, easily recognized words like *my, by* and *fly;* then the student is shown a similar but unknown word, perhaps *shy* or *cry* in this example. If the student can use the shared feature of the example words to figure out the new word, *the ability to generalize from the known to the unknown* is demonstrated. This generalizing is the fundamental aspect of all word analysis and decoding, an ability that appears only after children have begun to develop a stable store of sight words and have a clear concept of what a written word is.

The ability to group words by shared features is an important one to assess in beginning readers because if it is not yet developed, instruction in word analysis strategies will be largely misunderstood and confusing for the child. Decoding instruction should be put off until the youngster can do this kind of thinking. The informal word sort is a fast, accurate, and nonthreatening way of keeping track of the child's progress in being able to categorize words by shared features.

A Sequence of Feature Learning

There is no hard-and-fast sequence in which children learn to recognize word features. They do not learn to recognize all the letter, sound, grammatical, structural, and meaning features of words at the same time. Nonetheless, as they advance toward fluent reading they do recognize features of words in a rather set order, and it usually goes like this:

□ First, beginning letters and consonant sounds, beginning consonant blends, and some ending letters and sounds are recognizable.
□ Second, middle parts of words begin to "firm up": short vowel sounds, especially in three- or four-letter words, can be matched as well as long vowel sounds, and both can now be contrasted.
□ Third, word parts begin to be recognizable, and words can be categorized by their number of syllables and shared affixes. Children can now also identify compound words with the same word in them (*butterfly*, *buttermilk*, etc.).
□ Fourth, spelling patterns begin to emerge. When youngsters are very familiar with sorting by letters and sounds, the various ways that the same sound can be spelled becomes understandable, as, for example, in words like *bake*, *maid*, and *weigh* or *meet* and *meat*.
□ Finally, both meaning and grammatical features begin to appear. At this stage youngsters know a great deal about the sounds and parts of words, and they find it interesting to investigate word meanings and see how words can function in sentences. Many students, however, reach this stage quite early.

Word sorts are not a new development. The sorting of word bank words has long been an aspect of the language experience approach, but using sorts as structured activities for teaching word analysis and spelling are fairly new innovations. Additional information can be found in Gillet (1980), Gillet and Temple (1978), and Sulzby (1980).

The Directed Reading-Thinking Activity (DRTA)

In a third-grade class the teacher, Ms. Bennett, is using a basal reader story to conduct a diagnostic-instructional activity with a reading group of eight students.

MS. B.: Today we're going to read a story called "Amy for Short." Look at the title and picture on page 207. What do you think this story might be about?

SARAH: A girl with a really long name, maybe, and they just call her Amy for short.

TOM: Or a girl who's really short.

(Ms. B. jots "really long name" and "short girl" on the board.)

NICK: She doesn't look short in the picture. Maybe she *wants* to be short.

MS. B.: These are all good ideas. Let's read the first page and see if any turn out to be true. (The students read silently. Amy, the main character, is introduced and then her pal Mark. Amy is very tall.)

MS. B.: Now what do we know about the title? Were any of our first guesses right?

ANDY: She does have a really long name, it says here, but that's not what the title means.

SARAH: She's not real short, she's real tall. She's as tall as her best friend, that boy.

MS. B.: Sarah, please read us the part that told you she was really tall.

SARAH: "But I'm tall. The tallest girl in my class."

MS. B.: Good. Now, with this title, and what we've read so far, what do you think might happen in this story?

SUE: Maybe she'll grow up to be *real* tall, like a basketball player! I saw some girl basketball players on TV.

TOM: Yeah, maybe she'll get to be taller than the boy and he'll get jealous.

NICK: Maybe she'll just keep growing and never stop!

MS. B.: (jotting these ideas on the board) Any other ideas? Okay, read the next three pages of the story and stop.

(The students go on reading. In this part, Mark and Amy save up to buy a secret code ring, but Amy leaves for camp before they have enough money. Amy is the tallest girl at camp. When she returns, she has grown an inch taller than Mark, and she fears for their friendship.)

MS. B.: Were any of our earlier guesses right?

TOM: She's afraid Mark won't be her friend anymore because she's gotten so tall. It didn't say anything about playing basketball.

MS. B.: Tom, what sentence told you how she felt about getting taller?

TOM: (after a lengthy search) Here it is. "I was afraid Mark wasn't going to be my best friend anymore, just because I was an inch taller than he was."

MS B.: Good. Do you think they might stop being friends?

MARY: She can't help it that she's so tall. He shouldn't stop being her friend because of that.

DAVY: Maybe he's afraid she'll beat him up!

MS. B.: Tracy, what do you think? Do you think she might beat him up?

TRACY: I don't know. I guess not.

MS. B.: Why do you think so?

TRACY: She doesn't look mad.

MARY: I think they'll work it out okay. In the picture on the next page it looks like she's going to have a party. Maybe the party is for Mark.

MS. B.: (writes "party for Mark?" on the board) Okay, let's look at that picture. What might happen next?

DAVY: Maybe the boy won't go.

SUE: Maybe she won't even ask him!

MS. B.: (jotting these ideas down) Okay, read the next two pages and see if any of our predictions turn out to be true.

(The silent reading continues. Amy plans a birthday party and Mark makes a weak excuse for not planning to come. Amy is really worried about their friendship now.)

MS. B.: Tracy, what did happen in this part?

TRACY: He's not gonna go to the party. He says he's gonna play baseball.

MS. B.: How might the story end up?

SARAH: Maybe she'll go to the baseball game instead of having the party. Then he'll see she really does like him.

MARY: He *knows* she likes him all right. Maybe she'll go play baseball too, and she'll beat him!

TOM: Naw, it's gotta turn out happy. And it's gotta have something to do with the code ring, remember? Maybe she'll get one for her birthday, and she'll give it to him, and they'll be friends again.

MS. B.: How many think Mark will go to the party? How many think he won't? (She counts hands after each question.) Let's read the next two pages and see what happens. We're almost at the end of the story now. (The students read: On the day of the party Amy finds a mysterious package at the door, with a coded note on it.)

MARY: It's gotta be from Mark, because it's in code. He's going to come and be friends now.

DAVY: Maybe he's giving her a mitt or something.

ANDY: Maybe it's something to make her short again!

MS. B.: Any other, final guesses as to how it will turn out? Okay, read the end of the story. (The story ends with Mark giving Amy the code ring and saying he'd rather go to her party than play ball. All ends well.)

MS. B.: Did the ending surprise you?

ANDY: We forgot about the ring. We should have guessed that's what he'd give her.

TOM: I didn't forget it! I knew it all the time.

MS. B.: Okay, let's see if we can answer these questions now that we've read the story.

In the scene described here, the teacher has used a procedure called the *directed reading-thinking activity* (DRTA) to guide the reading of a basal story. The DRTA is a teaching method that helps students improve comprehension of and interest in fiction and nonfiction text. In essence, it is a set of procedures for guiding prereading and postreading discussion, which can particularly maximize comprehension of basal reader stories (Hall, Ribovich, and Ramig, 1979). In a fiction DRTA, children develop critical reading and thinking by predicting possible story events and outcomes, then reading to confirm or disprove their hypotheses. As described by Stauffer (1975), in a DRTA the student forms a set of purposes for reading, processing ideas, and testing answers by taking part in a predict-read-prove cycle. The teacher *activates thought* by asking "What do you think?"; *agitates thought* by asking "Why do you think so?"; and *requires evidence* by asking "How can you prove it?" (Stauffer, 1975, p. 37). The DRTA format helps students to read more critically and with improved comprehension because it engages them in this process of fluent reading in a structured fashion, slowing down and making concrete the phases of the prediction process.

The DRTA method has been shown to have significantly improved reading comprehension (Hammond, 1979; Stauffer, 1975). When students read in order to prove or disprove the correctness of predictions made prior to reading, they understand and remember more information than when they engage in the traditional read-and-answer-questions format of the directed reading activity.

The DRTA differs from the traditional group reading discussion in two major aspects: the *types* of questions asked and the *timing* of the questions. Table 5.1 shows the fundamental differences between these activities.

In a DRTA, the teacher asks open-ended questions that can be answered in many ways and that encourage divergent thinking. Most of the questions are asked prior to the reading because they require predictions and hypotheses rather than specific facts, and the reading is done to test the veracity of the predictions. When the students read, they are reading not to determine the answer to somebody else's question but to find out if they were correct. Thus the students set their own purposes for reading.

There are two "basic" DRTA questions used by Stauffer (1975), who de-

TABLE 5.1. Comparison of guided reading activity and DRTA.

	TRADITIONAL GUIDED READING ACTIVITY	DIRECTED READING-THINKING ACTIVITY
QUESTION TYPES	Generally convergent and closed-ended; often there is one right answer.	Divergent and open-ended; call for predictions; several answers are possible.
QUESTION TYPES	Asked after passage is read, to gather information; few pre-reading questions are generally used; when used they are more often for general "motivation" than to focus expectation on the story.	Asked before passage is read to elicit predictions and after passage is read to confirm or deny predictions; questions in both cases are story-dependent rather than general.

veloped the method: What do you think will happen? and Why do you think so? These two open-ended questions, or variations of them, usually form the backbone of DRTA questioning, although an occasional closed-ended question is helpful. As long as the majority of the questions are open-ended, it is a good practice for the teacher to ask some convergent or factual questions in order to ensure that students understand important details and to challenge and extend their thinking. In our example, Ms. Bennett asked a number of convergent questions that helped the students summarize what they had read and then put the story events in order.

A DRTA with Fiction

In our example, Ms. Bennett used DRTA questioning with material from fiction. Before the reading, students hypothesized about the story's title and the first illustration. They could have been asked to look at other illustrations or to read the first sentence, paragraph, or page. They were asked to predict what might happen in the story and how it might end up, and at times they were asked to justify their predictions. The predictions were recorded on the board and all were accepted as possible unless they contradicted previous story facts.

Then the students read a portion of the story and were asked to stop reading just prior to some event or some important piece of information. Stopping before, rather than after, an event allowed the students to predict what might happen next. Prior predictions were reviewed, and those no longer probable could be erased with new hypotheses replacing them. At some points students were asked to prove their ideas by finding and reading a sentence aloud. The cycle of predict-read-prove continued throughout the story, and as the students got closer to the end, their predictions became somewhat more convergent and specific since they had now gained more information.

In our example, Ms. Bennett stopped four times within the story to let students predict, but fewer or more stops may be better for a particular story. To complete a DRTA in one sitting, it is better to limit the number of stops to less than five; otherwise it takes a long time to finish the story, and too many enforced stops can fragment the children's thinking and cause them to lose interest in the activity.

The passages between stopping points need not be of equal length. Students might read a single paragraph that contains a lot of new information, stop to predict, then read several pages at one time. The important factor is not the length of the passage but its *content*. You should stop just prior to some crucial event or outcome, whether the passage is short or long. As you move toward the ending, fewer alternative outcomes are possible, so the discussions will be shorter and more specific. If the DRTA is going well, student interest will be growing, so don't keep them out of the story too long.

A DRTA with Nonfiction

A DRTA with nonfiction material is conducted quite differently from one with fiction. To see the differences, let's observe a nonfiction DRTA.

In his sixth-grade social studies class, Mr. Taylor summons a group of twelve students to a discussion circle and tells them to bring their social studies textbooks.

MR. T.: Today we're going to begin reading Chapter Four, which starts on page 116. We won't read the whole chapter today, but we'll read the first part, up to page 125. Open your books to page 116 and I'll give you three minutes to look at all the illustrations and maps on those pages and to read the section headings in dark print. Don't begin reading, just *look over* these pages and get a feel for what it's about.

(The students scan nine pages as the teacher watches.)

MR. T.: Okay, now let's try to answer some questions, or make some guesses about what's in the chapter before we read it. First, what's the *topic* here?

JANE: It's about the old West.

BRIAN: It looks like it's about the olden days when there were covered wagons and settlers.

MR. T.: Why do you think so?

JANE: Because there are old pictures of cowboys and maps of where the covered wagons went.

A *group directed reading-thinking activity (DRTA) with a fiction selection.* *The teacher elicits predictions of upcoming story events from the group* *and records the predictions on the board. Students read to confirm or* *change their predictions. The teacher checks confirmed predictions on the board and* *elicits new predictions.*

RUTH: Also the title was something like "The Westward Expansion."

MR. T.: Okay, let's get specific. *When* did the opening of the West take place? Brian, you said "olden days." When were they?

BRIAN: You know, like a hundred years ago.

MR. T.: Give me a year.

BRIAN: 1880.

JOY: No, earlier than that; 1800.

ANNE: After the Revolution, after 1776.

(Mr. T. writes these dates on the board under "When?")

MR T.: When do you think the expansion was completed? How long did it take?

TIM: Less than 100 years. By about 1850 or so.

ALEX: No, it was still going on during the Civil War.

MR. T.: When was that?

ALEX: I think 1860 or so.

BILL: I think it was pretty much settled by the 1900s; I think I read that someplace else.

MR. T.: Okay, that gives us a rough time span, sometime between 1800 and 1900, but we're not sure. Now, where did "The West" start?

MIKE: In the movie "Centennial" they talked a lot about St. Louis. I think they left from there.

MR. T.: Who did?

MIKE: The wagon trains.

MR. T.: What other cities were settled first?

ANNE: Abilene? Isn't that where they had the cattle drives?

KEN: Yeah, they drove them from Texas through Abilene to Chicago, I think. They sold them in Chicago.

(Mr. T. lists "Abilene — cattle drives, Chicago — cattle markets, St. Louis — wagon trains.")

MR. T.: What problems did the first settlers encounter?

BONNIE: Indians!

MR. T.: What tribes, specifically?

KEN: The Sioux and the Apaches.

BONNIE: Yeah, they were the ones that attacked the wagon trains.

JANE: Also I think the Cherokee, and, uh, another one, Pawnee?

MR. T.: Where did these tribes live?

CARTER: All over — Kansas, Wyoming, all the way to Canada.

MR. T.: What other problems besides Indians?

ARLENE: Deserts — not enough water.

RUTH: Yeah, they had to cross Death Valley. They were always dying.

JOY: Also mountains; sometimes their carts went right off the cliffs.

TIM: And they got sick too, and had no doctors, and a lot of the women and children died off.

MR. T.: (Mr. T. lists "Problems: Indians — Sioux, Apache, Cherokee, Pawnee; deserts; water shortages; mountains.") Now, how long might this journey take? How far do you think a wagon train could go in one day?

ARLENE: Just a few miles. In the movies they're always walking real slow.

KEN: Oh! Sometimes the horses died, too, and they needed mules or something to pull the wagons.

MR. T.: Anything else?

CARTER: Poisoned water? There were some places you couldn't drink from, I don't know why.

MR. T.: Okay, we've gotten a lot of information. We said the time was between 1800 and 1900. The settlers used wagon trains, leaving from St. Louis. They drove the cattle from Abilene to markets in Chicago. They suffered from illness and lack of water. They crossed mountains and deserts and fought with many Indian tribes, and they traveled very slowly. We tried to answer specifically *when, where, how, what problems, how long*. Now, read pages 116 to 125. Make a little check mark in the margin next to any information that might answer these questions. (As the students read, Mr. T. moves among them answering questions and helping with unfamiliar words.)

In this example, Mr. Taylor asked his students to bring forth any information they had, from any source, regarding the topic they were reading about. He asked broad general questions about dates, places, and problems and pressed them for as much specificity as they could provide. He accepted all hypotheses noncommitally and organized them topically on the board for later reference. After the students had provided most of the information they had available, they read the selection with the goal of finding specific information.

Following the reading, original hypotheses were reviewed, and the answers the selection provided for the original questions were discussed. From this point, any desired comprehension exercise, like completing a study guide or writing an outline, could be used.

In this activity the prereading discussion helps the students recall and organize what they believe or already know about a topic. With "old information" activated, acquiring "new information" is easier. Also, the hypothesizing helps awaken students' curiosity and sends them into the reading assignment with increased interest.

The Directed Listening-Thinking Activity (DLTA)

A useful variation of the DRTA is the *directed listening-thinking activity,* (DLTA). A DLTA is simply a DRTA wherein the reading passages are read aloud to the students (see Chapter Three). The thinking required and the questioning are the same. The only difference is that the information is gathered by listening rather than reading. It is productive and enjoyable for students of all ages, particularly for older poor readers who benefit from exposure to texts they cannot read themselves and from practice in critical listening and thinking.

Using the DRTA Diagnostically

The DRTA format provides a vehicle for obtaining informal diagnostic information on how students approach a story and how they react to what they read. A diagnostic DRTA can be used with an individual child, with certain minor adaptations, if you are particularly interested in one student, or it can be used with a group of students.

As described in Chapter Three, a group DRTA or DLTA can be used to investigate a child's sense of how stories are structured, the ability to follow a sequence of events to a logical conclusion, and the willingness to take the psychological risk of predicting what might happen in a story.

A DRTA inventory can be made up along the lines suggested by Stauffer (1975, pp. 321–323) and modified to fit an individual teacher's needs and interests. An example is shown in Table 5.2.

These checklist items are generally appropriate, whether you are using a group or individual DRTA, although some of the items may not be relevant in an individual DRTA. The exchange of others' ideas in a group DRTA helps to extend and refine an individual's ideas. With only one student, it is somewhat difficult to elicit very many different predictions. Also, of course, the interaction of children disagreeing and convincing one another is missing.

When asked to make predictions in an individual DRTA, some students can come up with only one or possibly two ideas. In this case, the teacher should focus on the quality of the student's "best guess." The student should be asked to evaluate prior predictions, change or refine predictions based on new information, and offer substantiation at each stopping point. The teacher can, if desired, offer two or three alternative predictions and ask the student to choose the one that seems most likely. This requires the student to make a "forced choice." The student must evaluate several alternatives and defend one the most likely. If the teacher offers only one prediction and asks for a reaction to it, some students will defer to the teacher rather than really evaluate the prediction. A forced choice requires a more thoughtful response and is an effective way of drawing students who will not volunteer into participating in a DRTA.

TABLE 5.2. Sample DRTA checklist.

DRTA Inventory

Student _____

	USUALLY	OCCASIONALLY	RARELY
Offers spontaneous predictions			
Predicts without coaxing			
Participates from the start			
Makes logical predictions			
Predictions show awareness of story structures			
Changes predictions when necessary			
Refines predictions as DRTA proceeds			
Can explain predictions clearly			
Can justify predictions from text			
Can relocate specific information			
Uses both explicit and implied information			
Shows awareness and tolerance of others' positions			
Uses others' predictions to extend or modify own ideas			
Shows original thinking			
Seeks confirmation of unconfirmed ideas from other sources			
Uses illustrations to get information			
Can effectively scan material before DRTA			
Uses context to analyze new words			

Using Diagnostic-Instructional Procedures

The Cloze and Maze

Because the major focus of the cloze and maze is on using context to get meaning, these activities are very useful for students who need help in reading for meaning. It is virtually impossible to complete a cloze or maze successfully without understanding what was read. Therefore, these activities help students to focus on comprehension and to develop an awareness of how context conveys meaning in several ways simultaneously. They are particularly beneficial for students with good word recognition but poor comprehension.

Do you remember Brian? He was the very anxious fourth grader from Chapter Four whose reading comprehension was poor in spite of excellent word recognition. A fast, accurate decoder who read rapidly but with little comprehension, Brian represented the type of reader who is a word caller. He was very concerned with precisely accurate word recognition and oral reading but paid little heed to the ideas expressed. Cloze and maze procedures on a regular basis would be ideal for Brian because they would force him to attend to the author's message.

In the case of a very anxious student like Brian, it would probably be wise to introduce him to a maze activity first. The maze is generally easier, and thus less threatening, for a reader who has to be right every time. Another way to handle the anxiety factor might be to begin using cloze procedures but omit fewer words. Instead of omitting every fifth word, every tenth or twelfth word could be deleted. This approach would provide more context for each deletion and would ease the student into the activity.

The cloze and maze are also good for a reader with a small sight vocabulary and poor word recognition, like Jerry in Chapter Four. He read poorly but not because he couldn't comprehend. Jerry's problem was that his sight vocabulary was too meager to read much of anything for meaning. The cloze could help Jerry learn to use context as a word recognition strategy and to identify unknown words in text by asking himself, What would make sense here? Moreover, particular kinds of words could be deleted systematically, for example all verbs or all articles, to help him concentrate on certain word features while he works with words in context. Both cloze and maze procedures could be made up from any fairly easy text that he is capable of reading.

Cloze passages made up from Jerry's dictated stories and his own creative writing, with deleted words to be supplied from his word bank, would help reinforce his use of new sight words. Because dictated stories are easy to remember and highly motivating, this activity would also be a very supportive one for Jerry.

Word Sorts

Word sorts would aid students like Brian and Jerry, but for very different reasons. Brian, a word caller, had excellent word analysis and could decode most words he saw and therefore word sorts featuring sound or structural aspects of words would not contribute much. In word study, however, Brian's biggest problem lay in word meanings, and he or students like him could profit by experiencing many meaning sorts, both open and closed types. Brian would particularly enjoy the "read my mind" open sort game in which others had to guess the meaning relationships among the words he sorted.

Jerry, who needed word study in all areas, would benefit from a program of word sorts dealing systematically with all features of words. You may recall that his word recognition test showed he had fairly good control of initial single consonants and blends, and also final sounds in words, but that he had much difficulty with medial parts of words, especially vowel sounds. Jerry's teacher might begin sorting with him by sound features, giving him many opportunities to think about and compare vowel patterns. When he reached the point where he could sort words easily by sound, he could begin working with spelling patterns as well as sounds, and words used in sorts could be used again in his spelling instruction. Sound and spelling sorts could help Jerry in word analysis, which is a critical area for him. If he could gain facility with sorting and if he acquired a sight vocabulary of 100 or more words, he could begin sorting by meaning and word type. These sorts are relatively advanced for very remedial readers like Jerry, and they should find them challenging.

DRTAs and DLTAs

For Brian and other youngsters with reading comprehension problems, DRTAs and DLTAs could be extremely worthwhile. Like the cloze procedure, a DRTA would channel Brian's efforts to comprehend and to organize and remember what he has learned about the topic. DRTA activities would induce him to become actively and thoughtfully *involved* in reading and would probably stimulate his interest in reading because he would want to find out if his prediction were right.

A word caller like Brian should participate in a group DRTA several times a week. In addition, he could be taught to listen critically and think carefully about stories by taking part in DLTAs. Both activities would help him to develop better comprehension.

Many word callers have to read aloud, to hear themselves say the words, in order to understand, but for these students, continued oral reading just makes silent reading harder. Therefore, Brian should stop reading aloud, and his DRTAs should be conducted with silent reading. With word callers, oral reading even in a DRTA should be deemphasized.

Jerry, who could comprehend adequately what little he was able to read, could also benefit from sustained exposure to DRTAs. We might expect that DRTAs would encourage his interest in reading, which was certainly lacking according to his teachers, and they might well bring back to life some of his interest in and curiosity about print.

As a barely literate older student, Jerry had been out of contact for some time with the general information print conveys. DRTAs with nonfiction material would certainly provide him with new information and allow him to use relevant information he had acquired elsewhere.

A particularly important activity for Jerry would be DLTAs. He could gain so much by listening to someone read to him. He could get information about the world, a sense of story, an expanded vocabulary, and perhaps even the notion that reading is rewarding. A DLTA format would actively involve him in the listening task and help sharpen his critical thinking. Ideally a remedial student like Jerry should be read to nearly every day from the best of children's literature, with DLTA questioning used at least as often as straight listening.

Summary

Four procedures were described in this chapter: the *cloze* and the *maze, word sorting,* and the *directed reading-thinking activity* — all valuable tools for gathering diagnostic information and for instruction.

The *cloze,* in which words are systematically deleted from connected test, is often used to determine whether a student can comfortably read particular material, and it is also used diagnostically by analyzing the responses. The *maze,* an alternative to the cloze, consists of multiple-choice responses instead of deletions from the text. The maze is somewhat easier to complete than the cloze, and it is often used for young readers and for older poor readers.

Word sorting is a group or individual activity wherein students categorize words that they are studying. By classifying words according to shared word features, they are led to discover similarities and differences in sound and letter patterns, structural elements, grammatical features, and possible meanings of words. In *closed sorts,* which develop convergent thinking, the word feature to be searched for is specified in advance, and examples of words sharing that feature are given. In *open sorts,* which foster divergent thinking, no sorting criterion is stated an advance. Instead, the children form categories of words based on a word feature they discern for themselves. Both open and closed sorts aid in developing awareness of word features and word recognition strategies. By forming generalizations about the features of known words, students can apply these generalizations to the new words they encounter. Word sorting can be adapted to a number of game formats.

The directed reading-thinking activity (DRTA) is a procedure for developing reading comprehension and critical reading skills. With fiction, students read a portion of a story and are asked to predict what will happen next in the story and how it might end up. Then they read to prove, disprove, or modify their hypotheses. With nonfiction, they hypothesize about the text content by listing the information they have acquired in advance. The teacher leads the prediction by probing for details and guiding the questioning toward information the text contains. Students read to prove or disprove their prior beliefs about the topic and recap by summarizing the new information they have acquired.

Either format can be adapted for use as a critical listening activity, called a *directed listening-thinking* activity (DLTA). Reading is replaced by listening. The teacher reads text portions to the students, and the DRTA questioning cycle is used. Reading and listening comprehension can often be increased by using these procedures as supplements to traditional read-and-question comprehension activities.

Extension Activities

1. Pick out a student in your own or someone else's classroom and determine his or her approximate instructional level. Construct a maze procedure from a portion of the student's basal reader, or other graded text, and a cloze procedure from another portion of the same book. Administer both to the child. Score each and compare the results. Is the student in the same reading category according to both devices? Can he or she truly read comfortably from that book? What, if any, instructional changes might be necessary?

2. Make up (or buy) a batch of picture cards and try several simple closed sorts with one or two beginning readers. Experiment with sorting by initial sounds, final sounds, vowel sounds, number of syllables, and spelling patterns.

3. Make up (or buy) a batch of simple word cards (start with basal words listed in the back of your basal manual). Try out a few word sorts with a beginning reader, then with a more proficient reader. Compare the different features each student was able to perceive and use them for sorting. Play "Read My Mind" with each student. Compare the bases each student used for forming groups. What kinds of features are the most interesting to each reader?

4. Using the format of a simple familiar card game (Old Maid, Go Fish, Concentration, or even poker) or board game (Candy Land, Tic-Tac-Toe), make up an original game for one or more players using word cards and word sorting. Play it with some of the students.

5. Using a new basal story or a trade book, plan and conduct a group DRTA or DLTA. Evaluate the group's predictions, their interest in the activity, and their comprehension of the story.

6. Do a modified individual DRTA or DLTA and use the DRTA inventory to form some judgments about how the student approaches written text. Share your evaluation with someone else who works with that student.

Suggested Readings

Hall, Maryanne; Ribovich, Jerilyn; and Ramig, Christopher. **Reading and the Elementary School Child, 2nd ed.** *N.Y.: Van Nostrand, 1979.* A "methods text" filled with sensible, practical suggestions including DRTAs, language-experience, cloze and other diagnostic-instructional procedures.

Stauffer, Russell G. **Directing Reading Maturity as a Cognitive Process.** *N.Y.: Harper & Row, 1969.*

Stauffer, Russell G. **Directing the Reading-Thinking Process.** *N.Y.: Harper & Row, 1975.*

Stauffer, Russell G. and Cramer, Ronald L. **Teaching Critical Reading at the Primary Level.** *Newark, Del.: International Reading Association, 1968.* All three volumes deal directly with development and use of DRTAs.

Vacca, Richard T. **Content Area Reading.** *Boston: Little, Brown, 1981.* (Chs. 7, 9, 10.) An excellent practical guide to teaching reading in content subjects; Vacca's treatment of comprehension activities such as DRTAs, ReQuest and study guides, vocabulary activities and readability are particularly useful.

References

Anglin, Jeremy M. *Word, Object, and Conceptual Development.* N.Y.: Norton, 1977.

Blachowicz, Camille. "Cloze Activities for Primary Readers." *The Reading Teacher* 31, no. 3 (Dec. 1977): 300–302.

Bormuth, J. "Readability: A New Approach." *Reading Research Quarterly* 1, no. 3 1966: 79–132.

Bormuth, John R. "The Cloze Readability Procedure." *Elementary English* 55 (April 1968): 429–436. (a)

Bormuth, John R. "Cloze Test Reliability; Criterion Reference Scores." *Journal of Educational Measurement* 5 (fall 1968): 189–196. (b)

Bortnick, Robert and Lopardo, Genevieve S. "An Instructional Application of the Cloze Procedure." *Journal of Reading* 16, no. 4 (Jan. 1973): 296–300.

Botnick, Robert and Lopardo, Genevieve. "The Cloze Procedure: A Multi-Purpose Classroom Tool." *Reading Improvement* 13, no. 2 (summer 1976): 113–117.

Estes, Thomas H. and Vaughan, Joseph L. Jr. *Reading and Learning in the Content Classroom: Diagnostic and Instructional Strategies.* Boston: Allyn and Bacon, 1978.

Gillet, Jean Wallace. "Sorting: A Word Study Alternative." *The Journal of Language Experience* 2, no. 2 (1980): 17–20.

Gillet, Jean and Kita, M. Jane. "Words, Kids and Categories." *The Reading Teacher* 32, no. 5 (February 1979): 538–542.

Gillet, Jean Wallace and Temple, Charles. "Developing Word Knowledge: A Cognitive View." *Reading World* 18, no. 2 (December 1978): 132–140.

Ginsberg, Herbert, and Opper, Sylvia. *Piaget's Theory of Intellectual Development: an introduction.* Englewood Cliffs, N.J.: Prentice Hall, 1969.

Guthrie, John; Seifert, M.; Burnham, N.A.; and Caplan, R. I. "The Maze Technique to Assess, Monitor Reading Comprehension," *The Reading Teacher* 28, no. 2 (November 1974): 161–168.

Hall, Maryann; Ribovich, Jerilyn; and Ramig, Christopher. *Reading and the Elementary School Child*, 2nd ed. N.Y.: Van Nostrand, 1979.

Hammond, W. Dorsey. "The Effects of Reader Predictions on Prequestions in the Recall of Relevant and Incidental Information Found in Expository Material"; paper presented at the annual meeting of the International Reading Association, Atlanta, April 1979.

Jackson, Shirley. "Trial by Combat." In *The Lottery*, N.Y.: Fawcett Popular Library, 1949 (renewed 1976), 35–39.

Jones, Margaret & Pikulski, Edna. "Cloze for the Classroom." *The Reading Teacher* 17, no. 6 (Mar. 1974): 432–438.

Jongsma, Eugene. *The Cloze Procedure as a Teaching Technique*. Newark, Delaware: International Reading Assoc., 1971.

Miller, G. R. and Coleman, E. G. "A Set of 36 Prose Passages Calibrated for Complexity." *Journal of Verbal Learning and Verbal Behavior*, 6 (1967): 851–854.

Piaget, Jean and Inhelder, Barbel. *The Psychology of the Child*. N.Y.: Basic Books, 1969.

Rankin, Earl F. and Culhane, Jos. W. "Comparable Cloze and Multiple Choice Comprehension Test Scores." *Journal of Reading* 13 no. 3 (Dec. 1969): 193–198.

Ruddell, Robert. "A Study of Cloze Comprehension Technique in Relation to Structurally Controlled Reading Material." *Proceedings of the International Reading Association*, 9 (1964): 298–303.

Spache, George D. *Diagnosing and Correcting Reading Disabilities*. Boston: Allyn and Bacon, 1976.

Stauffer, Russell G. *Directing the Reading-Thinking Process*. N.Y.: Harper & Row, 1975.

Stauffer, Russel G. *The Language-Experience Approach to Beginning Reading*, revised ed. N.Y.: Harper & Row, 1980.

Sulzby, Elizabeth. "Word Concept Development Activities." In James W. Beers and Edmund H. Henderson, eds., *Cognitive and Developmental Aspects of Learning to Spell*. Newark, Del.: International Reading Assoc., 1980.

Taylor, Wilson. "Cloze Procedure: A New Tool for Measuring Readability." *Journalism Quarterly*, 30 (Fall 1953): 415–433.

Williams, Margery. *The Velveteen Rabbit*. N.Y.: Doubleday, 1926.

Chapter Six

Spelling and Reading

The relation between children's spelling and their beginning reading processes is highlighted in this chapter. It has been noted that spelling and reading may not be closely related in mature readers, but with beginning readers, there is a relation between word recognition and the production of spelling patterns (Frith and Frith, 1980).

Research during the past decade has shown that most children are capable of inventing their own approach to spelling, even before they begin to read. This early *invented spelling* ability depends on their being able to do at least three things:

1. They must be familiar with many letters of the alphabet and recognize that letters are related to the sounds of words.
2. They must have an ability to "hold words still in their minds" while they decide how to spell them, which entails having a stable concept of word (see Chapter Two).
3. They must be able to recognize and mentally manipulate the component sounds of spoken words (referred to as *phonemic segmentation*).

All three of these competencies are intimately involved in beginning reading. Since they may be demonstrated in spelling behavior *before* the children begin to read, early spelling is a useful route to an assessment of their prereading competencies.

Spelling is an important language skill on its own. In this chapter we therefore discuss spelling development (for learning to spell is developmental) beyond the early stages, that is, beyond the point where it seems to be closely related to reading growth. In order to assess their development in spelling, it is necessary to explore the complex patterns of errors that children make at different stages. As we shall see, there is a logic strongly evident in these errors, although it will take some careful explication to make it clear.

In this chapter we look into the logic of children's spelling and define the five stages of development that have been identified in research: the *prephonemic stage*, the *early phonemic stage*, the *letter-name stage*, the *transitional stage*, and the *correct spelling stage*. We also describe an assessment device that determines the spelling stage of individual children. Then, for each stage we suggest teaching strategies that are more sharply focused on concepts about spelling than the traditional spelling lists that children memorize. These strategies may be used either as an alternative or as a supplement to the traditional teaching methods.

Spelling and Early Reading

All of us know more than one well-read adult whose spelling is embarrassingly poor. Because fluent reading is not a letter-by-letter process, it seems neither to contribute to, nor to be enhanced by, correct spelling. It is possible for adults to read without paying much conscious attention to the spelling of words, and that possibly explains why some highly literate people can be terrible spellers. With young children, however, the situation is different. Beginning readers do rely more heavily on spelling patterns of words in order to read them (Doehring and Aulls, 1979; Chall, 1979; Gray, 1956), and their spelling is rather closely related to their early reading.

Given encouragement, children will begin to write before they begin to read (Chomsky, 1979; Read, 1975; Temple *et al.*, 1981). This fact is not widely appreciated, probably because few parents or teachers give children the chance to demonstrate what they *could* do with writing. Writing entails spelling, and spelling entails both working judiciously with letters of the alphabet and analyzing spoken words into their component sounds. Analyzing sounds in words requires an ability to make words hold still in the mind while the analysis is carried out, which in turn depends on having a stable concept of what a word is. Because of the way these competencies are related, examining children's early writing can provide a rich source of insight into their development of these important prereading competencies.

Nelson (1980) has hypothesized that we use two different approaches to spelling words. First, we may spell by finding matches in letters for sounds in the words we want to spell. By this process, the spelling of each word we write is the result of invention. On the other hand, we also have the spellings of some words stored intact in our memories. For these words we are able to go directly from the whole word to the whole spelling without resorting to the rules that link the individual sounds in the word to the letters of the alphabet. According to Nelson's hypothesis, beginning spellers rely on the spelling-by-rule route to a large extent, while more mature spellers rely more heavily on the whole-word-to-spelling route.

Some young children are unaware that writing words by figuring out the spellings (Nelson's first approach) is possible, but many others have no such inhibition. They begin making up spellings on their own anywhere between the ages of four and seven. The more reluctant ones can often be coaxed to produce spellings by invention, or "invented spellings," as these have come to be called. Figure 6.1, from Chomsky, 1971, is an example of invented spelling produced by a four-year-old child.

This child's spelling is clearly invented: nobody taught her to spell those words the way she did! The words are not randomly spelled, however. They clearly show an effort to spell individual speech sounds with alphabet letters. Nearly all the sounds in each word have been spelled, and no silent letters have been included. Were we to examine the writing of other children who produced invented spellings, we would discover at least three things:

1. The spellings would almost all be systematic, resulting more from deliberate choices of letters to represent sounds than from guessing what a half-remembered spelling might have looked like.

FIGURE 6.1. "Once a lady went fishing and she caught Flipper."

KUTz A LADE YET FEH
Ee AD HE KOT FLEPR

SOURCE: From Carol Chomsky, "Invented Spelling in the Open Classroom," *Word*, vol. 27, nos. 1–3 (April–December 1971), pp. 499–518. Reprinted by permission of the author and the International Linguistic Association.

2. From child to child, the spellings would be quite similar, even though they looked very little like the adult spellings for the same words.
3. There would be developmental stages through which the children's spellings passed, ranging from highly primitive productions to those that looked much like standard spellings.

These points have been fully developed elsewhere (Beers and Henderson, 1977; Gentry, 1978; Henderson and Beers, 1980; Read, 1975; Temple *et al.*, 1981). In order to understand the relationship between invented spelling and early reading, we must examine in some detail the processes of invented spelling and their evolutionary stages.

The Stages of Spelling Development

Most young children develop a number of different strategies for spelling out the sounds they hear in words. These strategies can be classified, and they help us determine where children are in a developmental sequence and what they have internalized about letters and speech sounds.

Children begin to write by representing only a few sounds in words, but with experience and maturity they are able to represent more sounds in their invented spelling. This ability to isolate speech sounds is an important aspect of prereading competence. We can watch this competence develop as we see children advance through the stages of invented spelling. Table 6.1 shows some sample spellings from children in kindergarten, first grade, and second grade when they were asked to spell a list of words in a study by Gentry (1977). Note how the spelling of each word changed at different levels of development.

Studies have indicated that children pass through the following stages in their invented spelling: *prephonemic spelling, early phonemic spelling, letter-name spelling, transitional spelling.* Let us look at each of these in turn.

Prephonemic Spelling

Figure 6.2 shows eight spellings done by a six-year-old. He was asked to try to write eight words (*fish, bend, jumped, yell, learned, shove, witch, piece*) that he did not know. Figure 6.3 shows the attempts by another youngster to spell the same eight words.

TABLE 6.1. Examples of developmental spelling.

BRIAN KINDERGARTEN	ANGELA KINDERGARTEN	CHRIS 1ST GRADE	JOYCE 2ND GRADE	LORRAINE 2ND GRADE
MPRMRHM	J	GAGIN	DRAGUN	DRAGON
BDRNMPH	P	PRD	PURD	PURRED
Prephonemic	Early phonemic	Letter-name	Transitional	Correct

FIGURE 6.2. Kenny's spelling: prephonemic.

1 SRY   fish

2 LVh   bend

3 YEB   jumped

4 RB   yell

5 SB   learned

6 LS   shove

7 Be   witch

8 YVL   piece

Although the second youngster wrote more letters for most words, the spellings share a basic attribute: *there is no discernible relation between the sounds of the word spelled and the letters put down to spell those sounds.* No one looking at these inventions could guess what words the children were attempting, and

FIGURE 6.3. Rob's spelling: prephonemic.

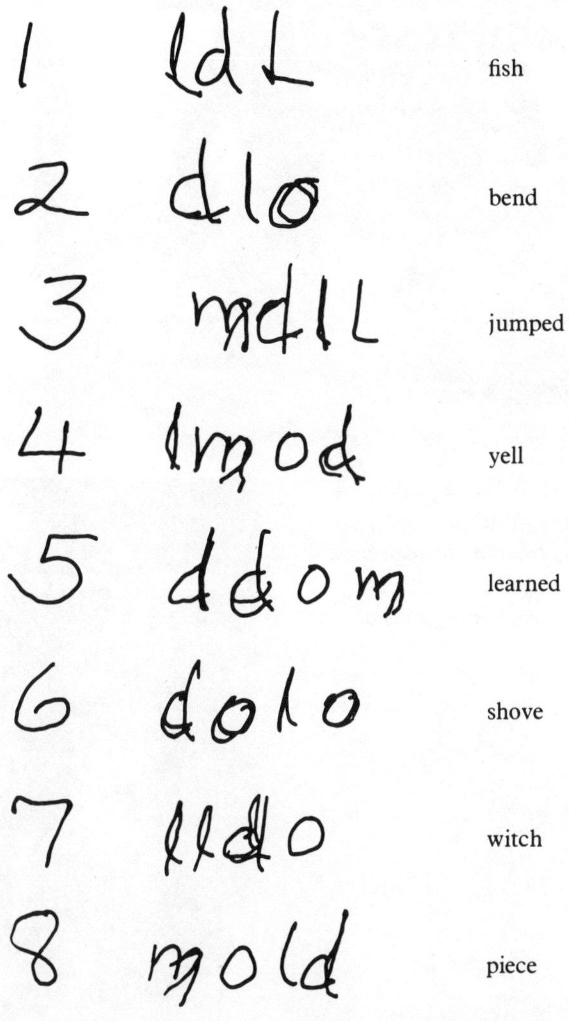

1	*ldL*	fish
2	*dlo*	bend
3	*mdlL*	jumped
4	*lmod*	yell
5	*ddom*	learned
6	*dolo*	shove
7	*lldo*	witch
8	*mold*	piece

even the children themselves could not remember a few minutes later which word was which. The productions are made up entirely of alphabet letters, however, so they are not completely random markings. There are no numerals, stars, or "squiggles" even though many preschoolers include them when they pretend to write. The children who produced Figures 6.2 and 6.3 do know that words are made up of letters and they know how to produce at least some letters fairly accurately.

*T*he development of writing ability is
a creative, thoughtful process.
Young writers learning to spell need
many opportunities to invent their own spellings and reflect on their approximations of
adult spellings.

Prephonemic spelling is not spelling in the usual sense. It is the written production of children who know what writing is supposed to look like but who have not yet discovered the phonetic relation between letters and parts of words, upon which our spelling system is based. We classify spelling as prephonemic when we cannot discern any relationship between the sounds in the words and the letters that are written. Prephonemic spelling looks like random strings of letters in groups.

Early Phonemic Spelling

At the next developmental stage children discover that spelling honors a relationship between speech sounds (phonemes) and letters. In this stage of early phonemic spelling a child's representation of phonemes in words is severely limited.

Figure 6.4 shows early phonemic spellings by Jerome, a six-year-old pre-reader. Here it can be seen that he represented at least one of the phonemes in each word he wrote. When he wrote FSS for *fish,* he represented the initial sound and attempted the final sound, which does sound something like *ss;* ND for *bend* represents the sounds we represent with the letters *en* as well as the final sound. Likewise each of the rest of Jerome's attempts show at least one of the sounds in the word (HD for *shove* may confuse you, but we'll consider this use of H in the next section).

Unlike prephonemic spelling, in the early phonemic stage there is a clear link between the letters a child writes and some speech sounds in the words being spelled. It is clear, however, that the spelling is incomplete. Only one or two phonemes are spelled for each word. Some of these are the first phonemes in the word, some the last. What defines early phonemic spelling is that *the letters represent phonemes but only an incomplete number of phonemes for each word.*

Why don't children represent more phonemes per word? Because they cannot. The difficulty lies not in the number of letters they know, nor so much in their notions of which letters should represent which phonemes. It is rather that they are unable beyond a very limited extent to break a word down into its phonemes, a task called *phonemic segmentation* by psychologists. Their inability to segment phonemes is related in turn to another factor: children at this stage lack a stable concept of word in print (Henderson, 1980).

Let us explore the relationship between phonemic segmentation and the concept of word somewhat further. When children try to spell a word, they must perform several different tasks in close harmony. They must first say the word over to themselves; they may do this out loud, as many children do, or silently in the "mind's ear." Next they must mentally break off the first sound. To spell *tooth,* for example, they must rehearse the word, then mentally break off the /t/ sound. Now they must think of a letter to match with the

FIGURE 6.4. Jerome's spelling: early phonemic.

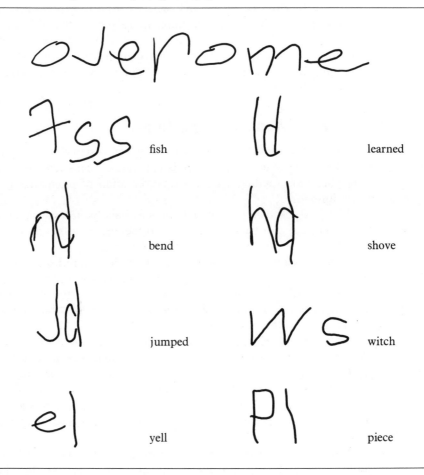

Jerome

Tss   fish   ld   learned

nd   bend   hd   shove

Jd   jumped   Ws   witch

el   yell   Pl   piece

phoneme, /t/. Now they must remember how to write the letter *T*, then decide where it should go on the page, then carry through the motor activity of forming the letter with their pencils. That done, they must remember what word it was they were trying to spell! If they can remember the word, then they must rehearse it again mentally and remember which phoneme they had already broken off. Then they must mentally break off the /t/ phoneme again and decide which phoneme comes next. If they get this far and arrive at the vowel sound, they must decide which letter represents it. Then they must recall how to write *that* letter and decide where to write it. Does it go to the left or to the right of the *T?* Now they write down that letter, then recall the word again, and so on.

If all of this were not complex enough, there is also the fact that phonemes are not so easy to separate from one another as this scenario may have suggested (Liberman et al., 1974). In fact, when we say the word *tooth*, we do not pronounce the /t/ and the /u/ distinctly from each other. We pronounce them practically at the same time. To separate them from each other is really an abstraction that we impose on the sounds of the word *tooth*, much like what we do when we separate a wave from the surface of the ocean, though in fact no objective dividing line is present in nature between the two. As adults it is easy to separate /t/ from /u/, but this is because we can already read, and we are used to seeing the separate phonemes depicted in writing. For beginning readers, this act is much more difficult.

Children in the early phonemic stage will fall by the wayside in the middle of the steps we described above. Part of the reason will be the difficulty of phonemic segmentation, but part of it will be because they lack a stable concept of word. Their words will not hold still in their minds while they carry out the series of acts that are necessary to spell them (Morris, 1980). Both the ability to segment phonemes (Liberman et al., 1980) and the concept of word (Morris, 1980) have been shown to be intimately related with beginning reading. Although a causal relationship has not been firmly established, it is believed that children must be able to reflect on words and segment phonemes before they can make real strides in beginning reading (Ehri, 1980). Since they are able to produce early phonemic spelling before they have begun to read, their reaching this stage may be taken as a predictor of reading development to come and a sign that an important prerequisite for that development has been met.

Letter-Name Spelling

As children move closer to the point when they begin to read and acquire more experience looking at printed words, their invented spelling strategies undergo many changes. From being able to represent only one or two sounds in a word, their spelling productions reflect most or all the sounds they hear. Their productions may look somewhat bizarre at first, but when considered carefully these productions do make sense. As they try to represent more and more sounds in words, they begin to use what has been called the *letter-name strategy* (Beers and Henderson, 1977); that is, they analyze the words they want to spell into their component sounds and then find a *letter name* to represent each sound. *To spell each sound, they choose the letter name that most closely resembles the sound they want to represent.*

In many languages, the relationship between speech sounds and letter names is very close. Finnish is one such language. In Finnish children's use of the letter-name strategy often results in correct spelling (Temple and Salminen, 1981). In English, however, there is quite a bit of variance between the names of our letters and the sounds in words. Many letters that appear in words do not represent sounds at all but rather serve to indicate the pronunciation of other letters in those words (Venezky, 1970). It has been said that modern English spelling most closely represents the way English words were pronounced five hundred years ago, before many substantial changes in pronunciation took place. One writer thus has called English spelling "historically phonetic" (Vallins, 1954). Because of all these factors there is not a very close relation between letters and sounds in English. Our spelling system is learnable, to be sure, but it is complex and not very directly phonetic.

Beginning spellers seem to expect a close relationship to exist between letters and sounds and thus their spelling is very different from standard spelling. When they choose letters to represent sounds, they don't use silent letters. They represent many sounds with letters that adults would not choose, both out of ignorance of the way standard spelling works and because they perceive similarities among sounds that years of experience with print have conditioned adults to ignore.

Let's observe this process in action by looking again at Figure 6.1. Consider the spelling YUTS A LADE YET FEHEG AD HE KOT FLEPR for "Once a lady went fishing and she caught Flipper." This work was generated by using the letter-name strategy. Can you decide *why* the child used the letters she did to spell each sound in those words?

The letter-name strategy yields some spellings that appear immediately reasonable and others that seem very peculiar. We can understand this better if we consider how a letter-name speller handles several aspects of words.

Long Vowels. Long vowels "say their names" in English and thus they are usually spelled with the letter name that sounds like them. Although standard spelling requires that a marker letter be present in most cases to indicate when a vowel letter is to have a long pronunciation, such markers are usually absent in letter-name spelling. For instance, the word *name* has a silent *e* marker that indicates that the *a* is long. But in letter-name spelling, the same word would be spelled NAM. Figure 6.5 shows other examples of long vowels spelled by letter-name spelling: *hates*, *likes*, and *playing*.

Short Vowels. How the short vowel sounds in English should be spelled is not so easy to guess. By simply saying the names of the vowel letters, *a*, *e*, *i*, *o*, and *u*, we cannot find a letter name with the sound of the vowels in *bet*, *bat*, *bit*, *but*, or *bottle*. The solution that letter-name spellers most often find for this problem is to choose the nearest fit — to choose a letter whose name sounds the most like the short vowel sounds they want to spell, which leads to some interesting pairings of sound and letter. In reality the long and short vowels that are paired in standard English spelling do not sound much alike. Consider /ā/ and /ă/; /ē/ and /ĕ/; /ī/ and /ĭ/; /ō/ and /ŏ/; /ū/ and /ŭ/. These pairings are not the ones children who use letter-name spelling produce (see Figure 6.6).

FIGURE 6.5. Frank's spelling: letter-name.

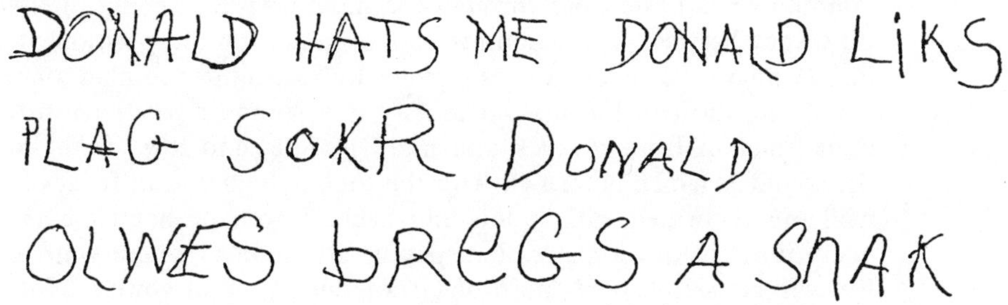

DONALD HATS ME DONALD LIKS
PLAG SOKR DONALD
OLWES bREGS A SnAK

"Donald hates me. Donald likes playing soccer. Donald always brings a snack."

In "My Teeth" the writer has used *o* to represent the vowel sound in *pulled* (POLD), *put* (POT), and *under* (ONDR). He has used *i* to represent the short vowel sound in *dollar* (DILR). He has used *e* to represent the short vowel sound in *pillow* (PELR) and *bill* (BEL). These are common substitutions because letter-name spellers often substitute short vowel sounds:

> *a* for *ĕ:* BAT for *bet*
> *e* for *ĭ:* BET for *bit*
> *i* for *ŏ:* HIT for *hot*
> *o* for *ŭ:* BOT for *but*
> (Read, 1971, 1975)

FIGURE 6.6. Billy's spelling: letter-name.

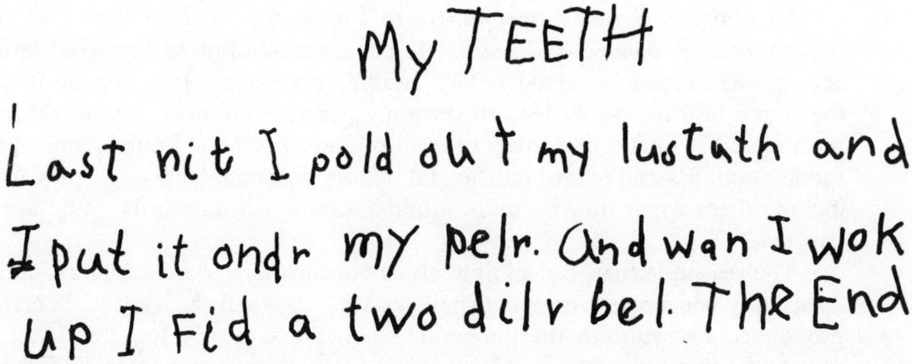

My TEETH

Last nit I pold ou t my lustuth and
I put it ondr my pelr. And wan I wok
up I Fid a two dilr bel. The End.

"Last night I pulled out my loose tooth and I put it under my pillow. And when I woke up I found a two dollar bill."

Though at first these pairings seem strange, on reflection they are not if we consider how vowel sounds are made in the mouth. Vowels are formed when vibrated air is passed out through the mouth without being interrupted. The difference between vowel sounds is determined by the position of the tongue in the mouth. The tongue can move to an infinite number of positions as vowels are formed, but it is customary to refer to its positions in terms of the dimensions of front to back and high, middle, and low. Take, for example, the sound $\bar{e}$, which is formed with the tongue high and in front of the mouth, while *ah* is formed with it low and back. If you pronounce *ē-ah, ē-ah, ē-ah* many times in quick succession, paying attention to where your tongue goes, you will get a feel for its positions in the formation of vowels. Now as it turns out, there is another important factor in the formation of vowels, and that is whether or not the tongue is tense or relaxed as the vowel is made. A tense high front vowel is $\bar{e}$, for example. A vowel made in the same position but with the tongue relaxed is $\bar{\imath}$. Similarly, a vowel made in the front of the mouth midway between high and low is $\bar{a}$ if the tongue is tense, but if the tongue is relaxed, the vowel is $\breve{e}$ (Langacker, 1973).

The tense-relaxed dimension can be demonstrated in the following manner: Hold your thumb and forefinger against the flesh beneath your jaw. Alternate saying the vowels $\bar{e}$ and $\bar{\imath}$. You should be able to feel the muscle in the bottom of your mouth literally tense up for the sound $\bar{e}$ and relax for the sound $\bar{\imath}$. The same tensing and relaxing can be felt with $\bar{a}$ and $\bar{e}$.

The vowel pairings that letter-name spellers make are exactly these tense-relaxed pairings. The vowels that they consider similar for the purpose of spelling are made in the same positions in the mouth and differ only according to whether or not the tongue is tense or relaxed in forming them. Again, they are *paired* in the sense that the letter name containing the name of the tense vowel is used to spell the corresponding relaxed vowel phoneme.

Ns and Ms Before Consonants. In Figure 6.7, look at how Daniel has spelled *monster, bumpy,* and *lunch.* He consistently omitted the nasal letters *n* and *m* when either occurred before another consonant. In *stamp* he included the *m* and omitted the *p*. He can certainly perceive the nasal sound, for he has represented it in the beginning of *monster* and in *bottom.* Letter-name spellers usually omit *n*'s and *m*'s when they fall before consonants, though they usually include them when they occur in other positions within words. Why are they omitted?

The reason is that in deciding which consonants a word contains, children apparently concentrate on what their mouths do when they say it. When they pronounce a word with the phoneme /t/, they can clearly feel the tip of their tongue touching the fleshy ridge behind their upper front teeth and then releasing a little blast of air. Letter-name spellers know that this movement in the mouth indicates the necessity of writing a letter *t*. Similarly, when their

FIGURE 6.7. Daniel's spelling: letter-name.

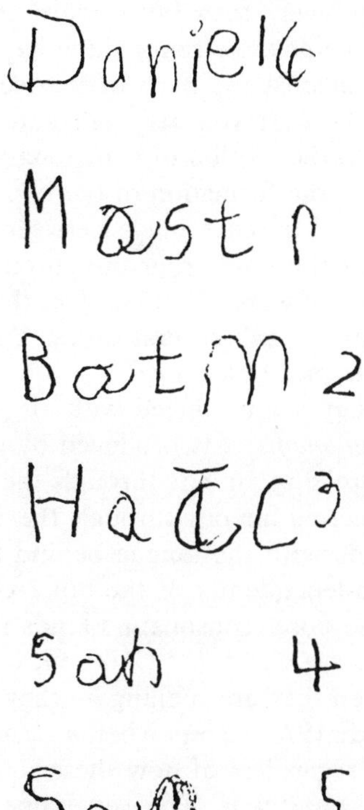

Daniel

Mostp 1   monster

Batn 2   bottom

HaTC 3   hiked

5ab 4   sock

Sam 5   stamp

ParD 6   purred

Boe 7   bumpy

Chp 8   chirp

Lach 9   lunch

two lips close, followed by a puff of air, they know that there must be a letter *p* in their written version of the word.

When, however, they say a word that has the phoneme *n* coming just before the phoneme *t*, a strange thing happens. There is nothing in the motion of the tongue against the back of the teeth to indicate that the sound of *n* is present with the *t*. If you say *can't* and *cat* in alternation several times, and pay attention to the motion of your tongue, you will find that there is virtually no difference in the formation of the two words in the mouth.

How is the difference made between the two words? In saying the word *can't*, we direct the flow of air out through the nose when we pronounce the second part of the word. You can feel this if you hold your nose while saying *cat — can't, cat — can't* several times. You will feel a vibration in the nose as you pronounce *can't* but not *cat*.

Because they are produced with air going through the nose, *n* and *m* are called *nasal consonants: n* is produced by touching the tongue behind the front teeth while directing air out through the nose; *m* is produced by closing the lips while directing air out through the nose. When *n* occurs before another consonant made with the tongue behind the front teeth we still can recognize its presence independently of the other consonant because of the vibration of air through the nose (consonant sounds that can be made in this position are /t/, /d/, /ch/, /s/, /z/, and /j/). Children, however, attend only to the motion in the mouth when they are spelling — they ignore the passing of air out through the nose (Read, 1975). Thus when *n* occurs before the sounds of /t/, /d/, /ch/, /s/, /z/, or /j/ (regardless of how these sounds may be spelled), youngsters are likely to leave out the *n*. The very same thing happens with *m* before /p/ or /b/ as in *bumpy* or *mumble*.

Syllables Without Vowels. Another strategy of letter-name spellers is to let a consonant sound or a consonant letter's name represent a whole syllable in which the vowel sound is reduced. In Figure 6.8 Joey used *l* for the last syllable in *little*, which he spelled LETL. Look again at Figure 6.7, in which Daniel wrote MASTR for *monster* and BATM for *bottom*. Here Daniel used *r* and *m* to represent whole syllables in which an adult would include a vowel. As we saw in Figure 6.6, the child who wrote "My Teeth" used *r* to represent the final syllable in *under* (ONDR), *pillow* (probably pronounced *piller*) (PELR), and *dollar* (DILR).

What LETL, MASTR, BATM, ONDR, PELR and DILR have in common is the absence of a vowel in the final unstressed syllable. In English, when words end in unstressed syllables containing the consonant *r*, *l*, *m*, or *n*, it is difficult to tell what vowel they are spelled with. Note the sound of the second vowel in *castle, common, letter,* and *bottom*. It is not very distinct; in fact it is hard to discern a vowel sound at all that is separate from the sound of the consonant itself. There are only a few English words that allow these syllables

FIGURE 6.8. Joey's spelling: letter-name.

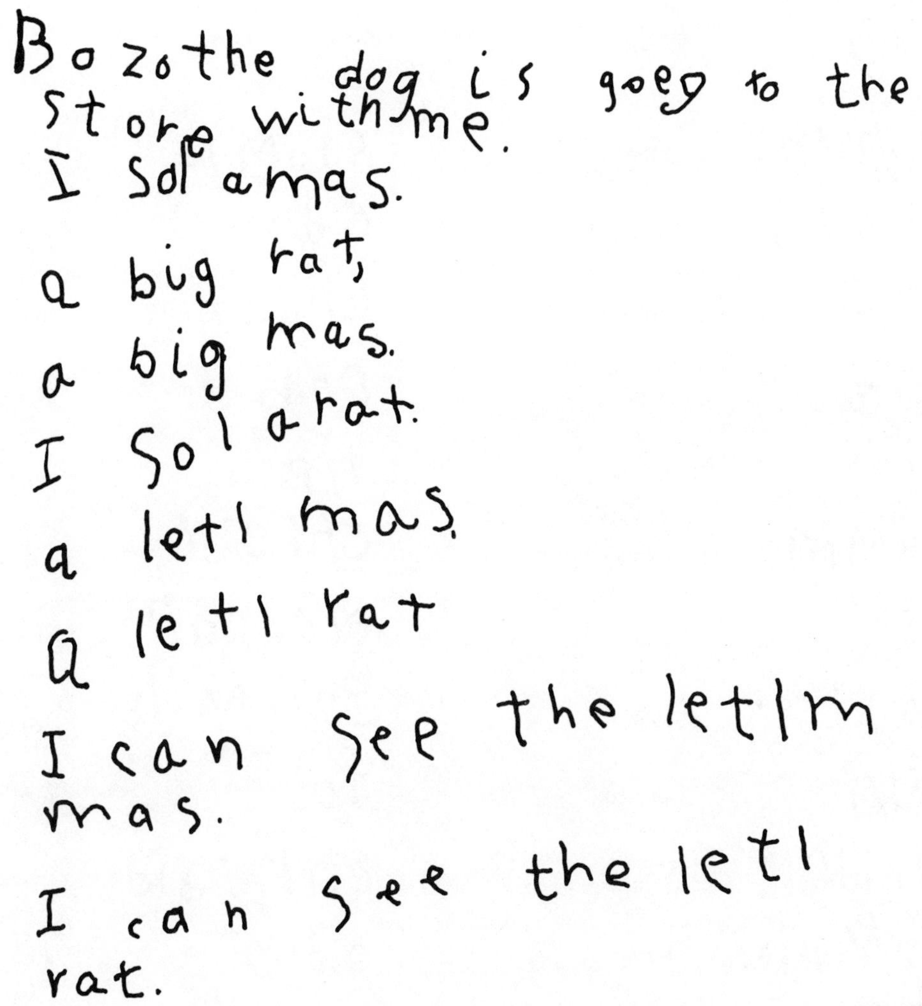

Bozo the dog is goeg to the
Store with me. I Sol a mas.
a big rat,
a big mas.
I Sol a rat.
a letl mas.
a letl rat
I can See the letlm mas.
I can See the letl rat.

to be spelled without a vowel: for example, *prism* and *chasm*. Children usually spell these syllables without a vowel at all (Gentry, 1977, 1978).

Tr and Dr. In normal speech, our pronunciation of the consonant blend at the beginning of *truck* sounds like *ch*, and our pronunciation of the blend at the beginning of *dragon* sounds like *gr* or *jr*. Few of us say *t-ruck* or *d-ragon*

FIGURE 6.9. Fergus's spelling: letter-name.

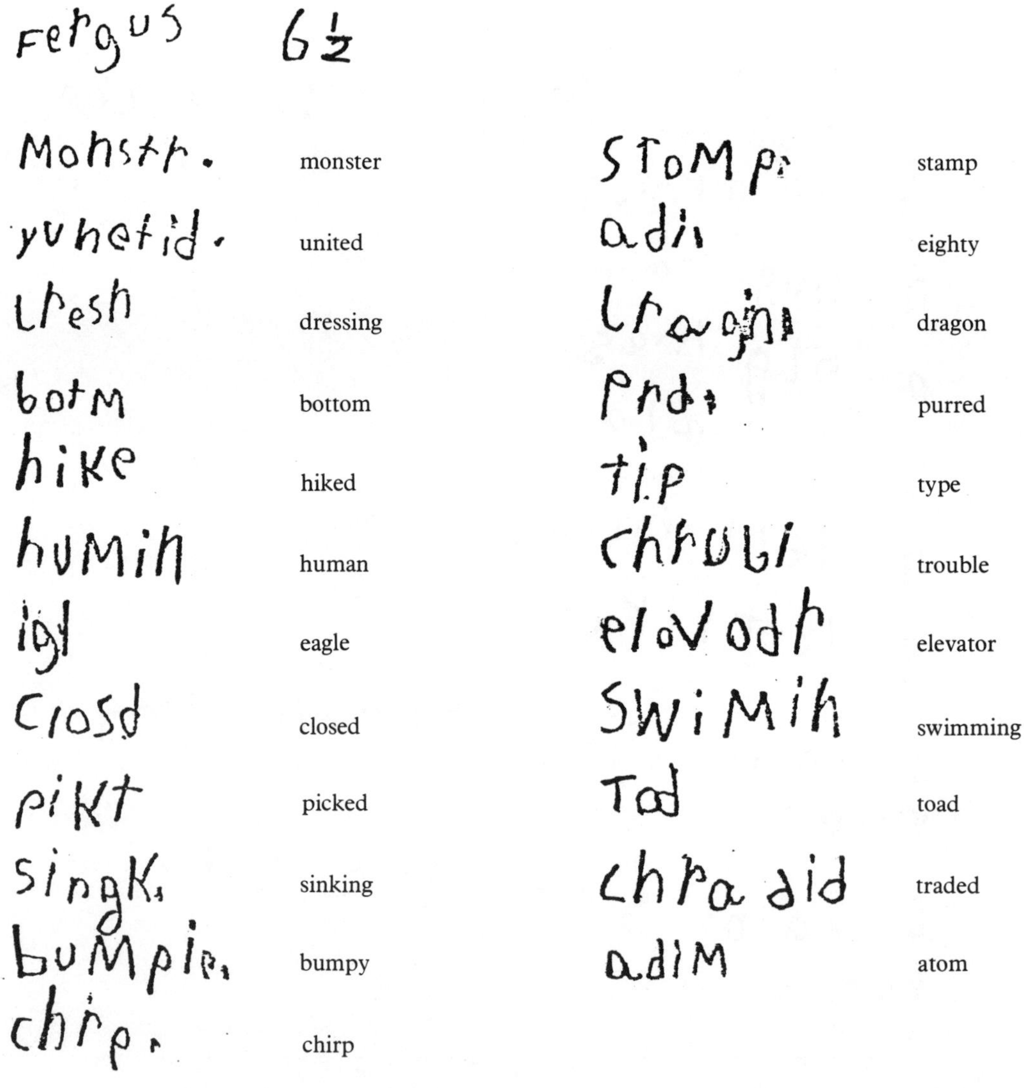

Fergus   6½

Mohstr.	monster	SToMp.	stamp
yuhetid.	united	adi	eighty
Lhesh	dressing	Lragni	dragon
botm	bottom	Prdi	purred
hike	hiked	tip	type
humih	human	chrubi	trouble
igl	eagle	elovodr	elevator
Closd	closed	SwiMih	swimming
pikt	picked	Tod	toad
singK.	sinking	chra did	traded
buMpi.	bumpy	adiM	atom
chrp.	chirp		

unless we're calling out words in a spelling test! Because beginners spell what they hear, they are likely to write JRAGN or GAGN for *dragon* and CHRUK or even HRUK for *truck*. The latter spelling needs further explanation because *ch* represents a sound that children could not possibly guess on their own.

FIGURE 6.10. Carla's spelling: letter-name.

Carla

6 munster	monster	Stamp	stamp
unidede	united	aĝey	eighty
dresing	dressing	dra6an	dragon
Bottem	bottom	pried	purred
hike	hiked	Tipc	type
Yumin	human	chrubm	trouble
igul	eagle	eluvader	elevator
closed	closed	swiming	swimming
picked	picked	tode	toad
Singck	sinking	traded	traded
Bumpy	bumpy	adem	atom
chrip	chirp		

There is only one sound, but two letters, and the relation between the two letters and the sound is not at all obvious. Letter-name spellers use the strategy of finding a match between a speech sound and the name of a letter of the alphabet. In our alphabet, the only letter name that contains the sound *ch* is the name of the letter *h:* "aitch." Thus *truck* might be spelled HRUK: *h* for

FIGURE 6.11. Some prominent features of letter-name spelling.

LONG VOWELS

Closely matched letter names are used for long vowels, but without silent letters as markers:

BAT (*bait*), STAN (*stain*), JRIV (*drive*), BOT (*boat*)

SHORT VOWELS

Short vowels are represented by pairing the desired short vowel sound with the long vowel sound that is similarly produced in the mouth and then spelling by means of a letter-name match:

BAT (*bet*), PAT (*pet*), BET (*bit*), STAP (*step*), BITL (*bottle*)

N'S AND *M*'S BEFORE CONSONANTS

When *n*'s and *m*'s come before "hard" consonants, such as *d*, *t*, *ch*, or *p*, they are omitted:

STAP (*stamp*), BOPE (*bumpy*), TET (*tent*), PEH (*pinch*)

UNSTRESSED FINAL SYLLABLES

With words that end in unstressed syllables the vowels in those syllables are usually omitted:

LATR (*letter*), LEDL (*little*), PECHR (*pincher*), BIDM (*bottom*)

TR AND *DR*

Words that begin with *tr* or *dr* are often pronounced as if the letters were *chr* and *jr*, respectively. *H* is often given for the digraph /ch/, and *g* or *j* for the sound, /j/. These sounds are spelled as they are heard:

HRUK (*truck*), GRIV (*drive*), CHRUBL (*trouble*), JEK (*drink*)

---

the sound /ch/ which is the sound actually heard at the beginning of truck (Gentry, 1977, 1978). And look again at Figure 6.4, where Jerome wrote HD for *shove*. The presence of the letter *d* is random, which often happens in early phonemic spellings, but the *h* is used there because of the similarity between the letter name "aitch" and the /sh/ sound. The letter name "aitch" is as close as one can come to the sound of /sh/.

In Figure 6.9, Fergus used JR and CHR to represent the initial sounds in *dragon*, *trouble*, and *traded*. In Figure 6.10, Carla used CHR to begin *trouble* but TR to begin *traded*. Like Fergus, Carla used JR for the initial sounds in *dragon*.

Letter-name spelling has a number of characteristic features, which are summarized in Figure 6.11.

Transitional Spelling

When children produce spellings like Eric's in Figure 6.12, the spellings look a lot more "wordlike" than Daniel's, Fergus's, or Carla's. More word features are present in Eric's spellings of CETER (*setter*), SHUVE (*shove*), SAILER (*sailor*), SPASHAL (*special*), and FECHER (*feature*).

Unlike the highly original forms produced by the letter-name strategy, *transitional spellings take on many of the features of standard spellings*. They employ short vowels appropriately, if not correctly: HAV, (*have*), GURL, (*girl*), LITL (*little*). They use silent letters for markers: WEPE (*weep*), REDE (*read*),

FIGURE 6.12. Eric's spelling: transitional.

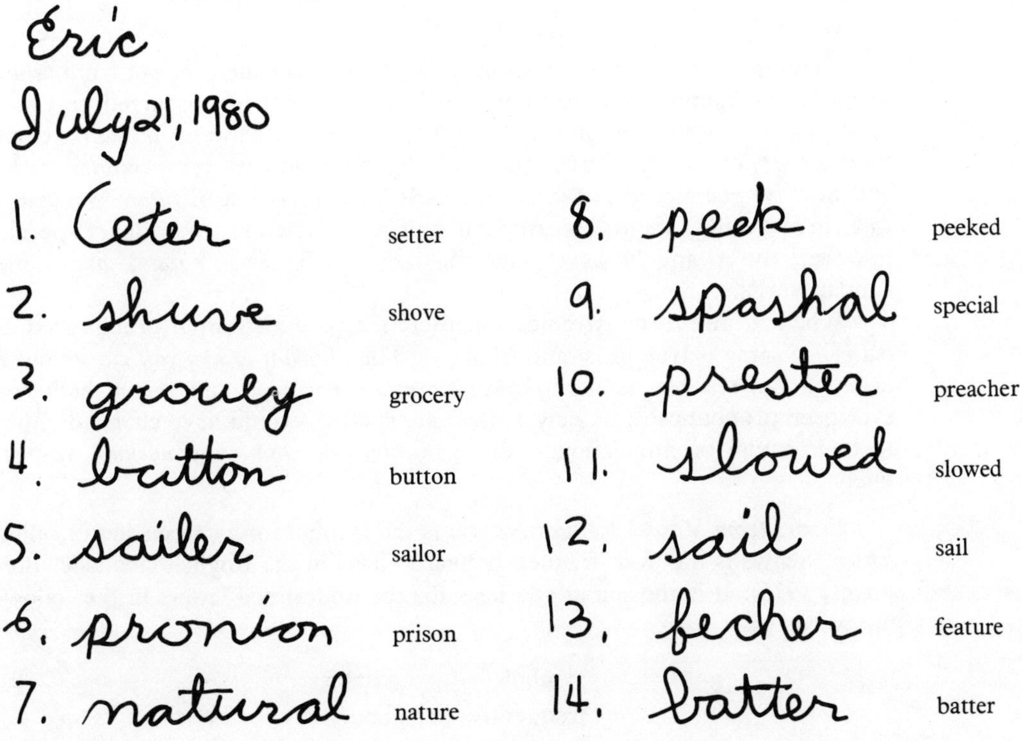

Eric
July 21, 1980

1. Ceter	setter		8. peek	peeked
2. shuve	shove		9. spashal	special
3. grouey	grocery		10. prester	preacher
4. batton	button		11. slowed	slowed
5. sailer	sailor		12. sail	sail
6. pronion	prison		13. fecher	feature
7. natural	nature		14. batter	batter

BIEK (*bike*), and ROAP (*rope*). Sometimes they use long vowel markers for short vowels and vice versa: GETE (*get*), GOTE (*got*), RALL (*rail*), and STELL (*steal*). Transitional spellers often forget to double the consonants when syllables are added to one-syllable words with short vowels: GETING (*getting*), BEDER (*better*), LITLE (*little*) (Gentry, 1981).

They also spell the grammatical ending *ed* the way it sounds. In some words *ed* sounds like *t* and is spelled that way by both letter-name and transitional spellers: PEEKT (*peeked*), TRAPT (*trapped*), BUNCHT (*bunched*). In other words it sounds like *id:* WONTID (*wanted*), CARRID (*carried*), TAS-TID (*tasted*), and sometimes *ed* sounds like *d*: SLODE (*slowed*), USDE (*used*), STADE (*stayed*).

Transitional spelling takes in a wide range of spelling behaviors that can be observed from first or second grade through high school. Those that affect older students are discussed in the following sections.

Errors from Pronunciation Changes. Some characteristic posttransitional spellings for words with /ch/ and /sh/ sounds are:

VACASHUN (*vacation*)	SPESHLE (*special*)
FORCHUN (*fortune*)	GROSHRY (*grocery*)
NACHER (*nature*)	FUCHURE (*future*)

Words from Latin origin with /ch/ or /sh/ sounds in them are troublesome for many children because they seem illogical: How does one ever get from *future* to its pronunciation which sounds like *fewcher?* What has occurred here is a very common pronunciation change. It happens that whenever /t/ and /y/ come together we tend to pronounce them as /ch/. Note how *got you* becomes *gotcha* and how *bet you* becomes *betcha*. An early pronunciation of *future* was *fyute-yure;* in fact BBC announcers still favor this pronunciation. In ordinary speech, however, the /t/ and /y/ have come together as /ch/, as in *nature, suture,* and similar words.

When /t/ and /i/ or /y/ come together, they are also often pronounced as /sh/. The same is true of /s/ and /i/ or /y/. Thus *I want to kiss you* comes out *I wanna kisha; this year* is often *thishyear*. *Initial, vacation,* and *nation,* had they ever been pronounced precisely as they are spelled, would have changed either to their actual pronunciation — or to *inichle, vacachun,* and *nachun,* respectively.

Errors from Vowel Reduction. /ə/ is the symbol for a speech sound called *schwa.* Schwa is the most frequently heard vowel in the English language (Bollinger, 1975). It is the sound you hear for the underlined letters in the following words:

symb<u>o</u>l	syll<u>a</u>bl<u>e</u>s
frequ<u>e</u>ntly	<u>a</u>bout

vow<u>e</u>l   <u>e</u>nough

langu<u>a</u>ge   <u>i</u>niti<u>a</u>l

bott<u>o</u>m   lib<u>e</u>rate

Schwa can be spelled by any vowel letter if it occurs in a syllable that is unstressed. Since the schwa sound can be spelled by any vowel letter, it is often very difficult to tell which letter should be used to spell it. Thus we see spellings such as:

LITTUL (*little*)   INUFF (*enough*)

BOTTUM (*bottom*)   NASHUN (*nation*)

UBOUT (*about*)   BUSHLE (*bushel*)

Linguists say that schwa occurs in reduced vowels, vowels that are unstressed to the point where their identity is indeterminate. Herein lies a useful key to their identity. A word that has a schwa for a certain unstressed vowel will often have a related form in which that vowel is stressed and, therefore, identifiable.

Likewise, words that have the /ch/ or /sh/ pronunciation for *ti* or *ty* can have related forms that make the identity of the letters in question easier. *Vac<u>a</u>tion* can be related to *vac<u>a</u>te; national* can be related to *inn<u>a</u>te* and *n<u>a</u>tive. Special* can be related to *spec<u>i</u>fic.*

Errors Stemming from Scribal Traditions. Spellings like LUV, ABUV, SHUV, SUME, CUM, DUN, and WUNTS are reasonable guesses for some seemingly unreasonable words, but the correct spellings turn out to have a common and interesting source. If the source is learned and remembered, the errors can be reduced, if not completely eliminated.

Before the printing press was invented and all reading material had to be copied by hand, the professional copiers of the Middle Ages, the scribes, proudly cultivated a beautiful handwriting called *Gothic script.* Unfortunately, this script sacrificed legibility for beauty. This fact, as well as some holdovers from Latin traditions of spelling, led to some curious spellings (Scragg, 1974; Vallins, 1954).

In writing Latin, there was no clear distinction between the letter *u* and the letter *v.* One was as likely to be used as the other when either was intended. In early English writing, also, *love* could be written *loue* and *very* could be written *uery,* or they could be written the other way around. Apparently it didn't make much difference, except to the scribes. While they failed in trying to separate the use of the two letters, they did establish the following rule: whenever a word ended in the sound of *v,* the consonant would be followed by the letter *e.* Thus *love,* which had originally been spelled *luv,* became *luve* (or *luue*) and *abuv* became *abuve* (or *abuue*). That rule has stayed with us, and to this day you won't find an English word that ends in the letter *v.*

Why then did the *u*'s turn into *o*'s? That change was deliberately made to distinguish the vowel from the consonant in words where *u* and *v* came together, as in *love, above, shove,* and *move* (all of these were originally spelled with *u* vowels). To make reading these words easier, the scribes changed the *u*'s to *o*'s when they came before *v*'s. While they were at it, they extended this practice to *o*'s that fell before *m*'s and *n*'s: the repetition of short vertical lines in such words made it easier to read the vowels if the *u*'s were closed and made into *o*'s.

Although these changes did not affect very many words, they were words of such high frequency that today we see many spelling errors if writers are not sensitive to the patterns that have come down to us from medieval times.

Consonant Doubling Errors. The necessity to double the consonants in the middle of two-syllable words results in many errors like:

LITLE (*little*)	BUTER (*butter*)
BATER (*batter*)	BOTLE (*bottle*)
MITEN (*mitten*)	SETLE (*settle*)

The principle behind consonant doubling goes back to the system of vowel markings (Venezky, 1970). As we all know, single vowel letters that come before single consonant letters are given a short pronunciation: b<u>a</u>t, b<u>u</u>t, b<u>i</u>t, and b<u>et</u>. The vowel would be pronounced long if another vowel came after the consonant: B<u>a</u>tes, b<u>i</u>te, P<u>e</u>te, N<u>A</u>TO, d<u>a</u>ta, v<u>e</u>to, and cr<u>e</u>do. (Note that whether or not the following vowel is silent does not affect its function as a marker for the preceding vowel). If we add another syllable directly onto a single vowel word like *bat*, it has the effect of making the vowel long and we get *bāter*. The remedy, of course, is to double the consonant at the boundary between the original word and the new syllable: *bătter*. This solution is very common, and most two-syllable words are spelled by this pattern. For children, however, the consonant doubling pattern presents more complexity than they can handle. It is easier to write *bat* and simply append *er* to it, without considering the effect of the *e* on the preceding vowel.

Transitional spelling has a number of characteristics, which we have summarized in Figure 6.13.

The Stages of Spelling Development and Reading

Children's progress through the stages of spelling development and their advancement as readers are related, at least in the beginning.

Prephonemic spellers are not yet readers. They have not yet discovered the alphabetic principle that governs writing, namely, that words are divisible into phonemes and that letters represent the phonemes. Before they make that discovery, not much progress toward reading will be forthcoming.

FIGURE 6.13. Some characteristics of transitional spelling.

LONG AND SHORT VOWELS

The letters used are correct, but there are problems with the ways these vowel sounds are marked:

METT (*meet*), PIKE (*pick*), BOT (*bought*), SPRINGE (*spring*)

PLURAL AND PAST TENSE MARKERS

The *ed*, *s*, and *es* markers, which are pronounced several ways, are spelled as they are pronounced:

PICKT (*picked*), SLODE (*slowed*), CRIZE (*cries*), HUGZ (*hugs*)

PRONUNCIATION-CHANGE ERRORS

Here words are spelled as they sound rather than by the predictable rules adults use:

VACASHUN (*vacation*), SPESHLE (*special*), GROSHRY (*grocery*),
NACHER (*nature*)

VOWEL-REDUCTION ERRORS

Vowels in unstressed syllables, which are reduced to schwas, are confused with other short vowels:

BUSHLE (*bushel*), FORCHUN (*fortune*), INDIUN (*Indian*),
LITTUL or LITTEL (*little*)

SCRIBAL TRADITION ERRORS

The rules made to make the writing of Latin easier to read are treated phonetically:

LUV (*love*), SUM (*some*), BRUTHER (*brother*), DROAV (*drove*)

CONSONANT-DOUBLING ERRORS

The rules for marking short and long vowels in syllables before consonants are frequently confused:

BETER (*better*), GETING (*getting*), SCRAPPING (*scraping*),
FINNISH (*finish*)

Early phonemic spellers are not yet readers either, but they are within a few months of making the breakthrough (Morris, 1980). Such children have discovered the alphabetic principle: they know that words are divisible into phonemes and that letters relate to those units, but as we saw earlier they are not yet adept at dividing a word into phonemes. Nor do they yet have a stable concept of a word in print: they cannot readily hold a word mentally while they analyze it into its parts.

The concept of a word in print is just as necessary for reading as for spelling. As indicated in our discussion of prereading in Chapter Two, the concept of a word in print is essential if children are to make the connection between the spoken words in their heads and the same written words on the page. This is an important step in beginning reading, and it is probably why many children are successful with early reading in the home: they hear their favorite stories read again and again while they sit in the reader's lap and observe the print as someone reads. Eventually they will "lock onto" the right units of print by hearing the story line and noticing the connections that exist between print and words — if, that is, they are aware of the word as a unit of written language.

Letter-name spellers are in the process of making the bridge into active reading. They have developed a stable concept of a word in print and have become adept at dividing words into phonemes. They may be reading material with a limited vocabulary, or material for which they have been well prepared, such as dictated-experience stories. They have not, however, yet developed a systematic sense of the structure of words in standard English spelling. They are just facing the task of building up a set of generalizations that will help them move from the spelling to the pronunciation of words. That they have not yet formed such generalizations is evident in the highly unorthodox way they have of spelling features of words that are seen very frequently, such as short vowels, *th* and *ch* digraphs, and others.

It is a mistake to expect their concepts of structures they look for in reading to be immediately reflected in their spelling. In language development in general, it has been found that children can comprehend language structures before they can reliably produce them. The same is true of spelling. They can read orthographic, or spelling structure, patterns before they can apply them. They are happy for a time to read words one way and write them another. A child may even write RAN for *rain* but then go back later and read it as *ran*.

Transitional spellers may be at least beginning readers. They have advanced to the point where they are developing increasingly strong concepts of word structure. These concepts make it possible for them to read words they have not learned beforehand because they can use spelling-to-speech patterns together with grammatical and semantic cues in the text to render the printed symbols into words they know. That they are not using spelling patterns correctly in their writing is a matter of inexperience. Concentrated practice not only with reading and writing, but also in word study (described in the next section) will help them establish control over these patterns.

When children reach the transitional stage, reading and spelling diverge from each other; that is, they may continue to make progress as readers at the same time that they continue to make many spelling errors. As their strategies develop, many students concentrate more on meaning contexts and grammatical structures to recognize words, which reduces the necessity of attending closely to spelling structures of words in order to read the words (Gilooley, 1973; Gray, 1956). Thus reading may appear to leave spelling behind, like a childhood friend one has outgrown. Once the transitional stage is reached, it is not particularly productive to analyze spelling to learn about children's reading. It is still useful, however, to look analytically at the spelling of these more advanced children for its own sake. Spelling errors tend to come in patterns in these youngsters, and they slowly yield to instruction that stresses spelling patterns.

There is no doubt that English spelling is a very complicated matter. Although it seems that English spelling is unsystematic and that a speller must learn hundreds of exceptions to weak rules or be doomed to incorrect spelling, recent research has demonstrated that it *is* systematic and that it is built on a strong system of patterns far more regular than realized (Chomsky and Halle, 1968; Venezky, 1970). These patterns are more abstract and complex than many had thought, however, because instead of simply relating the sounds of words to written letters they include pronunciation changes, writing practices of medieval scribes, the grammatical status of words, and the derivational relationship among words. It's a tall order, but if writers are sensitive to these complexities, they will avoid many spelling errors (Templeton, 1979).

Using a Features List to Assess Spelling Development

It is possible to evaluate samples of writing to determine the stage of spelling development that children have reached. For this evaluation to work properly, we must work with their errors because correct spellings might have been copied or memorized. To make an accurate assessment it is important to study the words they have generated by using their own rules or concepts about spelling.

There are two ways to elicit spelling errors for analysis. One is to have the children write free compositions. The trouble with this method, however, is that many youngsters are inhibited about their writing. They often believe they *cannot* write, since they equate writing with correct spelling, neat handwriting, and correct punctuation. A better approach is to dictate a word list. If the teacher provides enough reassurance, the task of spelling individual words is normally not as intimidating as free composition may be.

The *features list* is a list of words selected to test spellings of certain word features that invoke characteristic invented spelling strategies. The features are such things as long and short vowels, *n*'s and *m*'s before other consonants, unstressed final syllables with *l, r, m,* or *n,* and others. We have set up two levels so that we can test the particular strategies of both younger and older students. The beginners' list (Table 6.2) is designed for children in kindergarten through second grade (though it may be used with older children who are poor spellers). The advanced list (Table 6.3) is for grades three and up (though it may be used with advanced youngsters in lower grades).

When the features list is administered, several conditions should be observed. Assure the children that you do not expect them to know how to spell all, or even *any,* of the words correctly but that you simply want to know how they *think* the words are spelled. You should encourage them to do their best, however, and if they don't know how to spell a whole word, they should try to spell as much of it as they can.

Read the word clearly, illustrate it with a sentence so they understand the meaning, and then repeat the word, but don't *exaggerate* the parts of the words and distort their pronunciation. We once heard a teacher giving a spelling test

TABLE 6.2. Beginners' features list (for grades K–2).

1.	late	Kathy was late to school again today.
2.	wind	The wind was loud last night.
3.	shed	The wind blew down our shed.
4.	geese	The geese fly over Texas every fall.
5.	jumped	The frog jumped into the river.
6.	yell	We can yell all we want on the playground.
7.	chirped	The bird chirped when she saw a worm.
8.	once	Jim rode his bike into a creek once.
9.	learned	I learned to count in school.
10.	shove	Don't shove your neighbor when you line up.
11.	trained	I trained my dog to lie down and roll over.
12.	year	Next year you'll have a new teacher.
13.	shock	Electricity can shock you if you aren't careful.
14.	stained	The ice cream spilled and stained my shirt.
15.	chick	The egg cracked open and a baby chick climbed out.
16.	drive	Jim's sister is learning how to drive.

NOTE: With younger children, this list should be administered over two or three sessions. Do not give more than six to eight words in one sitting.

TABLE 6.3. Advanced features list (for grades 3 and up).

1.	setter	My dog is an Irish setter.
2.	shove	Don't shove your neighbor in the lunch line.
3.	grocery	I'm going to the grocery store.
4.	button	A button popped off his jacket.
5.	sailor	A person who sails the seas is a sailor.
6.	prison	If you break the law, you may go to prison.
7.	nature	The park just put in a nature trail.
8.	peeked	The spy peeked out from his hiding place.
9.	special	The store had a special sale on blue jeans.
10.	preacher	The preacher talked for an hour.
11.	slowed	The truck slowed down for the curve.
12.	sail	The boat had a torn sail.
13.	feature	The drive-in showed a double feature.
14.	batter	The first batter struck out.

say, "Banana, Bay-nay-nay." This sort of well-intentioned help is hopelessly confusing to children.

Scoring for the Features List

Scoring on the features list is done holistically; that is, for each word, the teacher makes an overall determination as to whether the spelling is prephonemic, early phonemic, letter-name, transitional, or correct.

To make this determination easier, the categories of spelling errors are summarized below:

1. Prephonemic Spelling. None of the letters written for a particular word has any apparent relation to any sound in the word. Example: LDLL for *wind*. Give each word spelled prephonetically 1.
2. Early Phonemic Spelling. Sounds *are* represented by letters, according to the letter-name strategy, but *fewer than half of the sounds* are represented, and the missing letters are those that the more advanced letter-name speller would have included. Example: YN, YE, WN, or YBBAR for *wind*. (The *y* can represent the sound /w/ in letter-name spelling; the *w* represents the same sound by conventional spelling.) Each early phonemic spelling is given 2.
3. Letter-Name Spelling. *Half (or more) of the sounds in the word* are represented by letters. The relation between the letters and sounds rests on the similarity between the sound of the name of the letter and the sound to be represented. Examples: YUTS for *once*, FEHEG for *fishing*. Each letter-name spelling is given 3.

4. Transitional Spelling. More than half of the sounds in the word are represented, but here *the relation between the letters and the sounds is not based on letter names but on conventions.* Short vowels, consonants, and digraphs are spelled correctly. Marker letters appear, but they may be used incorrectly. Examples: GETT or GETE for *get;* THAY or THAE for *they.* Each word classified as transitional is given 4.

5. Correct Spelling. The entire word must be spelled correctly to qualify. If only a minor part of it is incorrect, the spelling is coded as transitional. Correct spellings are given 5.

To score a particular child's paper, the teacher must first classify each spelling into one of the above categories. The category in which a majority of the spellings fall represents the strategy or stage of spelling that best describes that child. Table 6.4 is worked out for you as an example.

TABLE 6.4. Analysis of beginner's features list: second grader.

	RESPONSE	TEST WORD	SCORING
1.	LAT	late	3
2.	WND	wind	3
3.	SEAD	shed	4
4.	GEES	geese	4
5.	GOMT	jumped	3
6.	UL	yell	3
7.	CUTP	chirped	3
8.	UOS	once	3
9.	LUD	learned	3
10.	SUF	shove	3
11.	TRAD	trained	3
12.	YER	year	3
13.	SOCK	shock	4
14.	SAD	stained	3
15.	CEK	chick	3
16.	DRIF	drive	3

STAGE	NO. OF EXAMPLES
Prephonemic	0
Early phonemic	0
Letter-name	13
Transitional	3
Correct	0

KEY: 1 = prephonemic, 2 = early phonemic, 3 = letter-name, 4 = transitional, 5 = correct.
NOTE: This eight-year-old second grader is clearly in the letter-name stage of spelling.

TABLE 6.5. Analysis of advanced features list: fourth grader.

	RESPONSE	TEST WORD	SCORING	STAGE	NO. OF EXAMPLES
1.	SETTER	setter	5	Prephonemic	0
2.	SHUVE	shove	4	Early phonemic	0
3.	GROSHERY	grocery	4	Letter-name	0
4.	BUTTON	button	5	Letter-name	0
5.	SAILER	sailor	4	Transitional	9
6.	PRIZIN	prison	4	Correct	5
7.	NATCHER	nature	4		
8.	PEKED	peeked	4		
9.	SPEICLE	special	4		
10.	PRECHER	preacher	4		
11.	SLOWED	slowed	5		
12.	SAIL	sail	5		
13.	FETCHER	feature	4		
14.	BATTER	batter	5		

KEY: 1 = prephonemic, 2 = early phonemic, 3 = letter-name, 4 = transitional, 5 = correct.
NOTE: This ten-year-old fourth grader is predominantly in the transitional stage of spelling.

The child who wrote the words in Table 6.4 was a second grader who had a preprimer instructional reading level. Though some features of standard spelling show up in her words (the two e's in GEES, the ck in SOCK), she has been remarkably little influenced by her year and a half in school.

In addition to determining a child's predominant spelling strategy, the features list can also be used to identify features of spelling that are causing problems. Note the fourth grader's spelling in Table 6.5. This boy's spelling is transitional, but we can go further and note some specific difficulties. He must learn to preserve long vowels in two syllable words, as we can see in NATCHER, PRECHER, and FETCHER. He has to become aware of the phonological spellings of *tu* in words like *nature* and *feature*. He also must learn how the short *u* sound is spelled before *v* (SHUVE).

Relating Spelling Development and Instruction

Children entering the different stages of early spelling development think differently about written language, and therefore our goals for them differ accordingly. In general, we want to take them from where they are and coax them up through the higher stages, but the strategies for doing so are different for different children.

Teaching Prephonemic Spellers

Prephonemic spellers are usually found in preschool, kindergarten, and early first grade, although occasionally an older child will be a prephonemic speller.

Children in the prephonemic stage are really not spellers at all because they have not advanced very far toward a working grasp of written language. With a four-year-old, this is not surprising or alarming, but with a six-year-old, perhaps a child from a home where no one reads, it is a signal that a rich saturation in written language must begin immediately.

Prephonemic spellers have to be shown that books and magazines carry messages and that the messages are interesting and pleasurable. The best way to do this is by reading to them as often as we can fit it into the daily schedule. Half an hour a day is certainly not too much, even if it preempts so-called skills instruction. At this stage, it is far more important.

It is also important to find out what books they like best, read the same book to them several times, and then leave it in the reading area so they can look through it on their own. If children do not have favorite books at home, find some way to provide them. The *Reading Is Fundamental* program (RIF, The Smithsonian Institution, Washington, D.C. 20560) is one possible source; the local parent-teacher group may be another. Try to get the children and their parents interested in the local public library's programs for young people. Talk to the children's librarian there, so she can pass on word of these offerings to parents.

Prephonemic spellers have to learn that the print in a book conveys a message. As Marie Clay (1979) has pointed out, many youngsters believe the pictures tell the story. Such children have to be taught that print corresponds to words and that it is arranged in lines running left-to-right, top-to-bottom on the page. To get this information across, read familiar books to them and run your finger along the print as you do so. Another valuable procedure is to take dictation from them, perhaps with a group of other children. It will not make readers out of them right away, but it will help them begin to see that there is a relation between language and print.

Prephonemic spellers should be induced to write, even if it is just in play. When they draw a picture, they should be encouraged to try to write a caption underneath. Even though they cannot provide real writing, we can honestly assure them that if they put down whatever they think looks most like what they want to say, they will eventually get the hang of it and learn to write the way writers do. The purpose behind this approach is to put the issue of "making print" squarely before them. Even if they don't know how to write, they can begin to learn by comparing their own graphic productions with the print they see around them.

Teaching Early Phonemic Spellers

Early phonemic spellers are concentrated in kindergarten and early first grade. Those making a slower entry into literacy, however, are still at this stage late in first grade. Such spellers have discovered much that is still unknown to prephonemic spellers. They know that "print talks" and that letters correspond to phonemes, but they are lacking in three areas:

1. They have only a fragile facility at breaking a spoken word down into phonemes; thus it is difficult for them to match the phonemes with letters.
2. They lack a stable concept of a word in print; it is difficult for them to perform much of a mental operation on a word because words won't hold still for them in their minds.
3. They have not fully worked out which letters should represent which phonemes; in fact, they may not be able to form more than a dozen different letters in print.

The third deficit, not knowing very many letters with which to spell phonemes, will work itself out in the next stage, letter-name spelling. The first two problems are the ones that instruction should deal with at the beginning.

Everything we have recommended for prephonetic spellers is advisable for the early phonemic spellers as well. They still have to be read to, not so much to initiate an interest in written language, but to deepen and broaden such interest. They also need supported encounters with print. Read to them and point to the words as you read. Read a line of print and see if they can read it back to you, pointing to the words as they go. Then point to the first word in the line and see if they can read it; then the last; then one in the middle. This exercise is very important because it leads the children to practice thinking of words as units of print that correspond to the units of language that they can speak. (See the discussion of voice pointing in Chapters Two and Three.)

Early phonemic spellers must have allowances made for their inexperience in writing letters. One successful means of doing so is to provide preformed letters for them to use in composing words, such as Milton Bradley's Link Letters. Every kindergarten and first grade should have several boxes of Link Letters readily available because they are excellent for helping children to form words. Plastic letters are more durable, although more expensive.

Another approach is to encourage them to spell words part by part, spelling what they can and drawing a line for the parts they don't know how to spell (Stauffer, 1980). Thus an early phonemic speller might write M ___ KT S S ___ K for "My cat is sick." The important thing is that their uncertainty over some parts need not prevent them from writing something.

Finally, early phonemic spellers should be encouraged to write. They should be induced to take risks, to write things as best they can even when they know they cannot be correct. Two specific steps can be taken to encourage risk taking. One is to talk to them about what they are achieving. If they write KT for *cat* you can congratulate them on hearing the first and last sound in the word. You can also applaud them for putting the last letter to the right of the second, showing a grasp of left-to-right order in writing. Early phonemic spellers know many things about our writing system. Our job is to tune into some of these things, talk about them, and prod the children to make further efforts.

The second specific strategy is to convey your teaching strategies to the parents and to any other teachers who work with these children. Your efforts to get them to write the way they think words are spelled can be seriously undermined by well-meaning parents or teachers who point out that their spelling is wrong. This is likely to happen unless you stress the importance of encouraging the child to write freely at this stage. You may assure them that a little freedom from mechanics now is very likely to pay off in enthusiasm for and fluency in writing later on.

Teaching Letter-Name Spellers

Letter-name spellers have a stabilizing concept of a word in print, and their phonemic segmentation ability is well developed. At this stage there is a period of exuberant spelling, where invention has reached its highest point and the examples of the correctly spelled words around them are rarely reflected in their own approach to spelling.

The inventions of letter-name spellers look so little like the other words in their environment that it is apparent they are not studying the features of the words they encounter in any detail. Hence it is still too early to teach them very much directly about the spelling patterns of words. It is more productive to wait until the next stage. For now, it is enough to encourage them to write copiously and to help them learn the spellings of interesting words as wholes. We can do this by keeping a variety of stimulating writing tasks before them at all times — not just "Once upon a time" stories but instructions to friends on how to carry out some activity; suggestions in a suggestion box; secret messages to the teacher; notes on a science experiment; reports on a field trip; letters home to a parent; and so forth.

Studying words as wholes can be done in various ways. Word bank cards are an excellent vehicle (Stauffer, 1980). Cut from three by five inch index cards, the word bank cards constitute a tangible record of the words a child can read at sight. Since the words are spelled correctly on the cards, they will enjoy spreading them out and choosing words to use in creative writing. At this stage they will frequently ask someone else how to spell words. When they ask you, tell them, so they can go on creating. If some children seek such help too frequently, encourage them to take a guess. Tell them to write down at least one letter and leave a line for the rest.

Another approach is to write and post word lists on newsprint or on the blackboard after they have had an experience they are eager to write about. Labeling objects around the room is a good idea, as is hanging pictures of favorite objects with captions: motorcycle, starship, skateboard, minibike, etc. Picture dictionaries are also useful.

Teaching Transitional Spellers

Transitional spellers are concerned with the patterns of standard spelling, which is evident from their inclusion of long and short vowel markers and other features that could not arise from invention. Their need is to sort out these conventions and use them correctly. Transitional spellers are found from late first grade on up, including many youngsters in third or fourth grade.

A most productive activity for this group is the word sorting activity described in Chapter Five. Word sorts have two features to recommend them:

1. They employ words the children are very familiar with and thus enable them to see relations between spelling and meaning and grammar, not just spelling and pronunciation.
2. They proceed inductively; that is, children study patterns of words they already know to form generalizations to test against words they do not know. Thus they have to contend only with generalizations they are able to see in concrete form.

Helping Older Students
to Develop Word Knowledge

Older poor spellers often have one thing in common: they try to spell all words the way they sound, and it is no wonder. With all the emphasis given phonics instruction in the early grades and even greater emphasis in many remedial reading programs, it is natural to conclude that spelling is a simple matter of relating letters to sounds.

In order to spell correctly, we have to go well beyond phonics and look very carefully at words. We have to consider what words mean, what other words they are related to, and how they function syntactically. We also have to be open and curious about our written language, learn something of its history, and be sufficiently reflective to apply our learning to spelling.

There is more involved than memorizing hundreds of spellings, although that in itself does provide patterns that can be extended to the spelling of unknown words. We have to do more than memorize dozens of phonics rules and all their exceptions. We should be curious about language, explore it, and play with it to see how it works.

Many approaches to word study can be useful. Word games of all sorts, whether they play on meaning or structure, are recommended: Perquackey, Boggle, Spill 'n Spell, Hangman, Password, and other commercially available games. Frequent trips to the dictionary can also be beneficial. If teachers regularly raise challenging questions that can be resolved by the dictionary, they will be helping to develop good habits in children. Take, for example, the following questions:

"What do *nature* and *national* have to do with each other?"

"Why are the *u*'s in *united* and *uninterested* pronounced differently?"

"Where does the word *boycott* come from?"

At least one dictionary in the classroom should have etymologies. There are also many fascinating books that tell stories about the origin of words. The

Older spellers add to their knowledge about words by learning etomology and relationships between meanings. A good dictionary is a valuable classroom tool, and students can be taught to refer to it routinely.

linguist Mario Pei has written several fact-filled books on words, language, and the English language in particular for a general audience (1952, 1962). Wilfred Funk's *Word Origins and Their Romantic Stories* (1950) and Charles Funk's *Thereby Hangs a Tale: Hundreds of Stories of Curious Word Origins* (1972) are amusing, engaging introductions to etymology. *Word People* (Sorel, 1970) is similar. A more difficult, but perhaps even more informative, book on the background of our language and its relation to other languages is Lancelot Hogben's *The Mother Tongue* (1964). Geared to a high school audience, it is a fascinating excursion into, among other sources, the Latin, Greek, and Old English roots of our language.

Etymological dictionaries provide information on word origins, original meanings of words, and the relationships among words. Some paperback versions are available at moderate cost. Perhaps the best of these is the Dover reprint of Ernest Weekley's *Etymological Dictionary of Modern English* (1967).

Summary

Mature reading, utilizing as it does syntactic structures, information structures, and words recognized as wholes, is not a letter-by-letter operation, but beginning reading makes fairly heavy use of spelling patterns. More specifically, it demands some working familiarity with the alphabet, the ability to think about and mentally manipulate words (the concept of word), and the ability to mentally isolate component sounds in words (phonemic segmentation). All three of these abilities are demonstrated in *invented spelling*. Since children can begin invented spelling before they begin to read, it serves as an early indicator of the development of some centrally important prereading competencies.

Spelling growth advances developmentally, and progress is related to the emergence of prereading competencies as well as the child's reading and writing experience. Spelling ability advances through recognizable stages. These stages, and the reading advancement related to each one, are as follows:

1. *Prephonetic spelling.* At this stage children have a notion of what written language ought to look like, but they have not discovered the phonetic principle, the link between letters and speech sounds. These youngsters may be a year or more away from beginning to read.

2. *Early phonemic spelling.* At this point children have discovered the phonetic principle and try to spell words by matching phonemes (speech sounds) with letters of the alphabet. The matching of letters is incomplete, however, because of an unstable concept of word and/or undeveloped ability to segment phonemes in words. Early phonemic spellers are approaching beginning reading and are often within a few months of the period when rapid sight word acquisition begins.

3. *Letter-name spelling.* At this stage children give full renditions of the sounds in words by matching them with letters of the alphabet according to

the similarity between the speech sound and the letter name. Letter-name spellers are just at the threshold of beginning reading; they may begin to read while still using the letter-name strategy to write.

4. *Transitional spelling.* Children in this group have begun to read and are aware of the spelling patterns on which standard English writing is based. These standard patterns begin to show up in short vowel spellings, silent letters, and consonant digraphs, but the patterns are not used with full accuracy and the words are often still misspelled. Transitional spelling is not very informative in reading assessment, although children in third grade or above who are still transitional spellers may lack exposure to written materials and an awareness of the patterns of written language.

5. *Correct spelling.* These children have memorized the spellings of some words and learned to employ those patterns to spell other words. Correct spelling varies, of course, with the level of difficulty of the word. Faced with too difficult a word, normally correct spellers may revert to phonetic strategies or give up altogether.

The various levels of development can be determined by using a *features list,* which is designed to elicit spelling errors. These errors can be analyzed according to the strategy that seems to have produced them, and the teacher can make an approximate judgment as to a child's level of development. Features lists for young children (kindergarten to grade two) and older children (grade three and up) were included in this chapter.

Instructional strategies should be based on the stages of development. At first, the strategies should build competencies that are important both to reading and writing, such as an orientation to written language, the concept of word, and the ability to segment phonemes in words. Later, the instruction should work on sensitizing children to letter-sound patterns in words and eventually to grammatical considerations and spelling concerns related to scribal traditions, etymologies, and pronunciation habits.

Extension Activities

1. The following spellings were written by an eight-year-old boy in response to the beginners' features list (see Beginner's Features List).
   a. Using the categories and scoring system described in the chapter (see pages 189–191) decide which stage of spelling this child is in.
   b. Where would you say he might be in his reading development?
   c. What learning activities would you recommend for him?
2. The following responses were given for the advanced features list by an eleven-year-old girl (see Advanced Features List).
   a. Where is she in her spelling development?
   b. What features of spelling does she need to learn?
   c. What learning activities would you recommend?

BEGINNER'S FEATURES LIST

	TEST WORD	RESPONSE	STAGE	NO. OF EXAMPLES
1.	late	LAT	Prephonemic	
2.	wind	WNED		
3.	shed	SHUED	Early Phonemic	
4.	geese	GAEESE	Letter-Name	
5.	jumped	JUNPT		
6.	yell	HALL	Transitional	
7.	chirped	HRED	Correct	
8.	once	ONES		
9.	learned	LRNED		
10.	shove	SHUV		
11.	trained	TRANED		
12.	year	YERE		
13.	shock	SHIK		
14.	stained	STANED		
15.	chick	CHEK		
16.	drive	DRIVE		

ADVANCED FEATURES LIST

	TEST WORD	RESPONSE	STAGE	NO. OF EXAMPLES
1.	setter	SETTER	Prephonemic	
2.	shove	SHUV		
3.	grocery	GROSRY	Early phonemic	
4.	button	BUTTER	Letter-name	
5.	sailor	SALER		
6.	prison	PRESEN	Transitional	
7.	nature	NACHER	Correct	
8.	peeked	PECKED		
9.	special	SPESHEL		
10.	preacher	PRECHER		
11.	slowed	SLOWED		
12.	sail	SALE		
13.	feature	FECHER		
14.	batter	BATTER		

3. Study the teachers' manuals of the first two or three levels of a locally used commercial spelling program. How do those teaching instructions and activities compare with the stage theory of development described here? How would you predict young children would spell some of the required words if they hadn't memorized them? On the basis of your prediction, how would you advise a teacher using these materials?

4. Go back and review the word sorting procedure in Chapter Five. Using words that children in an age group of your choice are likely to know, write up sets of about twenty cards each that could be used in word sorts to study:
   a. *o*'s around *v*'s, and so forth (pages 183–184)
   b. phonological spelling changes (page 182)
   c. consonant doubling (pages 184–185)
   d. vowel reduction (pages 182–183)

Suggested Readings

Bissex, Glenda. **GNYS AT WRK: A Child Learns to Write and Read.** *Cambridge, Mass.: Harvard University Press, 1980.* A teacher-mother's account of her son's journey to literacy.

Chomsky, Carol. **"Approaching Reading Through Invented Spelling."** *In Lauren Resnick and Phyllis Weaver, eds. Theory and Practice of Beginning Reading, Vol. 2. Hillsdale, N.J.: Lawrence Erlbaum Associates, 1979.* Advocates encouraging children to explore writing as a means of developing prereading competencies.

Henderson, Edmund and Beers, James, eds. **Developmental and Cognitive Aspects of Learning to Spell.** *Newark, Del.: International Reading Association, 1980.* These papers discuss children's spelling and word knowledge as well as teaching strategies.

Read, Charles and Hodges, Richard. **"Spelling."** *The Encyclopedia of Educational Research (1982, in press).* A recent definitive compilation of research findings on spelling and how it is learned.

Temple, Charles; Nathan, Ruth; and Burris, Nancy. **The Beginnings of Writing.** *Boston: Allyn and Bacon, 1982.* Four chapters provide a detailed coverage of invented spelling, and teaching word study.

Weber, Kenneth J. **Yes They Can! A Practical Guide for Teaching the Adolescent Slow Learner.** *Evanston, Ill.: McDougal, Littell, 1974.* A step-by-step account of teaching reading and writing to older children with achievement problems.

References

Beers, James and Henderson, E. H. "A Study of Developing Orthographic Concepts Among First Graders." *Research in the Teaching of English 11* (Fall 1977): 133–148.

Bollinger, Dwight. *Aspects of Language,* 2nd ed. Cambridge, Mass.: Harvard University Press, 1975.

Chall, Jeanne. "The Great Debate: Ten Years Later, with a Modest Proposal for Reading

Stages." In Lauren Resnick and Phyllis Weaver, eds. *Theory and Practice of Early Reading*, Vol. 1. Hillsdale, N.J.: Erlbaum, 1979.

Chomsky, Carol. "Invented Spelling in the Open Classroom." *Word* 27, nos. 1–3 (April–Dec. 1971): 499–518.

Chomsky, Carol. "Approaching Reading Through Invented Spelling." In Lauren Resnick and Phyllis Weaver, eds. *Theory and Practice of Early Reading*, Vol. 2. Hillsdale, N.J.: Erlbaum, 1979.

Chomsky, Noam and Halle, Morris. *The Sound Pattern of English*. N.Y.: Harper & Row, 1968.

Clay, Marie. *Reading: The Patterning of Complex Behavior*, 2nd ed. Exeter, N.H.: Heinemann Educational Books, 1979.

Doehring, Donald G. and Aulls, Mark W. "The Interactive Nature of Reading Acquisition." *Journal of Reading Behavior* 11, no. 1 (Spring 1979): 27–40.

Ehri, Linnea. "The Development of Orthographic Images." In Uta Frith, ed. *Cognitive Processes in Spelling*. N.Y.: Academic Press, 1980.

Frith, Uta and Frith, Christopher. "Relationships Between Reading and Spelling." In James Kavanaugh and Richard Venezky, eds. *Orthography, Reading and Dyslexia*. Baltimore: University Park Press, 1980.

Funk, Charles E. *Thereby Hangs a Tale: Hundreds of Stories of Curious Word Origins*. N.Y.: Warner Paperback Library, 1972.

Funk, Wilfred. *Word Origins and their Romantic Stories*. N.Y.: Bell, 1950.

Gentry, J. Richard. "A Study of the Orthographic Strategies of Beginning Readers." (doctoral dissertation, University of Virginia, 1977). *Dissertation Abstracts International 39* (1979): 4017–A. (University Microfilms order no. 7901152).

Gentry, J. Richard. "Early Spelling Strategies." *Elementary School Journal* 79, no. 2 (Nov. 1978): 88–92.

Gentry, J. Richard. "Learning to Spell Developmentally." *The Reading Teacher* 34, no. 4 (Jan. 1981): 378–381.

Gilooley, William. "The Influence of Writing System Characteristics on Learning to Read." *Reading Research Quarterly* 8, no. 2 (winter 1973): 167–199.

Gray, William S. *The Teacher of Reading and Writing*. Chicago: Scott Foresman (for UNESCO), 1956.

Henderson, Edmund H. "Developmental Concepts of Word." In E. H. Henderson and J. W. Beers, eds. *Developmental and Cognitive Aspects of Learning to Spell*. Newark, Del.: International Reading Association, 1980.

Henderson, Edmund H. and Beers, James W., ed. *Developmental and Cognitive Aspects of Learning to Spell*. Newark, Del.: International Reading Association, 1980.

Hogben, Lancelot. *The Mother Tongue*. N.Y.: Norton, 1964.

Langacker, Ronald W. *Language and Its Structure: Some Fundamental Linguistic Concepts*, 2nd ed. N.Y.: Harcourt, 1973.

Liberman, Isabelle; Liberman, Alvin; Mattingly, Ignatius; and Shankweiler, Donald. "Orthography and the Beginning Reader." In James Cavanaugh and Richard Venezky, eds. *Orthography, Reading and Dyslexia*. Baltimore: University Park Press, 1980.

Liberman, Isabelle Y.; Shankweiler, Donald; Fischer, F. W.; and Carter, B. "Explicit Syllable and Phoneme Segmentation in the Young Child." *Journal of Experimental Child Psychology*, 18 (1974): 201–212.

Morris, R. Darrell. "Beginning Readers' Concept of Word." In E. H. Henderson and J. W. Beers, eds. *Cognitive and Developmental Aspects of Learning to Spell*. Newark, Del.: International Reading Assoc., 1980.

Nelson, Hazel E. "Analysis of Spelling Errors in Normal and Dyslexic Children." In Uta Frith, ed. *Cognitive Processes in Spelling*. N.Y.: Academic Press, 1980.

Pei, Mario. *The Story of English*. Philadelphia: Lippincott, 1952.

Pei, Mario. *The Families of Words.* N.Y.: St. Martin's, 1962.

Read, Charles. "Preschool Children's Knowledge of English Phonology." *Harvard Educational Review* 41 (1971): 1–34.

Read, Charles. *Children's Categorization of Speech Sounds in English.* National Council of Teachers of English Research Report #17. Urbana, Ill.: National Council of Teachers of English, 1975.

Scragg, D. G. *A History of English Spelling.* N.Y.: Manchester University Press, 1974.

Sorel, Nancy. *Word People.* N.Y.: American Heritage Press, 1970.

Stauffer, Russell G. *The Language-Experience Approach to Beginning Reading*, revised ed. N.Y.: Harper & Row, 1980.

Temple, Charles; Nathan, Ruth; and Burris, Nancy. *The Beginnings of Writing.* Boston: Allyn & Bacon, 1981.

Temple, Charles and Salminen, Jaakko. "Invented Spelling in Finnish First, Second and Third Graders." Unpublished manuscript. Victoria, Texas: University of Houston-Victoria, 1981.

Templeton, Shane. "Spelling First, Sound Later: The Relationship Between Orthography and Higher Order Phonological Knowledge in Older Students." *Research in the Teaching of English* 13, no. 3 (1979): 255–264.

Vallins, G. H. *Spelling.* Philadelphia: Richard West, 1954.

Venezky, Richard. *The Structure of English Orthography.* The Hague: Mouton, 1970.

Weekley, Ernest. *An Etymological Dictionary of Modern English.* N.Y.: Dover, 1967.

Chapter Seven

Reading in the
Content Areas

You have a child who makes nearly average progress in acquiring reading skills in the first and second grades. In the third grade she still does nearly average work in her reading group, but is beginning to have difficulty with her science and social studies assignments. By the time she reaches the upper elementary grades her work in these subjects is suffering, resulting in poor grades, and her problems are attributed to a reading problem that manifests itself only in content subjects, not in language arts.

This pattern is not uncommon. Children who progress adequately in beginning reading instruction often have difficulty in the upper grades applying their reading abilities in their content subjects. Why does this happen? Chall (1979) attributes the problem to the differences between the tasks of beginning reading and later reading. In early elementary years, the focus is on *learning to read*. In later years, it is on *reading to learn*.

In beginning reading, children concentrate on building sight vocabularies, learning basic comprehension skills, and learning to decode unknown words. Early instruction attempts to get students to the point where they can respond quickly and automatically to written language and relate print to oral language as well as to meaning.

In later school years, pupils in content subjects are expected to read long passages of text, under minimum supervision, and learn content from the reading. Their learning will usually not be tested by having to answer short comprehension questions directly after reading, as is common in basal reading programs. Rather, they are expected to use what they learn in a discussion, or on a quiz a day or more after the reading, or in carrying out some study task. In short, it is expected that what older students read will influence and perhaps change their way of thinking about the topic (Broudy, 1977). Later reading thus demands that they engage their ideas and prior experiences to an extent that beginning reading often does not.

Schematically, we can depict some of the most basic differences between beginning and later reading (see Table 7.1).

Older students must make a transition from beginning reading to reading as a medium for learning. The strategy of rendering print out loud or practicing sentence-by-sentence comprehension may be fine at the beginning, but it will be inadequate later on. Reading to learn requires the student to (a) do active thinking about the content of the material; (b) be familiar with and responsive to different structures of text; (c) learn new words encountered in books, not only decoding them but also determining their precise meaning in context; and (d) develop certain study skills for locating information and remembering it.

In this chapter we explore each of these requirements and present techniques for their development and instruction.

We also address some other concerns of teachers of older readers. One is readability, the difficulty level of textbooks, and ways to measure it. Another

TABLE 7.1. Some differences between beginning reading and later reading.

	BEGINNING READING (PRIMARY GRADES)	LATER READING (MIDDLE ELEMENTARY GRADES AND UP)
FOCUS	Learning to read	Reading to learn
MATERIAL	Mostly fiction Short passages, changing topics	Mostly nonfiction Long sections, continuous topics
PURPOSES	Short term, explicitly set by teacher ("Read this sentence [perhaps aloud] and tell me what it says")	Long term, generally set by teacher or by student ("Study pages 140–158 for a quiz on Friday")
TEACHER RESPONSE	Immediate and directly related to the act of reading ("You missed three words, Jerome")	Delayed and indirectly related to reading ("You didn't know the material, Linda")
EVALUATION	Oral reading, comprehension of short, explicit questions	Silent reading, learning of longer material, the ability to use information

is the use of recorded textbooks, an onerous but useful task. Finally we briefly outline a means of coping with widely divergent reading abilities within the same class.

A Theory of Comprehension: Schemata and Reading

In recent years educators and psychologists have been studying the question of how readers understand and learn from text. One explanation that has gained wide support is called *schema theory* (Adams and Collins, 1979; Anderson, 1977; Bartlett, 1932; Minsky, 1975). When authors write about some topic, they are putting ideas about the topic in written form. The authors' ideas are organized into mental frameworks called *schemata* (the singular form is *schema*). Schemata are complex idea structures existing in the mind, which relate ideas, things, and events bound together in a person's experience. A person might, for example, have a "birthday party" schema. This schema would typically include the ideas of guests coming together, a one-way giving of gifts, a birthday cake with a certain number of candles, singing of a particular song, and so on. Now if that person who had the birthday schema came to or heard about a particular birthday party, the schema would serve as a framework for making sense of details he or she encountered. People mentioned would be interpreted as guests or hosts, objects named interpreted as gifts, and so on.

When authors convey their ideas they do not write out their entire schemata; that is, they do not express everything they know about the topic or the relationships among all the ideas. They usually write out only those aspects of the schemata that they judge to be most informative to readers.

Readers have schemata too. Reading the text makes them think about their mental schemata, add other ideas, and forge new connections among them. Although the author hasn't communicated any entire schema, just *reminding* readers of their own schemata is enough for communication to take place, since they can mentally supply for themselves many details that were left out.

Here is an example:

"May I take your order, sir?" inquired the waiter.

"Yes, I believe so," I said.

"No!" Hilda hissed through clenched teeth. "I won't eat a thing. We're through! Do you hear me?"

"Sir!" said the waiter, drumming his pencil on the pad.

"I know," I interrupted hastily. "Hilda, this is not the place for a scene. We'll talk about it later," I urged in a strained whisper.

In order to make sense of the above passage, you yourself have to supply meaning that was not given by the author. You first have to summon up your schema for "restaurant scenes." The author never said the exchange took place in a restaurant, but by mentioning "waiter" and "order" in the first line enough information was supplied to suggest that you should interpret the rest of the episode in terms of what you know about restaurants. Because the waiter referred to the person as "sir," you imagine not just any old diner but a sophisticated restaurant. Perhaps your schema for "swanky" restaurants also implies that one should be on one's best behavior in such a place and that there is cause for embarrassment if one does not observe proper form.

The swanky restaurant schema prepares the reader to expect that the narrator might have been embarrassed by Hilda's behavior. The fact that Hilda says "We're through!" may suggest another schema: courtship.

When the waiter says "Sir!" you may assume that there are other patrons in the restaurant who shouldn't be disturbed. Again, this was not explicitly stated; it just comes with the swanky restaurant schema, as does the feeling that the narrator wants to observe proper decorum and try to head off an embarrassing scene.

Thus we understand this passage to be about a harried suitor who is embarrassed by Hilda's behavior in a fancy restaurant and who may also be chagrined by an apparent bad turn in the courtship. Yet most of this meaning is supplied by the reader; the author makes very little of it explicit. The author communicates the message, the theory goes, by mentioning items that form parts of certain schemata, which lead us to summon up our corresponding schemata. Our schemata have stored in them an array of details the author may not make explicit, but which help us understand the passage. We could not understand it otherwise.

According to some theorists, all comprehension employs the summoning up of schemata, from the recognition of letters and spelling patterns to the interpretation of nuances and literary allusions. For our purposes in this chapter, it is important that we recognize two general kinds of schemata. The first is the kind just dealt with: those that organize our knowledge and experiences of the world in our memories and that help us construct the meaning of what we read. We sometimes call this *world knowledge*. The second type consists of schemata for kinds of text structure. These cause us to respond one way to the information in a story, another way to the information in a political campaign speech. Both types play an important role in reading for meaning, and we will discuss each of them below.

We should first make another general observation about the role of schemata in reading. We have said that writers have their ideas organized in their heads. When they write, they put only certain aspects of their schemata on

*E*very reader uses prior information and experiences, organized in mental categories called schemata, to understand and interpret what an author has written. Each reader's schemata are different from other readers.

paper. When things work as they should, these bits will be a sufficient cue for readers to summon up the appropriate schemata in their own minds. They can use the information stored in their own schemata to fill in the gaps for themselves. This generalization assumes that everything is working, but in reality many things can go wrong that would prevent readers from constructing an adequate meaning on their own.

First, authors sometimes cause problems. If they are too stingy with details, we will not know which schema to summon. In the sample passage on page 206, for instance, the first line might have read, " 'May I help you?' asked the man." In this case it would not have been clear whether the setting was a restaurant, a store, a library, or an office reception area.

Second, we may lack some necessary schemata in our memories. If we had never been in a fancy restaurant, or seen a TV show or movie about one, we would not understand the narrator's discomfiture in the passage. Likewise students may not understand what they read if they lack compatible experiences to which they can relate. In schema theory, these experiences are the material out of which the author's meaning is made clear. When students lack important background experiences the teacher must make sure this background is provided, through such means as films, field trips, demonstrations, and class discussions, or else they will not be able to learn from reading and studying a topic.

A third problem may arise. The author may have written clearly and we may have the appropriate schemata in memory, but we fail to summon up the schemata. In other words, we are not reading actively. Say, for example, that you are reading a textbook in bed, and you stop yourself at the bottom of the page, only to find you cannot remember what you read on the last two pages. If you can make yourself pay attention, however, you find that you can understand the material, thus demonstrating that you do have the necessary schemata but are not summoning them up as you should. Unfortunately some students read in this innattentive fashion as a matter of habit.

Understanding Patterns of Text Organization

The way that information is organized in text makes a difference in the way we understand and use the information. Good readers recognize and correctly respond to different arrangements of text while poor ones often do not (Marshall and Glock, 1978–1979). Let's look at some typical patterns of text structure and consider how these patterns affect the reader's response to the text.

Taxonomy. What pattern of organization do you perceive in this passage?

FIGURE 7.1. A taxonomic outline.

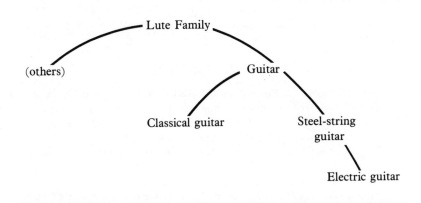

THE GUITAR

The guitar is one of the most popular stringed instruments. Because it has a fretboard, and strings stretched across a soundbox that are played by plucking, the guitar is considered a member of the lute family.

For centuries the guitar had a rather small wooden body with soft strings fashioned of animal gut. In the present century, however, several distinct classes of guitars have emerged. The traditional version has lived on as the "classical" guitar, but there are now steel-string guitars and electric guitars as well.

The steel-string guitar has a long, narrow neck and an enlarged body. It makes a louder, more piercing sound than the classical guitar. The electric guitar, an offshoot of the steel-string guitar, has its sounds amplified and its tones modified by electronic devices. It can make sounds loud enough to deafen a rock musician. It can also make a variety of tones, many of which do not sound guitarlike at all.

This piece of text is organized by classifying, by listing and defining the different instruments collected together under the label "guitar," and by showing their relationships to one another. Classifying is a fundamental act of the intellect, and text such as the above is usually the result. This passage could also be outlined by means of a tree diagram, as in Figure 7.1. Classification charts like this are called *taxonomies*.

If readers are to understand the above passage they must perceive the taxonomic structure. If you asked them to recall what the passage said, you would expect them to remember the kinds of guitars discussed, what makes them different from one another, and how they are related within the "family." Taxonomic text structures are frequently encountered in science materials, especially in biology.

Chronology. What pattern of organization do you perceive in this passage?

BURTON

The town of Burton, in the Midlands of England, has a history that is typical of trading villages of the region. Nothing of the town existed before the ninth century A.D. The hill overlooking the Avon River where the town now sits was covered with an impenetrable wood.

In about 870 A.D., Northumbrian knights cleared the hillside and erected a rude fortress as an outpost against the South Saxons lurking across the Avon, which then served as the southern frontier of Northumbria. By the time peace was effected some thirty years later, a stone castle had been built, surrounded by about thirty dwellings. Some crops had been grown nearby.

With the peace and political stability of the tenth century, Burton grew in earnest. Pastures were cleared for five miles during the first half of the century, and fine manor houses erected from the wood and the profits of sheep raising. Trails that crisscrossed the settlement grew to well-traveled roads, and by the middle of the eleventh century Burton served as the chief market center for the surrounding thirty- or forty-mile area. The town grew comparatively wealthy.

But prosperity came to an end when Cromwell and his Roundheads burned the town in the seventeenth century. They marched the residents of Burton off into captivity, and few ever returned.

This account is arranged according to a sequence of events. Its most prominent organizational feature is *chronological*. In order to comprehend the passage successfully, readers have to picture the unfolding of events across the perspective of time. If you asked them to recall this passage you would expect them to remember the events that were described, the time they occurred, and the order in which they occurred. Chronologically organized text can be reduced to a timeline, as shown in Table 7.2. Chronological structures are frequently encountered in historical text.

Cause and Effect. The passage about the town of Burton also used cause and effect for organization. How would you outline the following passage in which this pattern is more pronounced?

BLACK ROBES IN THE DESERT

Scientists sometimes question the wisdom of "folk wisdom." The case of the Tuaregs' robes is a case in point. These nomadic people live in the area of the southern Sahara desert, the hottest terrain on earth. For centuries they have worn the same head-to-toe black wool robes. Since black absorbs more

TABLE 7.2. **A chronological outline.**

BEFORE 870 A.D.	AFTER 870 A.D.	TENTH CENTURY	ELEVENTH CENTURY	SEVENTEENTH CENTURY
No town; thick woods	Northumbrian fortress built	Pastures cleared; manor houses built	Roads; market center	Town sacked by Cromwell; town abandoned

heat from the sun than any other color, scientists wonder why they've kept them through the years. Some people speculated that they had only black sheep as a source of wool, but an inspection of their herds dispelled that notion. Others speculated that black might have been chosen for its protection against the nightly desert cold, but scientific tests showed that black robes held heat no better than white ones.

Finally, through a series of experiments it was discovered that the black robes are actually cooler than white ones. The explanation is that the sun heats the upper part of the robe, which causes air to rise up through the loose-fitting robe and out through the open neck. In this way a constant draft is maintained through the robes. This draft evaporates perspiration, which cools the wearer.

In order to understand this passage readers must operate on at least two levels: they must recognize the larger cause-and-effect question, Why do the Tuareg wear black robes in the desert? and recognize its answer, Because their black robes keep them cool. They must also recognize the more specific set of cause-and-effect relations that explain the seemingly contradictory statement that black is cooler in the desert. An outline of this passage that would link causes and effects is shown in Figure 7.2. Cause-effect writing is found in many content subjects, including health, social studies, the sciences, and home economics.

FIGURE 7.2. **A cause-effect outline.**

CAUSE	EFFECT
Black robes keep Tuaregs cool ⟶	Tuaregs wear black robes
Sun heats black robes ⟵	Air rises inside robes
Air rises ⟵	Perspiration evaporates
Perspiration evaporates ⟵	Tuaregs are cooled
Tuaregs are comfortable ⟵	Tauregs prefer black to other colors

Written Directions. Some written materials give instructions for carrying out a procedure or performing some action. Simpler materials of this sort communicate a series of tasks that must be performed in some order:

HOW TO START YOUR CAR

Making sure the emergency brake is fully engaged, depress the clutch and move the gear shift lever to NEUTRAL. Pull the choke out all the way. Push the throttle to the floor, release it, then push it halfway down. Now, insert the key in the ignition and rotate the key forward to the START position. After the car has started and warmed up, push the choke in fully.

To understand this passage adequately, readers must attend to the steps described and to the order in which they are given. They could show that they understand by getting into the car and trying to follow the steps. Short of that, they could write a list of the steps in the proper order or properly arrange a set of pictures detailing each step.

Some descriptions are more complicated than the one just described in that they set up *contingencies,* or alternative sequences.

WHAT TO DO IN CASE OF FIRE

In the event of a fire in this building, students must immediately and quietly stand beside their desks. The teacher should press his or her hand against the classroom door. If the door feels hot to the touch, the door must *not* be opened. Instead, the teacher is to lower the rope ladder stored in each classroom from the window ledge. The children will then climb down the rope ladder one at a time. As they reach the ground they are to proceed at a walk to the west end of the playground where they will line up and remain silent.

If the door is not hot to the touch, the teacher may open it and inspect the hall for flames or smoke. If the fire is at the north end of the building, the class will exit by the south stairway. Conversely, if the fire is at the south end of the building the north stairway will be used. Each class will proceed at a walk to the west end of the playground to line up and remain silent. Each teacher will ascertain whether all the pupils are present at that time.

The understanding of this passage cannot be done by carrying out one sequence of tasks, because no *one* sequence is appropriate for all situations. Readers must recognize not only the tasks and their sequence but also the situations in which each alternative sequence should be followed. They should be able to role-play the correct procedure for each situation or answer questions like "What should you do if the fire alarm rings and the teacher tells you the door feels hot?"

The relationship of the ideas in the fire drill passage may be outlined as in Figure 7.3. Material that takes the form of written directions is seen most frequently in math, science, home economics, and vocational education.

FIGURE 7.3. An outline of written directions containing contingency sequences.

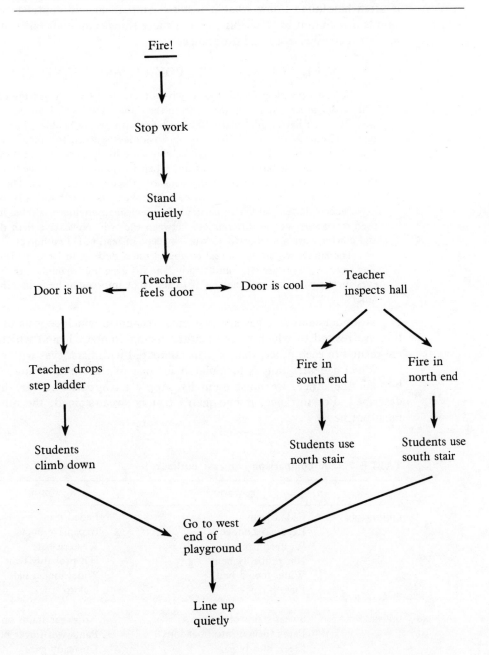

Comparison and Contrast. In order to understand what something *is*, it is often helpful to know what it *is not*. Comparison and contrast go beyond simple description by describing two or more things simultaneously and pointing out their likenesses and differences.

WILL THE REAL COWBOY PLEASE STAND UP?

So many people pretend to be cowboys these days that it is getting harder and harder to tell the real cowboys from the dudes. Dudes and cowboys both wear Western hats, wide, tooled leather belts with ornate buckles, jeans, and boots. The jeans of both dudes and cowboys may be worn and faded in contrast to their boots. Both dudes and cowboys are likely to wear shiny, expensive-looking boots, but the real cowboy's belt is usually sweat-stained around the top edge, and he often tucks his jeans into the tops of his boots. The brim of the cowboy's hat is sometimes tipped at a rakish angle, but so is that of the experienced dude. Neither is particularly bowlegged anymore, although this used to be one way to differentiate between the two. Nowadays both dudes and cowboys are apt to drive pickups or jeeps instead of riding horses.

The surest way to tell a real cowboy from a dude is to look at his eyes. The cowboy's eyes are clear and steady, and his gaze holds yours. The dude's eyes flicker this way and that, as if to see what impression he is making on others.

To understand this passage, we must recognize which aspects of description are related to which of the features being compared, and which aspects are related to each other; that is, hats compared with hats, eyes with eyes, etc.

When a description is formulated for one of the things being compared but not the other, we must mentally supply its opposite to the things not described. For instance, if one man's belt is sweat-stained, the other's belt must not be so.

TABLE 7.3. A comparison-contrast outline.

	COWBOY	DUDE
LIKENESSES	Faded jeans	Faded jeans
	Expensive boots	Expensive boots
	Western hat	Western hat
	Hat probably bent	Hat probably bent
	Wide, tooled belt	Wide, tooled belt
	Pickup truck	Pickup truck
DIFFERENCES	Sweat stains on belt	No sweat stains on belt
	Pants tucked into boot tops	Pants worn over boots
	Clear, steady gaze	Unsteady gaze

The ultimate test of a reader's comprehension of this passage would be to distinguish between actual people, one of which was a real cowboy and the other a dude. To demonstrate comprehension by means of an outline, the reader might produce something like Table 7.3. Comparison-contrast structures are found in many content subjects, especially social studies and science.

Explanation or Exposition. Much text material in schools is used to describe or explain. Since the organization of such material varies widely, it does not lend itself to a cut-and-dried description. The material may be entirely verbal, as the example below, or it may include numbers and formulas, charts, graphs, and pictures.

THE DEADLY COBRA

The cobra is one of the most deadly snakes in the world. Many wildlife experts consider it *the* deadliest animal. Its venom, its mobility, and its behavior are legendary.

The cobra's venom is more powerful even than that of the rattlesnake. Its large fangs do not inject the venom as do the fangs of other poisonous snakes; instead the fangs are used to pierce deep wounds in the victim's flesh, and the cobra releases venom from sacs in its mouth into these punctures. The deadly venom is carried by the bloodstream and attacks the victim's central nervous system. One African variety spits its venom at its victim's eyes; it can spit up to eight feet with almost pinpoint accuracy, and the highly corrosive venom blinds the victim unless it is immediately washed away.

The cobra's mobility is chilling. In spite of its size it can move with great speed almost soundlessly. It creeps up on its intended victim undetected and can move on or above the ground with equal efficiency. It glides silently along the branches of trees or building rafters as well as along the ground. Its mottled skin provides a good camouflage since it blends almost perfectly with dead leaves, tree bark, grasses, and dusty earth.

The cobra may be the only snake that seeks out humans. Most snakes and other animals avoid contact with humans at all costs and attack them only when escape is blocked or in defense of their young, but cobras seem to have no such avoidance instinct. Instead, they have been known to seek out and follow humans before attacking them without provocation. Their actions are those of a predator hunting, and the prey is man.

Comprehending expository material usually entails recognizing main ideas and supporting details. Expository material is often captured nicely by the traditional outline format because it explicitly shows the relation among ideas of different levels of importance. Table 7.4 shows an outline of this expository piece. Expository writing is encountered in virtually every subject in the curriculum. Whenever information has to be explained, expository prose is the choice.

Textbooks from elementary school through college employ a wide variety

TABLE 7.4. Expository outline.

THE DEADLY COBRA

I. Venom
   A. More deadly than rattlesnake
   B. Puncture wounds made by large fangs
   C. Released from sacs in mouth
   D. Attacks central nervous system

II. Mobility
   A. Has great speed in spite of size
   B. Moves silently
   C. Moves on or above ground easily
   D. Is camouflaged by coloration

III. Behavior
   A. Does not avoid human contact
   B. Seeks out, follows humans
   C. Attacks without provocation

of patterns for organizing information. The mental activity involved in comprehending a passage written in one pattern may be somewhat different from that required to comprehend a passage written a different way (Estes and Shibilski, 1980).

We can demonstrate this point by studying the questions that are asked for each pattern (see Table 7.5).

Schema Theory and Reading Diagnosis

Thus far we have discussed two types of schemata, or mental frameworks of understanding. The first type was world knowledge, or background information. This type encompasses the general understanding of people, things, and events that we bring to the comprehension of any kind of writing. Schemata for world knowledge are of great importance inasmuch as we can easily comprehend what we read only when we already have existing schemata in our heads to help us make sense of it. For reading diagnosis, the important questions are, What schemata for world knowledge do readers have? and, Are the readers able to summon up these schemata when necessary? We cannot observe schemata directly, however, so it is more productive to word these questions as follows:

□ What do the readers already know about the topic?
□ Do they recall what they know, and can they link it up to what they are reading?

TABLE 7.5. Information patterns and questions.

ORGANIZATIONAL PATTERN	TYPES OF QUESTIONS
Taxonomy	What kind of thing is X?
	What defines it as such?
	What varieties of X exist?
Chronological	What happened first?
	What happened next?
	What did these events lead to?
Cause-Effect	What caused X?
	What were the effects of X?
Comparison-Contrast	How are X and Y alike?
	How are they different?
	How are X and Y related to Z?
Direction Sequences	What do I do first?
	How do I do it?
	What do I do next?
Expository-Explanatory	What is the main idea?
	What supports that idea?

The second type discussed were schemata for text structure. Good readers seem to have schemata for the different structures of text and can use these schemata to read efficiently. Those who do not may have background experiences and schemata for the *content* of the text, yet still respond haphazardly or passively to its *organization*.

An important question in assessing students from about the fourth grade and up is, What schemata for text structure do the students have? Since we cannot observe schemata directly, however, a more practical wording of that question is, Do the students adjust their expectations for information appropriately for different structures of text?

Assessing Schemata for Reading Comprehension

The advent of schema theory has contributed much to our understanding of reading comprehension and its problems. Schema theorists have not as yet proposed any new classroom techniques for teaching or assessing comprehension, however. What they have done is explain why some of the best techniques that have been around for some time work for us. *The directed reading–thinking activity, the ReQuest procedure, pattern guides,* and the *structured overview* are such techniques.

Nonfiction DRTAs. The directed reading-thinking activities were described in Chapter Five, pages 143–153. We suggest you review those pages before reading on.

The DRTA is a technique of guided inquiry where the teacher invites the students to raise questions about a topic and then read to answer them. The DRTA follows a cycle of *predicting, reading,* and *proving.* The students predict; that is, they hypothesize answers to their own questions and then confirm or modify their predictions. Finally they prove that a prediction was right or wrong depending on what a passage actually said.

Questioning and predicting reveal schemata for both world knowledge and text structure. In a nonfiction DRTA, the teacher presses the students to explain as much as they know about a passage before reading it. In practice, this stage of a DRTA may take much longer than the reading and often generates more information than the passage contains — especially when the DRTA is done with a group.

The questioning time yields the best indication the teacher is likely to get about students' knowledge of the subject prior to reading. With a group, it is an indication of the general level of knowledge; with an individual, the teacher may ask probing questions to get a fair idea of a student's background concepts about a topic. One of the authors did a DRTA with a seventh-grade girl, using a passage about Austria. It was not surprising that she didn't know where Austria was. It *was* surprising that she got no help from the cue that it was next to Germany. As it turned out, she could not find Europe on the globe either. Teachers are often appalled at these occasional glimpses of the things students do not know even after spending many years in classrooms. The DRTA is one of relatively few regular indicators of world knowledge in widespread use.

The DRTA also indicates schemata for text structure patterns. During the questioning session before or between readings, the teacher can ask not only *what* students think they will learn from reading a particular passage but also *what kind of information* the passage will contain. They will indicate their knowledge of text structure by the kinds of questions they predict the passage will answer. When, for example, teacher and students are reading a historical piece arranged chronologically, after previewing the title and the headings the teacher should ask, "What questions do you think will be answered in this passage?" A response such as "When did X happen?" reveals a sensitivity to the chronological pattern.

With regard to schemata for text structure, it becomes obvious in the course of a DRTA if the students' questions and predictions are missing the point. The teacher can find out by asking the students to pencil in a light check mark ($\sqrt{}$) beside sentences that confirm predictions that were made, a minus ($-$) beside sentences that refute predictions, and a plus ($+$) beside new, unanticipated information. If plus marks outnumber checks and minuses, it is apparent that the students did not ask the right questions about the text. The teacher should review with them the questions they predicted would be answered and the actual structure of the text. Then they should formulate questions that would have been better suited to that passage.

The ReQuest Procedure. Designed by Manzo (1969), this activity gives insights into a child's sense of text structure. The ReQuest is an individual procedure, though it can be adapted for a small group. It proceeds as follows:

1. The teacher and student both read the first sentence of a passage to be studied. They read it silently.
2. After they both have read the passage, the student asks as many questions as he or she can think of. The teacher answers the questions clearly and completely.
3. Then it is the teacher's turn to ask the questions about the same sentence, and the student answers as fully as possible. By forming questions which call upon the student's grasp of text structures, the teacher models good questioning strategies. This helps the student see how good readers ask themselves questions about text as they read.
4. When the student has finished answering, teacher and student read the next sentence and proceed as before.
5. When the teacher feels that a sufficient amount of the text has been read in this way to make comprehension of the remainder of the passage possible, the student is asked to read to the end (Manzo, 1969, p. 125).

The ReQuest procedure can be modified in several ways. First, a group of two to five students can team up against the teacher and take turns asking questions. Second, the reading can be increased to cover a paragraph at a time if proceeding sentence by sentence does not generate many questions. Third, the teacher and student can work on interpretative and predictive questions — the latter especially before the ReQuest is suspended and they read to the end.

This procedure is indirectly diagnostic. By noting the kinds of questions the students ask for each kind of text structure, the teacher can tell whether or not they are on the right track, as in the DRTA example above.

Pattern Guides. Pattern guides focus on text structure (Estes and Vaughan, 1978). Used instructionally, they encourage students to organize their thinking about a passage in terms of its structure. Used diagnostically, they show how well students are able to use structure in organizing their search for information in a reading task.

Pattern guides, like all study guides, are written questions that are given to students before they read an assignment and which must be answered while they read it. The intention of the guide is not only to enhance their comprehension of a particular reading assignment but also to develop habits of organizing their search for information in other reading tasks along the lines they are required to do by a study guide.

There are as many different kinds of pattern guides as there are patterns of text structure. Figures 7.4 and 7.5 show some sample guides. Figure 7.4 is, of course, simply a timeline, but since the outline was not explicitly presented in the passage, filling in the timeline indicates a student's ability to find and categorize information chronologically.

As can be seen from these two examples, in order to construct a pattern guide, you must (a) decide what pattern of text structure organizes the reading assignment and (b) create an exercise that requires students to manipulate information according to the structure. This might entail producing or filling in an outline or some other graphic rendering of the text's structure.

You should introduce and discuss the procedure of using a pattern guide before assigning one. After the students have completed their guides, discuss with them what they did and why, which is just as important as completing the study guide. Filling in blanks is a mindless procedure unless the purposes are discussed. After they have had some experience with pattern guides, let them construct their own pattern guides or outlines, since this leads to more thought about text structures than does filling in a teacher-made guide.

During the discussion of the pattern guide activities, listen to find out (a) how aware the students become of the structure of the text and (b) how well they were able to use it to gain information.

FIGURE 7.4. A chronological pattern guide for "Burton."

A. Fill in the blanks with an event or events that happened in Burton in each time period:

BEFORE 800 A.D.	AFTER 870 A.D.	TENTH CENTURY	ELEVENTH CENTURY	SEVENTEENTH CENTURY
_____	_____ .	_____ .	_____ .	_____ .
_____ .	_____ .	_____ .	_____ .	_____ .
_____ .	_____ .	_____ .	_____ .	_____ .

B. Fill in the blanks with a brief description of what the town of Burton might have looked like in each period:

BEFORE 800 A.D.	AFTER 870 A.D.	TENTH CENTURY	ELEVENTH CENTURY	SEVENTEENTH CENTURY	PRESENT
_____ .	_____ .	_____ .	_____ .	_____ .	_____ .
_____ .	_____ .	_____ .	_____ .	_____ .	_____ .
_____ .	_____ .	_____ .	_____ .	_____ .	_____ .

FIGURE 7.5. A taxonomic pattern guide for "The Guitar."

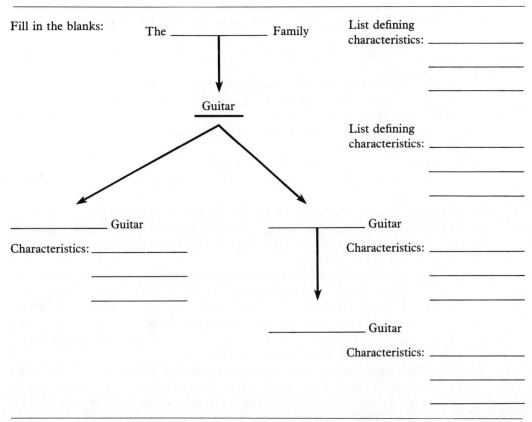

The *Structured Overview* (Barron, 1969; Tierney, Readence, and Dishner, 1980). The structured overview is an illustrated discussion led by a teacher for a group of students before they read an assignment. The teacher raises the major concepts dealt with in the assignment. Using the blackboard or overhead, the teacher elicits and writes down the students' own terms for the concepts. Then, in diagram form, he or she illustrates (or asks the students to suggest ways to illustrate) the relationships among the concepts.

The following example is taken from a discussion conducted by a fourth-grade teacher prior to making a reading assignment in a health book.

MS. LEE: This chapter is about *stress*. When you feel stress how do you think you feel?

PETER: Kind of scared.

ANDREA: Worried.

LIVONA: I feel like somebody's hassling me.

JAMES: It's like you do your homework but you forget it, and you remember on the bus that you forgot it, and you feel like jumping off the bus but you can't.

CINDY: Yeah, like you don't want to do this but you have to — that's stress.

(Ms. Lee writes: *Stress* — scared; worried; hassled)

MS. LEE: James and Cindy are describing times you feel stress. Can anyone think of some more?

PETER: Like when you have to fight someone after school and you don't want to.

JAMES: Yeah, but you know you have to or people will say you're chicken.

CINDY: Or when you broke a bowl or something and you know your parents will be mad.

ANDREA: . . . and you hear them drive up in the driveway!

(Ms. Lee writes: *Times we feel stress* — forgot homework; having to do things you don't want to; about to have a fight; broke something — waiting for parents)

MS. LEE: Now think. At times like those when you felt stress, how did you deal with it? What happened to make your stress go away?

JAMES: Well, when I lost my homework once and I wanted to jump off the bus, I just made up my mind, I was going to go to school and tell the teacher I forgot the homework and see what happened. She was kind of mad, but it wasn't too bad.

PETER: Once this boy told me to meet him after school and we'd fight and I was kind of scared and I didn't want to go but I went. And then he came and he said I better never call him names again or he'd beat me up. Then he just got on his bike and rode off.

MS. LEE: How did you feel?

PETER: Well, kind of better, I guess, but I really thought we were going to have a fight. It was like it wasn't so bad once I went. I don't know. . . .

(Ms. Lee writes: *Ways of dealing with stress* — do what you have to do; things don't turn out as badly as they seem)

When she finished, her diagram on the blackboard looked like Figure 7.6.

Then she explained that stress, kinds of stress, causes of stress, and ways of dealing with stress were going to be the subject of their reading. She asked them to look for the points they had already made as well as things they hadn't thought of as they read.

When a structured overview is used diagnostically, its function is to determine how well students can relate personal experiences or world knowledge to a topic they are about to read. It does not yield generalizable data about their

FIGURE 7.6. Diagram of a structured overview.

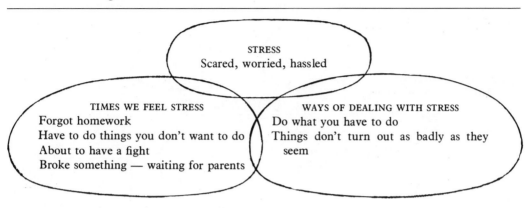

STRESS
Scared, worried, hassled

TIMES WE FEEL STRESS
Forgot homework
Have to do things you don't want to do
About to have a fight
Broke something — waiting for parents

WAYS OF DEALING WITH STRESS
Do what you have to do
Things don't turn out as badly as they
seem

levels of comprehension. Rather, it reveals, *for a particular assignment,* to what extent they can relate experiences and the terms they normally use to think about the topic.

As an instructional device, the structured overview makes students think about relevant experiences before reading and helps them match book terms with words in their own vocabulary. They often read with better comprehension after building a structured overview than they do without this activity.

Vocabulary

Vocabulary is an important and troublesome issue in content area reading. By the time they reach third grade, students must be able to read and understand many words they usually do not use in speech (Chall, 1979). When they are successful at gleaning new words we rightly conclude that reading has made a major contribution to their education. For those who do not succeed, however, vocabulary constitutes a widespread problem in the middle and upper grades, especially in the content subjects.

We will deal with two main aspects of vocabulary: (a) background concepts to which vocabulary words can be related and (b) strategies to derive approximate word meanings from surrounding context.

Vocabulary and Background Concepts. Words are labels for concepts. Concepts are stored mental patterns that are derived from experiences. If, for example, we have enough experience with wildflowers, we may begin to recognize different varieties of them. With the help of a guidebook or other information source we can learn words to associate with the various wildflowers we have come to recognize, as illustrated in Figure 7.7.

FIGURE 7.7. Experiences, concepts, and labels: wildflowers.

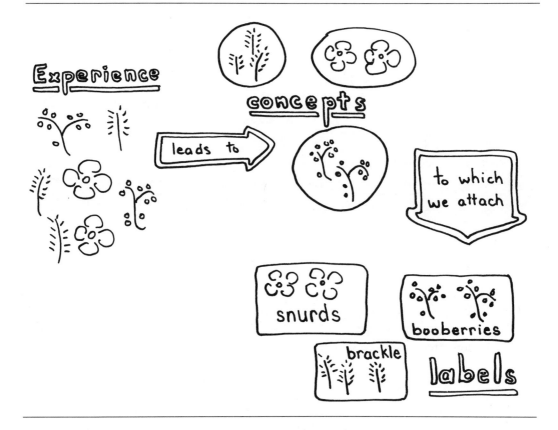

Relating new words to personal experiences. As Figure 7.7 suggests, in order to learn new vocabulary it is necessary to have experiences from which concepts can be derived. Words are then attached to concepts as labels. Often the experiences are there but have not been organized into concepts to which words can be applied, and sometimes the teacher must help children organize concepts. The discussion that Ms. Lee held to introduce the concept of stress is a good example (see "Structured Overview," page 221). The point was to see what words and personal experiences the children could associate with the word *stress.* This is good instruction because they learned that experiences they had associated with the words *afraid, hassled,* and *worried* could also be associated with the unfamiliar word *stress.* Moreover, it gave the teacher a chance to straighten out misconceptions, as she would have if a child had said stress was "what you did after you woke up from a nap" (stretch).

A discussion of this type yields diagnostic insights too because the teacher can find out if the children are able to associate words and ideas with the terms under study.

If discussion does not uncover many associations that the children have for words, the teacher should set up an activity to help build associations. In science or social studies this may involve field trips, experiments, demonstrations, or guest speakers. Or it may involve role plays: the children can act out *avaricious, hostile, laconic,* and other such words. Role play will often do as a substitute for real experience, and it has much potential for teaching vocabulary.

Treating meanings categorically. Semanticists, specialists in the study of meaning, suggest that it is useful to think of the meaning of one word in relation to the meanings of others. To semanticists, meanings come not by themselves but in family or hierarchical relationships. A duck can be thought of not just as a white or yellow creature with a beak and feathers but as a kind of bird. Moreover, it is useful to know that there are varieties of ducks: mallards, teals, wood ducks, and so on. Ducks are seen in stages, too. A little fuzzy yellow-beaked thing grows up to be a brown and green adult duck; ducklings and ducks are varied stages of the same bird.

One semanticist, Albert Upton (1973), has suggested a set of three questions that people should ask when they are striving for exactness in meaning:

1. What is it a kind of/what are the kinds of it?
2. What is it a part of/what are the parts of it?
3. What is it a stage of/what are the stages of it?

To these we have added a fourth:

4. What is it a product or a result of/what are the products or results of it?

These four questions will yield much information about any meaning or word under consideration. Depending on whether the item under scrutiny is a *class of things* (i.e., ducks in general) or a *particular thing* (that mallard over there with the twisted beak), one side of the questions or the other will be useful but not always both.

Hence for *duck* in general we can say:

1. It is a kind of bird; the kinds of ducks are mallards, wood ducks, etc.
2. (The first part of the question is not relevant.) Its parts are the wings, legs, body, neck, head, feathers, beak, gizzard, etc.
3. (The first part is not relevant.) Its stages are the egg, the chick, the young duck, and the mature duck.
4. (The first part is not relevant.) Ducks lay eggs that are good to eat, their feathers make soft pillows, the mature birds are thought by some to be tasty eating, good hunting, etc.

*T*he concept ladder is an activity that can help students incorporate new vocabulary terms into their existing schemata. Here, the teacher organizes and introduces the activity to a group, and students come to the board to add their own suggestions and examples.

Concept Ladders. An exercise called the *concept ladder,* which was developed around these four questions, is good for both instruction and assessment. Since it is a paper-and-pencil exercise, a concept ladder used instructionally may be given out for students to complete individually as they do a reading assignment or it may be given to a small group of students to be completed together.

In creating a concept ladder, the teacher sets up columns to correspond to Upton's questions and leaves blanks above or below the word in question, depending on the information that is relevant to understanding the term. The students fill in the blanks. Concept ladders are somewhat open-ended, since there may be several correct answers for each blank, but the teacher can limit the choices at first by restricting the answers to a set list from which the students must choose. (See Tables 7.6 and 7.7.)

Analogies. Analogies, another form of exercise in categorizing word meanings, are suitable for students in late middle grades or beyond. Analogies compare relationships between sets of things or ideas and thus go a bit deeper than synonyms in tapping vocabulary development. You set up analogies by (1) thinking of how the concept represented by your test word relates to another concept and (2) thinking of a familiar pair of concepts that share the same sort of relationship. For example:

Nests are to birds as _____ are to beavers.

(a) dams, (b) lodges, (c) hives, (d) trees.

It is advisable to provide multiple choices, since choosing from alternatives is easier than guessing from scratch. If all the analogies in a single exercise draw

TABLE 7.6. Concept ladder for "The Guitar."

A. Kind of?	B. Part of?	C. Function of? (How is it made?)
musical instrument	*a band?*	*out of wood, I guess*
GUITAR	GUITAR	GUITAR
electric, classical, folk	*neck, strings*	*makes good music*
Kinds of it?	Parts of it?	Functions of it?
(name 3)	(name 4)	(what does it do?)

TABLE 7.7. Concept ladder for amphibians.

What kinds of amphibians are there?	What is an amphibian a stage of?	What is an amphibian a product of?
AMPHIBIAN	AMPHIBIAN	AMPHIBIAN
What are the kinds of an amphibian?	What are the stages of an amphibian?	What are the products or results of an amphibian?

POSSIBLE ANSWERS:

frog legs (some folks eat them)   young amphibians on land
frogs   waste products
eggs in water   mature amphibians on land
salamanders   help control mosquito population
neophytes in water   more amphibians
turtles

from a single pool of possible responses, the students have an opportunity to check themselves. Here is an example:

Fill in the blanks with the appropriate word:

1. Fresh water is to salt water as the desert is to _____.
2. Water is to a fish as land is to _____.
3. Gills are to tadpoles as _____ are to frogs.
4. Ammonia is to fish as _____ is to land animals.
5. Urea is to a grown bird as uric acid is to _____.
6. Jelly-like coating is to frogs' eggs as _____ is to chickens' eggs.

(Asimov and Gallant, 1975, pp. 306–308)

Vocabulary and Surrounding Context. When authors use unfamiliar vocabulary, it is not always possible for the reader to determine the meaning directly from context. Hittleman (1978) suggests that the best strategy in such cases is to formulate a hypothesis as to what the word might mean and then test that hypothesis against the other occurrences of the word in the text. To do so, readers must be aware of structural devices authors use to signal meaning. According to Deighton (1959) and Hittleman (1978), writers generally use five types of signals:

1. *Definition.* They may use sentence forms like "*X* is (or "is called") *Y*." These sentences communicate an explicit definition of the word.
   An iconoclast is a person who deliberately breaks other people's traditions.
   A person who deliberately breaks traditions is called an iconoclast.
2. *Example.* When examples are given of an idea named by an unknown word, we may be able to figure out the word if we recognize the example. Sentences so constructed often use words or phrases like *for example, such as, like,* and *especially.*
   Venomous snakes, such as the rattlesnake, the copperhead, or the coral snake, are to be avoided.
3. *Modifiers.* Even when a word is not known, the modifiers used to describe it may give an indication of what it is. Modifiers are not only adjectives and adverbs but also relative clauses.
   The minaret that the Moslems built stood tall, slender, and graceful above the other buildings in the town.
4. *Restatement.* Sentences sometimes state the unknown idea a second time using other, more familiar words. One such device is an appositive, a group of words following the word defined and set off by commas or dashes. Restatement is also done by using key words or phrases like *or, that is,* and *in other words.*
   Chauvinism, an aggressive loyalty to one's own group at the expense of others, originally applied to national patriotism only.
   They fired the attendant because of her indolence; in other words, she was lazy.
5. *Inference.* There are several grammatical patterns writers employ that signal the meaning of unknown words:
   a. *Parallel sentence structure.* When series are used either in the same sentence or in groups of sentences, we can often get an idea of the nature of an unknown word by recognizing a known word in the series.
      Each office contained some type of medical specialist. In one was a family practitioner; in another, an obstetrician; in another, a radiologist; and in another, a hematologist.
   b. *Repetition of key words.* Sometimes, if an unknown word is of sufficient importance in a passage, the author will repeat it enough times in enough contexts for its meaning to be figured out.
      It is sometimes said that only primitive people have taboos. That is not necessarily so. Even advanced cultures like ours have them. In America, for example, it is taboo to speak directly about death, or about a grown person's age or weight.

    c. *Familiar connectives.* Some familiar connectives, especially subordinating or coordinating conjunctions, show us the relationship between ideas and thus allow us to associate an unknown idea with a known one.
John was very excited about the award, but Judith seemed indifferent.

The devices for identifying meanings in context can be taught. If they are clearly introduced, well practiced, and returned to often, they can become a valuable addition to a reader's strategies for dealing with difficult material. Assessing vocabulary in context should include exercises that deliberately test familiarity with and sensitivity to these contextual clues to word meaning.

Readability

Readability refers to the level of difficulty in written material. It is an important but controversial concept.

Every time we say that a person has an independent or instructional reading level of X we operate from an assumption that reading matter comes to us in perceivable gradations of difficulty and that the gradations affect everyone in the same ways. If this were not the case, we could not conclude from an informal reading inventory that a given student reads independently on, say, a fifth-grade level. This conclusion assumes that there is such a thing as a fifth-grade level of difficulty. We further conclude that ten hypothetical students with the same reading level and same general reading skill development would have about equal difficulty with material written at a given level.

Right? Wrong. Schema theory tells us that ten hypothetical students with approximately equal reading abilities would *not* read the same text with equal ease or difficulty. They would have different experiences, and therefore the schemata they brought to the text would vary. As a result, those with prior experiences closely related to the subject of the text would have an easier time than those whose experience was more remote. We see this happen all the time, and it does cast doubt on the concept of readability.

There is something to the concept, however. It is possible to find two passages *on the same subject* that are quite different in terms of the effort required to read them. We sometimes call this *relative readability* (Hirsch, 1978), which is of great concern, particularly to content subject teachers.

When two pieces of text on the same subject are analyzed to account for the relative difficulty of one vis-à-vis the other, two factors stand out in accounting for the difference: (a) the degree of familiarity of the words used and (b) the grammatical complexity of the sentences (Klare, 1974). These two factors form the basis of most formulas of estimating readability. Since there is usually an inverse relationship between familiarity and the length of individual words, difficulty is commonly measured by means of letter or syllable counts.

The same is true of grammatical complexity: the more words in a sentence, the greater, in general, is the difficulty. Thus we think of highly readable words as short words and highly readable sentences as short sentences.

Researchers using these factors have examined what happened when hundreds of readers read pieces of text with varying densities of long words and long sentences. From this research they derived the norms that are used in the formulas presented below.

The formulas we will discuss operate by averaging the number of sentences per 100 words of running text and averaging the number of syllables per 100 words. If, for example, the average number of sentences per 100 words is 10, each sentence averages 10 words in length, a moderate length. If a passage averages 110 syllables per 100 words, each word is very short. When these formulas are applied to a particular book, they can predict whether that book will be difficult for a particular group, fifth graders for example. Since reading fluency varies widely in all but the most homogeneous groups, however, such a book would vary in difficulty for students even if the effects of their prior knowledge were not considered. Nevertheless, the formula would alert a fifth-grade teacher to the danger of adopting a book written, say, on the seventh-grade level.

This very situation is a common problem because many textbooks used widely in schools have readability levels well above what can normally be expected in the grades for which the book is intended. Since many programs do little to prepare students for the demands of reading textbooks independently and learn content from them, it seems doubly merciless to give them material written in a style that is too difficult. For this reason, it is good practice for the teacher to assess the readability of the text material used in the classroom, particularly the material assigned for homework reading. The readability formulas described in the next section provide an easy means of doing so.

The Raygor Readability Estimate. This formula (Baldwin and Kaufman, 1979) can be used to estimate the readability level of a long reading selection or an entire book so long as it is written at the third-grade level or higher. To use the formula, follow these steps:

1. Count out three 100-word passages from a selection or book: one from near the beginning, one from near the middle, and one from near the end.
2. Count the number of sentences in each passage, estimating to the nearest tenth of a sentence. If, for example, the 100th word in the passage occurs halfway through the ninth sentence, the sentence count for the passage is 8.5 sentences.
3. Count the number of words in each passage containing six or more letters ("long words").
4. Average the number of sentences and the number of long words for the three passages. (Add the number of sentences for each of the three pas-

sages and divide by 3; do the same for the number of long words in all three passages.) If one sample of 100 words yields very different numbers from the other two, add one or more samples to the total and adjust the averages accordingly. If, for example, you see that two of the passages have about 25–35 long words and the third has only 4, use one more sample.

5. Find the point on the graph (Figure 7.8) where the average number of sentences and the average number of long words intersect. The number of the band running across the chart tells you the grade level of the text. If the intersection falls in the areas marked "Invalid," do not try to interpret this finding. The text you have used in this case is so unusual that it does not conform to typical norms on grade levels of difficulty. Before you make your decision, check your arithmetic and perhaps try three more samples from other places in the text.

Let's try an example. Suppose upon examining three passages from a fourth-grade science book, we arrived at these figures:

	SENTENCES	LONG WORDS
Passage 1	7.2	18
2	6.7	17
3	6.9	19
Total	20.8	54
Average	6.9	18

By moving to the right from the 6.9 for sentence length and moving up from the point between 16 and 20 for the number of long words, we arrive in the band marked 5. This textbook thus has a fifth-grade readability level.

Interpreting the Raygor estimate. What does the score of fifth-grade level on the passage above mean? The results reported by this formula are interpreted to correspond to a student's *instructional* reading level — that is, an average fifth grader could be expected to read the science book in our example with about 70 percent comprehension. This book was intended for fourth grade use, however, it would not be surprising if fourth-grade students found it too difficult.

What level of reading ability would a student need to read this book *independently*, for homework assignments or as a source of information when writing a report, or if 90 percent or higher comprehension is necessary? The Raygor estimate does not give us this information. To determine the required level for independent reading we may use the SMOG readability formula.

The SMOG Readability Formula. The SMOG (McLaughlin, 1969) also estimates readability at the third-grade level or higher by computing word and

FIGURE 7.8. Raygor readability formula chart.

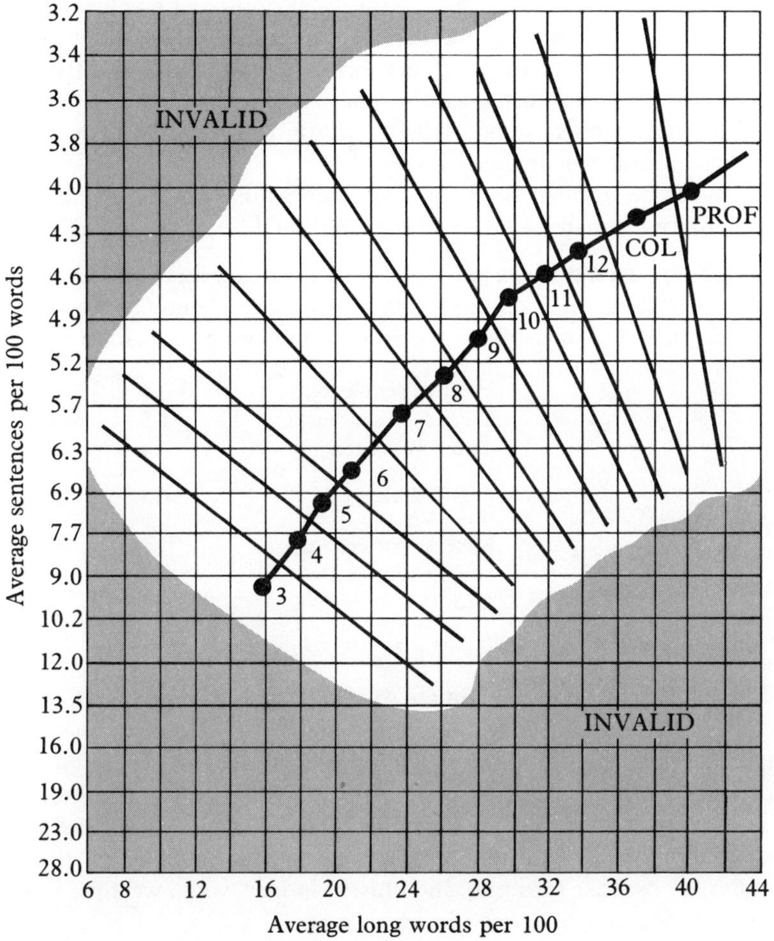

SOURCE: From R. Scott Baldwin and Rhonda K. Kaufman, "A Concurrent Study of the Raynor Readability Estimate," *Journal of Reading*, November 1979, pp. 148–153.

sentence length. It involves different computational procedures and yields the reading level needed for 90 to 100 percent comprehension.

To use the SMOG formula, follow these steps:

1. Count ten consecutive sentences near the beginning of the material being tested, ten near the middle, and ten more near the end.

2. Read the thirty sentences aloud and count every word with three or more syllables (polysyllabic words).
3. Estimate the square root of the total number of polysyllabic words. (An exact square root is not necessary — simply take the square root of the nearest perfect square. If, for example, the total is 40, the nearest perfect square is 36, so use 6 as the square root.)
4. If the number of polysyllabic words falls exactly between two squares, take the lower of the two.
5. Add the number 3 to the estimated square root. The result is the readability estimate of the material (McLaughlin, 1969, p. 639).

As an example, let us analyze the same fourth-grade science book on which we tried the Raygor formula. Taking ten sentences near the beginning, middle, and end of the book we find the following sums of polysyllabic words:

First 10 sentences	4
Second 10 sentences	5
Third 10 sentences	4
Total	13
Nearest perfect square	16
Square root of 16	4
Add 3	+3
Total	7

The SMOG readability estimate of this book is seventh grade.

Interpreting the SMOG formula. The score yielded by the SMOG formula indicates the level of ability required of a student to read a given text with 90 percent comprehension or better, which is considered the independent level. The creator of the SMOG formula, Harry McLaughlin (1969), indicated that the instructional level tends to fall *two years below* the independent level as indicated by this formula, and this is indeed what we found to be the case with the fourth-grade book in our example.

Assessing Study Skills

The Group Instructional Inventory (GII). An instrument developed by Thomas Rakes (1975), the GII tests study skills and general comprehension of a particular textbook. It is a paper-and-pencil test normally given to a whole class at the beginning of the year. It is used to:

1. place students in textbooks
2. yield diagnostic information for small group instruction to improve certain reference or study strategies

3. pinpoint those students whose general reading ability will be a handicap to them

Construction. A group instructional inventory can be constructed as follows:

1. Select a two- or three-page passage from within the second fifty pages of a textbook. The passage should pertain to a unified topic and should completely develop one or more ideas.

2. Count the total number of words in the excerpt.

3. After studying the selection, construct ten general reading questions covering its content. Questions that tap (a) facts, (b) inferences, (c) main points or applications, and (d) vocabulary are generally recommended (see the directions for writing questions for the informal reading inventory in Chapter Four).

4. Construct ten to fifteen questions that require reference, location, or other special study skills. These questions should reflect skills that the teacher thinks are important in a particular course. They might include questions that demonstrate ability to use the table of contents, the index, chapter headings, previews and summaries, and the glossary. Some teachers would add map reading or table and graph interpretation. The more concrete the question, the better. It is preferable to ask "What does *parabola* mean?" rather than "What is the glossary for?" as a test of the student's ability to use the glossary.

5. Prepare a response sheet on which students can write their answers.

6. Prepare an answer key for yourself. Write a detailed answer to each question and the pages on which the answers may be found (this will come in handy if other teachers use the inventory or if you use it again in future years). On your answer key, code each question by type — for example, vocabulary, map reading, table of contents, etc.

7. Develop a summary chart on which you can enter the performance of each student for each type of question. You can use this chart as a guide in assembling small groups for later instruction on specific skills.

Administration. The group instructional inventory can be given to large groups of students at one time. It usually takes a whole class period. Here are the steps:

1. Hand out the student response forms.
2. Explain the purpose of the activity. Alert the students that each question will be read two times.
3. Explain that they will be asked to read silently.
4. Ask them to place their texts on their desks.

Begin with the questions related to locational/study skills.

5. Ask the students to open their texts to the designated section of the book.
6. Provide a brief introduction of the material to be read.

FIGURE 7.9. Group instruction inventory.

PART I. TEXT USAGE SECTION

Use your textbook to find the answers to these questions.

1. According to the chart on page 96, what is the body temperature of a goat? (interpreting charts)
2. Write out the definition of the term *half-life*. (using the glossary)
3. According to the figure on page 314, what do *carbohydrates* and *fats* turn into? (interpreting figures)
4. According to the figure on page 315, what do *proteins* turn into? (interpreting figures)
5. On what page do you find a discussion of mammoths? (using the index)
6. On what pages is *lead* discussed? (using the index)
7. On what pages is the *table of contents* found? (locating the table of contents)
8. What is the subject of the *appendix?* (using the appendix)
9. Locate the *pronunciation key* on page 407. How would you use these symbols to write the word *bacon?* (using the pronunciation key)
10. How would you use these symbols to write the word *those?* (using the pronunciation key)

SOURCE: Based on a selection from Isaac Asimov and Roy A. Gallant, *Ginn Science Program: Intermediate Level C*, Ginn and Company, Lexington, Mass., 1975.

7. Explain that as soon as they finish reading the assignment, they should write down the exact time on their paper. Be sure to make a note of when they begin. Later you can compute their reading rate by dividing the total number of words in the passage by the number of minutes they required to read it.
8. After the students have read the passage tell them to put their books away. Now read aloud each of the comprehension questions twice and direct them to write down their answers after each question is read.
9. Collect the papers. Later you may wish to redistribute the papers so the students can mark their own answers and calculate their reading rates (Rakes, 1975, 596–597).

Interpretation. Students who answer 85 percent or more of all the questions correctly should have no trouble carrying out assignments. Those who score in the range from 60 to 85 percent will require assistance. This assistance may include not only general instruction in locational or study skills but also careful development of reading purposes and vocabulary. A sample group instructional inventory follows (Figure 7.9).

FIGURE 7.9 (continued)

PART II. COMPREHENSION SECTION

Read the section, "Life Begins in Water," pages 306–308. Start reading at the signal and record your time when you finish. Then close your book and write out the answers to the questions written below.

1. How long ago do scientists believe evolution began? (fact)
2. In what parts of the earth did living things first develop? (fact)
3. What two main groups of organisms developed first? (main idea)
4. What things did these first living organisms need to stay alive? (fact)
5. What does *freshwater* mean? (vocabulary)
6. What disadvantages would freshwater organisms face? (main idea)
7. From the information presented in this section, are you more likely to catch fish in a big lake or in the ocean? Why? (inference)
8. Explain what the term *selection* means in this sentence: "By this process of selection, scientists think that a whole new world of life came to occupy . . . freshwater. . . ." (vocabulary)
9. Could the offspring of a freshwater fish live in saltwater? Why or why not? (inference)
10. What are some things that would have to exist on the moon for living things to survive? (inference)

Instructional Strategies for Disabled Readers

Recording Reading Material. There are many disabled readers, students with instructional levels of fourth grade or lower, in our high school and middle school classrooms. They often sit unobtrusively in the back of the room, nodding agreement with the teacher's statements, praying that they won't be called on to answer any questions. There are not enough remedial reading classes in the higher grades to accommodate them all. If there were, they would still be enrolled in content area classes like history, English, civics, and home economics for some part of the school day.

What should a content area teacher do for the student with a lower elementary independent reading level who is placed in a middle or high school class?

The best coping strategy is also the most time-consuming: have the textbook recorded on tape. Let the student take the tape home or to the library, play it on a tape recorder, and read along with the textbook. Providing a taped version of the book accomplishes two purposes:

1. It leads to improvement. For many students who are not in any remedial program, the practice of reading along with the tape recorder is the only reading they are likely to do. If the textbook is not too far beyond them, a few weeks or months of listening to tapes may be all they need to get going. If their reading level is well below the writing style of the book, however, they may not improve enough to read independently.
2. It exposes the students to text material they would not otherwise see. Again, however, a caution is in order. If their reading levels are several years below grade placement level, it is likely that their ability to understand material read to them will fall below grade placement as well.

Hearing capacity, or the ability to comprehend text read aloud, is in large part a measure of students' familiarity with written language and their schemata for world knowledge and text structure. We can expect their hearing capacity to improve somewhat from listening to text on tape, since they can develop schemata through listening as well as reading, but in the meantime we must provide all the boosts to comprehension we can. These aids include discussing the assignments before they read them, previewing the major concepts the assignments contain, and elucidating the structure of the presentation of the text material. We should ask questions in the style of the DRTA: What do they already know about the topic? What do they still need to know? What do they think the text will tell them?

Some teachers make their own tapes of text material. Others assign their older students to do it, rotating the assignment so that several students share the responsibility. It is desirable to save the tape so it can be used year after year. To avoid scheduling problems in using the tapes, it is wise to assign readings at least a week in advance, and longer if possible. This routine allows time for several students to listen to the tape before the material is brought up in class.

If the school library is set up to accommodate tape lessons, allowing the library staff to handle the scheduling and playing of the tapes can save the teacher trouble. Some libraries or media centers have multiple listening areas. Others have high-speed tape reproduction facilities. You should check to see what your school library or media center can provide. If checking ov recorded text can be made into an everyday library transaction, the students are far less likely to "lose face" than they would if they were put in the position of getting a lot of obvious extra help from the teacher.

The Unit Teaching Approach. Students with widely varying reading ability constitute a fact of life in content area classrooms, and if a teacher relies too heavily on reading and discussing textbook assignments many students will be left behind. An alternative that circumvents this problem is the unit approach.

Unit teaching is a planning and teaching procedure that attempts to ac-

TABLE 7.8. Categories of activities for unit teaching.

CATEGORY: *Physically and Mentally Active*
Out of class concept-related activity
Construct artifacts, models, diaramas, etc.
Simulation
Do experiment, investigation, or demonstration
Role play or dramatization
Field trip

CATEGORY: *Creative*
Participate in debate
Complete directed and independent readings with various study guides
Illustrate concept with pictures or examples
Content reading lesson
Participate in a discussion
Write a report or research paper
Categorization exercise
Complete vocabulary activities

CATEGORY: *Watching and Listening*
Watch a demonstration
Guest speaker
View still pictures
View films or filmstrips
Listen to a record or tape
Listen to oral reading or lecture

SOURCE: From Thomas H. Estes and Joseph Vaughan, *Reading and Learning in the Content Classroom*, pp. 212–213. Copyright © 1978 by Allyn and Bacon, Inc. Reprinted by permission.

complish the same goals as might be accomplished through heavy textbook reliance. The unit plan, however, uses a wide range of alternative media to supplement the textbook.

Teachers engaged in unit teaching might still pursue the same goals and follow the same progression of ideas presented in the textbook, but they will not depend solely on the textbook for material. Usually they will carry out the following steps:

1. Analyze a section of the textbook to identify the *concepts* it presents and then choose all or some of them for the unit.
2. Identify from the textbook, from the subject area curriculum guide, or from their own judgment the *process goals* the students should work on as they study the concepts in the unit. Process goals are those such as classifying, comparing, charting, solving problems, finding references, con-

ducting interviews, making careful observations, keeping notebooks, building models, conducting opinion surveys, performing experiments, and disseminating information.

3. Take an inventory of all the available sources of information that might contribute to the conceptual goals or the process objectives. In planning for learning activities and organizing resources, it is helpful to consider the categories shown in Table 7.8.

4. Discuss the options with the students and draw up contracts with each student. The contracts should include: the material and activities the student will cover, the deadlines for each component activity, a description of the evaluation procedure to be used, the grade the student will receive after satisfactorily completing X amount of work (this is optional), and the signatures of student and teacher.

5. Schedule the activities, class discussions, films, guest speakers, field trips, and whatever else is required.

The amount of variety in a unit will depend on the teacher's willingness to coordinate multiple activities simultaneously. Many teachers delight in this activity; others do not. Unit teaching does offer the advantage of providing alternatives for those students who simply cannot read long assignments in a textbook, but in a setting where much independent work is going on the teacher must provide strong direction because students who don't read well usually don't perform scholastic tasks efficiently either. On the other hand, films, discussion, visiting speakers, presentations by other students, class skits, demonstrations, field trips, and other activities will certainly do more for nonreading students than reading assignments and discussions alone.

One final advantage of unit teaching: the participating students can write up case studies and monographs of their findings during the unit study. The teacher should ask them to write the reports and monographs for the information of others, and then in following years they can be added to the materials used in the units. They can also be used as short-cut material for reading disabled students.

Summary

Some children experience reading problems in content subjects in later elementary and secondary grades even though they made fair progress in early reading instruction. These problems usually arise because there is a difference between learning to read in early years and reading to learn in later years. Reading to learn requires familiarity with and responsiveness to different types of text structures, broad vocabulary skills, and a variety of comprehension and study skills.

Schema theory helps us to see how readers understand and learn from text material. *Schemata*, or cognitive frameworks, contain information we have about the world. When ideas are expressed in print, they are related by the reader to other ideas and information, which are organized in mental schemata. Two schema types are especially important: those containing our world knowledge and those concerning different text structure.

Perceiving the organizational structure of text helps readers to understand and remember what they read. Some common text structures are: *taxonomic*, classifying information in superordinate and subordinate categories; *chronological*, organizing facts sequentially across time; *cause and effect*, linking events with their causes and outcomes; *written direction*, sequencing the steps to be followed, sometimes with alternate contingency sequences; *comparison and contrast*, describing by pointing up similarities and differences among things; and *expository or explanatory*, featuring hierarchies of main ideas and supporting details. To adequately comprehend different types of text structures, the reader must tacitly ask different types of questions.

The use of schemata can be informally assessed to determine (a) what information readers already have about the topic and (b) how they relate new information to already acquired information. Activities such as the *directed reading-thinking activity* for nonfiction material, the *ReQuest procedure* for reciprocal questioning, *pattern guides* to perceive text organization, and the *structured overview* are suggested as aids in making assessments.

Vocabulary activities help students develop labels for existing schemata, remember new information, relate new words to personal experiences, learn and construct categories of meaning for new words, and derive meanings from the context in which new words appear. Concept ladders, analogies, categorizing activities, and context activities are worthwhile vehicles for vocabulary study.

Readability estimates or formulas are arithmetic scales to determine the approximate grade level of difficulty of text. These estimates are based on the idea that short words and short sentences are more easily readable than long words and sentences. The Raygor estimate and SMOG formula are simple methods of determining the grade level of a book. Such estimates, however, deal only with superficial aspects of text, not with the ideas expressed, and they should not be overinterpreted.

The Rakes *group instructional inventory* is a two-part written test that assesses skills in locating book parts and visual matter as well as comprehension of text passages.

Two instructional strategies suggested for helping disabled readers deal with difficult content areas materials are *recording textbooks* on tape for listening and *unit teaching*, which relies on the wide use of nontextbook materials to teach the same material contained in textbooks. Necessary concepts are analyzed, ways of teaching concepts other than by assigning textbook readings are outlined, and alternate sources of information are gathered for classroom use. Unit teaching gives poor readers a chance to learn necessary concepts and information without having to do extensive reading in textbooks that are too difficult for them.

Extension Activities

1. What level of reading ability is required to read *this* textbook at the independent level? At the instructional level?
2. Interview a random group of five students in any grade between the fourth and twelfth. It is better if all five are in the same grade and, if you are teaching, that they not be your students. Find out:
   a. in what subjects they have reading assignments for homework or in-class reading
   b. approximately how many pages they are assigned per day in each subject
   c. what portion of the assignments they actually read
   d. whether they find the reading of these assignments easy or hard, interesting or boring

   Take your findings to class and discuss them. What generalizations can you draw about the use of assigned reading in content classes?
3. Select three different textbooks on the same subject from your curriculum laboratory or school bookroom. Randomly select three pages of running text from each book and analyze all three passages.
   a. What text structures are prominent in the three? Is there a consensus?
   b. How would you construct a pattern guide for the structures you find?
   c. Compare your findings with those of classmates who selected books from different disciplines. Is there a preferred text structure for each discipline?
4. Select a content area textbook and decide what features students should know how to use: glossary, charts, chapter overviews, etc. Construct the text usage portion of a group instructional inventory for that text.
5. Construct a concept ladder for the term reading. Exchange your views with another student in your class.
6. Devise a set of analogies involving each of the following terms (you will have to think up other terms to give shape to the analogies):

frustration level	purposes for reading
readability	concept
content areas	tape recording (as a verb or noun)

Suggested Readings

Estes, Thomas and Shibilski, Wayne. **"Comprehension: Of What the Reader Sees Of What the Author Says."** *In Michael L. Kamil and Alden J. Moe, eds. Perspectives in Reading Research and Instruction. National Reading Conference, 1980, 99–104.* An early report from a research project investigating the demands different forms of text structure placed on reading strategies.

Klare, George. **"Assessing Readability."** *Reading Research Quarterly 10, no. 1 (1974): 62–102.* Explains the concept of readability and summarizes the major approaches to measuring it.

Upton, Albert. **Design for Thinking: A First Book On Semantics.** A concise treatment of issues of definition, word usage and meaning.

Vacca, Richard T. **Content Area Reading.** *Boston: Little, Brown, 1981.* Covers many aspects of assessing and teaching reading in the content areas.

References

Adams, Marilyn J. and Collins, Allan. "A Schema-Theoretic View of Reading." In Roy O. Freedle, ed. *New Directions in Discourse Processing.* Norwood, N.J.: Ablex, 1979.

Anderson, Richard C. "The Notion of Schemata and the Educational Enterprise." In Richard C. Anderson, Rand J. Spiro, and William Montague, eds. *Schooling and the Acquisition of Knowledge.* Hillsdale, N.J.: Erlbaum, 1977.

Asimov, Isaac and Gallant, Roy A. "From Land to Water: How Organisms Adapted." *Ginn Science Program: Intermediate Level C.* Lexington, Mass.: Ginn, 1975.

Baldwin, R. Scott and Kaufman, Rhonda K. "A Concurrent Validity Study of the Raygor Readability Estimate." *Journal of Reading* 23, No. 2 (Nov. 1979): 148–153.

Barron, Richard C. "The Use of Vocabulary as an Advance Organizer." In Harold Herber and P. L. Sanders, eds. *Research in Reading in the Content Areas: First Year Report.* Syracuse, N.Y.: Syracuse University Reading and Language Arts Center, 1969.

Bartlett, F. C. *Remembering.* Cambridge, England: Cambridge University Press, 1932.

Broudy, Harry S. "Types of Knowledge and Purposes of Education." In Richard C. Anderson, Rand J. Spiro, and William Montague, eds. *Schooling and the Acquisition of Knowledge.* Hillsdale, N.J.: Erlbaum, 1977.

Chall, Jeanne. "The Great Debate: Ten Years Later, With a Modest Proposal for Reading Stages." In Lauren Resnick and Phyllis Weaver, eds. *Theory and Practice of Early Reading,* Vol. I. Hillsdale, N.J.: Erlbaum, 1979.

Deighton, Lee. C. *Vocabulary Development in the Classroom.* N.Y.: Teachers College, Columbia University, 1959.

Estes, Thomas H. and Shebilski, Wayne. "Comprehension: Of What the Reader Sees of What the Author Says." In Michael L. Kamil and Alden J. Moe, eds. *Perspectives on Reading Research and Instruction, The 29th Yearbook of the National Reading Conference.* Washington D.C.: National Reading Conference, 1980.

Estes, Thomas H. and Vaughan, Joseph. *Reading and Learning in the Content Classroom.* Boston: Allyn and Bacon, 1978.

Hirsch, E. Donald. *The Philosophy of Composition.* Chicago: University of Chicago Press, 1978.

Hittleman, Daniel R. *Developmental Reading: A Psycholinguistic Perspective.* Chicago: Rand McNally, 1978.

Klare, George. "Assessing Readability." *Reading Research Quarterly*, 10, No. 1 (Fall 1974): 62–102.

Manzo, Anthony V. "ReQuest Procedure." *Journal of Reading* 13 (1969): 123–126.

Marshall, Nancy and Glock, Marvin D. "Comprehension of Connected Discourse: A Study into the Relationships Between the Structure of Text and Information Recalled." *Reading Research Quarterly* 14, No. 1 (1978–79): 10–56.

McLaughlin, Harry. "SMOG Grading: A New Readability Formula." *Journal of Reading* 12, No. 8, (May 1969): 639–646.

Minsky, Marvin. "A Framework for Representing Knowledge." In P. H. Winston, ed. *The Theory of Computer Vision*, N.Y.: McGraw-Hill, 1975.

Rakes, Thomas A. "A Group Instructional Inventory." *Journal of Reading.* 18, No. 5, (May 1975): 595–598.

Tierney, Robert J.; Readance, John E.; and Dishner, Ernest K. *Reading Strategies and Practices: A Guide for Improving Instruction.* Boston: Allyn and Bacon, 1980.

Upton, Albert. *Design for Thinking: A First Book On Semantics.* Palo Alto: Pacific Press, 1973.

Chapter Eight

Formal Measures of
Reading Ability

Ms. Jones was troubled. A number of her seventh-grade English students were having difficulty reading the literature anthology assigned by the school division. Ms. Jones retrieved their cumulative record folders from the principal's office files and began reviewing the accumulated records. What she found in their folders did little to enlighten her.

Along with report cards, school pictures, and attendance records, each folder contained a number of standardized record sheets and related papers. Most of the folders included reading scores from the general achievement test battery given in May of sixth grade. Some contained a placement test from the basal reading system used in the elementary schools, but in seventh grade basals were not used. Others had Stanford Diagnostic Reading Tests or skills profiles from the Wisconsin Design for Reading Skill Development. Ms. Jones was not sure what the Wisconsin Design was, or if the skills profiles represented test results at all.

Most of the tests, she found, seemed to be reporting very different information in very different forms. One reported the scores in grade equivalents, others in stanines and percentiles. Some had no apparent scores at all but instead gave lengthy lists of skills with some checked off, or with holes punched in corresponding boxes.

Ms. Jones pondered how these various forms of scores and checklists of skills could be applied to her curriculum and her students, each one with unique talents and interests. Should she try to supplement her present English unit with work on these reading skills? Were all the tests equally good ones? Ms. Jones had seen enough of her "average" students receive spuriously low achievement test scores to have a healthy degree of skepticism about these tests. And she had never heard of some of them. Yet every year, at least a full week of teaching time was taken up with giving such tests schoolwide.

Ms. Jones needed answers to these questions:

□ What are the major types of reading-related standardized tests?
□ How do I interpret these tests to derive the information I need?
□ How can I use these scores to improve the reading ability of my students?

The purpose of Chapter Eight is to help answer these questions. Most teachers realize, as Ms. Jones did, that standardized tests of various kinds are widely administered in all subject areas, but it is often difficult to make some sense out of the many kinds of tests and the many ways in which they yield results.

This chapter covers two basic kinds of measurement devices: *norm-referenced tests* and *criterion-referenced tests*. Within those generic categories we discuss different kinds of tests given for different purposes, some basic concepts of measurement such as the reliability and validity of tests, how scores are distributed, and how to interpret various forms of test scores.

The use of formal testing measures is so widespread that it is hard to imagine a school where they are not used. All teachers, regardless of grade or subject, must know how to evaluate tests and interpret their results. Educators are *consumers* of formal tests, and only informed consumers can guard against the misuse and misinterpretation of these products. This chapter is aimed toward developing a critical awareness of the characteristics, strengths, and limitations of formal reading tests.

Basic Test Concepts

There are over two thousand educational tests available. A measurement expert has estimated that at least 200 million standardized achievement tests are given yearly, as well as hundreds of thousands of standardized diagnostic, survey, aptitude, and other types of tests (Gronlund, 1976). Every teacher must understand basic test concepts in order to interpret different kinds of numerical results of standardized tests, and proper evaluation involves much more than skill in calculating. Many schools use machine-scored test forms or hand-scored tests with tables for easy score transformations, but no machine or table of numbers can evaluate or interpret the results.

There are two qualities that every reading (or other) test should possess: *reliability*, the degree of consistency of test scores, and *validity*, the degree to which a test measures what it is supposed to measure. Validity is the more important, but since validity involves a degree of reliability, we will discuss reliability first.

Reliability

Reliability is a measure of how stable test scores are. It refers to the results obtained from a test, not to the test itself. Thus it is more appropriate to refer to the reliability of the measurement or the results yielded rather than to the reliability of the measure itself (Mehrens and Lehmann, 1978).

There are several aspects of reliability to be considered. One is *stability*, or the consistency of test scores across time, from one administration to another with the same group of subjects. Another is *internal consistency*, or the consistency of items within a test. A third is *equivalence*, or consistency across different forms of the same test. All three aspects are important but they are estimated through different methods.

Stability. If a group of students took Test 1 several times, each individual's score would be somewhat different each time. If the scores are consistent, or reliable, their *rank order* would remain very similar from one testing to another. Therefore, the student with the highest score the first time would have the highest, or nearly the highest, score the second time; the student with the lowest score would retain very low standing, and the order of students between highest and lowest would remain nearly unchanged (Thorndike and Hagen, 1977). If stability is lacking, a score attained once is unrelated to the score attained another time; students with high scores on the first administration may get very low scores on a retest. Obviously, such scores would have little meaning or usefulness because they would be heavily affected by random chance.

There are several ways stability can be built into a test. One way is through standardized administration procedures: administering the tests at the same time of day under the same or highly similar physical conditions and utilizing identical directions, examples, and time limits.

Another, more important, way of building in stability involves the nature of the test itself. It must be developed so that students will rank about the same each time the test is given to them. Test length is a critical factor.

Generally speaking, the longer a test is, the more reliable the scores from it will be (Sax, 1980). Since any test represents only a sampling of what students know and can do, a longer test yields a more accurate estimate of their capabilities. On a longer test with many items, random effects tend to cancel out. Therefore, random chance has less effect on the total score of a long test vis-à-vis a short one.

Of course, there are limits to *how* long it should be. A test with 50 items will yield more reliable scores than one with only 5 items, but a test with 500 items will only exhaust those trying to take it. There is no particular rule of thumb for length, but standardized test developers try out different lengths and add or delete items to arrive at an optimum length.

Stability is estimated using the *test-retest method*. The same test is given twice to the same group of subjects, and the rank order of their scores on each one is compared. If the interval between administrations is fairly short, students will remember a number of items and will be familiar with the format. This method will tend to raise everyone's scores, but the rank order of the scores will remain much the same. It should be remembered that the rank order of the scores, not the numerical value of the scores themselves, is what is important here. If the interval between administrations is very long, maturation and the acquiring of new information will affect performance. If all students made identical progress in the interval, the rank order would not be affected, but this is never the case because students learn and develop at different rates.

Internal Consistency. The factor of internal consistency refers to the degree to which items within a test are related. We can determine internal consistency by comparing a student's performance on an entire test to his or her performance on two halves of the same test administered separately, but since the more difficult items often come toward the end, it would not be a good practice to split a test at the middle. Instead, alternate items should be selected: one-half with all the odd-numbered items, the other half with all the even-numbered items. If the scores on each half are closely related, a measure of good internal consistency has been provided. If performance on the two halves is not closely related, the total test score will not be reliable, and its value questionable.

Internal consistency is dependent in part on clarity. Items must be precisely worded and clearly understandable or else they will be interpreted and answered differently by different students with equal knowledge and understanding of the topic.

Sometimes internal consistency is estimated by the *split-half method* in which students take the two halves of a test as separate tests. The scores on each half are correlated, and an arithmetic formula is applied to relate the correlation to the entire test. Other ways of estimating internal consistency involve giving the whole test once and applying one of several arithmetic formulas to the total score. These computations are beyond the scope of this discussion, but you will find detailed information in almost any text on tests and measurement methods.

Equivalence. When alternate forms of a test are being used, equivalence is important. Many standardized reading tests feature alternative forms that are used for pre- and posttesting, but they must be highly equivalent for the scores to have any usefulness.

The *equivalent forms method* is used to estimate this aspect of reliability. It requires the construction of two different tests, each one an equally good sampling of the content being tested. Each form must also be equivalent in difficulty and length. The two forms are administered to the same students in close succession, and the scores on the two forms are correlated. This method usually yields the lowest, most conservative estimate of reliability of the three methods discussed.

Every standardized reading test being considered for use should have reported reliability estimates, and it should indicate what methods were used to determine such estimates. Reliability can be expressed in numerical terms by a *reliability coefficient.* This coefficient, a decimal number between zero and one, shows how consistent the scores were after using the test-retest, split-halves, or equivalent forms assessments. The closer to 1.0 the reliability coefficient is, the more reliable the scores. Some experts recommend that for evaluation of a single student, a test should have an overall reliability coefficient of at least .90; somewhat lower figures would be acceptable if the test is to evaluate groups of students rather than individuals. In the case of groups, the overall reliability estimate should not be less than about .70. If it is, you should look for another test.

Overall reliability can be profoundly affected, for good or bad, by the consistency of individual subtests. Survey reading tests, generally used for screening large numbers of students, usually have few subtests, and the expressed reliability coefficients refer to the test as a whole. Quite a few reading achievement tests and most standardized reading diagnostic tests, however, have many separate subtests, and the reliability of subtest scores can vary widely. These tests should have reported subtest reliabilities as well as a coefficient for the entire test, and scores on subtests of questionable reliability must be discounted. If a test under consideration has more than one or two subtests of low reliability, another one should be considered.

A final point about judging reliability concerns the standard error of measurement. This term does not mean there are mistakes in the test; it refers to the fact that no score is absolutely precise. The standard error of measurement (SE) is a number that indicates how much an individual's score might have varied depending on random chance factors. Take, for example, a test with a reported SE of plus or minus three points (± 3) and a student with a raw score of 67. We can be about 70 percent sure that the student's true score lies somewhere between 64 and 70. If we double the SE to ± 6, we can be 90 percent sure that the student's true score lies between 61 and 73 (Bertrand and Cebula, 1980).

The standard error shows numerically how accurate any score is likely to be. A small standard error indicates high reliability because we can be fairly confident that the student's test score and the true score closely approximate each other (Nunnally, 1972).

Validity

High reliability is necessary, but not sufficient, for a test to be a good one. A test can yield consistent scores but still not truly measure what was intended to be measured. This quality of actually measuring what was supposed to be measured is referred to as *test validity*. The difference between reliability and validity, and the necessity for both, can be illustrated by a simple example. Let's say that someone developed an intelligence test for children on which the only measurement was how fast each child could run a fifty-yard dash. If each child were retested several times in a few months, or even at the beginning and end of the school year, scores would probably not differ much. The fastest runners in September would very likely be the fastest in June, even though everyone would have grown somewhat. Therefore, these scores would be quite reliable. Would anyone, however, consider a test of running speed a *valid* test of intelligence? Obviously not. A valid test of intelligence requires problem solving and many types of cognitive operations while a valid test of running speed requires only that subjects actually run. Reliability only provides the consistency that makes validity possible (Gronlund, 1976).

There are several types of validity that are often referred to in test reviews and manuals, and teachers should understand how validity is developed in test evaluation. While reliability is quantitatively estimated, validity involves qualitative judgments as well.

Content Validity. In assessing content validity, we ask if the test is an adequate sample of the content area or process being tested. Content validity is particularly important in achievement tests, which are designed to show subject mastery (Mehrens and Lehmann, 1978). An elementary spelling achievement test with only very long, difficult, infrequently used words from college texts would lack content validity because it does not represent what elementary children study in spelling. Content validity is established when test makers study both school curricula and tests and submit their tests to the scrutiny of subject area experts. Some authorities claim, however, that many reading achievement tests lack content validity because they measure only a narrow range of real reading behaviors.

Construct Validity. Human traits or qualities that are not directly observable or measurable, but which are widely inferred from behaviors, are called *constructs*. Running speed or hand width are directly observable or measurable entities. Traits like attitudes, intelligence, or aptitudes are not directly measurable and must be inferred from observable behaviors. Thus intelligence, musical or mechanical aptitude, judgment, problem solving, attitudes, and interests are constructs.

If a test has good construct validity, it allows the student to demonstrate behaviors directly related to the construct. In a test of attitudes toward reading, for example, students should be able to show how positively or negatively they would feel about getting a book for a gift, hearing a book discussed, going to the library or bookstore, or seeing someone vandalizing a book. A test of intelligence with construct validity will elicit many behaviors associated with intelligence: verbal and spatial reasoning and problem solving will be required as well as memory, factual knowledge, and word meanings. Construct validity is important in all tests, but it is critical in psychological and personality tests and attitude inventories.

Criterion-Related Validity. Another way of establishing a test's validity is to relate it to other validated measures of the same ability or knowledge. The predetermined *criterion* may be other test scores, grades or subject area performance, or other observable behaviors. A test has criterion-related validity if it calls for responses that relate closely to actual performance. Concurrent and predictive validity are criterion-related.

When a new test is found to be highly correlated to an existing test of established validity, it is said to have *concurrent validity*. The one measure is found to "concur" with the other. Coefficients of concurrent validity are frequently reported by test makers. It is important for teachers to satisfy themselves that the test used as the criterion is itself valid. Just because two tests are closely related is no guarantee that either one is valid, only that they measure the same attribute.

When a score is found to be closely related to later performance on some criterion, the test is said to have *predictive validity*. This aspect is critically important in aptitude tests, since they purport to determine whether someone has the potential to become skilled in a particular field at a later time. If students who do well on a test of mechanical aptitude later excel in school courses like "shop" and drafting and then go on to college engineering and technical schools or seek careers as engineers, architects, and machinists, that test is a good predictor of mechanical aptitude. The well-known Scholastic Aptitude Test (SAT), used to predict the potential of high school students for college studies, is believed to be high in predictive validity because SAT scores and subsequent college grade-point averages are closely related.

Simple Descriptive Statistics

Many teachers and reading specialists cringe when they face information given in statistical terms, which is unfortunate as well as unnecessary. Standardized tests often yield numerical information in statistical terms that must be understood for appropriate interpretation, and although teachers don't usually have to compute statistics, they must understand some of the basic principles. Test manuals and reference works like Buros's *Mental Measurement Yearbooks* (1978) contain a wealth of information in numerical terms, but too many educators cannot make use of such information. The following discussion is aimed toward developing this understanding so that teachers can avoid the overinterpretation and outright misuse of tests and scores.

Distributions. This term refers to the span or array of test scores achieved by any group. From highest to lowest, scores are "distributed" across a range of numbers. The nature of this distribution is an important concept.

If a large number of people were assessed according to some attribute and their scores were rank-ordered, they would form a distribution. Let's say we measured the height of a hundred adult men and women and asked them to stand on a line with the tallest person at one end and the shortest at the other. At each end of the line, the extremes, there would be a few very tall and a few very short people; toward the middle there would be many people of average height all clustered together.

A symmetrical distribution with many scores in the middle and a few arrayed at the extremes is called a *normal distribution*. It is sometimes called a *bell-shaped curve* because it looks like a bell (see Figure 8.1).

FIGURE 8.1. Normal distribution.

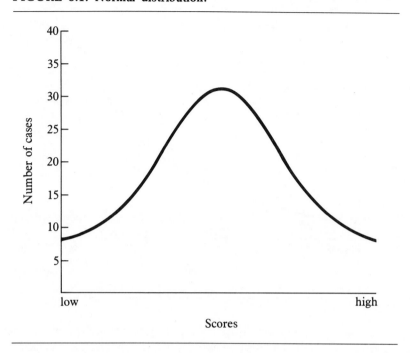

The normal distribution is a hypothetical construct similar to the distribution of scores on most standardized tests and similar to many human characteristics, like height. If large numbers of people are assessed, the scores may approach the normal distribution on many attributes. If a distribution is normal, or is assumed to approach this model, we know that most of the scores will be clustered around the center with progressively fewer and fewer scores arrayed near or at the two extremes. Test makers and publishers use this distribution to report individual scores in a variety of ways, which we will discuss in the next section.

Not all distributions are normal. Instead of most of the scores clustering in the middle, a test may yield a distribution with many very high or very low scores. This is called a *skewed* distribution; it is not symmetrical, as is the normal curve. If most people get high scores, with few average or low scores, the distribution would be skewed toward the high end of the scale, as in Figure 8.2.

Likewise, a test yielding many low and few average or high scores is skewed toward the low end of the scale, as in Figure 8.3. Many, but not all, standardized tests assume a normal distribution. Some "minimum competency" tests have a positively skewed distribution if they are easy for most of

FIGURE 8.2. Positively skewed distribution.

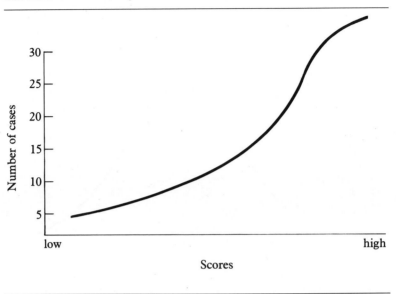

the students, as they should be if they truly test "minimum" competencies. A negatively skewed distribution usually means the test is too difficult for the intended testees; that is, most of them got low scores (Mehrens and Lehmann, 1978).

Indices of Central Tendency. Scores are most often throught of in relation to where they lie on a distribution. Two important indices of central tendency are the mean and median, which are used in computing grade-equivalent scores.

A *mean* is an arithmetic *average* calculated by adding all scores and dividing the sum by the number of scores used.

The *median* is the point in a distribution where there are equal numbers of scores above and below it. If we had scores of 14, 15, 16, and 17 the median would be 15.5, with two scores below that point and two above it. In general, the closer together the mean and median are, the more the distribution of scores will be symmetrical in shape.

Indices of Dispersion. This term refers to ways of numerically indicating how spread out a set of scores are. Two indices of dispersion are the range and the standard deviation.

The *range* indicates the span of scores attained, from highest to lowest. It is calculated by subtracting the lowest from the highest score. The range is less informative than the standard deviation.

FIGURE 8.3. Negatively skewed distribution.

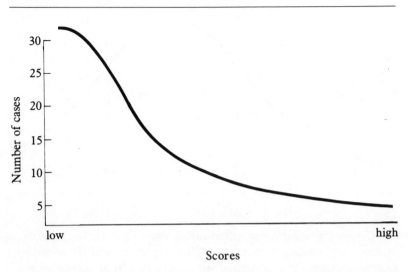

The *standard deviation* is an index of how spread out scores are around the mean, regardless of the shape of the distribution. For convenience, we will return to the normal distribution concept to illustrate the standard deviation.

In a normal distribution we said that most of the scores would be grouped near the mean. How many is "most"? How near is "near"? Statisticians have determined that 68 percent of the scores would be arrayed around or at the mean, with smaller percentages near the extremes, as in Figure 8.4.

If a student's score was 1SD below the mean, we would know where the score lay on the distribution; we would know that the student did as well or better than 16 percent of the norm group but that 84 percent did better. The range around the mean, from −1SD to +1SD, is considered the average range. A score of −1SD would be at the bottom of the average range.

Say, for example, a test has a mean of 50 and a standard deviation of 6. The distribution would look like the one in Figure 8.5. Where would a score of 53 lie? Halfway between the mean and +1SD, in the upper half of the average range. Where would a score of 36 be? Between 2 and 3 SDs below the mean, in the bottom 2 percent of the group.

The concepts of mean and standard deviation are integral in understanding how most scores such as those described below are reported.

Forms of Test Scores. A *raw score* is the total number of correct items on a test or subtest. Raw scores are usually converted to another form to facilitate comparisons.

FIGURE 8.4. Percentages of scores within standard deviation (SD) units.

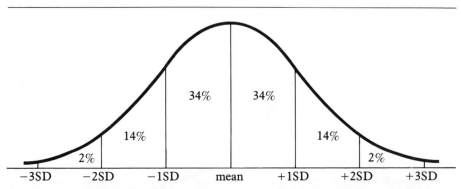

Grade-equivalent scores, often called simply *grade scores,* are frequently used in reporting reading test scores. They represent a level of achievement considered average for a particular grade and month of school within that grade. Grade scores are expressed in two-part numbers; the first number indicates the grade level, and the second number indicates the month within that grade. The two numerals are usually separated by a dash. A grade score of 3-1, for example, stands for the first month, September, of third grade. (There are *nine* months in a school year. Grade-equivalent scores use a dash because using a decimal point implies a 10-unit scale.)

Grade scores infer that there is some objective, generally accepted standard of achievement for every month of each school grade. In reality, no such

FIGURE 8.5. Distribution with mean of 50 and SD of 6.

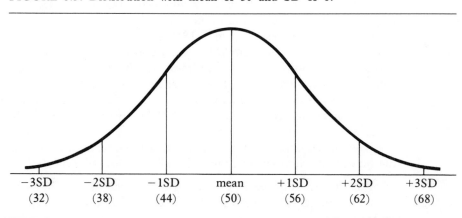

agreement exists on what skills or competencies should be attained by all, or most, readers at any given point. Such expectations are too heavily influenced by local standards, curricular goals, scope and sequences of skills within commercial programs, and learner characteristics for there to be any one standard of achievement. Grade scores are often considered, and interpreted to parents, however, as though there *were* such objective standards and thus they are often overinterpreted.

Percentiles, another common form of score, are more easily understood than grade scores. Percentiles range from 1 to 99; wherever a score lies within this range indicates relative performance compared with the norm group. A score at the tenth percentile means the student did better than 10 percent but worse than 89 percent of the students in the norm group. A score at the ninety-eighth percentile means that the student did better than 98 percent of the norm group and that only 1 percent attained higher scores. Sometimes percentile scores are frustrating for parents who believe the score represents the number of items correctly answered. Such a parent, whose child scored at the fiftieth percentile, would judge that the child had done poorly, with only 50 percent of the items right, instead of correctly viewing the score as average.

Stanines are similar to percentiles; the term is derived from "standard nines," which means that the distribution of possible scores has been divided into nine equal parts. Stanine scores range from one to nine; five is the mean, and scores from just below four to just above six are considered average.

T scores and *z scores* are fairly common standard scores. They indicate how close to the mean of the normal distribution a score lies. T scores range from a low of 20 to a high of 80, with a mean of 50 and a standard deviation of 10. z scores use positive and negative numbers distributed around a mean of zero with a standard deviation of 1; z scores between -1.0 and $+1.0$ are considered average.

Norm-Referenced Tests

Norm-referenced tests are developed by publishers who administer them to large numbers of students in order to develop *norms*. The norms represent average performances of many students in various age, grade, and demographic groups and are used to compare the performance of individuals or special groups to the performance of those in the norm group.

Some test makers go to great lengths to include students from various geographic areas, urban and rural communities, racial and ethnic groups, and economic groups. Many tests feature several different sets of norms for local groups that are unlike "national averages" — for example, center-city schools, rural populations, schools receiving federal funding for education, high-achieving gifted populations, highly affluent areas, and the like.

The information yielded by norm-referenced tests is primarily quantitative, which has relatively little diagnostic value but is useful for comparing achievement patterns. The scores on standardized diagnostic tests must be combined with qualitative information, however, if they are to have real diagnostic usefulness.

Norm-referenced reading tests generally fall into three rough categories: (a) *survey tests*, screening devices that feature a few broad, general subtests and yield a small number of global scores; (b) *diagnostic tests*, given to show skill strengths and needs, with a number of subtests assessing particular skills and yielding a half dozen or more subtest scores; and (c) general *reading achievement tests*, which are given to assess past learning rather than for diagnostic purposes.

Survey Tests

Survey tests are most commonly used to screen large numbers of students for approximate reading levels and identify those with severe problems. Their purpose is to determine general, overall levels of proficiency rather than to pinpoint specific skill strengths and needs.

Because they are intended to be general rather than specific, survey reading tests usually have from one to four subtests, and the subtest scores are combined into a total reading score. Subtests are usually for comprehension and vocabulary, although some include reading speed or study skills. Figure 8.6 shows sample vocabulary and comprehension items from the Gates-MacGinitie Reading Tests.

Survey tests are quite simple to administer to large groups. Because they have few subtests, there are fewer sets of directions, examples, and time limits to monitor. They can easily be given by the regular classroom teacher with no special preparation beyond a careful reading of the test manual, and they can usually be completed in one sitting. They are simple to score by hand and some can be machine-scored. The manuals include tables for conversion of raw scores to standard scores, usually grade scores, percentiles, and stanines.

Some typical group survey tests are the Gates-MacGinitie Reading Tests, Iowa Silent Reading Test, Metropolitan Reading Test, and the reading sections of the Comprehensive Test of Basic Skills and the California Achievement Test.

Advantages. Survey tests in reading are widely used and popular because they have a number of advantages. First, they can be administered to large groups. Second, they can usually be completed in a short time, often in one sitting. Third, they are usually easy to administer and score without special preparation. Fourth, they are useful for screening large numbers of students to identify those who are reading very poorly; for example, a survey test might

FIGURE 8.6. Sample vocabulary and comprehension items from a primary form of the Gates-MacGinitie Reading Tests, a survey instrument.

Practice Page

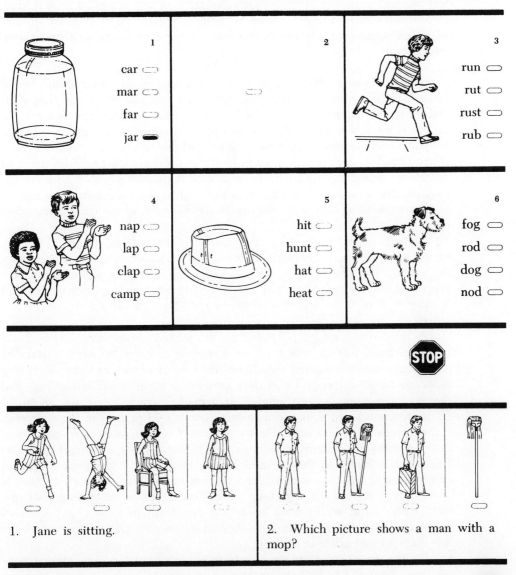

be given to all entering sixth graders in a consolidated middle school. Fifth, test manuals generally allow simple conversion of raw scores to several kinds of common standard scores, which facilitates comparisons of different groups. Many publishers supply norms for special populations as well as national norms.

Disadvantages. Survey tests also have a number of shortcomings. First, because of their very general nature they often lack content depth. Scores are yielded in very broad areas like reading comprehension and knowledge of vocabulary, but low scores in these areas do little to indicate specifically what the student knows or has trouble with. When subtest scores are combined into a general reading score it is difficult to interpret precisely what abilities the score represents. Some experts advocate examining individual items on a survey test to determine a student's specific strengths and weaknesses, but this would be so time-consuming that it would negate the survey's advantage of time economy.

Second, grade scores frequently overestimate reading ability. They are supposed to represent instructional levels, but more often than not they show the student's *frustration* level. If the scores are used to place children at a proper textbook level, a common use, they will often end up overplaced, thus leading to frustration and discouragement. This is a misuse of survey test scores.

A third disadvantage is related to the second. Most survey tests use a multiple-choice format, which allows a student to get some items correct by guessing. Scores are derived by adding the number of correct items, including those answered correctly by chance as well as by true understanding, and therefore the scores will be inflated. If items have three alternative multiple-choice responses, students could answer correctly 33 percent of the time even if they guessed at every item. For the typical, four-alternative response, a student's guesses on all items could lead to a 25 percent rate of correct response. Fry (1971) referred to this as the "orangoutang score," the score a diligent primate might get on a standardized reading test if it could mark an answer sheet. Fry generated "orangoutang scores" for a number of reading tests that were widely used at the time his article appeared; in most cases, students guessing at *every* item got grade-equivalent scores only two or three years below their present grade in school!

Fourth, because survey reading tests are intended for large general populations, they tend to be better estimates of true ability for students with average performance than for either very good or very poor readers. The scores at either the high or low end of the performance scale are less accurate: superior readers are often underestimated while very poor readers can get scores years above their actual instructional levels. Although survey tests can be useful in identifying very poor readers, a low score indicates only that a reading difficulty exists, but it does not reveal the nature or degree of the difficulty.

Diagnostic Tests

Because survey reading tests offer little in terms of diagnosis, standardized *diagnostic tests* are often given to those students performing poorly on a survey test.

Diagnostic tests differ from survey tests in three major ways (Gronlund, 1976): (a) they have a large number of subtest scores (sometimes called "part scores") and a larger number of items; (b) the items are devised to measure specific skills; and (c) difficulty tends to be lower in order to provide adequate discrimination among students with reading problems.

Diagnostic tests, both the group and individual types, have numerous subtests and yield a profile of scores. Each subtest assesses a particular skill area. Developers of these tests maintain that analysis of a profile of subtest scores will reveal strengths and weaknesses in skill areas and that it is this analysis that makes them more "diagnostic" than survey tests.

Diagnostic tests for group administration frequently include subtests assessing some or most of the following skills: reading comprehension, vocabulary, visual and auditory discrimination, structural analysis, numerous aspects of phonic analysis, sound blending, skimming and scanning, syllabication, sight word recognition, and spelling. Because of the number of separate subtests, they usually have to be administered in several sittings.

A typical group diagnostic test is the Stanford Diagnostic Reading Test. The Stanford, testing grades one through thirteen with four levels and two alternate forms of each level, includes subtests assessing auditory discrimination, word meanings, phonic and structural analysis, and literal and inferential comprehension. Levels for grade four and above include reading speed and skimming and scanning subtests. Scores are reported in grade scores, percentiles, and stanines. The Stanford test takes about two hours to administer.

There are also a number of diagnostic tests for individual use, many of which focus on one or two particular aspects, such as word recognition or phonic analysis skills. Others are like informal reading inventories in that they assess word recognition and comprehension with word lists and story passages. Some attempt a broad-based analysis of skills while others cover a narrower range of skills. When the latter type is used, several different tests must be given in order to derive a more complete picture of a reader's strengths and needs.

Some tests focus on word recognition or oral reading only. The Slosson Oral Reading Test (SORT) is one of the most extreme of these. Its name is misleading because it is not a test of oral reading as most of us would define that term. It is made up entirely of lists of words in isolation. The student pronounces each word in an untimed presentation. No attempt is made to assess knowledge of word meanings since the words are in lists and there is no reading comprehension involved. On the basis of sheer word pronunciation, the SORT purports to furnish an instructional reading level for each student.

The instructional level, however, must be based on comprehension ability, and so the reading level this test yields is largely useless.

Several individual tests assess oral reading skill in a slightly broader sense than the SORT. The Gray Oral Reading Test and the Gilmore Oral Reading Test assess recognition of words in context, oral reading fluency, and accuracy. Comprehension questions are usually asked, but in both the Gray and the Gilmore comprehension is not reflected in the score. When comprehension questions are included, these tests take about as long to administer as the oral passages of an IRI, but the results are less helpful because there is no direct assessment of comprehension.

There are a number of "standardized IRIs" that are more comprehensive than the oral reading tests, while saving the teacher the time needed to a make up an IRI. The Durrell Analysis of Reading Difficulty, Diagnostic Reading Scales by Spache, Silvaroli's Classroom Reading Inventory, and the Ekwall Reading Inventory are among the better known. All four of them assess sight vocabulary, word analysis in isolation and in context, and silent and oral reading comprehension, as in a teacher-made IRI. Their components include word lists, graded passages with comprehension questions, occasional supplemental tests, and usually some kind of system for determining independent and instructional levels by counting errors. Although most of these tests have some simple system of coding oral reading errors, there is no qualitative analysis of the errors. The *number* of oral reading errors, not *types*, is what is considered.

In his Diagnostic Reading Scales Spache uses the terms Independent Level and Instructional Level differently from others. Spache uses the term instructional to mean the level just below the grade where *oral* reading broke down either in word recognition *or* comprehension. He uses the term independent to refer to the highest grade level at which the student can read *silently* with adequate comprehension. Teachers referring to a student's independent or instructional level as indicated by the Diagnostic Reading Scales will mean something very different from those using another IRI, and they should be careful of this difference in terminology. Spache's independent level means silent reading level, and his instructional level means oral reading level.

Some of the standardized IRIs feature phonics or word analysis subtests. The Durrell Analysis of Reading Difficulty contains a number of subtests for students reading at or below a particular level. These include two different "Visual Memory of Words" subtests where the student matches a word flashed on a tachistoscope to a word on the answer sheet as well as several auditory discrimination and auditory analysis subtests called "Hearing Sounds in Words," "Learning to Hear Sounds in Words," and "Sounds of Letters." Subtests on "learning rate," spelling, and handwriting complete the Durrell battery. The Diagnostic Reading Scales contain eight phonics subtests that assess letter sounds, blends, syllables, auditory discrimination, and other aspects of word analysis.

The IRIs by Ekwall and Silvaroli are similar, both featuring word lists and reading passages. The Ekwall IRI has preprimer through ninth-grade passages, word lists, four alternate forms, a phonics survey test, and student pages that are not illustrated. Silvaroli's test has three alternate forms, illustrated passages from preprimer through eighth grade, word lists from preprimer through sixth grade, and a spelling test. (Refer to Chapter Four for other published IRIs.) Figure 8.7 shows a passage and comprehension questions from Silvaroli's Classroom Reading Inventory.

The Woodcock Reading Mastery Test is often used in special education. The Woodcock consists of five subtests: letter identification, word identification, word attack, word comprehension, and passage comprehension. Designed for use in all grades from kindergarten through twelfth, it takes about thirty minutes to administer.

The letter identification subtest requires the student to name letters shown in eight styles of type. The word identification subtest consists of 150 words in order of difficulty from preprimer through twelfth grade. They are listed in isolation, and the student pronounces the words in an untimed presentation. The word attack subtest consists of 50 nonsense words to be decoded and pronounced. Items range in difficulty from *bim* to *wubfambif*. The word comprehension subtest contains 70 items presented as verbal analogies: "boy — girl, man — _____." The subject reads the analogy silently and says a word to complete the set. Figure 8.8 shows items from the word comprehension and word attack subtests. The passage comprehension subtest consists of 85 modified cloze items; a word is omitted from a sentence, and the subject reads the item silently, then gives a word to complete it. Early items are single sentences with a picture clue; later items contain two or three sentences and have no picture.

The Woodcock yields grade-equivalent scores and age-equivalent scores for each subtest and for Total Reading, which represents the combined subtest scores. Scores can be converted to percentiles, and there are separate norms available for males and females as well as for different socioeconomic groups.

Like other standardized tests, the Woodcock yields entirely numerical data. A grade-equivalent score, or any other form of numerical score, on subtests like Word Identification or Passage Comprehension does not tell the teacher what the student can or cannot do. The examiner still does not know *what* letters the student can identify or what phonics skills have been mastered without detailed item analysis, which is not discussed in the manual.

Some individual diagnostic tests focus particularly on word analysis skills and not comprehension as such, like the Botel Reading Inventory and Sipay Word Analysis Test.

The Botel does not measure comprehension of sentences or paragraphs but does include comprehension of single words. The Botel is made up of a Word Recognition Test for identification of isolated words, Word Opposites subtests, both reading and listening, for selection of opposites in a multiple-choice format, and a Phonemic Inventory for the usual phonics skills like con-

FIGURE 8.7. A fourth-grade story passage and examiner's page from a commercial IRI.

THE CONESTOGA WAGON

People riding in wagon trains did not have our easy ways of traveling. Their trip was made in what was called a Conestoga Wagon. These were good wagons but they were not comfortable. The wagons were large. They had broad wooden seats. Sitting on these seats was a weary task. The bumping and churning of the ride could be compared to being on a ship in rough water. When this old wagon reached a river the wheels were removed. Then the wagon was made into a flat boat. These are but a few of the interesting facts about these old wagons.

FIGURE 8.7.
(continued)

FORM B, PART II — *Level 4* (101 words)   **W.P.M.**

6060

MOTIVATION: The Conestoga Wagon was a kind of covered wagon that people used long ago. I wonder how people who traveled in these wagons might have felt? Read the story to find out more about this wagon and how people traveled.

THE CONESTOGA WAGON

People riding in wagon trains did not have our easy ways of traveling. Their trip was made in what was called a Conestoga Wagon. These were good wagons, but they were not comfortable. The wagons were large. They had broad wooden seats. Sitting on these seats was a weary task. The bumping and churning of the ride could be compared to being on a ship in rough water. When this old wagon reached a river the wheels were removed. Then the wagon was made into a flat boat. These are but a few of the interesting facts about these old wagons.

COMPREHENSION CHECK

(F) 1. ___What made riding in a Conestoga Wagon unpleasant?
(Bumps, sitting on wooden seats, etc.)

(F) 2. ___According to the story, riding on a wagon was like what other type of ride?

(I) 3. ___What are some ways of travel found today?
(Airplane, car, train, etc.)

(F) 4. ___How did the people get the wagon across deep streams?
(Used the wagon as a flat boat by taking off the wheels)

(V) 5. ___What does the word "weary" mean?
(Tired, uncomfortable, etc.)

SCORING GUIDE: FOURTH

WR Errors		COMP Errors	
IND	2	IND	0–1
INST	5	INST	1½–2
FRUST	10	FRUST	2½+

SOURCE: From Nicholas J. Silvaroli, *Classroom Reading Inventory*, 3rd Ed. © 1969, 1973 Wm. C. Brown Company Publishers, Dubuque, Iowa. Reprinted by permission.

FIGURE 8.8. Sample items from the word comprehension and word attack subtests of the Woodcock Reading Mastery Test.

WORD COMPREHENSION SAMPLE ITEMS —
DO NOT RECORD ON THE RESPONSE FORM

Point to the first sample item and say: **Listen carefully and finish what I say** (point to each of the three words and the blank space, in turn, while reading the item).

A dog walks; a bird . . . (pause). (*flies*) If the subject gives an incorrect response or does not respond, read the item again, completing it with the correct word.

Continue with the remaining sample items in the same manner (point to each word as the item is read to the subject):

One is to two as three is to . . . (pause). (*four, six*)
He is to she as boy is to . . . (pause). (*girl*)
Grass is to green as snow is to . . . (pause). (*white*)

dog — walks	bird —
one — two	three —
he — she	boy —
grass — green	snow —

sonant and vowel sounds, blends, syllabication, and accents. The Botel is sometimes administered along with a commercial or teacher-made IRI to assess reading comprehension.

The Sipay test begins with a survey test that indicates which of the subsequent sixteen subtests should be administered. The survey portion serves as a pretest; adequate performance in any area means that the teacher can delete the corresponding subtest in further testing — a good feature since administering all sixteen subtests would be very time-consuming. Subtests are very specific, ranging from simple Letter Names to such discrete analysis skills as Vowel Combinations, Final Silent-*E* Generalization, Vowel Sounds of *Y*, and Visual Blending. It is hard to imagine a test that would partition word analysis into more molecular units. It does a thorough job of assessing a very narrow range of reading behaviors.

FIGURE 8.8.
(continued)

WORD ATTACK SAMPLE ITEM —
DO NOT RECORD ON RESPONSE FORM

Say: **I want you to pronounce some words that are not real words. I want you to tell me how they sound.** Point to "tat." **How does this word sound?**

Sample: **tat**

If the subject incorrectly responds to "tat," point to "tat" and say it clearly. Do not pronounce any other words during the Word Attack Test.

Proceed to the next page and begin the test. Continue testing until the subject has missed five or more consecutive words, or has responded to Item 50.

How do these words sound? Point to each word if necessary. If the subject fails to respond in a few seconds, encourage a response. If the subject still fails to respond, continue the test by pointing to the next word.

1. **ift**	2. **bim**	3. **ut**	4. **rayed**	5. **kak**
(ift)★	(bim)	(ət)	(rād)	(kak)
6. **maft**	7. **nen**	8. **ab**	9. **tash**	10. **wip's**
(maft)	(nen)	(ab)	(tash)	(wips)

★Pronunciation symbols used by permission of the publishers of the Merriam-Webster Dictionaries. See test manual for further explanation.

SOURCE: From Richard W. Woodcock, *Woodcock Reading Mastery Tests*, Form A, © 1973. Reprinted by permission of American Guidance Service, Inc.

Advantages. First, as with group survey tests, the most obvious advantage is economy of time. With a *group diagnostic test* like the Stanford, a large group can be tested in under two hours. Second, some teachers find the information generated by such a test more specific, and thus more helpful in planning instruction, than the results of a general survey test with its relatively undifferentiated subtests and global scores. Third, group diagnostic tests, like their survey counterparts, are easy to administer without special preparation and are usually easy to score.

An advantage of using a standardized individual diagnostic test lies not in saving time but in the opportunity to closely observe one student's reading. A second advantage is the detailed analysis of discrete skills that many of these tests allow. Also, an advantage of standardized IRIs over similar informal measures is that the teacher does not have to make up or find word lists, comprehension passages, or comprehension questions. As long as the passages and questions are interesting and of high quality, the teacher can save valuable time. Just because an IRI is commercially available, however, does not guarantee the quality of its components.

Disadvantages. Diagnostic reading tests, including those mentioned here, have several drawbacks of which the user should be aware. Some of these drawbacks are shared by many tests of this type; others are unique to one test or another.

First, a disadvantage of using multiple subtests is that they may represent a very limited sample of the desired behavior. They are usually kept very short in order to save time, but subtest length can critically affect reliability. Although there is no general rule of thumb, tests in which individual subtests have few responses should be suspect because they may sacrifice in-depth analysis of specific things for a quick glimpse at many things.

Second, tests that feature reading or listening comprehension passages like the standardized IRIs can be seriously flawed by poor passages and poor questions. The passages are usually written to conform to readability formulas, which make them sound stilted. Often they are bland, dull, and sometimes very short. It should be remembered that a student's comprehension will be radically affected by interest in what is read, and dull passages written poorly do little to promote anyone's reading comprehension.

Poor questions can also detract from a test. It seems hard to believe that questions sometimes call for information not available in the story, but it is occasionally true. The number of questions following a passage is another important variable. Ten questions of different types will make a fairly good sample, but ten questions all requiring literal recall will not, and asking only four or five questions is usually not enough to really test comprehension.

Third, tests that yield an overall reading level but do not assess comprehension are of dubious value. The heart of reading is comprehension, and a reading level that has not included comprehension, even indirectly, is not very useful. The Gilmore and Gray tests both ask comprehension questions, but the questions play no part in the resultant score. The Slosson Oral Reading Test does not even have the student read sentences, only lists of undefined words. The Word Opposites parts of the Botel test do include word meanings, but again the reader has no opportunity to read connected text. The reading assessed by these tests is actually a group of reading-like behaviors. Their diagnostic usefulness is limited to precisely what they test, which is *not* reading for meaning.

Fourth, some diagnostic tests have so many subtests that they artificially partition reading into numerous isolated acts. The Sipay Word Analysis is an example of a test with a very narrow focus that attempts to isolate molecular reading behaviors. Just how much can that be done without doing violence to reading as an integrated act? This question should be considered when tests are being evaluated because just as a test can be too general it can also be too specific and narrow in focus.

Achievement Tests

Reading achievement tests are somewhat difficult to characterize because they share certain characteristics with both survey and diagnostic tests. The ones most commonly used are actually batteries. A *battery* is a collection of tests in separate subject areas, administered separately but based on the same norm group. The results on various parts of a battery, like tests in math, science, and language arts, are easily comparable since all the parts are based on similar norms. It is misleading to try to compare scores on two completely different tests because each one has been standardized using different groups, and yet this error is made quite often. Achievement test batteries were developed specifically to meet the need for tests in different subject areas that shared the same norm group. Their format makes it easy to compare results of the different parts of the same battery.

The reading or language arts portions of these batteries may be broad and general, yielding global reading and language scores like a reading survey test. Or they may be as detailed and specific as a group diagnostic test. So it is not the type or number of subtests or scores that helps us differentiate an achievement test from other types but rather the testing purpose.

Achievement tests are designed to show the depth of one's knowledge and mastery of subject area curricula. Because they are designed to assess mastery, or achievement, they are usually administered *after* the appropriate instruction has been given. Tests used for diagnostic purposes are often given *before* a program of instruction, or early on, to reveal strengths and so that instruction can be modified appropriately. Diagnostic and survey tests are usually given "before the fact," achievement tests "after the fact." Their content is sometimes very similar, but the purpose and timing of the testing differ.

Standardized achievement tests are probably the most common type of formal tests used in schools except for the teacher-made ones that are used in individual classrooms. Most students take a standardized achievement test of some kind yearly, often a battery covering the major curricular areas. Because subtests are usually given in separate sittings completion of a battery can take several days or a week. Achievement tests must be given under strictly standard conditions in order for results to be compared across groups, so sometimes a team of school personnel administers all the tests, and sometimes the regular daily schedule is suspended so that all students can be tested simultaneously. They are machine-scored by the publishers and results are sent back to the school.

Almost all achievement tests are group tests and should be used to evaluate groups of students, not individuals. For this reason, they are of very lim-

FIGURE 8.9. Reading comprehension items from the reading subtest of the SRA Achievement battery.

Color serves a protective function for many animals. It makes some hard to see against their backgrounds. This helps to protect them from their predators — other animals that kill and eat them. Color also serves to protect some predators. It warns them that some animals they would like to eat can harm them.

5   Many insects are the color of leaves, twigs, or bark. When they rest quietly on a plant or tree, their predators have a hard time spotting them. For example, the underwing, a kind of moth, has gray-and-brown wings that blend with the color of bark.

The color of some animals changes to blend with their backgrounds. The arctic hare, a rabbit, is brown in summer. In winter its fur becomes white to match the snow on the

10   ground. The color of some animals changes more quickly. The mosquito fish, for example, becomes darker or lighter to match its background as it moves around.

Some investigators experimented to see if color really does protect animals from predators. They put mosquito fish in a tank with a white bottom. A few hours later all the fish were light-colored. The investigators then put half the fish in a tank with a black

15   bottom. They immediately freed penguins, seabirds that eat mosquito fish, near the two tanks. After several hours they counted the number of fish in each tank. Most of the fish in the black tank had been eaten. Most of the fish in the white tank were still alive. Thus the investigators found that color does protect mosquito fish. But color is not a foolproof source of protection.

20   Color serves as a warning to some predators. Some animals are poisonous, sting, give off a bad smell, or taste bad. Many of these animals are brightly colored. They are easily seen by predators.

Investigators experimented to see whether predators know instinctively which bright-colored animals to avoid or whether they learn only by experience. In their experiments

25   they used monarch butterflies and blue jays. Monarchs have bright orange-and-black wings and are believed to taste very bad. The investigators put a hungry young blue jay into a cage with the monarchs. The blue jay caught and ate just one. It did not chase any others.

ited diagnostic use. They are useful for evaluating the progress of large groups like whole schools, or all the students from one grade.

Publishers attempt to make the content of their achievement tests represent typical school curricula. A math test, for example, will generally be made up of problems and calculations common to most school math programs for a particular grade. What is "typical" is decided by consulting subject area experts, by studying textbooks and material in wide use, and by field-testing experimental test forms. Content validity, or how well a test represents the major aspects of the subject area, is of particular importance, but how closely the curriculum of an individual district, school, or classroom coincides with national trends is difficult to say. Achievement tests in any subject area should be carefully evaluated in light of how well their content matches the local programs and materials in use.

FIGURE 8.9.
(continued)

11. In line 7, <u>bark</u> means

    A. the sound a dog makes
    B. a loud and angry cry
    C. the outside of a tree trunk
    D. a kind of beetle

12. Where would you be LEAST likely to find animals like the arctic hare that change color in winter and summer?

    A. Canada
    B. Florida
    C. Alaska
    D. Colorado

13. In the test with mosquito fish, what did the investigators find when they counted the fish?

    A. All the fish in both tanks had been eaten by the penguins.
    B. About half the mosquito fish in each tank had been eaten.
    C. The penguins had eaten more fish from the black tank than from the white tank.
    D. Penguins don't like mosquito fish and so had eaten only a few.

14. What was the investigators' last step in the test with the mosquito fish and penguins?

    A. They counted the number of fish in each tank.
    B. They freed penguins near the tank.
    C. They placed mosquito fish in a white tank.
    D. They put half the mosquito fish in the black tank.

15. After they placed the mosquito fish in the white tank, the investigators waited before placing half of them in the black tank. Why did they do this?

    A. They wanted to make sure the penguins would be hungry.
    B. It took several hours for the mosquito fish to become light-colored.
    C. It took several hours for the mosquito fish to become dark-colored.
    D. They had to count the fish in the tank.

Most of the widely used achievement batteries measure reading, language (English), science, math, and social studies. Most have forms for every grade from early elementary through high school, although some school districts do not begin using them until third or fourth grade. Some batteries have reading readiness tests for kindergarten and first grade. Fig. 8.9 shows reading subtest items from an achievement battery. Among the typical wide-ranging achievement batteries are the following: the Metropolitan Achievement Test, with reading comprehension, language, social studies, science, and math subtests and a separate readiness test; the Comprehensive Test of Basic Skills, with readiness, reading, language, arithmetic, and study skills; the Stanford Achievement Test, with reading, spelling, language, math, science, social

FIGURE 8.10. Items from the Reading Recognition subtest of the PIAT.

(Point to "was" in the stimulus area.) **Find one like this — down here.**
(Point in a sweeping motion to the response area.) **Point to it.** (1)

was

was	mas
SAW	man

For subjects progressing to item 19 and beyond or starting at this level

(Say the following:) **Now we are going to do some reading aloud. This page has rows of words on it.** (Point, in a sweeping motion across each of the rows from the subject's left to right.) **Read each of the words aloud going across the rows this way.** (Point again across the rows from the subject's left to right.) **As you finish each row, go on to the next one. Start here** (Point to the first word to be attempted) **and read them to me.** (If necessary, elicit responses by pointing to each word in turn, and using such phrases as: What is this word?) **Give me a pronunciation you would expect to find in the dictionary.**

studies, and listening; and the California Achievement Test, with reading, spelling, language, math, and reference skills subtests. All those mentioned, except the Stanford, are designed for kindergarten through grade twelve; the Stanford is for grades one through nine.

There are a few achievement tests for individual administration. Two examples are the Peabody Individual Achievement Test (PIAT) and the Wide Range Achievement Test (WRAT). These instruments are hybrids that have characteristics of both group achievement tests and individual survey tests. They are most often used like individual survey or diagnostic tests.

The PIAT contains reading recognition, reading comprehension, spelling, math, and general information subtests. Because it includes math as well as various reading skills and general information, the PIAT measures mastery of the largest part of typical elementary curricula. The WRAT has reading, spelling, and arithmetic subtests. Like the PIAT, it covers the areas most heavily concentrated on in elementary school. Both tests are often given as diagnostic screening devices to students experiencing difficulty in either reading or math or those with generally poor school achievement. Like other achievement tests,

FIGURE 8.10. (continued)

19. **run**	20. **play**	21. **jump**
ˈrən	ˈplā	ˈjəmp

22. **kit·ten**	23. **wag·on**	24. **fishing**	25. **brook**
ˈkitən	ˈwagən, ˈwaig-	ˈfishiŋ, -ēŋ, ȯn, -ēn	ˈbrük, ˈbrük

26. **gloves**	27. **smile**	28. **colt**	29. **round**
ˈgləvz	ˈsmīl	ˈkōlt	ˈraund

NOTE: Accept the first scoreable response, unless the subject spontaneously corrects it. Ask the subject to repeat a word only if the response is not loud and clear enough to score. If the subject is hesitant about pronouncing the words, encourage responses by such phrases as: Try it. Say it as best you can, etc. (See Part I of the manual for further instructions.)

Items 19 to 29   Plate 16

run	play	jump

kitten	wagon	fishing	brook

gloves	smile	colt	round

SOURCE: From Lloyd M. Dunn and Frederick C. Markwardt, Jr., *Peabody Individual Reading Achievement Test,* © 1970. Reprinted by permission of American Guidance Service, Inc.

the results they yield are solely quantitative, and they have little, if any, diagnostic value.

The PIAT, for kindergarten through twelfth grade, has two reading sections. Reading Recognition includes letter and single word identification; word recognition is on an untimed basis. Fig. 8.10 shows items from this subtest. The comprehension subtest requires reading of one or several sentences and then matching a picture to the text. Pictures are in a multiple-choice format, and written sentences cannot be referred to by the student. At the upper levels the comprehension sentences are extremely complex and words are highly unusual. The picture selection process is unlike any other reading comprehension test but is similar to the format of the Peabody Picture Vocabulary Test.

The WRAT, often used in screening students for special education programs, is designed for ages five years old through adulthood. The reading subtest deserves special attention. Like the Slosson Oral Reading Test, the reading portion of the WRAT is made up entirely of lists of single words. Pronunciation within ten seconds is the only criterion. It does not measure comprehension of either text or words, and no reading of connected text is included. Consequently, it does not measure real reading at all. If the test makers do not include comprehension in their view of reading, they should at least acknowledge what the test does *not* do. Far from doing that, the manual states that the test allows for accurate diagnosis of reading disabilities and placement of students in instructional groups, all without reading of words in sentences! We believe that these claims and the content validity of the reading subtest are doubtful.

Advantages.   First, like other group tests, group achievement measures offer schools a reliable, uncomplicated way to gather information on large numbers of students.

Second, a maximum of data can be gathered in a minimum of time. If the batteries include a number of subjects, many curricular areas and processes can be assessed at one time.

Third, if properly administered and scored, they yield potentially informative data on the progress of groups of students, such as the total population of a given grade. When patterns of progress or lack of progress are discerned, curricular changes at the school and district levels can take place.

Fourth, these tests are usually extensively field-tested and standardized with great precision. Norming and validating achievement batteries is a big and complex business, and since millions are taken yearly, test manufacturers try to make them as reliable and valid as they can.

Disadvantages.   Standardized reading achievement tests are not designed to give diagnostic data, so they cannot be criticized for not doing so, but if used for their proper purposes, they can be effective measures of prior learning. There are some cautions, however, that should be kept in mind.

First, administration procedures must be followed to the letter. Students should take these tests in their regular classrooms rather than in huge groups in the cafeteria or gym, as sometimes happens.

Second, as with diagnostic reading tests, subtests are sometimes quite short, and their reliability coefficients may be low because of this and other factors.

Third, the time and cost involved sometimes contribute to gross overinterpretation of their scores. Retention of students because of scores on a single achievement battery or public humiliation of school groups and personnel because of score comparisons are clear abuses of test scores, and yet such abuses are not uncommon.

Fourth, achievement tests tend to call upon recall of factual material more than other higher-level thinking skills (Bertrand and Cebula, 1980). Factual learning and recall are among the easiest processes to measure, but they do not represent all learning or achievement. We must not lose sight of the many additional aspects in reading and other subject areas, such as learning rate, interest, or creative thinking, which achievement tests do not measure.

Criterion-Referenced Tests

During the 1960s and 1970s a new approach to test construction was developed: *criterion-referenced* evaluation. As educators began to give more thought to the need for individualized instruction, criterion-referenced tests gained in popularity. They enabled teachers to compare a student's performance to a predetermined goal or outcome, while norm-referenced tests, on the other hand, aid in comparing one student's performance to someone else's. Since criterion-referenced tests provided a way of determining whether a student had met instructional goals, or *criteria*, they quickly became the major kind of measurement device for many different kinds of individualized programs.

Characteristics

In individualized reading programs each student works toward mastery of skills that he or she has not yet learned. Pretests are most often used to determine which skills need improvement. In theory, every student in a classroom might be working on mastering a different skill at any given time. In practice, few teachers can effectively manage such a program, and students are temporarily grouped with others who need work on the same skill or process. Even though the instruction usually takes place in groups, these programs are called individualized because each student works on those particular skills in which he or she is thought to be deficient.

This instructional model requires a measurement method that helps the teacher determine not how students compare to one another but how each student's performance compares with the goals of the program. Individual differences among students are less important than whether or not an individual student can meet the stated criterion (Sax, 1980; Thorndike and Hagen, 1977).

When criterion-referenced tests are used, the instructional outcomes to be aimed for are always determined and defined before instruction takes place. Therefore, instruction is deliberately aimed toward "teaching to the test," which is not a criticism in this case. When goals and outcomes are predetermined, instruction must be directed toward achieving those particular goals.

In reading and language arts, where criterion-referenced tests and individualized programs have gained great popularity, the result has been that the skills tested came to define the reading program. Reading instruction in many cases became little more than a cut-and-dried sequence of skills to be mastered, with the major goal that of passing the mastery tests. We believe, with many others, that reading is more than a set of mastered skills and that mastering sequenced skills does not guarantee that the student will read effectively or enthusiastically.

Specially designed programs for the teaching, mastery, and testing of specific skills, often referred to as *skills management systems*, usually rely on criterion-referenced tests for their evaluation component. Developed to make the teaching of reading skills systematic and sequential, these systems have become popular adjuncts to basal reading programs in recent years. They have found a particularly enthusiastic market in compensatory and remedial programs, where it has been thought that students would benefit from "extra doses" of skills instruction. The Wisconsin Design for Reading Skill Development, the Fountain Valley System, and the Read System are typical management systems.

Whether commercial or locally developed, a management system usually features specific skill objectives arranged in some sequence, materials and activities coded to the objectives, criterion-referenced pretests and posttests, record-keeping procedures and materials, and suggestions for teaching and practicing the skills (Cheek and Cheek, 1980). By systematic use of the pre- and posttests and careful record keeping, these programs claim that it is possible for the teacher to determine quickly and precisely what skills have been mastered by any individual student at any given time. The availability of this precise information on each student has done much to satisfy public demands for increased teacher accountability. Some educators, however, remain unconvinced that reading can or should be partitioned in this manner, or that better readers emerge from this type of reading instruction.

For a criterion-referenced test to achieve its purpose, each item must define the task, skill, or process to be demonstrated. These definitions, called *objectives*, must clearly state what is to be demonstrated, under what conditions, and at what level of quality or accuracy. These three characteristics of good objectives are referred to as the *performance, condition*, and *criterion* aspects (Bertrand and Cebula, 1980; Mager, 1962). The performance is the statement of what the student must do; the conditions are the ways in which the student will participate in the learning process and any special conditions under which the task is to be performed; and the criterion is the statement of the level of performance quality required.

As with any other kind of test, criterion-referenced test items should represent essential skills or knowledge. Do they adequately and fairly sample the whole domain of possible items? This is a basic question of content validity, which is a crucial aspect of these tests as well as other types. Figure 8.11 shows the list of skills making up the reading subtest of a criterion-referenced

FIGURE 8.11. List of skills making up the reading subtest of a criterion-referenced test battery.

TEST TITLE	II. READING	PAGE #
A. WORD RECOGNITION		
A-1	Word Recognition Grade Level	25
A-2	Basic Sight Vocabulary	26–29
A-3	Direction Words	30
A-4	Abbreviations	31
A-5	Contractions	32
A-6	Common Signs	33–34
B. READING		
B-1	Oral Reading Level	35–41
B-2	Reading Comprehension Level	35–41
B-3	Oral Reading Rate	42
C. WORD ANALYSIS		
C-1	Auditory Discrimination	43
C-2	Initial Consonant Sounds Auditorily	44
C-3	Initial Consonant Sounds Visually	45–46
C-4	Substitution of Initial Consonant Sounds	47–50
C-5	Ending Sounds Auditorily	51
C-6	Vowels	52
C-7	Short Vowel Sounds	53
C-8	Long Vowel Sounds	54
C-9	Initial Clusters Auditorily	55
C-10	Initial Clusters Visually	56–57
C-11	Substitution of Initial Cluster Sounds	58–61
C-12	Digraphs and Diphthongs	62
C-13	Phonetic Irregularities	63
C-14	Common Endings of Rhyming Words	64–66
C-15	Suffixes	67
C-16	Prefixes	68
C-17	Meaning of Prefixes	69
C-18	Number of Syllables Auditorily	70
C-19	Syllabication Concepts	71–72
D. VOCABULARY		
D-1	Context Clues	73
D-2	Classification	74–75
D-3	Analogies	76–77
D-4	Antonyms	78–79
D-5	Homonyms	80

SOURCE: From Albert H. Brigance, BRIGANCE® Diagnostic Inventory of Basic Skills, 2nd ed., © 1976, 1977 Curriculum Associates, Inc. Reproduced by permission of the publisher, Curriculum Associates, Inc.

test battery. Figure 8.12 shows how one-word analysis skill is to be tested, with objective statements describing the performance, condition, and criterion.

Developing an adequate sample of the behavior desired sounds easy enough, but in reading it is very difficult because no agreement exists about what specific skills, attitudes, and/or information are essential. This situation is not surprising when we consider the fact that reading experts are still not in complete agreement on whether or not comprehension is necessary for reading!

It is easier to develop a multitude of goals than to determine what is important. Like other tests, criterion-referenced tests frequently include tasks that are easily measured but not very closely related to reading. Stauffer, Abrams, and Pikulski (1978) give the example of an objective measuring the student's ability to put stress on the proper syllable in three-syllable words. The test item required the student to choose, from three alternatives, the word *incorrectly* accented. Locating an incorrectly placed accent mark is not much like being able to correctly apply stress when pronouncing a word. Saying the word correctly, or putting in an accent mark correctly, would have been much more productive. Either would have been a better way of assessing mastery of the skill.

Criterion-referenced tests usually have items arranged in some sort of learning sequence or hierarchy. Many reading programs that feature criterion-referenced tests are built on the assumptions that there is a set *number* of required skills and that these skills must be mastered in a particular *order*. Although there is no evidence from research to support either assumption, these tests imply that the assumptions are valid.

What is important is not *which* hierarchy is accepted as absolute truth but how closely the sequence of reading skills on the test matches what was taught. In commercial programs that supply their own criterion-referenced tests, this consistency is built in, but in some schools, tests are purchased separately from programs, or test packages are bought but instructional goals locally developed. In these cases the tests may set forth a required skills sequence that does not match the way the students were taught. If a commercial test locks students and teachers into a particular sequence of skills, instructional programs must be made to dovetail with it or else students may appear to have learned less than they really have. Of course, tests should be tailored to meet instructional procedures, not the reverse. They are a means to the end: better instruction. They are not an end in themselves.

Gronlund (1978) suggests certain criteria that we have adapted for judging the adequacy of objectives for a commercial criterion-referenced test package:

1. Do these objectives call for learning outcomes that are appropriate to the subject area? What are the most important outcomes to be desired? Are they included?

FIGURE 8.12. A criterion-referenced test item assessing one word analysis skill.

SKILL: Can give correct ending letter or letters when word is given orally.

DIRECTIONS:

Say: *I'm going to say some words. I want you to listen carefully and tell me the last letter you hear in the word.*

Use *one* word listed after each letter below. Say the word and pause for the student to respond. If the student responds incorrectly,

Say: *No, I want you to give me the letter you hear at the end of the word.*

Say:

t-*fat, let*	k-*back, sack*
n-*ten, men*	m-*harm, jam*
b-*tub, dab, cab*	p-*stop, top*
d-*sad, lad, bed*	l-*fall, tall, call*
r-*far, tar, car*	g-*log, leg*
s-*bus, fuss, us*	x-*ox, ax, tax*

At this point in the testing,

Say: *Now I want you to tell me the last two letters you hear at the end of the word.*

Continue by using *one* word listed after each of the two letters listed below.

Say:

st-*west, best, must*	nt-*sent, bent, went*
ng-*song, bang, wrong*	ld-*bold, mold, gold*
ch-*church, match, hatch*	sh-*dish, wish, fish*
ck-*kick, wick, chick*	lt-*belt, wilt, melt*
nk-*sink, sank, wink*	mp-*lump, stump, stamp*
nd-*bend, send, wind*	th-*fifth, sixth, fourth*

DISCONTINUE: After 3 consecutive errors.

TIME: Your discretion.

ACCURACY: Give credit for each correct response.

OBJECTIVE: When the examiner pronounces words with final consonants, the student will demonstrate his or her ability to recognize final consonant sounds auditorily by naming the correct final consonant(s) for _____ (quantity) for a total of 24 different consonant combinations.

SOURCE: From Albert H. Brigance, BRIGANCE® Diagnostic Inventory of Basic Skills, 2nd ed., © 1976, 1977 Curriculum Associates, Inc. Reproduced by permission of the publisher, Curriculum Associates, Inc.

2. Do these objectives represent a balance of thinking and learning skills? Is factual knowledge overrepresented, with higher cognitive and affective thinking shortchanged?
3. Are these outcomes attainable by our students? What modifications should be made to fit our students' needs and our teaching facilities?
4. Do these objectives fit the philosophy of our school(s) and teachers? Is it reasonable to expect that our teachers and students can achieve these ends?

Advantages. One of the most important assets of criterion-referenced tests is their diagnostic potential. They can indicate with great clarity and precision what a student can or cannot yet do and thus appropriate instructional modifications can be made, which is the major goal of any diagnostic procedure. They have much greater diagnostic power than norm-referenced tests because they yield information related to specific goals rather than information in numerical or quantitative terms.

Second, it is possible for parents and students to see how test scores are related to instructional methods and materials, whereas ordinarily it is difficult for them to see any relationship. This advantage can help to eliminate a misunderstanding between home and school.

Third, criterion-referenced tests make it very clear to the public what goals the school has developed and how these goals are to be attained. There is therefore greater public confidence in the accountability of schools.

Fourth, they can be made to conform to local standards, teaching conditions, and practices and thus more accurately reflect the actual abilities and achievement of local students than standardized norm-referenced tests.

Fifth, they tend to minimize damaging competition among students, since a student's achievement is not measured in terms of someone else's achievement but rather in terms of a preset criterion. Both parents and students can then concentrate on the goals to be attained rather than on invidious comparisons among individuals or groups.

Sixth, they are particularly useful for evaluating the effectiveness of a program innovation or a completely new program. Standardized tests, which measure broad, widely accepted trends within a subject area, rarely show whether or not a new or modified program is effective.

Disadvantages. Like any other form of test, criterion-referenced tests must be approached with some cautions. First, they may be top-heavy with objectives that are easiest to measure, such as factual material. The higher-order learning processes, like evaluation and application of knowledge to novel situations, are naturally harder to assess, and they may be underrepresented in the objectives.

Second, the necessity of being clear and precise may encourage partitioning of reading acts into many molecular units. Excessive partitioning leads to a proliferation of objectives, and reading as an integrated process can get lost. Criterion-referenced tests tend to encourage teachers to think of reading as a conglomerate of hundreds of discrete skills instead of a complex thinking and language process.

Look again at Figure 8.11, which shows the skills tested in the reading subtest of that particular battery. Thirty-three discrete skills are assessed, including nineteen word analysis skills, each assessed in isolation.

Third, since criteria of quality or accuracy are always arbitrary, they should be considered carefully. There is nothing magical about 80, 90, or 100 percent accuracy. If skills are truly hierarchical, as with some math skills, then 100 percent accuracy may be necessary before the student goes on to more difficult skills. If there is no particular sequence of skills in one area, or no generally agreed-upon progression, then all quality criteria are arbitrary and one may be just as good as another. Teachers using any test with criteria for mastery predetermined should decide for themselves if the criteria seem unnecessarily rigid. In Figure 8.12, the objective does not state the minimum number students must get correct. Purchasers of this test battery determine their own criteria.

Fourth, we must remember that we don't want students to demonstrate mastery only on a one-time basis. We want them to retain what they have learned and be able to apply it to new situations. Important objectives should be tested more than once and mastery should be shown in more than one way.

Perhaps the biggest drawback in criterion-referenced tests is the point made earlier: that objectives to be tested have a way of becoming the reading curriculum itself. Some educators maintain that programs that emphasize testing of discrete skills encourage teaching the skills in the same manner. It is difficult, if not impossible, to isolate skills in actual reading because meaningful reading requires the use of many skills and processes simultaneously, and partitioning overlooks this important factor.

Sources of Test Information

Information on a commercial test or battery can be obtained from a number of sources such as measurement yearbooks, test publishers' catalogs and technical reports, bulletins, and journals.

Yearbooks and Indexes

These sources are compendia of information and reviews of all current published tests. They can be found in libraries, although many school divisions have a set of their own.

Measurement Yearbooks. The most valuable source, and the first place many teachers turn to with questions about tests, is the series of *Mental Measurement Yearbooks* (*MMY*) edited by the late Oscar K. Buros. Buros produced the first volume in 1938; the *Eighth Mental Measurement Yearbook* was issued in 1978. They are revised about every six years.

Each *MMY* lists tests that have appeared or been revised since publication of the previous volume. Age and grade levels, time needed for administration, subtests included, publishers and costs are listed for each test. This information is helpful when initially screening a number of tests, and it makes ordering sample sets easy. Most important, these yearbooks contain extensive reviews of many tests written by qualified experts in the field; synopses of reviews appearing in journals and other sources; lists of pertinent books and monographs; and the names of people and journals that review tests.

Measurement Indexes. The *MMY*s are not cumulative; a test reviewed in a previous *MMY* may not appear in subsequent volumes. To aid in locating reviews and pertinent information without having to go through each *MMY*, Buros developed *Tests in Print I* (1961) and *Tests in Print II* (1974). These volumes are very helpful as indexes to those previously published.

Buros also edited nine monographs, each containing test information and reviews on a single topic: English, foreign languages, math, science, social studies, reading, intelligence, personality, and vocational tests. *Reading Tests and Reviews I* (1968) contains all the reviews of reading tests found in the earlier yearbooks. *Reading Tests and Reviews II* (1975) contains more current reviews.

Additional Sources

There are several other places where you can get critical information about tests, after you have checked the *MMY*s and indexes.

Test Publishers' Catalogs. Publishers of commercial tests usually provide informative catalogs and technical manuals without charge to educators. They can provide a wealth of very current information to add to what Buros's reference books provide. The catalogs usually provide descriptions of the tests, subtests included, time limitations, normative information, types of scores yielded, scoring services, costs, and related specific information. Because catalogs are sales devices, they tend to present the tests in the most positive light, so the publisher's claims should be compared with the critical reviews in the *MMY*s and current journals.

The eighth *MMY* lists names and addresses of all test publishers as of 1978. The Educational Testing Services (ETS) (Rosedale Road, Princeton, N.J. 08540) publishes the *Test Collection Bulletin*, a quarterly publication listing the most current addresses and services of test publishers.

Technical manuals often accompany specimen sets of tests, which usually must be purchased from the publisher. They provide detailed information about the populations used in standardizing the tests, reliability and validity estimates for individual subtests and the entire test, and other statistical data that are very useful for evaluation purposes.

Bulletins. Free or inexpensive bulletins about tests, publishers, and measurement issues are available from a number of sources. ETS publishes the nominally priced *Tests and Measurement Kit,* which includes guides for developing teacher-made tests and selecting commercial ones. ETS also publishes *TM News* and *TM Reports,* bulletins reporting on measurement trends and issues and summarizing papers presented at national meetings of the American Educational Research Association (AERA). *TM Reports* also includes bibliographies on a wide variety of testing topics, which are extremely helpful to those interested in extended readings. In addition to the above bulletins, ETS issues *A Directory of Information on Tests,* which will help in locating other information sources.

The National Council on Measurement in Education (NCME) (1230 17th St. N.W., Washington, D.C. 20036) publishes quarterly reports (*Journal of Educational Measurement, Measurement in Education* and *Measurement News*) on a wide variety of topics such as performance contracting, criterion-referenced testing, grading practices, reporting of test scores to parents, and interpreting of national norms.

The Psychological Corporation (757 Third Ave., New York, N.Y. 10017) publishes a number of free or inexpensive bulletins on topics like aptitude testing, test score accuracy, interpretation of reliability coefficients, the costs of tests, and the development of local norms. The Psychological Corporation also provides free single copies of their *Test Service Notebooks,* including reports on such topics as secondary school testing and what parents must know about testing and test selection, as well as their *Focus on Evaluation* monographs, which cover topics like mandated assessment and the political use of test results.

The American Psychological Association, Inc. (APA) (1200 17th St. N.W., Washington, D.C. 20036) publishes a valuable bulletin entitled *Standards for Educational and Psychological Tests* (1974) to guide test developers and test users. It contains information on the proper development and reporting of tests, results and research findings, and the use and interpretation of tests.

Journals. Published several times yearly, professional journals often contain the most current information. Many routinely review new or revised tests in many areas as well as reporting research findings related to testing. In the area of measurement and evaluation are such journals as the *American Psychologist, Journal of Educational Measurement, American Educational Research Jour-*

nal, Psychological Bulletin, and *Applied Psychological Measurement.* Reading journals such as *Language Arts, The Reading Teacher, Journal of Reading,* and *Reading Research Quarterly* often include test reviews and critical articles.

Summary

Formal measures of reading ability are of two types: *norm-referenced* and *criterion-referenced.* Norm-referenced tests are used to compare an individual's performance with that of others. They include *survey, diagnostic,* and *achievement tests.* Survey tests are general reading tests with few subtests and are most often used to screen large numbers of students. Diagnostic reading tests have a number of subtests, each stressing a particular skill area, and are usually given to diagnose specific strengths and weaknesses. Achievement tests may be either general or specific; they are intended not to provide diagnostic information but to assess overall effectiveness of instruction in broad curricular areas.

Criterion-referenced tests assess a student's mastery of a predetermined criterion or goal. They do not compare students to one another but to a stated objective. They provide specific diagnostic information on the mastery of instructional objectives.

The basic test characteristics that teachers should be familiar with are *reliability* and *validity.* Reliability refers to the consistency of scores a test yields. Aspects of reliability are *stability,* or consistency across repeated administrations; *internal consistency,* or consistency among test items; and *equivalence,* or consistency across alternate test forms. Validity refers to how well a test measures what it was intended to measure. *Content validity* is the quality of adequately sampling the subject area or process being assessed. *Construct validity* refers to how well the test measures traits, or constructs, that are not directly observable but must be inferred from observable behavior. Intelligence is an example of a construct. *Criterion-related validity* is made up of *concurrent validity,* or how closely a test is related to another test of established validity, and *predictive validity,* the degree to which test performance is related to some other established criterion, such as grades in college or job success.

Commonly used descriptive statistics include *distributions, indices of central tendency and dispersion,* and forms of *standard scores.* A distribution is an array of scores from highest to lowest. Many standardized tests assume a *normal distribution,* a symmetrical array with most scores falling near the mean and progressively fewer scores at the extreme high and low ends. Asymmetrical distributions are referred to as *skewed.* Indices of central tendency in distributions include the *mean,* an arithmetic average, and the *median,* the point in a distribution at which there are equal numbers of higher and lower scores. Indices of dispersion in a distribution describe how far apart scores are from one another. They include the *range*, or the span from highest to lowest score, and the *standard deviation*, which shows how far from the mean each score is in standard or equal increments.

Standardized reading tests usually yield several forms of test scores. *Grade scores* are two-part numbers that indicate achievement such as we might expect at a given grade level and a number of months within that grade. These scores are meant to represent the performance of an average student in the grade and month indicated. *Percentiles* are standard scores that show what percentage of the norm population scored higher or lower than the individual tested. *Stanines* are scores in which the distribution has been divided into nine parts; a stanine score indicates which ninth a score fell in. *T scores* and *z scores* use the concepts of mean and standard deviation to show where a score lies in relation to the mean of a normal distribution.

Extension Activities

1. Find out the name of a standardized reading test used in your school (or use one mentioned in this chapter). Look up the test in *Reading Tests and Reviews* (look first in Volume II). Read the reviews and the information listed there. Does the test sound like one you would want to use? Why or why not?

2. Find a review or description of a standardized reading test or battery in a recent issue of a professional journal. Do you understand the information given on the test itself and statements of a critical nature? If you are unsure of what some of the information means, what sources could you use to help you make sense of it?

3. Compare a teacher-made and a commercial informal reading inventory. Look critically at the reading passages, comprehension questions, and illustrations, if any. List the strengths and weaknesses in the content of each test.

4. Imagine that your local newspaper published reading achievement scores, showing grade-equivalent averages for the grades tested in each school. Say, for example, the fourth grades in each school attained the following averaged scores:

   School A: 4–8
   School B: 4–3
   School C: 2–9

   What data would you need to interpret these scores and the differences among them?

5. If you had access only to norm-referenced test scores for a class but you had to make criterion-referenced interpretations of the scores, what problems would you encounter?

Suggested Readings

Bertrand, Arthur and Cebula, Joseph P. **Tests, Measurement and Evaluation: A Developmental Approach.** *Reading, Mass.: Addison-Wesley, 1980.* One of the most readable texts available on test and measurement concepts and devices.

Farr, Roger. **Reading: What Can Be Measured?** *Newark, Del.: International Reading Association, 1969.* Concise summary of research on measurement of reading abilities and achievement.

Nunnally, Jim C. **Introduction to Statistics for Psychology and Education.** *New York: McGraw-Hill, 1975.* Comprehensive text on measurement concepts, descriptive statistics and interpretation of test data.

Sanders, Norris M. **Classroom Questions: What Kinds?** *New York: Harper & Row, 1966.* Classic volume on teachers' questioning strategies and how questions affect what is understood and remembered, critical aspects of reading comprehension assessment.

Schreiner, Robert. **Reading Tests and Teachers: A Practical Guide.** *Newark, Del.: International Reading Association, 1979.* Informative description of current reading tests and their use.

References

Bertrand, Arthur and Cebula, Joseph. *Tests, Measurement, and Evaluation.* Reading, Mass.: Addison-Wesley, 1980.

Buros, Oscar K., ed. *Eighth Mental Measurement Yearbook.* Highland Park, N.J.: Gryphon Press, 1978. (Previous editions: 1972, 1965, 1959, 1953, 1949, 1940, 1938)

Buros, Oscar K., ed. *Reading Tests and Reviews II.* Highland Park, N.J.: Gryphon Press, 1975. (Previous edition: 1968)

Buros, Oscar K., ed. *Tests in Print II.* Highland Park, N.J.: Gryphon Press, 1974. (Previous edition: 1961)

Cheek, Martha and Cheek, Earl. *Diagnostic-Prescriptive Reading Instruction.* Dubuque, Iowa: William C. Brown, 1980.

Fry, Edward. "The Orangoutang Score." *The Reading Teacher* 4, no. 4 (Jan. 1971): 360–361.

Gronlund, Norman E. *Measurement and Evaluation in Teaching,* 3rd ed. N.Y.: Macmillan, 1976.

Gronlund, Norman E. *Stating Objectives for Classroom Instruction,* 2nd ed. N.Y.: Macmillan, 1978.

Mager, Robert. *Preparing Instructional Objectives.* Palo Alto, Cal.: Fearon, 1962.

Mehrens, William A. & Lehmann, Irving J. *Measurement and Evaluation in Education and Psychology,* 2nd ed. N.Y.: Holt, Rinehart & Winston, 1978.

Nunnally, Jim. *Educational Measurement and Evaluation,* 2nd ed. N.Y.: McGraw-Hill, 1972.

Sax, Gilbert. *Principles of Educational and Psychological Measurement and Evaluation,* 2nd ed. Belmont, Cal.: Wadsworth, 1980.

Stauffer, Russell G.; Abrams, Jules; and Pikulski, John. *Diagnosis, Correction and Prevention of Reading Disabilities.* N.Y.: Harper & Row, 1978.

Thorndike, Robert L. & Hagen, Elizabeth P. *Measurement and Evaluation in Psychology and Education,* 4th ed. N.Y.: Wiley, 1977.

Chapter Nine

Assessing Reading-Related Factors

In this chapter we discuss intellectual, physical, and emotional factors, topics often thought to be secondary or contributing causes of reading problems.

It is true that these topics are peripheral to reading, but actually it is for this reason that they deserve careful attention. Most classroom teachers are more or less accustomed to testing reading skills within their classrooms. The testing of intelligence, vision and hearing, emotional and personality development, and special learning problems, however, is usually done outside the regular classroom by the school nurse, school psychologist, counselor, and other specialists. As a result, many teachers feel personally uninvolved in the assessment of these factors and often do not know much about how they affect reading.

In the past, children with special intellectual, physical, or emotional needs were largely excluded from the regular curriculum, and many teachers in areas other than special education have felt they had little need for such information. Now, however, no educator can remain unaware of the important changes education has undergone regarding children with special needs. New laws and growing public awareness have led to changes in educational policy toward all "special" children. By far the most important piece of legislation is Public Law 94–142, enacted in 1975. PL 94–142, the Education for All Handicapped Children Act, affects not only special educators but also every teacher at every level.

PL 94–142 has four major provisions, which will be detailed in the next section. In essence, the law requires that all handicapped students be provided with appropriate special education and related services. Since the team evaluating each handicapped student must include a regular classroom teacher or equivalent generalist (Wallace and Larsen, 1978), regular classroom teachers have to be familiar with the special education issues and procedures.

Special-Needs Students and PL 94–142

PL 94–142 is often referred to as the "mainstreaming law," but that term refers to only one of its provisions. In reality, it mandates a number of far-reaching changes in the education of students with special needs. Below we have listed the law's major provisions, the immediate implications of each provision for the classroom teacher, and a summary of the basic rights of handicapped students under the law.

Provision: Free public education will be provided for all handicapped persons between the ages of three and twenty-one years of age.

Implications: Schools must serve the needs of students both older and younger than those served in the past. The traditional concept of "school-age children" between five and eighteen has been drastically modified. Since the law provides for grants that create financial incentives for schools to identify handicapped preschoolers and provide special services for them, kindergarten and primary grade teachers are involved in early identification programs.

At the other end of the age scale, teachers in all grades are affected by the mainstreaming of handicapped older students into regular classes (see below). This is particularly important in high schools where pupils up to the age of twenty-one may be included in regular classes. Teachers must be aware of the special needs and interests of handicapped older students and young adults who are placed in classes with younger pupils.

Provision: Handicapped students will be placed in the least restrictive environment whenever and wherever possible. This often means mainstreaming handicapped children into the regular classroom and curriculum.

Implications: The inclusion of handicapped students in regular classrooms for part or all of the school day affects nearly every teacher. All teachers must clearly understand how the handicaps of students affect their learning, how materials and activities must be adapted appropriately, how their performances are to be evaluated, and how to deal positively with their social and interpersonal problems. In addition, regular classroom teachers have to be routinely involved in the assessment of these students' special needs.

Provision: Each handicapped student will be provided with an individualized educational program, called an IEP, which spells out present abilities, short- and long-term goals, and the means by which goals will be achieved. Each student's IEP will be developed jointly by teachers, parents, and the student where possible.

Implications: All teachers working with mainstreamed students have direct responsibility for the planning, implementing, and evaluating of instructional programs. They must expand their understanding of handicapping conditions, management techniques, teaching strategies, and materials (Rupley and Blair, 1979b) in order to develop and use IEPs. Assignment of grades, promotion, and awarding of diplomas are some issues directly tied to the fulfillment of IEP goals. In developing IEPs, teachers have to join forces with the parents of handicapped students for greater parental involvement and teacher accountability. In many cases the students can be included in the development of their IEPs, to the extent that they are able to participate.

Provision: All tests and evaluative instruments used will be prepared and administered so as to eliminate racial and cultural discrimination.

Implications: Tests and assessment devices have to be closely scrutinized to eliminate discriminatory aspects. Some intelligence tests, for example, appear to place some ethnic minority students at a disadvantage because they call upon a background of experience limited to higher socioeconomic groups. Results from such tests have sometimes been used in the past to erroneously classify minority children as mentally retarded.

Results of a single test or measure cannot be used to classify students, a practice that has sometimes been followed in the past. In addition, tests must be modified when necessary so that handicapped students can respond to them in ways that are best for them, for example in Braille or in a sign language. They must be administered in the student's native language, which may include sign languages or in cued speech for hearing-impaired students. These modifications entail widespread changes both in test construction and in the ways tests are administered and interpreted.

The provisions of PL 94–142 also establish certain basic rights for handicapped students:

1. The right to due process, which protects the individual from erroneous classification, capricious labeling, and denial of equal education;
2. Protection against discriminatory testing in diagnosis, which ensures against possible bias in intelligence tests (and other tests) used with ethnic minority children;
3. Placement in an educational setting that is the least restrictive environment, which protects the individual from possible detrimental effects of segregated education for the handicapped;
4. Individual program plans, which ensure accountability by those responsible for the education of the handicapped. (MacMillan, 1977, p.1)

Individual school divisions differ in minor ways in the procedures they follow regarding referral and classification, but a sequence of events such as this is typical:

1. A teacher who suspects that a student needs special services requests special screening for the student by notifying the school principal.

2. The principal obtains parental permission for such screening and arranges for testing by a team that usually includes a school psychologist and a special educator. The team must also include at least one teacher or specialist with expertise in the area of the suspected disability. Since reading problems are often involved with many different handicaps, a reading teacher is frequently a member of such an evaluation team.

3. The principal or other administrator involved arranges a meeting to discuss the screening results with the parents, the evaluation team, the student's teachers(s), and the special education specialists. Other educators who have tested and/or taught the student, such as clinicians from a university reading center, are often included.

4. At this meeting, all relevant assessment and instructional data are detailed. The teachers should present the results of informal diagnostic procedures such as IRIs, miscue analysis, diagnostic DRTAs, word sorts, cloze procedures, and prereading assessment procedures. These informal measures are very useful in developing a picture of the student's abilities and needs, and they provide a valuable supplement to the formal tests given by the other members of the evaluation team. The information they yield is essential in

preparing the IEP and will ensure that it is truly based on the student's individual strengths and needs in reading.

After all data have been discussed, the team members individually indicate whether special education placement is warranted. Parental consent *must* be given for such placement.

5. If placement is agreed upon, an IEP is developed for the student. It must include a statement of the student's present levels of functioning, both short-term and annual goals, projected dates for initiation and duration of special services, specific criteria and evaluation procedures to be used to determine if goals have been achieved, the names of persons responsible for special services and evaluation, descriptions of special services to be provided, and the extent to which the student will participate in regular education programs. Parental approval must again be given for the IEP to be implemented; if they do not approve it, or do not approve any subsequent changes in it, an impartial due process hearing must be held. Special services cannot be provided until after the IEP is developed and approved.

6. The next step is to place the student in the least restrictive educational environment where special services are provided and implementation of the IEP proceeds. Every educator (or agency) involved is required to make good faith efforts to help the student achieve the goals set forth in the IEP. Parents can request program review and revision if they believe such good faith efforts have not been made, but if in spite of such efforts the student does not achieve the goals of the IEP, no individual is to be held accountable.

The Education for All Handicapped Children Act requires massive changes in attitudes and procedures for dealing with children who have special educational needs. A reading problem may be a symptom of an educational handicap, such as a learning disability, or may result from a handicap such as visual or auditory impairment. Reading teachers must expand their traditional knowledge base about the physical, intellectual, and emotional difficulties involved in order to effectively teach all students. This requirement cannot be overemphasized.

In the following sections we introduce some of the more common terms and their implications, outline the appropriate informal classroom assessment or observation techniques, and discuss the more common intellectual, physical, and emotional factors often involved in reading difficulties.

Intellectual Factors

Intelligence Tests

In diagnosing a reading problem, one of the most frequently used instruments is an intelligence test. When a teacher requests special testing for a student by the school psychologist or other specialist, the first (and sometimes only) test given is usually an I.Q. test. Why? Is intelligence so clearly and directly related to reading success or failure, or to the remediation of reading problems, that an I.Q. test will be helpful? What is the relationship between intelligence and reading?

Those questions cannot be answered simply because the relationship is unclear and poorly understood at best. Broad trends in the research literature show what seem to be contradictory findings: (a) that good readers tend to be smarter than poor readers, at least in terms of I.Q. test performance and (b) that reading problems are not limited to lower-I.Q. students but are found across the whole range of intellectual abilities. How are these findings to be interpreted?

There has long been some general agreement that intelligence and reading achievement are fairly well correlated, particularly in the upper grades. What this means is that better performance on reading tests and intelligence tests tends to occur together; students generally do well on both or poorly on both. It does *not* imply causation; we cannot infer from positive correlations that one factor causes the other, only that they coincide. It may be that above average intelligence encourages above average reading achievement. It may be equally true that good reading helps students do better on intelligence tests. Or it may be that *both* reading tests and I.Q. tests call upon the same kinds of abilities and knowledge.

The incidence of reading problems is certainly not limited to those students who are below average in intelligence. Ask a few remedial reading teachers if their students are all "slow learners"; most will tell you that their poor readers come from all ability levels. Perhaps the most puzzling cases are those bright, curious, verbal youngsters capable of sophisticated reasoning but dogged by years of continuing reading failure.

What *do* I.Q. tests tell us? That depends very much on which test is used. Not all measure the same skills, and in order to evaluate results we have to know something about their characteristics.

Some tests that yield an I.Q., or a kind of "ability quotient," are group tests; many of them require the student to read and mark answers. Some representative group tests are the California Test of Mental Maturity, the Lorge-Thorndike Intelligence Tests, the Kuhlman-Anderson Measure of Academic Potential, and the Short Test of Education Ability (STEA). These are more like reading tests than intelligence tests.

An individually administered I.Q. test that does not require the student to read or write will give a better estimate of real performance, but there are different types of individual I.Q. tests.

Two that can be given by teachers without specialized training are the Slosson Intelligence Test (SIT) and the Peabody Picture Vocabulary Test (PPVT). Both are individually administered and reading is not required.

In the Slosson Intelligence Test (Slosson, 1963) linguistic questions are asked and answered orally. Mathematical problems are done "in the head."

The questions, adapted from subtests of the widely known Stanford-Binet Intelligence Scale, call for general information, repetition of digit spans and sentences, arithmetic calculations, verbal similarities and opposites, and definition of vocabulary items. Each question represents an average mental age in years and months. The person being tested is given credit, in months of mental age, for items answered correctly. The I.Q. is calculated from chronological age and mental age. Mental age is calculated by the number of correct answers. Here are some representative questions from the Slosson, with the age for which each is supposed to be typical:

(7–8)   How is a *submarine different* from a *fish?* How are they alike? (p. 7)
(7–10) How many *months* in a year? (p. 7)
(10–8) If a boy had *45 cents*, how many *nickel* or *5 cent* suckers could he buy? (p. 8)
(11–4) Say these numbers *forwards* for me: 9 3 5 2 8 6. (p. 8)
(13–6) What is the *difference* between *contraction* and *expansion?* (p. 9)
(17–0) What does *mutilate* mean? (p. 10)
(21–0) A dog is canine. A cat is _____. (p. 11)

(Slosson, 1963)

The Slosson Intelligence Test clearly calls for different kinds of mental operations and information in its questions, but all the items are language-dependent because they must all be solved or responded to through language. The Slosson has no nonverbal component, and the I.Q. thus derived is an estimate of *verbal* intelligence. It is best used only for screening purposes.

The Peabody Picture Vocabulary Test (Dunn, 1959) yields I.Q. and mental age scores, but its content is more limited than that of the Slosson. The Peabody is a test of receptive vocabulary; for each item, the examiner pronounces a single word and the subject chooses one picture representing the stimulus word from a plate of four pictures. The subject responds by pointing; no oral response is necessary. Here are some sample items from Form A:

STIMULUS WORD	PLATE SHOWS
eagle	spider, whale, eagle, giraffe (Plate 43)
stunt	performing seal, deer, horse, penguin (Plate 70)
cascade	mountain, underwater scene, waterfall, garden maze (Plate 104)
ellipse	concentric circles, oval, circle with congruent line, angle (Plate 123)
legume	rose, palm tree, peanut plant, fern (Plate 137)
predatory	ape, sheep, fox eating hen, elephants (Plate 145)

(Dunn, 1959)

Like the SIT, the PPVT tests verbal intelligence only. In fact, it tests only one aspect of verbal intelligence: vocabulary. As a test of vocabulary it is a useful device. As a test of general intelligence, it has clear limitations and is probably better suited for screening purposes.

Some intelligence tests used in reading diagnosis require special training to administer and must be given under strictly standard conditions. The Stanford-Binet Intelligence Scale and the Wechsler Intelligence Scales are usually given by school psychologists or specially trained clinicians.

The Stanford-Binet, last revised in 1972, is descended from the Binet Scale developed in 1905, the first standardized intelligence measure. Alfred Binet was one of the first psychologists to conceive of intelligence as a dynamic, developmental concept rather than a fixed, static trait. His test, in all its revisions, has reflected his belief that intelligent behavior is largely dependent on the acquisition and use of language and the development of sound judgment. Binet developed the concept of mental age in 1908, and since then the tests have featured sets of questions appropriate for subjects of each sequential mental age. Thus items are arranged according to age level, and at each mental age level the subject is asked several questions of different types. The questions are very similar to those sampled from the SIT, because Slosson adapted questions from the Stanford-Binet subtests for his test. The Stanford-Binet, yielding an overall mental age and I.Q. scores, is not reading-dependent but is heavily influenced by verbal intelligence.

Probably the most widely used individual intelligence tests are the Wechsler Scales. With separate forms for preschoolers, school-age children, and adults, the Wechsler Scales represent an attempt to assess verbal and nonverbal aspects of intelligence separately.

The Wechsler Intelligence Scale for Children — Revised Form (Wechsler, 1974), known as the WISC-R, is widely used in schools and clinics. It differs from the Stanford-Binet in several ways. First, Wechsler has done away with the concept of mental age, retaining only I.Q. Second, items on the WISC-R are arranged by type, in ascending order of difficulty, and there are twelve subtests to measure different skills and operations. Third, scores from the subtests involving language operations are considered together, as are scores from the nonverbal (performance) subtests. In this way, separate Verbal and Performance Scale I.Q.s are derived, which can be compared to determine if both aspects of the subject's intellect seem to be equally well developed.

When the test is administered, verbal and performance subtests are given alternately, but for descriptive purposes it is simpler to consider all six subtests of each scale together. Tables 9.1 and 9.2 describe the subtests of the verbal and performance scales (Kaufman, 1979).

Raw scores from each subtest are converted to *scaled scores*, standard scores ranging from 1 to 19 with a mean of 10 and a standard deviation of 3.

TABLE 9.1. WISC-R Verbal Scale subtests.

VERBAL SCALE SUBTESTS	ABILITIES ASSESSED	SUBJECT TO INFLUENCE OF	SAMPLE ITEMS
Information	Range of factual information; acquired knowledge; memory (long term)	Life experience; reading; school learning	What does the stomach do? Who was Charles Darwin?
Similarities	Categorical thinking; abstract reasoning; verbal concept formation	Reading; interest; school learning	In what way are a hat and a shirt alike?
Arithmetic	Acquired knowledge; arithmetic reasoning; memory (long term); computational skill	Attention span; anxiety; concentration; time pressure	A workman earning $4.00 per hour was paid $36.00. How long did he work?
Vocabulary	Language development; knowledge; expression	Reading; school learning; environmental and cultural opportunities	What is a *donkey*? What does *gamble* mean?
Comprehension	Practical information; common sense and social judgment	Development of conscience and moral sense; cultural influences	Why are criminals locked up? Why should a promise be kept?
Digit Span (optional subtest)	Short-term memory	Attention span; distractability; anxiety	Strings of 3–9 digits

Transforming raw scores into standard units makes it possible to compare results of one subtest to another.

The Digit Span (Verbal Scale) and Mazes (Performance Scale) are optional subtests. When they are given, their resulting scaled scores are not included in the computation of the Verbal, Performance, or Full Scale I.Q.s. Wechsler (1974), however, recommended that Mazes be used instead of Coding when testing children below eight years of age because the Mazes subtest yields more reliable scores than coding when used with young children.

The Full Scale I.Q. represents the subject's overall intelligence as measured by performance on the ten key subtests. The Verbal, Performance, and

TABLE 9.2. WISC-R Performance Scale subtests.

PERFORMANCE SCALE SUBTESTS	ABILITIES ASSESSED	SUBJECT TO INFLUENCE OF	SAMPLE ITEM
Picture Completion	Visual alertness; attention to detail; long-term visual memory	Concentration, speed of response	Locate missing item in picture: ladder without rung
Picture Arrangement	Temporal sequence; anticipation of outcomes	Creativity, cultural influences; experience reading comic strips	Arrange 4–5 pictures in story sequence
Block Design	Whole-part analysis; spatial visualization; motor coordination	Time pressure; impulsivity; clumsiness	Reproduce design with blocks:
Object Assembly	Part-whole re-relationships; flexibility; visual perception and visual-motor coordination	Experience with puzzles; compulsivity; clumsiness; time pressure	Assemble puzzle pieces: face, car
Coding	Short-term visual memory; direction following; motor speed and accuracy	Anxiety, distractibility; lack of experience with writing tasks	Copy symbols corresponding to digits 1–9 in random order
Mazes (optional subtest)	Following visual pattern; anticipation of outcomes	Time pressure; experience with mazes; anxiety	Follow increasingly complex mazes with pencil

Full Scale I.Q.s all have a mean of 100 and a standard deviation of 15. The test uses the following classification scheme for I.Q. scores:

130 and above:	Very superior
120–129:	Superior
110–119:	High average
90–109:	Average
80–89:	Low average
70–79:	Borderline
69 and below:	Mentally deficient

Clinicians often look for differences between Verbal and Performance Scale I.Q.s (see Kaufman, 1979) and differences among subtest scores (see Searls, 1975). Although these analyses can sometimes be helpful, we must be wary of overinterpreting any set of scores that represent a sample of behavior taken at one point in time. We can avoid overinterpretation by considering I.Q. scores in terms of the range in which they occurred, rather than as a single, fixed score. The WISC-R has a standard error of measurement of about 5 I.Q. points; a Full Scale I.Q. score could thus be expected to vary by ±5 points because of probable random effects. For this reason it is much less misleading and more informative to speak of a student's I.Q. score as "falling within the high average range," for example, than to say that the same student has "an I.Q. of 117."

When interpreting scores on the WISC-R or any other intelligence test, it is most important to remember that the scores represent only a portion of one's intellectual functioning. Wechsler himself was critically aware of this when he wrote, "I have, however, become increasingly convinced that intelligence is most usefully interpreted as an aspect of the total personality. I look upon intelligence as an effect rather than a cause, that is, as a resultant of interacting abilities — nonintellective included" (Wechsler, 1958, p. vii). Personality, interests, motivation, social and moral values, home and cultural influences all are bound up with intellect and its manifestation on intelligence tests. Kaufman stresses the need for ". . . integration of background information, behavioral observations, and other test scores with the obtained WISC-R scores to properly interpret the intelligence-test data" (Kaufman, 1979, p. 59). Perhaps nowhere in assessment is the consideration of the *whole* individual as critically important as in the interpretation of intelligence tests.

The Role of Experience

When we consider the concept of intelligence in terms of a student's personality, background, interests, and other related aspects as well as in terms of subtest behaviors and I.Q. points, we come smack up against the role of experience. It is difficult to underestimate the importance of experience, both real and vicarious, in shaping intelligence and one of its manifestations: I.Q. test performance.

Kaufman (1979) and others have described some of the influences affecting performance on the various WISC-R subtests. Many of them are directly related to the degree of experience children have had with objects, events, and people in their home and school environments. It is easy to see how subtests like Information, Similarities, and Vocabulary are influenced by general knowledge and experiences in life. So too are the Performance Scale subtests of Picture Completion, Object Assembly, and Coding as well as nearly all items on the Stanford-Binet, Slosson Intelligence Test, and the Peabody Picture Vocabulary Test. The youngster who has grown up in an environment rich in concrete experiences, extended language use, and intellectual stimulation has an obvious advantage when it comes to taking these tests.

What kind of experience are we talking about? Essentially, we learn about ourselves and our world in two ways: by real, concrete experience with objects and events and, vicariously, by observing and remembering the experiences of others.

Real experiences in the formative years contribute to what most of us think of as an enriched environment. Enrichment has little to do with economics; it has much more to do with having opportunities to manipulate things, experimenting with causes, effects, and consequences, and being consistently encouraged to extend cognitive horizons and try new things. These characteristics of an intellectually enriching environment know no economic, ethnic, social, or linguistic boundaries. They don't depend on having brothers and sisters, or a yard to play in, or two parents in the home. They show up in every home, no matter how traditional or nontraditional, where adults respect and nurture children's attempts to become competent and where those adults give conscious thought to providing opportunities for children to become independent and capable.

Sometimes people do confuse an *intellectually* enriched environment with a *materially* enriched one. They believe that fostering real cognitive growth requires so-called educational toys, a high-priced nursery school, or expensive family vacations to distant places. Nothing could be farther from the truth. You have probably witnessed well-intentioned parents forcibly dragging hungry, exhausted children around a zoo, theme park, or museum, desperately trying to point out all the fascinating things while the children are screaming. Perhaps you have seen your own children abandon (or break) the latest in expensive, educational toys before Christmas Day is over and then happily return to the well-worn, simpler toys that have amused and engaged them in the past. Cognitive growth and the acquisition of information about the world come when adults provide the means for children to experiment and manipulate. These opportunities can be found on a neighborhood walk as well as a trip to the Grand Canyon; in an aquarium or terrarium as well as a park; in the kitchen cupboards as well as in the toy store.

Direct, concrete experience with things and events is one critical aspect; experience with language is another. Verbal intelligence flourishes in the home, and later the school, where children are talked to by adults, where adults really listen to their responses and encourage conversation, where events and behaviors are explained and verbal reasoning is demonstrated, where adults model language use by expanding and elaborating on what children say. In environments where children are rarely addressed except in commands, where their spontaneous utterances are rarely listened to or responded to, where their requests for explanations are routinely answered by "Because I said so, that's why!" and explanations are rarely given, verbal intelligence is stunted. These children enter the world of language poorly adapted to participate in it fully. Their learning opportunities are restricted by language rather than expanded by it. Whatever their socioeconomic status, they are disadvantaged in school.

The other important aspect of experience is vicarious experience. Fortunately for all of us, we can learn from observing others as well as by experiencing things ourselves. The value of vicarious experience has been codified in expressions like "Experience keeps a dear school; but fools will learn in no other" (Benjamin Franklin). Learning from the experiences of others saves us from having to experience everything personally, and we can derive nearly as much from those experiences as from our own.

Perhaps the greatest benefit of literacy is that through reading we can vicariously experience events, emotions, and ideas completely outside our own environment. We can travel to places we will never go to, including places that exist only in the mind; visit the past and the future with as much ease as the present; meet the most famous people of history and share their innermost thoughts; find the most exciting lovers, battle the most dangerous adversaries, experience joy, rage, grief, amazement, and every other human emotion by reading. All this makes good reading a lifelong joy and sustenance instead of just a useful skill.

R *eading provides a rich source of vicarious experience that extends our understanding of ourselves and our world. Through reading, we can imagine experiences that may never be lived in reality.*

Reading and books, however, are more than a source of pleasure. They remain, in spite of the inroads of TV and films, the largest source of information for many people. Schools still use books and other forms of print as the major vehicles for transmitting information.

Yet what happens to the students who cannot read or cannot read well enough to reap all those benefits? They are in large part closed off from those myriad sources of vicarious experience and information. Their literate classmates go on year after year acquiring knowledge and understandings, figuratively laying down layer upon layer of print-conveyed information in their minds. The poor readers or nonreaders don't have this information store, and every year they spend away from the printed word, the less they know in comparison to their age mates.

The calculation of mental ages and I.Q.s is built on the comparison of people of the same age. The tests of intelligence discussed here call for the kinds of learning an educated person would have acquired in school: facts, word meanings, arithmetic calculation, and the ability to make analogies and get meaning from print and visual arrays. No wonder the illiterate student usually does so poorly even on I.Q. tests that are not reading-dependent. In school, the act of acquiring knowledge is largely reading-dependent!

The brutal fact is that the longer older illiterates stay in school, the duller they are perceived to be. Their assessed I.Q.s often drop as they get older. Is this because their intellectual abilities are eroding year after year? Are they actually getting duller intellectually? Not really. These students themselves are not changing, but their age mates who can read *are* constantly changing in their level of information and vicarious experience. The illiterates or poor readers are simply left behind, and they fall farther behind every year.

The cruelest irony of this is that their apparent dullness, the acquired by-product of illiteracy, may be turned against them in the school. In trying to determine how to allocate their overburdened resources in remedial reading, school administrators may select for special programs those students who seem as though they could benefit the most. Usually they are the ones whose reading problems are less severe or less long-standing. Those who have not been in contact with print for a long time and do poorest on the tests sometimes get the least help.

These selection procedures have been justified on the basis that since everybody can't be served, there must be some way to choose those who will benefit the most. Also, when program funding is dependent on increases in scores, program administrators are forced to take only those students whose test scores are likely to go up fastest. These justifications are real, but the older illiterate is often the one left out in the cold.

Do illiterate older students do poorly on I.Q. tests because they are intellectually deficient or because they can't read? The question is like "the chicken or the egg?" The answer hardly matters. If they are ever going to begin to catch up, they must be able to read. Teaching them to read is probably the hardest task in teaching, but it must be attempted because otherwise they face a lifetime of being second class intellectually, and our society just cannot afford it.

Informal Assessment of Capacity

Teachers can use the hearing capacity (listening comprehension) measure from an IRI to gain informal information about a student's capacity.

Hearing capacity is not the same as I.Q. or mental age. It is a concept specifically related to reading ability. For this reason, it may be more directly useful to the teacher than I.Q. test scores or estimates of mental age.

The hearing capacity measure gives an estimate of students' potential for improvement in reading ability. It does this by allowing a comparison of students' reading levels to the level of material they can understand when hearing it read aloud. By listening to written language read aloud and answering comprehension questions on what they heard, they can use verbal intelligence to deal with information conveyed in print. By comparing the grade level of material the student can read to the grade level of material the student can understand by listening, the teacher can determine approximately how much improvement is possible.

When the passages read to them are school textbook passages, the way students deal with the material shows how they might be expected to deal with similar material in the classroom. When they attend lectures and demonstrations, listen to others read aloud, and watch films, they gain knowledge without having to read. For poor readers, these activities may provide the only way to keep up with their classes.

Administration of the hearing capacity measure is very simple. As described in Chapter Four, it is most often used together with an informal reading inventory. In that context, passages of increasing difficulty are read to the student after the frustration level of comprehension has been determined. The usual comprehension questions are asked after the passage has been read, and the procedure is continued as long as the student maintains 70 percent or better comprehension. The level of capacity is the highest grade level at which the student has 70 percent comprehension.

It is not necessary to use this procedure along with an IRI. Even if you use IRI passages and questions, hearing capacity can be estimated at any time without doing any other testing of reading comprehension. If IRI passages are not used, teachers can begin with their regular grade-level reader or other textbook. With questions prepared beforehand (see Chapter Four), a teacher can determine in a few minutes if a student is able to comprehend that text when it is read aloud or discussed in class. If the teacher determines that the text is too difficult for the student to understand on an aural level, an easier book could be attempted, or assessment could end there. One way or the other, the teacher can find out whether the book's concepts and vocabulary are too advanced for the student to deal with even by listening.

This finding is important because it helps the teacher set reasonable instructional goals. If students can neither read nor listen to the text and make sense of it, there is little reason to believe that they can be taught to read it effectively in the near future. The time-honored remedial practice of having poor readers listen to their textbooks on tapes or others read the books aloud will probably do little immediate good at this point. Materials at a lower level of difficulty must be substituted for the grade-level texts and discussions must be geared to the student's ability to understand. Expecting poor readers to learn from a taped text that is above their hearing capacity is not only futile, it is frustrating and humiliating for them.

If, however, teachers find that although students cannot read the text they can understand it adequately through listening, they have made an important finding. First, they can be confident that the students have the necessary verbal concepts to benefit from discussions, lectures, and other oral activities within their regular grade level. Second, the teachers know that these students have the potential to be able to learn to read at their grade level if they are given sufficient and appropriate corrective instruction. Third, while corrective instruction is going on, the students can gain enough information and vocabulary by listening to tapes to be able to keep up with their peers in classroom oral activities.

A very important point to remember about hearing capacity is that it is inseparably related to the processing of written language. Very poor readers or illiterates, who have been out of contact with print for a long time, may lack the necessary information and listening skills to deal aurally with text at anywhere near their grade level. An illiterate high school boy, for example, may have a hearing capacity level of only third or fourth grade, which means that information conveyed orally in his high school classes is largely beyond him. In addition, listening to his grade-level texts on tape in the reading lab is, for him, mostly a waste of time. He must be instructed from materials at about a third- to fourth-grade difficulty level, but written to appeal to adolescents. His hearing capacity level, however, is not all bad news: it shows that at this point in time he has the capacity to learn to read material of third- or fourth-grade difficulty. For an illiterate, that would constitute a great deal of progress.

A second critical point is that hearing capacity is not fixed, as I.Q. tends to be. If that same illiterate high schooler could improve his reading to the point where he *could* read fourth-grade level material instructionally, his hearing capacity would almost certainly increase by several grades. In learning to read even that well, he would have increased his experience with print, vocabulary, and verbal concepts to a point where he could then listen to and understand material well *beyond* fourth-grade level. Breaking the bonds of illiteracy means more than learning to read and write: it means that students can function intellectually more like others their age. In that sense, reading actually "makes you smarter," as one former remedial reader expressed it. Learning to read makes a student better able to learn other things that are important in school.

The dynamic, developmental nature of hearing capacity means that even if it is limited at first, a student will benefit from remedial instruction. Gains may not be spectacular; indeed, they rarely are. Some youngsters may not be able to read at their present grade level in spite of huge amounts of special help, but hearing capacity is an innately positive concept. It helps us to see that no matter how modest the gains, the student learns more than just better reading skills. Therefore, limited hearing capacity must *never* be used as a reason to deny a student special help; it must be viewed as dynamic, not fixed. If reading is improved, hearing capacity will grow and the student will show greater academic promise. In this regard, no effort is ever wasted.

Physical Factors

Many physical conditions and processes can be related to reading problems. The factors most commonly considered are visual, auditory, and neurological processes. Each of these areas has been extensively studied in relation to reading difficulties, but the research data and the various conditions and processes themselves are complex and sometimes confusing. In this section we will consider vision, hearing, and some disabilities often attributed to neurological functioning.

Vision

Reading is a visual act (for sighted persons) in that we cannot read in the dark. It is, of course, much more than just a visual act because, as discussed in Chapter One, more goes on behind the reader's eyes than in front of them, but some visual competence is needed to activate the cognitive processes involved in reading. In order to make sense of print, the reader must be able to gain information from print through vision. For this reason, poor readers are often subjected to vision screening in diagnosis. Before we explore vision problems, however, let's review how normal eyes operate and how eye movements play a role in reading. (An overview of this information was presented in Chapter One.)

Eye Movements. When you are reading comfortably and thinking about what is being read, rather than about what your eyes are doing, you are probably unaware of your eyes moving at all. If you are aware of anything, you probably feel as though your eyes are sweeping in a smooth, continuous motion from the left margin to the right, then smoothly back to the next line of text. Once in a while you are conscious of looking back to reread a word or phrase, but if you are concentrating on what you are reading you probably think you are looking back only rarely.

What you *feel* your eyes doing and what they really *are* doing are very different. Watch someone read the newspaper or a novel; if possible, watch them covertly. What do their eyes do? First, they don't sweep smoothly along at all but rather in a series of jerky little hops forward. They jerk forward, stop, jerk forward again. Second, they probably move backward a lot more often than the reader is aware. Most people's eyes move backward once every one or two lines, but they will usually report after reading a whole page that they looked back only once or twice in total.

The abrupt hop forward is called a *saccade*, a French word that sounds much more elegant than its definition: a jerk. The stops are called *fixations*, and the combination of saccades and fixations make the visual side of reading possible (Gregory, 1966). During the saccadic movements, the eyes do not take in visual information (Smith, 1978). If they did, you would be conscious of seeing a blur, much like what you see if you look at the ground outside the window of a fast-moving car or train. Yet when you read you are certainly never aware of a blurring-clearing-blurring-clearing cycle as your eyes move forward. (If you *were* aware of this, you would probably get carsick every time you tried to read!)

Visual information is taken in by the eyes during the fixation, when the eye is relatively motionless. Fixations can vary in duration, but about fifty milliseconds ($1/20$ second) is sufficient for perception of all the visual information the brain can handle at one time (Smith, 1978). During the fixation the eyes take in visual stimuli and transmit signals to the brain along the optic nerves. As the eyes move to the next fixation, the brain acts on the information it has been given. If the information is understood, the eyes move forward in the text. If there is some ambiguity or if what is received does not match expectations, the eyes travel backward to recheck and clarify (Hochberg, 1970). These backward looks are called *regressions*, and they occur much more often than we know. They are an entirely normal function in all reading, as you will see if you carefully observe a good reader read interesting material. Regressions have been the subject of much discussion and considerable misunderstanding, however.

A persistent misconception is that they are a cause of poor reading, or that *any* regressions are a symptom of poor reading, and as such they should be rooted out. In some localities vision specialists such as optometrists, who prescribe and make corrective lenses, carry out elaborate eye-training programs for children, eye-muscle exercises and training on machines that restrict the visual field while reading. By exposing only short portions of a line of text sequentially, the machine prevents the reader from looking back. Supposedly, continued practice of this type will help children "break the habit" of making regressions. The effectiveness of these programs was criticized even in the 1950s (Vernon, 1957), but worried parents continue even now to invest in months or even years of this type of training. Machines of similar kinds, which reveal portions of text for increasingly short exposures, are still used in some school reading programs, but since their effectiveness has not been convincingly demonstrated (Spache, 1976a; Witty, 1973), they are less common than they were a decade or more ago.

Fixations during reading have also been the subject of considerable argument. First of all, how many fixations per line should occur? If you observe people's eyes as they read a typical book page of print, with about ten to twelve words per line, you will see that they do not make ten or twelve fixations. If the reading is comfortable and not too difficult, most good readers will make two or five fixations per line. Obviously, then, we do not ordinarily fixate on every word but rather take in several words in each fixation. In 1908 Huey (reprinted 1968) summarized the classic studies that demonstrate these findings, and they have since been replicated countless times.

Two to five fixations per line is about average for a good reader who is comfortably reading easy material and adequately comprehending it. When reading very difficult material, or when confusion or anxiety are present, readers tend to make more fixations per line (Smith, 1978). Poor readers, who have difficulty with almost any material, or uncertain readers accustomed to failure may fixate as frequently as each word in the line. This slows the reading down, interferes with comprehension, and fragments the whole reading process. Mackworth (1965) used the term *tunnel vision* to describe this aspect of very dysfluent reading. It is an apt phrase, for instead of taking in several words at once and processing them in idea groups, dysfluent readers process text as though they were looking through a narrow tube, seeing only one word, or even part of a word, at a time.

It is important to remember that overly frequent fixations, or tunnel-vision reading, are *symptoms* of reading difficulty. They do not *cause* the difficulty. They are not "bad reading habits," as is sometimes charged. The eyes make more frequent fixations and regressions because the text is not making sense to the reader. The brain directs the eyes to take another look in order to get more information to process. Training on machines that prevent regressions or force the reader to make only a certain number of fixations doesn't help. Reading easier material *does* help. Those poor readers whose eyes seem to go all over the page will have much more normal eye movements if they are given material on their instructional or independent levels. This observation is not new. Tinker, a noted expert in eye movement research, demonstrated this nearly twenty-five years ago (1958). Inefficient eye movements are a symptom of reading frustration and are caused by reading text that is too difficult.

Common Vision Problems. Teachers are sometimes the first line of defense against vision problems. They are usually in the best position to spot potential problems and refer children for appropriate screening because they, more than parents, observe children in close contact with reading and writing materials. Also, children with vision problems often don't realize that others see differently, and they don't call adult attention to their difficulty. There-

TABLE 9.3. Vision problems.

TECHNICAL NAME	COMMON NAME	CONDITION	SYMPTOMS
Myopia	Nearsightedness	Clear vision at near point; blurring of distant images	Squinting at the board; holding print close to face; inattention to board work
Hyperopia	Farsightedness	Clear vision at far point; blurring of close objects	Holding print well away from face; disinterest in close work; eye fatigue during reading
Astigmatism		Distortion and/or blurring of part (or all) of visual field, far and near	Eye fatigue; headache; squinting; tilting or turning head; nausea during reading
Amblyopia	Lazy eye	Suppression of vision in one eye; dimming of vision without structural cause	Tilting or turning head to read; eye fatigue on one side; headache
Strabismus	Crossed eyes	Difficulty converging and focusing both eyes on the same object	Squinting; closing or covering one eye to focus; eyes misaligned
Phoria or fusion problems; binocular coordination		Imbalance of ocular muscles; difficulty converging and focusing both eyes equally	Squinting; closing or covering one eye
Aniseikonia		Differences in size or shape of image in each eye	Blurring; squinting; difficulty focusing or fusing image; closing one eye

fore, it is important for teachers to understand vision problems and their symptoms. Table 9.3 summarizes the nature and symptoms of some common visual difficulties.

These vision problems can be so minor that they have few if any symptoms, and even the reader may be unaware of any problem. Or they can be so severe that normal classroom activities are extremely difficult. Usually the teacher is in a position to detect fairly minor problems which, if treated promptly, are easy to correct. All of the aforementioned vision problems are correctable, most with glasses or contact lenses, some with a combination of corrective lenses and muscle exercises.

Astigmatism, hyperopia, and myopia are by far the most common problems. Astigmation (blurring of part of the image) can occur in conjunction with either near- or farsightedness, but both conditions are corrected simultaneously with lenses. Hyperopia, blurring of the image at the near point, makes reading and writing uncomfortable and tiring and has long been associated with reading problems. Mild hyperopia is fairly common when children enter school (Spache, 1976b; Woodruff, 1972). After more and more close work in the first few years of school, this developmental farsightedness disappears for most children, and many become mildly myopic as they learn to read. Myopia, better acuity (keenness) of vision up close than at a distance, does not interfere with reading; in fact, myopia is common in good readers and students with good school achievement (Ekwall, 1976; Spache, 1976b). There is some evidence that myopia may be largely developmental and environmentally produced by the demands of close work with print during the school years (Lanyon and Giddings, 1974). While nearsightedness does not contribute directly to reading problems, it can give children difficulty in doing board work and can be a cause of inattention during such activities.

Although vision problems may be very different, they often have identical symptoms. Teachers can do little more than guess about the precise nature of the problem in many cases, but they should be alert to the continuing presence of the symptoms that Spache claims have been validated by professional eye examiners (see Table 9.4).

TABLE 9.4. Symptoms of problems in vision.

APPEARANCE OF EYES	One eye turns in or out at any time
	Eyes or lids sometimes reddened
	Excessive tearing
	Encrusted eyelids or frequent sties (inflammation of sebaceous gland of eyelid)
COMPLAINTS FROM SUSTAINED CLOSE WORK	Headache in forehead, temples or eyes
	Burning or itching eyes
	Nausea or dizziness
	Blurring after reading awhile
POSTURE AND SEATED BEHAVIOR	Squints, closes or covers one eye
	Tilts or turns head constantly to read or write
	Blinks excessively during reading
	Strains forward to see board
	Holds head or book excessively near or far
	Fatigues quickly and avoids near-point tasks

SOURCE: From George D. Spache, *Diagnosing and Correcting Reading Disabilities*, pp. 30–31. Copyright © 1976 by Allyn and Bacon, Inc. Reprinted by permission.

As Spache and others have pointed out, many of these symptoms are sometimes demonstrated by poor readers whose vision is unimpaired. When any of these signs are displayed frequently, are not common to the rest of the class, and are evidenced even when performing easy tasks, they should signal a need for referral to an eye specialist.

There are many more elaborate lists of symptoms. Many include behaviors common to most poor readers even with no visual problems. Ekwall (1976), for example, cites a lengthy list of "Observable Clues to Classroom Vision Problems" published by the Optometric Extension Program Foundation, Inc. (1968). Included in this checklist are such ubiquitous reading behaviors as:

- Loses place during reading
- Short attention span in reading or copying
- Omits letters, numbers, or phrases
- Fails to recognize same word in next sentence
- Reverses letters or words in writing
- Confuses same word in same sentence
- Whispers to self while reading silently
- Comprehension reduces as reading continues

Most teachers would agree that "symptoms" like these are extremely common to many kinds of reading problems, including simply having to read at one's frustration level. Many of these behaviors can disappear spontaneously if the reader is given less frustrating material to read. They should not be ignored, but they should not automatically be attributed to visual deficits, either.

Vision Screening Measures. Whenever a teacher suspects that a student has an uncorrected vision problem, the student should be referred to a vision specialist for testing. Referrals should be made through the principal, school nurse, supervisor, or other designated personnel.

In some schools the nurse, reading or resource teacher, or other specialist will use a vision screening battery prior to referral to an outside expert. A *stereoscopic instrument* is often used for testing vision in each eye and both together. (Stereoscopes are commonly used to test vision for a driver's license; you may have had your vision checked this way.) The following are done with a stereoscope:

- Keystone Visual Survey Telebinocular Test: Screens for myopia, hyperopia, fusion problems, depth perception, and color blindness, using test cards.
- Ortho-Rater: Originally developed for adults, recently adapted for use with children; screens for acuity problems, depth perception, and binocular (both eyes) coordination.
- Titmus Professional Vision Tester and Titmus Biopter: Like the Key-

stone, tests for binocular fusion, myopia, hyperopia, astigmatism, depth perception, and color blindness.

There are two test batteries that can be used together with a stereoscopic instrument and the previously listed tests. Each one extends the scope of the other tests to include aspects of vision problems sometimes detected only by professional vision experts:

- □ Walton Modified Telebinocular Technique: Using a Keystone Telebinocular machine and an additional card, the procedure screens for amblyopia, myopia, hyperopia, and astigmatism and features revised scoring procedures for the muscular imbalance (fusion and phoria) tests. This procedure was found to be as effective in detecting vision problems as much more exhaustive professional exams and is practical for school use (Schubert and Walton, 1980).
- □ Spache Binocular Reading Test: Tests for suppression of vision in either eye and binocular vision in reading; test cards contain paragraphs to be read aloud at several difficulty levels; cards can be used with most models of stereoscope such as the Keystone Telebinocular or Titmus Biopter.

The Snellen Chart, that familiar wall chart with its rows of letters of decreasing size, deserves a comment. It is a device that measures one's ability to see letters from a distance of twenty feet. It can detect nearsightedness (myopia), but myopia rarely has any effect on reading. The chart is useless in detecting visual problems that *can* affect reading such as farsightedness, astigmatism, or binocular fusion problems. The exclusive use of the Snellen Chart is clearly inadequate for effective vision screening.

Hearing

The relationship between auditory problems and reading difficulties has long been established. Hearing and language are as intimately related as language and reading. As teachers observe the oral and written language of their students they can become aware of possible hearing problems.

When children learn to read, they employ their whole experience with oral language. We know that oral language development and learning to read are closely related and that the ability to process and understand *written* language depends in large part on being able to process and understand *oral* language. Hearing problems can interfere with, delay, or even prevent the development of oral language fluency, and it is in this respect that hearing problems can affect reading.

Another factor is the heavy reliance on oral activities and phonics instruction. Across the entire spectrum of approaches, some features of every beginning reading program are standard: learning of letter names and sounds, use of simple phonic analysis strategies to decode words, and frequent oral reading. These activities put a premium on clarity of hearing, and the youngster with auditory problems is at a distinct disadvantage.

Thus hearing problems that occur anytime in the first eight to ten years of life may affect a child's reading by interfering with language development in the preschool years or with the largely oral reading instruction of the primary grades.

Types of Hearing Problems. Testing of auditory acuity (keenness) involves assessment of the ability to hear speech sounds, music, and noises. In reading, it is the speech sounds that are critical.

Speech sounds are measured in terms of *pitch* and *volume*. Pitch refers to the frequency of a sound; speech sounds are high-tone or low-tone depending on their pitch. Pitch is measured in *hertz*, or cycles per second. High-frequency, or high-tone, sounds have a higher number of cycles per second than low tones. Speech sounds of the normal human voice range from 128 to 4000 cycles per second; consonant sounds are higher in pitch than vowel sounds (Bond, Tinker, and Wasson, 1979).

Volume or loudness is measured in units called *decibels*. Normal conversation is usually around sixty decibels, the volume necessary for classroom activities.

Hearing losses can affect the perception of pitch or volume or both. If the child can hear some sound frequencies but not others, it can be devastating in learning to read because it means that the child can hear some speech sounds accurately but not others. Hearing loss involving the high-frequency sounds is more common than loss of low-frequency sounds. Children with high-frequency hearing loss can accurately hear vowel sounds and maybe some consonant sounds but not all of them.

Those with high-tone losses may hear spoken words in a garbled, indistinct fashion, depending on how many consonant sounds are affected. If only vowels can be heard, words are almost totally meaningless because consonant sounds are what make spoken words intelligible. (Read a line of print aloud to someone, pronouncing only the vowel sounds; repeat the line pronouncing only the consonant sounds. Which version could the listener more easily understand?)

Hearing losses are not always as severe as the previous example. Often only a few consonant and blend sounds are affected, but phonics instruction is made very difficult by this loss, and the student may be very poor at word analysis and word recognition. Also, the words that are most often taught in beginning reading frequently vary only in their consonant sounds, as in the "word families" and rhyming word patterns (*cat-hat-pat-mat-sat*). Learning these words can be very difficult for the child with high-tone hearing loss.

Some hearing problems are caused by volume impairment at most or all frequencies. These cases can be helped by hearing aids, which amplify sound at all levels. Since volume loss affects the perception of all types of sounds, it is probably the most obvious and the easiest to spot in the classroom. Loss of only certain sounds is more difficult to spot because the student will hear many sounds normally and problems may be blamed on inattention or carelessness.

Symptoms of both types of hearing loss are similar. The main difference is that the child with volume loss will have trouble consistently while the child with selective frequency losses will hear many sounds normally. In general, the following physical signs may be apparent:

- frequent requests to have statements repeated
- frequent confusion of simple oral directions
- ringing, buzzing, or pain in ears
- turning or tilting head toward speaker
- strained posture in listening
- cupping of ears toward speaker
- unusually loud or monotonous voice

At first glance, some of these signs are similar to those of children with vision problems. Behaviors like inattention, strained posture, scowling, or squinting can be common to children with hearing or vision problems, or to children who are free of physical problems but who are simply frustrated in reading.

Another very important factor in the diagnosis of hearing problems is the *duration* of the problem. While volume losses are usually of a more or less chronic nature, many selective frequency losses are temporary. It is very common for children to experience temporary loss of some sounds during and after a heavy cold or upper respiratory infection. These hearing losses can last from a few days to a few months, and while they exist, they can interfere with normal classroom activities.

Upper respiratory infections are common in young children. Few nursery school or primary grades youngsters sail through an entire winter without one cold or bout with the flu. For many children these colds are chronic and result in weeks of illness every year, usually in the winter months. Others recover from one cold only to fall prey to the next one coming along. Children with colds or other viral upper respiratory infections and respiratory allergies are subject to middle ear impairments called *conductive hearing losses* (Dirks, 1978). Two types of conductive problems are particularly common in school-age children.

One condition is *otitis media*, a collection of fluid in the middle ear. The middle ear and outer ear are separated by the *tympanic membrane*, or eardrum. This membrane conducts sound by vibration to the middle ear structures. Fluid in the middle ear distends the eardrum outward, inhibiting its ability to vibrate freely and thus reducing the signal transmitted inward. In severe cases, the eardrum can rupture. Otitis media may result from respiratory infections and allergies and persist long after nasal and bronchial congestion have disappeared. The condition is treated medically with drugs and, in severe cases, by surgical draining (Dirks, 1978; Sanders, 1977).

A second common conductive loss occurs when air pressure on either side of the tympanic membrane is unequal. The tympanic membrane divides the middle ear from the outer ear. From the middle ear a tunnel, the *eustachian tube,* runs to the back of the throat at the level of the nose. This tube's function is to equalize pressure on both sides of the eardrum (Sanders, 1977). Unequal pressure on either side inhibits the conduction of sound to the middle ear. Some people experience discomfort and temporary hearing impairment when they fly, caused by air pressure in the airplane cabin.

When heavy upper respiratory congestion is present, the eustachian tube can collapse or close up. If this happens, air behind the tympanic membrane is absorbed and air pressure is exerted inward on the eardrum. As a result, the eardrum cannot properly conduct sound because the membrane becomes distended, as it does in otitis media. Implantation of plastic tubes in the eustachian tube now corrects the problem without surgery.

Children who do not receive the necessary medical treatment for chronic infections may suffer these temporary hearing losses. Those with chronic colds, or those returning to school after a particularly severe upper respiratory infection, should have auditory screening at regular intervals, with particular attention paid to perception of the high-tone sounds.

While middle ear disorders are more common in children, inner ear disorders can also cause hearing impairment. Within the inner ear the *cochlea,* a bony structure looking like a coiled shell, contains the sensory organs of hearing and the components of the body's balance system. Here the sound waves that have been transmitted by vibration to the inner ear are transformed into mechanical, electrical, and chemical signals and transmitted to the brain (Sanders, 1977). The cochlea and its delicate transmission functions can be damaged by excessive noise, certain drugs, and exposure to infections like mumps and rubella (German measles). Since mumps and various forms of measles are still considered childhood diseases, children returning to school after these illnesses should also be screened for hearing loss.

Auditory Screening Methods. The most reliable method examines volume in decibels and different frequencies in cycles per second. An instrument called an *audiometer* is used to produce pure tones generally ranging from 125 to 8000 cycles per second in pitch and from about 10 to 110 decibels in volume.

An audiometer can be used for screening groups of students, but the most accurate screening is done individually. The subject is seated so that the audiometer controls are not visible. Headphones are worn so each ear can be tested separately, and a buzzer or other signaling device is used as a means of responding to the test. The examiner uses the audiometer to produce each tone at a full range of volume from soft to loud, and the subject signals when the tone is first audible and also indicates its duration. The examiner can occasionally check to see that the subject is not just signaling randomly by using an interrupter switch to cut off the signal momentarily.

Audiometers are quite easy to use, are portable, and are not prohibitively expensive. They are good for determining which children should be referred to hearing specialists for extensive evaluation.

A topic related to auditory acuity is *auditory discrimination*, the ability to distinguish between highly similar sounds and to detect whether two (or more) sounds are alike or different. Being able to detect subtle differences in speech sounds helps students to master phonics; those with poor auditory discrimination may have persistent trouble with phonic analysis and may also have speech impairments (Wilson, 1981).

Auditory discrimination can be assessed formally or informally. The student is required to distinguish between pairs of words or syllables that differ minimally (*rat-rap, ome-ote*). Teachers frequently make up and give such exercises themselves. Formal auditory discrimination tests are also common, and some standardized readiness tests include such a subtest.

The Goldman-Fristoe-Woodcock Test of Auditory Discrimination uses tape recordings. The student looks at four pictures and selects one that corresponds to the word heard on the tape. The words for each picture have minimal sound differences (*goat, coat, boat, throat*). Correct selection can be adversely affected if the student does not recognize all the pictured objects (Wallace and Larsen, 1978).

Another common device is the Wepman Auditory Discrimination Test. Pairs of real and nonsense words are pronounced, some of which differ (*dumb-dump*) and some of which do not (*car-car*). The students indicate whether the words in the pair were "the same" or "different." Performance on the test can be severely affected by the students' understanding of the meaning of "same" and "different," as well as their understanding of what they are supposed to do (Blank, 1968). Since Wepman provides no normative data on the test, these factors combine to make it suspect, and its results should be viewed with caution (Wallace and Larsen, 1978).

In beginning reading it is common to combine phonics instruction with auditory discrimination practice. Beginning readers or prereaders who at first seem to have difficulty with auditory discrimination often need only to learn what to listen for and how to respond. In other words, they have no auditory disability but have to learn what the task is. Auditory discrimination skill seems to improve sharply as children progress through the primary grades (Ekwall, 1976; Thompson, 1963), which implies that it develops at least partly in response to instruction and experience with the task. It may well be a learned skill as much as an innate perceptual ability.

Special Learning Problems

Perhaps no other issue in reading has aroused as much controversy and contradiction as the subject of special learning problems. Two topics in particular have generated countless studies, dissertations, symposia, monographs, and plain arguments: *dyslexia* and *learning disabilities*. To some, each term means something very different; to others the terms overlap and may even be synonymous. The waters here are very muddy, but we will wade in and attempt to clarify where we can.

What Is Dyslexia? Richard Adams (1969) opened his article on dyslexia with an apt quotation:

> "When I use a word," Humpty Dumpty said in rather a scornful tone, "it means just what I choose it to mean — neither more nor less."
> "The question is," said Alice, "whether you can make words mean so many different things."
> "The question is," said Humpty Dumpty, "which is to be master — that's all." (Carroll, n.d., p. 110)

Adams extended the metaphor in this way:

> If man is master of his own inventions then he is free to manage the meaning of his words to suit his own conventions. But sometimes a word gets born which, rather than live as servant to man, moves out in life like a Frankenstein monster wreaking havoc in the discourse of sensible men. *Dyslexia is such a word. . . .* The time then has come for us to pause amidst our dialogue and examine this monster word dyslexia and tame its meaning. (Adams, 1969, p. 618)

Adams, however, was unable to "tame its meaning" in spite of his search for agreement in various definitions. His article lists numerous definitions from many scholarly sources; each definition contradicts the last and adds new synonyms to a growing list. Adams's collection of definitions tells us that dyslexia may be considered an *impairment,* a *syndrome,* a *disturbance* of reading ability, an *inability* to read, *decreased ability* to learn to read, *intact* reading ability but *distorted speech,* a specific *language* disability, a specific *reading* disability, an *inborn* disability, *developmental* in nature, or congenital *word blindness.* The term can imply *minimal cerebral dysfunction,* be caused by a biologically *abnormal brain,* be due to a *central lesion,* or to *constitutional factors* (heredity), or even to "*thwarting* of the sublimation of the *aggressive drive.*" See?

Of course, a number of these terms contradict one another. Spache (1976b) lists over a dozen definitions selected from the professional literature. Here, for example, we learn that dyslexia can mean, in the words of one definition, "the presence of all the causes discussed [visual, auditory, brain damage, low intelligence, emotional problems, cultural deprivation] or an absence of all. It can mean the presence of causes yet undiscovered. The term has as many meanings as the disorder has causes" (Dauzat, 1969, p. 633). Hittleman wrote, "Educationally, dyslexia is viewed as an inability to read when no specific causes are evident" (Hittleman, 1978, p. 407).

Does all this sound suspiciously like Humpty Dumpty? Can dyslexia possibly be innate and also developmental, due to such widely divergent causes as heredity, central brain lesion, and low motivation, marked by word blindness or intact reading but poor comprehension, specific and generic, a disease, a syndrome and a condition, an impairment and an inability? Dyslexia can apparently be "what I choose it to mean — neither more nor less."

In this spirit, Edward Fry (1968) produced a tongue-in-cheek "terminology generator" (Table 9.5). The results of this entertaining exercise sound very much like the list of definitions, synonymous terms, and symptoms Adams, Spache and others have compiled.

The experts agree on little except that there is widespread disagreement of

TABLE 9.5. Fry's Do-It-Yourself Terminology Generator.

Directions: Select any word from Column 1. Add any word from Column 2, then add any word from Column 3. If you don't like the result, try again. It will mean about the same thing.

1 QUALIFIER	2 AREA OF INVOLVEMENT	3 PROBLEM
Minimal	Brain	Disfunction
Mild	Cerebral	Damage
Minor	Neurological	Disorder
Chronic	Neurologic	Dissynchronization
Diffuse	C.N.S. (Central Nervous System)	Handicap
Specific	Language	Disability
Primary	Reading	Retardation
Disorganized	Perceptual	Impairment
Organic	Impulse	Pathology
Clumsy	Behavior	Syndrome

The above system will yield 1000 terms, but if that is not enough you could use specific dyslexia, aphasoid, neurophrenia, or developmental lag.

SOURCE: From Edward Fry, "Do-It-Yourself Terminology Generator," *Journal of Reading*, vol. 11, no. 6 (March 1968), p. 428. Reprinted with permission of Edward Fry and the International Reading Association.

the nature, causes, symptoms, and treatments of dyslexia. This disagreement appears not to have prevented the equally widespread use of the term. When two or more educators, doctors, or parents discuss dyslexia, it is more than likely that each may mean something different.

Clearly, dyslexia is a wastebasket term. Many reading experts have criticized its use because it seems to imply a condition that has clearly recognizable parameters. A medical doctor summed up the position of many experts in these unequivocal words:

> The use of the term dyslexia is disputed, its definition is unclear and continues to vary with different experts in the field, and it is of little or no use to the classroom teacher or the child's physician. Inasmuch as its definition has been inexact and bastardized, the use of this term may be more harmful than helpful in trying to understand children who are reading poorly. (Martin, 1971, p. 469)

In spite of all the confusion and criticism the term is still widely used. The question now is: What can be learned from all this wrangling?

First, there is no general agreement on what *causes* dyslexia. Genetic factors, central nervous system dysfunction, brain damage, and even hormonal factors have been suggested. Some authorities avoid any suggestion of causative factors (see Rutherford's [1971] concise literature review).

Second, there is no general agreement on the *symptoms* of dyslexia. Many authorities have attempted to learn whether there are symptoms unique to dyslexia, but whatever constellation of symptoms is considered, some of them will appear in poor readers who are not dyslexic and even in good readers (see Spache's [1976b] review of the literature on symptoms). There is also very little agreement on the degree of involvement of any given symptom. Some studies, for example, show conclusively that left-right confusion occurs significantly more often in dyslexic students; other studies show, equally conclusively, that this effect is due only to chance. Just about any symptoms you can think of meet the same fate: reversals, poor auditory discrimination, mixed dominance, clumsiness, faulty memory, poor spelling, and on and on. About the only symptom the experts agree on is difficulty with phonics (Rutherford, 1971).

We noted in our discussion of visual and auditory problems that very common reading behaviors are sometimes viewed as symptoms of these disabilities. The same is true with dyslexia. Every list of symptoms contains behaviors that can be found in many readers who are simply frustrated or anxious. Consider the following from Ekwall:

Reversals of letters or words
Short or erratic memory for words
Oral rereading not improved after silent or oral first-reading
Difficulty in concentration

Inability to see whole relationships, which Ekwall exemplified by "overly phonetic" spellings like LIKS (likes) or HAV (have)

Emotional instability

Tendency toward impulsiveness (characterized by a child who reads "bunny"
for "rabbit")

Poor eye-motor coordination

Inability to work rapidly

Omission of words or phrases

Poor syntax, stuttering or speaking haltingly

(Ekwall, 1976, pp. 226–227)

Ekwall uses the term "severe reading disability" as synonymous with dyslexia,
but he acknowledges that these symptoms could also describe "learning disability cases in general," an unclear distinction.

Third, there is no general agreement on the proper *treatment* of dyslexia,
which Spache (1976b) considered surprising in that there are relatively few
different treatments available. Perhaps the reason for disagreement lies in the
fact that in this area, as with other aspects of dyslexia, studies contradict one
another and conclusive evidence of effectiveness is lacking. Spache cites six
general trends in remedial programs:

Multisensory or VAKT (visual-auditory-kinesthetic-tactile impressions)

Avoiding intrasensory stimulation but using VAKT for reinforcement in word
recognition

Perceptual-motor or eye-hand coordination

Phonics

Language therapy

Auditory and/or visual perception and sequencing

(Spache, 1976b, p. 185)

These are components of many different remedial programs for dyslexics,
but they are also common in programs for learning disabled, mentally retarded, and other educationally "special" children. It is interesting to note the
inclusion of phonics here. Most authorities agree that dyslexics have a great
deal of trouble working with letter sounds and yet phonics instruction is the
foundation of a great many remedial approaches. Thus we could predict that
such instruction would meet with only limited success. Indeed, this is what
often happens.

In many cases remedial programs for dyslexics seem to be almost indistin-
guishable from programs for garden-variety reading difficulties (*Reading
Newsreport*, 1969). According to Rosner,

Differences between programs for youngsters with dyslexia, minimal brain
damage, and specific learning disability are frequently most clearly indicated
in the terminology which is used and least clearly seen in the actual treatment
practices. The techniques one uses to help the youngster overcome disability
are often more a function of where one has been trained than of what diagnostic label is applied to the child. (Rosner, 1971, p. 333)

If you take only one point from the previous discussion, let it be this one: the term dyslexia should be used with the utmost caution, if at all. No one would be harmed if we were to discard the term entirely, since seventy or more years of discussion have failed to adequately define or describe it, so be very, very careful about using it to describe a student. If others use it, try to determine precisely what they mean. Be wary of any diagnostic or remedial program that purports to identify or cure dyslexia. And don't thoughtlessly add to the already considerable confusion by the way you use this label.

What Are Learning Disabilities? This term is just as poorly defined, widely used, and generally misunderstood as its cousin, dyslexia. Learning disability, or LD, is a little more general; it usually is used to mean a puzzling and persistent learning problem in any area. When the area in question is reading, the learning disability is often called dyslexia, but sometimes it is called *specific reading disability* or *specific language disability*. According to Samuels (1973), "Terms such as *brain damage, neurologic impairment,* and *minimal cerebral dysfunction* have all been used somewhat interchangeably in the literature on learning disability" (p. 204), and "A diagnosis of *learning disability* is often made by systematically ruling out other factors. If, for example, the diagnostician can rule out emotional problems, mental retardation, inadequate instruction and the like, as causes of the learning problem, the student may be identified as one with a *reading disability*" (p. 203; emphasis added). Careful reading of Samuels's second quote reveals that even he uses learning disability and reading disability interchangeably. Likewise, dyslexia is often used to denote a type of learning disability that specifically affects the ability to read.

The obvious difficulty here is that frequently one undefined term is being used to define, categorize, or characterize another undefined term. Hence we have dyslexia as a kind of learning disability; meanwhile no one is sure what either term means. No clear set of criteria or definitions exist for either one (Hittleman, 1978).

Hartman and Hartman gave an operational definition of learning disability that is very common: "The definition of a learning disability . . . generally describes children with average or above intellectual potential whose academic achievement is significantly lagging, presumably because of minimal brain dysfunction. Definitions of the learning disabled child generally rule out social disadvantage, emotional disturbance, physical handicap, and mental retardation as causative factors" (Hartman and Hartman, 1973, p. 684).

This definition represents what Samuels referred to as diagnosis by elimination, by ruling out other factors first, a process that seems to beg the question. In his words, "To diagnose by elimination and then place the student in a category which implies that the cause of the problem is known, is scientifically untenable" (Samuels, 1973, pp. 203–204). In addition, the presence of minimal brain dysfunction is "presumed."

It may be bad science, but it is also common practice. Batteries of tests are given and, one by one, clearly definable factors are ruled out: the youngsters' WISC-R scores are too high for them to be retarded; their personality tests show no particular emotional problems; their medical histories show no gross positive findings; they have been in school regularly and have been adequately taught; they can hear, see, and speak within normal limits; and still they read poorly — therefore, they *must* have a learning disability. Remember Dauzat's (1969) definition of dyslexia as existing when no specific causes are evident? The same reasoning is commonly applied to learning disabilities.

Hartman and Hartman's provocative article focuses on what they call the "false dichotomy" between reading disabilities and learning disabilities. They posit that ". . . in fact, there is little if any difference between learning by disabled children and many of the other children being seen by the reading specialist. A false dichotomy has been created because the two specialists employ different terms, different diagnostic approaches and different remedial methods" (Hartman and Hartman, 1973, p. 685).

Hartman and Hartman demonstrated the basic difference between these two approaches by describing the tests administered and the diagnostic interpretations made by hypothetical-but-typical reading and LD specialists studying the same third-grade student. Reading specialists are most interested in the child's reading: what the student can and can't do in reading, which the authors referred to as a "task-oriented approach." LD specialists are most concerned with isolating the defective perceptual process or processes that they assume are causing the reading problem. The authors called this a "process training approach." Here is how they sum up these very different approaches to the same problem:

> The differences in the approaches can be clarified by stating the basic diagnostic question of each of the remedial specialists. The learning disability specialist asks "What's wrong with the child?" while the reading specialist asks "What's wrong with the child's reading?" (Hartman and Hartman, 1973, p. 692)

The point is a telling one. Perhaps we might ask ourselves, where can we make the most difference in remediation? At the present time we cannot repair minimal brain dysfunction, or perceptual handicaps, or most of the other neurological problems often attributed to learning disabled children. We cannot fix up dominance or laterality problems, change so-called modality preferences, or speed up growth of visual motor coordination. What we *can* affect is *how and what the youngster reads.*

Research studies indicate that the training procedure used for remediation should be as similar as possible to the desired outcome and that the further away the training activities are from the real academic task, the less we can effect a transfer of learning (Masland, 1969). It seems that reading problems can be best attacked by having the student read rather than working on "hypothetical perceptual process[es] underlying the academic skill" (Hartman and Hartman, 1973, p. 688), but as with nearly every other aspect of learning and reading disabilities, this point is a controversial one.

Emotional Factors

So far we have discussed many of the ways that things can go wrong for youngsters as they learn to read, such as physical problems, reading readiness, and a host of specific skill weaknesses. Our description of reading problems, however, would be incomplete, and our intention to deal with the whole child unfulfilled, if we did not turn our attention to emotional problems.

Every teacher or tutor attempting to work with a disabled reader has to acknowledge the emotional problems that often accompany reading failure. Affective factors complicate the picture for many remedial readers, and the longer the duration of the disability, the more severely the student's self-concept is damaged. Lecky (in Gillham, 1973, p. 82) described a "typical low achiever," a student you may recognize:

> . . . a child who sees himself as helpless and perhaps worthless. He sees himself . . . as having to be on the defensive in order to maintain integrity. He may simulate indifference or boldness; he may fight blindly and hopelessly, dig in his heels stubbornly, or withdraw into daydreams or unreachable passivity. While he may see himself as threatened and helpless, in the areas of academic achievement, he can be the winner. No one can make him learn anything.

Although Lecky wrote that description in 1945, it describes just as accurately many poor readers of the 1980s. It is fruitless to try to deal with a student's reading without giving thought to the emotional factors involved in reading failure.

However, a full, clinical description of severe personality and emotional disorders is beyond the scope of this discussion. What we are addressing here are the common, predictable kinds of emotional problems that often accompany reading difficulties.

Educators have long been interested in determining whether emotional problems are a cause or a result of reading problems, or whether the two simply go together. The question, like that of the chicken and the egg, has never been answered conclusively; all three conditions occur.

It is not surprising that there is no general agreement on whether reading instruction or counseling should be the primary remedial focus. Some claim that even excessive emotional problems show marked improvement if reading is attacked first (Rupley and Blair, 1979a). Others consider these gains temporary and superficial. They say that reading problems will reappear later unless personality factors are dealt with directly (Spache, 1976b). Our position here, from our own experience, is that improvement in reading ability never hurts, and many emotional difficulties improve when students become better able to cope academically. As with learning disabilities, we have to start where we can.

Reading and Anxiety

Because emotional problems are as varied and individual as the human beings they affect, there are no all-inclusive sets of criteria or symptoms to which we can refer. Our own experience in classrooms and reading clinics has shown us a few characteristic ways in which youngsters react to the anxiety that reading can produce.

Many young children, for example, believe that on the first day of school they will learn to read. They are, by and large, sadly disappointed. Learning to read generally takes a fairly long time, especially if you've been around for only six or seven years. Being able to accept this notion, and have the persistence to stick it out, is related to the early development of *competence* (White, 1973).

Children who have developed physical and emotional mastery in their early years, by extended experience with things and people, are *confident* and *error-tolerant*. They are secure in their own ability to succeed even if they fail on the first attempts, and they are able to shrug off and learn from mistakes without becoming unduly discouraged by them. Children who develop a sense of their own competence in their early years approach beginning reading with patience and persistence, confidence that they will probably succeed in the end, and knowledge that occasional failure happens to everybody.

Youngsters who lack these notions are often unable to stick to a task long enough to become good at it. They admit defeat after only a few days or weeks of reading instruction. They seem to be overwhelmed by the whole process and often become inordinately discouraged by mistakes or confusion. When they aren't sure of what to do next, they get depressed or panicky. Activities that involve some element of cognitive risk, like predicting what might happen next in a story, are just too threatening. By avoiding risk, these children sometimes appear to be uncooperative or disinterested, but their apparent disinterest is often a cover for fear.

Risk avoiding is a common strategy for children who have not developed the resilience of spirit that we see in a competent child. It is also an aspect of another problem, one related to reading readiness.

Educators, child psychologists, and parents generally agree that children develop at very different rates, each according to an individual timetable. We are rarely seriously concerned if milestones like the first step, first word, or first tooth come earlier or later than those of a sibling or neighbor's child. Likewise we know that children develop the social skills, attention span, self-control, and physical stamina required for school at different ages. Some are able to deal with full half-days of nursery school experience between the ages of three and four whereas some five-year-olds cannot sustain themselves for an entire half day of kindergarten. Kindergarten was instituted to provide a structured environment in which children could develop in areas like socialized interaction, group play, observance of simple rules, attentive listening, following directions, and waiting one's turn. It is certainly a crucial school experience for every child.

Many children who are happy and secure in kindergarten, however, are unready for the greater demands of first grade. First, there are the physical demands: staying at school all day, eating lunch at school, getting on the right bus, staying awake all afternoon. Then there are the social demands: listening, waiting, following directions, lining up, sharing, making friends, keeping your temper. Add the academic demands: remembering your letters, reading all the words, printing neatly, learning the sounds, finishing your seatwork. It can be all too much. For some children learning to read is too difficult right from the start, and their anxiety is soon manifested.

It is not hard to spot first graders who fall asleep every day after lunch, but other behaviors may be somewhat more subtle. Carll and Richard (1976) listed some common behaviors of the "overplaced child" who is developmentally unready for first-grade instruction:

PHYSICAL MANIFESTATIONS

□ Fatigue, especially in afternoon
□ Frequent colds and infections
□ Poor letter formation compared to others of the same age
□ Inattention to activities most others find interesting

SOCIAL MANIFESTATIONS

□ Has difficulty making friends
□ Prefers to play with younger children
□ Chooses individual activities rather than group ones
□ Lashes out in anger physically or verbally

EMOTIONAL MANIFESTATIONS

□ Feels unwanted, unable
□ Lacks self-confidence
□ Cries easily
□ Escapes stressful activities with bathroom visits, drinks, pencil sharpening, daydreaming, etc.

- □ Overanxious about right answers
- □ Bed wetting, nail biting, poor sleep or appetite
- □ Unusually fearful, especially about getting hurt during play

ACADEMIC MANIFESTATIONS

- □ Slow to finish work; checks and rechecks, erases frequently
- □ Quick to respond "I don't know"
- □ Afraid to guess
- □ May be compulsively neat or excessively sloppy
- □ Asks to have directions repeated time after time

Youngsters who chronically exhibit a number of these behaviors are signaling that something is very wrong. Since children cannot be forced or taught how to develop *faster*, the situation must be modified for them. Too often, we expect the *child* to change rather than changing the anxiety-producing environment.

What can be done? We have heard well-intentioned parents and teachers say things like "Well, he's got to grow up sometime," or "She's just got to tough it out. School shouldn't be too much fun anyway." These responses are brutal in their egocentrism: they assume that children are small adults, with the same coping strategies and defense mechanisms as adults. That is patently not so. Children are not able to change their school situations because they do not control them; adults do. Children who need more time to grow and develop, to experience and to adapt to school must be given that time, free of stigma. Often, this means an additional year in kindergarten. In some schools, an extra year option has been built into the curriculum. The extra year is a full day of pre-first-grade instruction, often focusing on extended reading readiness, language development, exposure to books, and concrete experiences. It can, in our experience, make all the difference in the world for youngsters not quite ready for a full first-grade experience because it has no connotations of having failed or not having been promoted. Another year of first-grade instruction is sometimes a good solution. However, the youngster's second trip through first grade should entail different materials and instructional methods, and perhaps a different teacher. It should not mean recycling the child through the same materials and methods that didn't work the first time.

The anxious behaviors being described here are fairly common in young poor readers or prereaders, but they can also be seen in very anxious youngsters who are actually good readers. Fear of failure is no respecter of ability.

Some high-achieving students drive themselves with an intensity that, in an adult, would make friends worry about a heart attack. Such students are often compulsively neat in their written work, scrupulous in attention to detail, and rely on prodigious memory stores. They may take an inordinate amount of time to complete reading or writing assignments because they review and check their work over and over; they may excel at recall of factual information and convergent thinking but have difficulty drawing conclusions, thinking of alternatives, and predicting; they often get deeply discouraged by a critical remark or a less-than-perfect paper. It is unfortunate that these signs of anxiety are often overlooked in the classroom if a student's reading ability is at or near grade level.

As children grow older they become more dependent on what their peers think of them and less dependent on teacher or parental feedback. Added to their growing concern for peer approval, though, is their awareness that reading is extremely important both in and out of school, and failure to master reading can severely affect their self-esteem. Faced with a situation in which they cannot conform to adults' expectations, they may bend every effort to win approval from other students. They may exhibit hostility, defiance, profanity, aggression, and other behaviors that put teachers in an adversary position. In a review of studies of good and poor readers' personality traits, Spache (1976b) listed the following traits as being common in poor readers: aggressiveness, anxiety, withdrawal, negativeness, depression, and feelings of helplessness in academic and problem-solving situations, while good readers are usually self-confident, persistent, compliant, and have feelings of self-worth, independence, and belonging.

Assessing Interests

Teacher-made interest and attitude inventories are very useful devices for learning how students feel about books, reading, school subjects, and common childhood problems. This information can be used in several ways:

□ to determine if a particular student has very negative attitudes about reading that may affect progress in reading
□ to reveal if a particular student is having serious personal problems that may affect classroom performance and social relationships
□ to discover what specific topics students are interested in reading about as well as what kinds of materials they prefer using

Figures 9.1, 9.2, and 9.3 are sample classroom interest inventories that you may find helpful. Depending on their reading and writing ability, the students can complete them in writing or orally, and you will probably want to add other questions. The incomplete sentences in Figure 9.3 are modeled on those developed by Strang (1969, pp. 262–263). Hall, Ribovich, and Ramig (1979, p. 236) give several excellent examples of reading interest inventories and suggestions for their use, and Figures 9.1 and 9.2 are adapted from these.

FIGURE 9.1. Interest inventory for primary grades.

(The questions are read aloud to students, and their oral responses are written down by the teacher.)

1. If *you* could decide what you would study in school next week, what would you choose? Why? _____

_____

2. If someone asked you to choose a book or story you'd like to have read to you, what would the book be about? _____

_____

3. If you could magically visit any person from now or from the past, who would it be? _____

_____

4. If you woke up one day and found you had superhuman powers, what would you do? _____

_____

5. If someone were giving you a book for your birthday, what would you want the book to be about? _____

_____

6. Do you think a book is a good present? _____
    Why or why not? _____

_____

7. If you could magically turn into any kind of animal or bird, real or make-believe, what would you become? _____

_____

    What would you do in your new form? _____

_____

8. If you could write a TV show or movie, what would it be about? _____

_____

_____

_____

FIGURE 9.2. Interest inventory for intermediate and upper grades.

(The questions may be given silently or orally, and the student can answer orally or in writing.)

1. If you had a "surprise day off from school," how would you spend the day? _____

_____

2. If someone wanted to give you a magazine subscription for a gift, what magazine would you choose? _____

_____

3. If you were hired to write a new TV show, what would it be about? Who would star in it? Would *you* be in it? _____

_____

4. If you won a contest and your grand prize was to meet and get to know any famous person in the world today, whom would you choose? What would you like to talk about? _____

_____

5. If you could transport yourself into any time and place in the past, where would you go? What would you do there? How long would you stay in the past? _____

_____

6. If you could somehow become a super-athlete overnight, what would your sport be? What would you do as a super-athlete? _____

_____

7. If you could go into a bookstore and get any three books free, what kinds of books would you choose? _____

_____

8. If *you* could choose the books or stories to be used from now on in English (or language arts), what kinds of things would you choose? What would you definitely *not* include? _____

_____

_____

*C*hildren's attitudes and interests are as different as the individuals themselves. We can help children enjoy reading more by learning about their
interests and attitudes and using this information in our planning.

FIGURE 9.3. Attitudes and interests survey.

(The sentences may be completed orally or in writing.)

1. I think reading _____ .
2. I wish I could _____ .
3. Someday I _____ .
4. I wish my teacher _____ .
5. My best friend _____ .
6. I'd rather read than _____ .
7. At home I _____ .
8. When I read out loud _____ .
9. Science books _____ .
10. When I don't know a word _____ .
11. I wonder why _____ .
12. Reading about the past _____ .

(*continued on following page*)

FIGURE 9.3. (continued)

13. On test days I _____ .
14. Spelling is _____ .
15. I really love to _____ .
16. Animal stories _____ .
17. I don't understand _____ .
18. I wish I could _____ .
19. Books about famous people _____ .
20. When I have to write a paper _____ .
21. I felt proud when _____ .
22. My mother _____ .
23. Sometimes I think I _____ .
24. Pictures in books _____ .
25. My father _____ .

SOURCE: Adapted from *Improvement of Reading*, 4th ed., by Ruth Strang et al. Copyright © 1967 by McGraw-Hill, Inc. Used with the permission of McGraw-Hill Book Company.

Orchestrating Success

What can we do to help those whose emotional reactions to school, reading, and academic success have become destructively involved with their learning to read? We believe it is as important to know what you *cannot* do as what you *can*.

Unless you have special training and expertise in working with disturbed children or in counseling, you will probably not be able to "cure" the severely anxious student singlehandedly. If it consistently takes more than a smile and sincere praise to get a student to try again, if the student is socially isolated, and if you can observe continued signs of frustration and anxiety, seek help from others. The intensity and duration of anxiety are important factors. Everyone has an occasional bout of depression or feelings of worthlessness, but emotionally troubled children cannot shake it off. We all lose our tempers at ourselves or others and let our anger show in words or gestures. Troubled children have difficulty with degrees of emotion, and annoyance may become rage or withdrawal before they can get control of it. If you at all suspect that a student's moods and reactions are beyond average limits, get some professional advice.

In the area of reading we can always do something to help. Two key concepts are *support* and *success*. The importance of success in every person's life cannot be overstated. Even B. F. Skinner, the acknowledged founder of the behavior modification movement who was often associated with an impersonal, unemotional approach to children, put it this way:

The human organism, fortunately for us all, is reinforced just by being successful. Consequently, if material is designed to facilitate correct responses, the resulting frequent success is enough reinforcement for most persons. Not only will the child's behavior change as he learns to do things he could not do before, but he will become highly motivated, his morale will improve, and his attitude toward teachers will change. (Skinner, 1972, p. 11)

Hewett and Taylor (1980) have written of "the orchestration of success" necessary in dealing with emotionally disturbed children. The concept is generalizable to remedial work with children whose reading difficulties have led to damaged self-concept.

In describing the orchestration of success Hewitt and Taylor recount the case of Peter, a subject in a now classic study of operant conditioning to overcome a phobia. Peter, almost three years old, was irrationally afraid of a white rabbit, and his fear had generalized to all furry white things — beards, cotton, fur, etc. In a series of forty-five "desensitization" sessions, Peter's fear was removed by "pairing" the rabbit with Peter's favorite foods. As Peter ate, the rabbit was very gradually moved closer to him in successive sessions. At first, the rabbit's presence in the room caused Peter extreme anxiety. Forty-five sessions later he let the rabbit nibble at his fingers and spontaneously commented, "I like the rabbit." His fear was gone.

We are not advocating using this type of desensitization, a complex psychological treatment, for unhappy children in the classroom. We use this account to illustrate a point: that by *successive positive experiences* we can help children replace fear and anxiety with confidence.

Hewett and Taylor relate this desensitization process to that of helping children overcome fear and aversion to school tasks. They write:

> In place of food we are concerned with giving the child as positive and successful an experience as possible in the classroom. We need to capitalize on the child's interests, ask no more than he or she can comfortably do, and provide meaningful consequences for the child's efforts. Gradually, we may be able to move the aversive "white rabbit of schoolness" with its demands for conformity, rules, competition, and complexity closer and closer until the child is functioning in a normal manner in school. (Hewett and Taylor, 1980, pp. 128–129)

For many children, the white rabbit is reading. By providing support through activities that children can do, appropriate recognition of effort and achievement no matter how modest, and extended opportunities to practice newly emerging reading abilities, we can gradually move that fearful white rabbit back into their lives. As they become able to do more, self-confidence will begin to reappear. Success begets success.

It will not happen quickly, however. Even with consistent encouragement and support from teachers, family, and peers and consistent, thoughtful instruction it can still take years to help a child become a functional reader. And many children do not enjoy even the minimal criteria of consistent support and instruction. The problem is further compounded when instruction is haphazard or inappropriate to the student's abilities, which is often the case. Sometimes no one really seems to care whether or not students succeed, and sometimes teachers forget that endless patience is required.

Then there is the matter of finding the right material. The truth is that easy-to-read material doesn't have to mean dull, stilted language written to conform to a readability formula. Any material that is *memorable* and highly *predictable* is easy to read. The most memorable materials are those dictated by the students; after all, they just said it. Dictated accounts are nearly failsafe because they are memorable, natural sounding (written in the student's own language patterns), and intrinsically interesting (involving the student's own experiences, opinions, and values). Students who can learn to read their individual dictated accounts can move easily into reading group-dictated stories and then into simple text in trade books.

High predictability is found in any written material containing rhythmic or repetitious elements. For young children, books featuring repeated lines, simple rhymes and poems, nursery rhymes, songs, and jingles are good. For older students, song lyrics, commercial slogans, and poetry are all common forms of highly predictable materials. They can be used as a jumping-off place, a source of easy-to-read words and phrases, which, once learned, can be found in other reading materials that may be too difficult to tackle at first. If, at any point in the lessons, the student begins to show the same signs of anxiety and frustration as before, we have to move the white rabbit back; in other words, move to easier, more supportive activities in which the student can succeed.

Echo reading and choral reading are good support techniques. In echo reading, the teacher reads a sentence or two of text and the student (one or more) echoes the teacher's words. Choral reading is a bit less supported since it requires the teacher and student(s) to read aloud simultaneously. Students may read fairly difficult material several times by echo reading and then move to choral reading of the same material. Sometimes students read comfortably and successfully in the echo setting but quickly begin to exhibit tension, fear, and frustration when they move to choral reading. In these cases we must move back and spend more time in the more supportive mode before we move that old rabbit closer again. Patience pays because every time children go through the text their confidence grows, and in time they will be able to choral-read fluently and, finally, without support. Rushing the early stages only delays the development of the confidence that is so necessary. The analogy of Peter and the white rabbit is an excellent model for reading remediation: by moving through gradual stages we can provide sufficient support and continuous success in reading, and by doing so we can modify negative attitudes and repair damaged self-concepts.

Summary

PL 94–142, the Education for All Handicapped Children Act of 1975, has profoundly affected the education profession. The law requires that every handicapped child be provided with special education services appropriate to the individual's abilities and/or disabilities. The major provisions of the law mandate free public education for all handicapped persons between three and twenty-one years of age, placement in the least restrictive learning environment, an individual educational program (IEP) for each handicapped pupil to be developed jointly by the student's teachers and parents (and the student, when possible), and the elimination of racial, cultural, and other forms of bias in testing and evaluation. Every handicapped student is guaranteed due process, equal educational opportunity, and accountability from teachers and schools in IEP implementation.

The implications of PL 94–142 are numerous and profound. Teachers of reading, and all other educators, must be aware of the effect of intellectual, physical, and emotional factors in reading, how children with special needs are diagnosed and taught most effectively, and how handicapped students are successfully dealt with in regular classrooms.

Intelligence tests are frequently given as a part of a reading diagnostic assessment. Reading achievement and intelligence are correlated, particularly in the upper grades, but many poor readers are of average or above average intelligence.

Group intelligence tests nearly always require the student to read and write. *Individual* tests, which are given orally, yield better estimates of intellectual ability. Some individual tests are language-dependent; they estimate only *verbal intelligence,* which is modified and expressed by means of language. The Slosson Intelligence Test, Peabody Picture Vocabulary Test, and Stanford-Binet Intelligence Scales are examples. The Wechsler Scales assess both verbal and *nonverbal intelligence.*

Intelligence test performance is heavily influenced by the amount and kind of experience one has had. Experience is gained concretely, by direct or real experience with people, objects, and events, and vicariously, by observing others' experience and by reading. Much of the learning in school is conveyed by print, and the poor readers who lack such information and experience generally do less well on intelligence tests than their age mates who do read, even when the test given requires no reading.

An informal alternative to an I.Q. test is the assessment of *hearing capacity,* the grade level of text a student can adequately understand through listening. Hearing capacity is assessed by reading text material aloud to the student and evaluating the answers to orally administered comprehension questions. Comparison of hearing capacity and instructional levels allows the diagnostician to estimate the student's present *potential for reading improvement.* Since it is specifically related to reading ability, the hearing capacity concept is more directly useful for instructional planning than I.Q. test scores.

If students can listen to and adequately understand text written at their present grade level and yet cannot adequately read the same text for themselves, they are still judged to have the verbal concepts and vocabulary necessary for learning to read at that level of difficulty. Very poor readers may have hearing capacity levels many grades below their present grade, but hearing capacity is *dynamic* rather than fixed, and as reading ability improves the hearing capacity level will probably rise also.

Physical factors in reading include *vision, hearing,* and *special learning problems.*

In the area of vision, *eye movements* are often misunderstood. The normal reading eye moves forward in jerky *saccadic* movements, moves backward occasionally in *regressions,* and takes in visual information only when at rest, during *fixations.* A fixation usually lasts about fifty milliseconds, and three to five fixations per line of print is usual. At this rate the reader sees about two to four words per fixation. *Visual training programs* attempt to prevent regressions or speed up fixations during reading, but their effectiveness has been widely questioned for many years. When few words are recognized quickly the reader makes more frequent fixations; very slow reading with nearly as many fixations as there are words per line results in poor comprehension. The term *tunnel vision* has been used to describe very slow, dysfluent reading. Overly frequent fixations or regressions are *symptoms, not causes,* of reading difficulty.

Common visual problems include *myopia* (nearsightedness), *hyperopia* (farsightedness), *astigmatism, amblyopia* (lazy eye), *strabismus* (crossed eyes), *muscular imbalance* (fusion or phoria), and *aniseikonia.* The first three are the most common. Hyperopia and astigmatism can make reading tiring and uncomfortable, but myopia affects only reading of distant images (blackboard, signs) and is common among good readers. All these problems are correctable. Different vision problems can share similar symptoms, but if any are persistent, *vision screening* should be sought. Vision screening is usually done with a *stereoscopic* instrument and test battery that test each eye separately and both together. *Ophthalmologists,* eye specialists, use more technical measures.

Problems of hearing can affect the child's production and use of oral language and interfere with primarily oral early reading instruction, including phonics instruction. Hearing is assessed by measuring perception of speech sounds in terms of *pitch* and *volume.* Pitch, the *frequency* at which sounds are produced, is measured in *hertz* or cycles per second. Consonant sounds are produced at a higher pitch or frequency than vowel sounds. Volume or loudness is measured in *decibels.* Hearing aids are used to amplify sounds and are used to correct volume losses.

Many children suffer temporary but recurrent hearing losses involving the high-frequency sounds, which severely affect phonics instruction and may make speech reception difficult. These losses, called *conductive hearing losses,* are commonly caused by conditions arising from upper respiratory infections, allergies, and childhood diseases. A collection of fluid in the middle ear can result from such infections and can inhibit conduction of sounds to the inner ear. Unequal air pressure behind the eardrum, caused by blocking or collapse of the eustachian tube, can inhibit conduction by distending the eardrum. Conductive hearing losses may recur chronically during the school years, when children often suffer many colds and upper respiratory infections.

In addition, common childhood diseases like mumps and measles, and exposure to excessive noise, can damage structures of the inner ear. Both middle and inner ear structures are involved in the transmission of sound signals to the brain. *Auditory screening* is done with an *audiometer,* an instrument that tests perception of sounds at a wide range of frequencies and volumes. Children who exhibit persistent symptoms of hearing problems, as well as those returning to school after mumps, measles, flu, or other upper respiratory illnesses, should be routinely screened.

Dyslexia and *learning disabilities* are terms that are the subject of much controversy and disagreement. *Dyslexia* is often used to mean a specific learning disability that severely affects the ability to read or to learn to read. There is no general agreement on its causes, symptoms, or treatment. The wide use of the term has been criticized because of its lack of specificity. Similarly, there is little consensus on the specific meaning of the term *learning disability.* It is often used to describe the difficulty of a child of at least average intelligence who appears to be free of physical, emotional, and intellectual handicaps. Minimal neurological damage or dysfunction is often presumed from behavioral, rather than neurological, evidence.

The same student with a reading problem may be considered "reading disabled" by a reading specialist and "learning disabled" by a learning disabilities specialist. A child's reading behaviors are frequently interpreted in very different ways by the two practitioners. Remedial methods also differ widely between the two specialties.

Students experiencing difficulty with reading often suffer *emotional* difficulties as a result of damaged self-concepts, loss of confidence, and aversion to school and reading. Those having problems learning to read often show particular *anxiety behaviors.* If preschoolers consider themselves *competent,* they will approach learning with confidence and tolerance for their own mistakes. Children who do not feel competent may not be persistent, may become easily discouraged, and may attempt to avoid risk by acting withdrawn, uncooperative, or disinterested. Some young children also lack the *maturity* to succeed in the early grades; they lack the physical stamina, emotional resiliency, or academic skills necessary to learn to read in first grade. They too exhibit characteristic physical, social, emotional, and academic reactions to the stress they suffer. Additional time for development must be provided for them. Older poor readers may also be withdrawn or disinterested, and their desire for peer admiration may result in episodes of aggressive physical or verbal behavior.

Anxiety is not limited to poor readers; some high achievers gain success at great physical and emotional cost, driving themselves for perfection. Their anxious behaviors are just as damaging but may be overlooked if their reading is at or near grade level.

Students experiencing difficulty can be helped by providing supportive measures, by using materials that can be read easily, by keeping tasks reasonable in terms of what they can accomplish, and by providing enough support for a long enough period of time for their confidence to rebuild.

Extension Activities

1. Choose one of the group intelligence tests and one of the individual tests listed in this chapter. Find the description and reviews of each test in the appropriate *Mental Measurement Yearbook* or *Intelligence Tests in Print*. What are the apparent strengths and weaknesses of each test? For what specific purposes would each test be more appropriate?

2. Interview a psychometrist or school psychologist about the uses of the WISC-R in reading diagnosis. In his or her opinion, what types of subtest score patterns are most characteristic of poor readers? What subtests seem most profoundly affected by poor reading? Are there any particular score patterns or responses the examiner might look for that could explain why the student has reading problems? In his or her opinion, of what use is an intelligence test in reading diagnosis?

3. Select a student and administer a hearing capacity assessment, using any IRI or your own selection of text passages and questions. *After* determining the student's hearing capacity level, find out what intelligence test or similar ability data exist for that pupil. Do your informal findings correspond to the other test scores? If not, why do you think the discrepancy exists?

4. Interview a preschool or kindergarten teacher about the role of experience in developing young children's intelligence. What experiences does he or she consider critical for school success? Which are necessary before school entrance? Which can be provided within the school curriculum? Are they being provided?

5. Find out who is responsible for doing visual and/or auditory screening in your school or division. What tests are used? What machines? How are students referred? If they have positive screening results, what follow-up is done to see if they receive treatment? Find out how the screening procedures work by learning how to use the equipment or see how it is operated. Have your own hearing/vision checked by someone else.

6. Select a "panel" consisting of as many of these people as you can: a reading specialist, a special education teacher and/or an LD specialist, several regular classroom teachers from both elementary and secondary levels, several parents, a doctor or nurse, and a university educator. Ask them to define *dyslexia* and describe its causes, symptoms, and treatment as fully as they can. Keep a record of what each one tells you and compare the responses. Are there agreements? Contradictions? Misinformation? What is the general state of understanding of this term?

7. Ask a reading teacher and an LD teacher to describe the tests each would use to diagnose the reading problem of a child you describe, the same child in each case. How would their assessments differ? Why do they differ? What information might each teacher have that the other could benefit from sharing?

Suggested Readings

Blackhurst, A. Edward and Berdine, William H. **An Introduction to Special Education.** *Boston: Little, Brown, 1981.* A comprehensive text with particularly informative chapters on special education legislation, language disorders, visual and auditory impairments, learning disabilities, and special intellectual needs.

Heward, William L. and Orlansky, Michael D. **Exceptional Children.** *Columbus: Charles Merrill, 1980.* Basic special education text, interestingly written and practical.

Kirk, Samuel A.; Kliebhan, Sr. Joanne Marie; and Lerner, Janet W. **Teaching Reading to Slow and Disabled Learners.** *Boston: Houghton Mifflin, 1978.* Reading instruction methods for special education students in a balanced and thoughtful presentation.

Landau, Elliott D.; Epstein, Sherry L., and Stone, Ann P. **The Exceptional Child Through Literature.** *Engelwood Cliffs, N.J.: Prentice-Hall, 1978.* Uses of literature to help teachers and students become aware of their feelings and attitudes about handicapped children.

Orlansky, Michael D. **Mainstreaminng the Visually Impaired Child.** *Hingham, Mass.: Teaching Resources, 1977.* Handbook for teachers with visually impaired students in regular classrooms.

Sagan, Carl. **The Dragons of Eden.** *New York: Random House, 1977.* Spellbinding discussions of brain and sensory activity, the nature of intelligence, language and human cultures written for the lay reader.

References

Adams, Richard B. "Dyslexia: A Discussion of Its Definition." *Journal of Learning Disabilities* 2, No. 12 (Dec. 1969): 616–623.

Blank, Marion. "Cognitive Processes in Auditory Discrimination in Normal and Retarded Readers." *Child Development* 39, No. 4 (Dec. 1968): 1091–1101.

Bond, Guy L.; Tinker, Miles A.; and Wasson, Barbara B. *Reading Difficulties: Their Diagnosis & Correction,* 4th ed. Englewood Cliffs, N.J.: Prentice-Hall, 1979.

Carll, Barbara and Richard, Nancy. *One Piece of the Puzzle: School Readiness.* Programs for Education: 1976.

Carroll, Lewis. *Through the Looking-Glass, and What Alice Found There.* N.Y.: Hurst, n.d.

Dauzat, Sam V. "Good Gosh! My Child Has Dyslexia." *The Reading Teacher* 22, No. 7 (April 1969): 630–633.

Dirks, Donald D. "Effects of Hearing Impairment on the Auditory System." In Edward Carterette & Morton Friedman, eds. *Handbook of Perception, Volume IV: Hearing.* N.Y.: Academic Press, 1978.

Dunn, Lloyd M. *Peabody Picture Vocabulary Test.* Circle Pines, Minn.: American Guidance Service, 1959.

Ekwall, Eldon E. *Diagnosis and Remediation of the Disabled Reader.* Boston: Allyn and Bacon, 1976.

Fry, Edward. "Do-It-Yourself Terminology Generator." *Journal of Reading* 11, No. 6 (Mar. 1968): 428.

Gillham, Isabel. "Self-Concept and Reading." In Eldon Ekwall, ed. *Psychological Factors in the Teaching of Reading.* Columbus: Charles Merrill, 1973.

Gregory, R. L. *Eye and Brain: The Psychology of Seeing.* N.Y.: McGraw-Hill, 1966.

Hall, MaryAnne; Ribovich, Jerilyn K.; and Ramig, Christopher. *Reading and the Elementary School Child,* 2nd ed. N.Y.: Van Nostrand, 1979.

Hartman, Nancy C. and Hartman, Robert K. "Perceptual Handicap or Reading Disability?" *The Reading Teacher* 26, No. 7 (April 1973): 684–695.

Hewett, Frank M. and Taylor, Frank M. *The Emotionally Disturbed Child in the Classroom: The Orchestration of Success,* 2nd. ed. Boston: Allyn and Bacon, 1980.

Hittleman, Daniel R. *Developmental Reading: A Psycholinguistic Perspective.* Chicago: Rand McNally, 1978.

Hochberg, Julian. "Components of Literacy: Speculations and Exploratory Research." In H. Levin & J. P. Williams, eds. *Basic Studies on Reading.* N.Y.: Basic Books, 1970.

Huey, Edmund Burke. *The Psychology and Pedagogy of Reading.* N.Y.: Macmillan, 1908; reprinted Cambridge, Mass.: MIT Press, 1968.

Kaufman, Alan S. *Intelligent Testing with the WISC-R.* N.Y.: Wiley, 1979.

Lanyon, Richard I. and Giddings, John W. "Psychological Approaches to Myopia: A Review." *American Journal of Optometry and Physiological Optics* 51 (April 1974): 271–281.

Mackworth, Norman H. "Visual Noise Causes Tunnel Vision." *Psychonomic Science* 3 (1965): 67–68.

MacMillan, D. L. *Mental Retardation in School and Society.* Boston: Little, Brown, 1977.

Martin, Harold P. "Vision and Its Role in Reading Disability and Dyslexia." *The Journal of School Health* 41 (Nov. 1971): 468–472.

Masland, R. L. "Children with Minimal Brain Dysfunction: A National Problem." In L. Tarnapol, ed. *Learning Disabilities: Introduction to Educational and Medical Management.* Springfield, Ill.: Thomas, 1969.

Optometric Extension Program Foundation, Inc. *Educator's Guide to Classroom Vision Problems and Educator's Checklist.* Duncan, Okla.: Optometric Extension Program Foundation, 1968.

Reading Newsreport "Early Help for Dyslexics." Vol. 3 (May–June 1969): 32–36.

Rosner, Stanley L. "Word Games in Reading Diagnosis." *The Reading Teacher* 24, No. 4 (Jan. 1971): 331–335.

Rupley, William H. and Blair, Timothy R. *Reading Diagnosis and Remediation.* Chicago: Rand McNally, 1979a.

Rupley, William H. and Blair, Timothy R. "Mainstreaming and Reading Instruction." *The Reading Teacher* 32, No. 6 (March 1979b): 762–765.

Rutherford, William L. "What Is Your D.L. (Dyslexia Quotient)?" *The Reading Teacher* 24 No. 3 (Dec. 1971): 262–266.

Samuels, S. Jay. "Success and Failure in Learning to Read: A Critique of the Research." *Reading Research Quarterly* 8, No. 2 (Winter 1973): 200–239.

Sanders, Derek A. *Auditory Perception of Speech*. Englewood Cliffs, N.J: Prentice-Hall, 1977.

Schubert, Delwyn G. and Walton, Howard N. "Visual Screening: A New Breakthrough." *The Reading Teacher*, 34 No. 2 (Nov. 1980): 175–177.

Searls, Evelyn F. *How to Use WISC Scores in Reading Diagnosis*. Newark, Del.: International Reading Association, 1975.

Skinner, B. F. "Teaching: The Arrangement of Contingencies Under Which Something Is Taught." In N. G. Haring and A. H. Hayden, eds. *Improvement of Instruction*. Seattle: Special Child Publications, 1972.

Slosson, Richard L. *Slosson Intelligence Test*. E. Aurora, N.Y.: Slosson Educational Publications, 1963.

Smith, Frank. *Understanding Reading*, 2nd ed. N.Y.: Holt, Rinehart & Winston, 1978.

Spache, George D. *Diagnosing and Correcting Reading Disabilities*. Boston: Allyn and Bacon, 1976a.

Spache, George D. *Investigating the Issues of Reading Difficulties*. Boston: Allyn and Bacon, 1976b.

Strang, Ruth. *Diagnostic Teaching of Reading*, 2nd ed. N.Y.: McGraw-Hill, 1969.

Thompson, Bertha B. "A Longitudinal Study of Auditory Discrimination." *Journal of Educational Research* 56 (March 1963): 376–378.

Tinker, Miles A. "The Study of Eye Movements in Reading." *Psychological Bulletin* 43 (1958): 215–231.

Vernon, Magdalen D. *Backwardness in Reading*. Cambridge: Cambridge University Press, 1957.

Wallace, Gerald and Larsen, Stephen C. *Educational Assessment of Learning Problems: Testing for Teaching*. Boston: Allyn and Bacon, 1978.

Wechsler, David. *The Measurement and Appraisal of Adult Intelligence*, 4th ed. Baltimore: Williams & Wilkins, 1958.

Wechsler, David. *Manual for the Wechsler Intelligence Scale for Children — Revised*. N.Y.: Psychological Corporation, 1974.

White, Burton L. & Watts, Jean Carew. *Experience and Environment: Major Influences on the Development of the Young Child*. Vol. I. Englewood Cliffs, N.J.: Prentice-Hall, 1973.

Wilson, Robert M. *Diagnostic and Remedial Reading for Classroom and Clinic*, 5th ed. Columbus: Charles Merrill, 1981.

Witty, Paul A. "Rate of Reading: A Critical Issue." In E. Ekwall, ed. *Psychological Factors in the Teaching of Reading*. Columbus: Charles Merrill, 1973.

Woodruff, M. Emerson. "Observations on the Visual Acuity of Children During the First Five Years of Live." *American Journal of Optometry and Archives of American Academy of Optometry*, 49 (March 1972): 205–214.

Chapter Ten

Assessing the Reading Environment

Assessment of reading problems sometimes takes place in university reading clinics and private remedial centers, outside the school setting. While the expertise of such sources varies widely, in most cases the examination is thorough and perceptive. A good clinical diagnosis will include tests of reading, writing, and spelling as well as an individually administered intelligence test, investigation of personality development and attitudes toward reading, screening of vision and hearing, detailed medical and school histories, and interviews with the student and parents.

In this way clinicians develop a detailed, generally accurate picture of the student's reading, but there is always a piece of the picture missing: What is the classroom setting like in which the student must operate? What kinds of teaching go on? What are the demands of the school reading program? If any of this information is available, it is often secondhand.

Morris wrote, ". . . learning or not learning to read is a product of the interaction between an individual child and his or her instructional environment. A child does not learn to read in a vacuum, and ultimately our understanding of the reading acquisition process must include an analysis of the environmental factors which facilitate or impede that progress" (Morris, 1979, p. 497). Diagnosis that takes place out of the school setting may ignore this interaction.

And after the assessment, what happens? Are the clinical recommendations implemented? Diagnosticians working in a clinic rather than in a school may never learn what happens after the students return to their classrooms.

When testing is done within the school, it is hoped that this kind of closure can be achieved — that diagnosis takes the *classroom* and *program* as well as the *student* into consideration and that the diagnosis is done in order to make instructional change possible.

Any reading assessment that does not result in classroom action is of little use. Even the most detailed discussion of the learning activities children need to overcome a reading problem or to meet their potential must be put in the context of teaching many children at once. Teachers have to teach children in groups, in classroom settings. When they work with an individual child, they still have to maintain responsibility for all the other children at the same time.

Some classrooms are better environments for learning to read than others and in this chapter we describe a set of factors that may explain why.

Setting Instructional Goals

Are classroom instructional goals set by teachers or dictated by commercial reading or language arts programs? There are really two important assumptions in this question: that the teachers who implement a reading program should have a solid understanding of how children learn to read and that they should be given *real* responsibility for making day-to-day decisions regarding instruction in their own classrooms.

We can illustrate this point with an example. A few years ago we were asked by a county public school division to conduct a study of reading achievement and instruction throughout all the county schools. There was widespread dissatisfaction with reading achievement, and we were asked to report the problems and recommend solutions.

As part of the study we selected students with low reading achievement in grades one through twelve and tested each one individually by using the measures and procedures described in this book. After our assessment was completed we formed independent judgments of what each one needed. Then we observed them in their regular classes, talked with their teachers, looked at materials, and finally determined whether their instruction matched their needs as we perceived them.

One day in the fall we tested Kevin, a third-grade nonreader. The son of a pulpwood cutter, Kevin had been given few material advantages in his life and had known little intellectual enrichment. We quickly realized that he did not express himself orally with much fluency, had few ideas about what writing or print were for, and had little exposure to books or story structures. In reading he could recognize only a few words at sight; he knew an assortment of letter sounds but not enough to be able to decode very much; and he spelled almost at random. In short, we could see that he was just getting ready to learn to read and that he would need to be supported by rich oral language practice and prereading experience with books. He should have been read to often and had his interest in books aroused in all of the dozens of ways that good kindergarten and primary grade teachers have practiced for decades. Because Kevin's background had poorly prepared him for the demands of literacy, we hoped that his school environment would be especially rich in oral and written language experiences.

When we returned with Kevin to his classroom we were unprepared for what we saw. Kevin walked over to his work folder and pulled out a duplicator sheet. After asking another student what to do with it, he went to his desk and began to color it. We looked over his shoulder and saw that he was coloring all the geometric shapes that looked the same. This, the instructions told us, was preparation for learning to discriminate letter shapes. We noticed that all of the twenty-odd children in the class were working on filling in different duplicator sheets. Later we queried the teacher about what Kevin had been doing. We asked why he had been assigned *that* duplicator sheet. Because it was prescribed by the management system that accompanied the basal reading series, she replied. Every child had been tested at the beginning of the year and placed in a sequence of skills to be mastered. Kevin, and a few others in the class, were at the bottom of the sequence. (The sequence, we later found, ran something like this: discriminating shapes, learning letter forms, discriminating sounds, learning letter sounds for word attack, reading single words, reading sentences, and so on). Kevin was working on readiness skills at his prescribed level, and in the few weeks since school started he had worked through a number of similar skill activities.

We naively asked the teacher why she was using the management system. She rolled her eyes and said that it "came with the job." She was an older teacher who had taught in the primary grades for many years. We asked, "If you were free to teach Kevin in any way you wanted, how would you go about it?" "Well," she said, "before the management system was instituted, I used to read to the children and they would learn their favorite stories, and they would put on plays about them." She smiled as she recalled the puppet shows and storytelling they did. "But," she said regretfully, "now there isn't time." For a large portion of their reading period, the children went to different teachers for a period of forty minutes to work on skills. Kevin had come from someone else's class, and he would go back shortly, so this teacher wouldn't see him the rest of the day.

We were saddened by what we saw happening with Kevin. He was being treated humanely, but he just wasn't being taught. As we talked with administrators and other teachers we heard over and over that the basal-and-management-system approach had allowed the district to "individualize instruction for every child." School personnel told us proudly that all the students in language arts were now working on their level, regardless of grade placement, and that reading achievement groups within the classroom had been replaced by a rotating system whereby each teacher taught children of similar ability. Nobody seemed to realize that in spite of their attempts to streamline instruction and "individualize" by the use of programming, children like Kevin were slipping through the cracks.

This is a sad story, but not an uncommon one. There are many teachers whose programs dictate the way they teach reading. Sometimes they are required to follow them explicitly, as in the case of Kevin's teacher. More often they understandably assume that the reading series is "right," or (sometimes from experience) that they will be reprimanded by a supervisor if they deviate from the teacher's manual. In truth, however, the reading series or method that will teach *every* child to read has not been written, and it probably never will be. Teachers will always have to make numerous modifications in the called-for procedures in the basal readers for one or several children. This is just as true for the individualized systems as for those that are more traditionally organized. The program Kevin was in had an elaborate system of skill lists, placement and checkup tests, and individual lessons, all for the purpose of "individualizing instruction." We believe, however, that most of the activities Kevin really needed to become literate were not included in the program. Since programs will have to be modified if they are to be right for all children, teachers must be more than just free to do such modifying — they must be actively *encouraged* and *helped* to do so.

Our position, that informed teachers should run the program and not vice versa, has another position embedded in it. Teachers must know *how* children learn to read. They should also know how to, and be willing to, use a variety of techniques for reading instruction. The contents of this or any textbook are not enough, but they do give us a starting point.

Think critically about reading in your classroom. Who (or what) dictates what individual children need to do, what they actually do, and how they are evaluated?

Time Spent Reading

It is self-evident that students should spend their time on the "right" tasks in order to learn to read, but this guideline is so regularly and routinely violated that it demands examination. Two crucial aspects here are the *quantity* of time spent on various activities and the *quality* of those activities. Both are essential and yet there are times when neither criterion is met.

What would an uninformed observer see in an elementary school class? Seymour Sarason (1971), a community psychologist, has noted that people who work in complex institutions like schools day in and day out sometimes overlook facts and conditions that would be obvious to another person who has never seen a school. To illustrate the point, he asks us to pretend that a Martian is hovering in a spacecraft right over a school. The Martian has X-ray vision and can see into all parts of the school. Being a careful observer, the Martian is skilled at finding patterns in the activity below but does not know Earth languages and therefore cannot understand what people *say* they are doing. The Martian can only watch what they *do*, and draw independent conclusions.

Morris (1979) applied the Martian's observation technique to a third-grade reading class to find out what it is that children actually *do* during reading time in a self-contained classroom. It appeared that they frequently move around from place to place; they spend much time marking in blanks or putting circles around items on printed sheets; and they spend a little time sitting in a circle with an adult. They also did something else: they pointed their eyes at the squiggles of print in books. How much of the time did they do this "pointing"? The Martian concluded that this activity usually accounted for a total of less than five minutes. The Martian in this classroom was Morris himself, who informally but carefully recorded the time each of two third-grade poor readers spent reading connected text (sentences or paragraphs, as in a story or article, rather than individual sentences or even smaller units) in a typical language arts period. Morris found that those poor readers averaged about two minutes of real reading per day during language arts.

We have replicated these depressing findings in a number of classroom observations involving different schools and grades. In each situation, the poorest readers spent the least time even *looking* at text, often five minutes or less per language arts period. The better readers, conversely, generally spent extended amounts of time reading basal stories, library books, and magazines. Even with all other considerations aside, it is not surprising that the poorer readers make such slow progress, if indeed they make any progress at all.

In addition to reading extended text themselves, let us consider what other things children in reading classes do. One activity that would strike any observer is *testing*. A surprising amount of time is taken up with tests of various kinds. A number of basal reading series have adopted a cyclical format for the teaching of skills, and a cycle of pretest-teach-retest-reteach-posttest is common. If teachers carefully follow this format and utilize the activities provided for each step (as many teachers are now *required* to do), as much as 40 percent of their instructional time may be taken up just by the reading series tests. This percentage does not include, of course, the time given to other tests: achievement tests in reading, state-mandated tests of basic skills or minimum competencies, teacher-made tests, and group diagnostic tests of various kinds. As testing proliferates, more and more instructional time is being sacrificed. After all, the time must come from somewhere; the school day has not been significantly lengthened, nor are there fewer subjects being taught now than a few years ago. Probably, the opposite is true. In many districts and states, the traditional elementary subjects of language arts, social studies, math, science, and supplementary subjects (music, art, and physical education) have been augmented by career education, languages, health, environmental awareness, and numerous other special subjects. There is more to teach and a good deal less time in which to do it! Is it any wonder that many children spend so little time reading?

Just as we must determine how much time is spent on real reading tasks, it is just as important to see to it that the instructional tasks themselves are really worthwhile. In many current individualized reading instruction programs, a lot of the prescribed activities are of dubious instructional value. Most duplicator work sheets, for example, do not involve real reading (of connected text, for meaning), yet in many programs children work on duplicator sheets more than half of the time.

Even the students come to believe that this is what reading instruction is. In a study of reading interests, students were asked if there should be more time in school for free reading. One child's answer was typical: "Yes, but it wouldn't work because then we wouldn't have enough time to do our work sheets." (Estes and Johnstone, 1977, p. 893). When asked to list the daily schedule of activities in her second-grade class, a daughter of one of the authors recited, "Homeroom, spelling, *dittos*, reading group . . ." (emphasis added).

Rather than list all the questionable instruction activities that might be encountered, however, let us list some activities that should be abundant in every reading class.

Reading to Children

One of the most positive activities is reading to the students. This is true at all grade levels, but it is imperative in the primary grades. Young children must be read to at least once every day, and for those who have not been read to at home, even once a day is not enough.

Why read to children? Aren't there more important readiness and beginning reading skills that they should be working on? In a word, no. Ronald Cramer, a reading and early childhood educator, put it this way:

> Teachers can't teach children to love books, but by reading to them every day they can create an atmosphere that will help children appreciate the gift of literature. The enjoyment of books can be shared. Reading to children helps them learn to read . . . provides models for writing . . . sparks the imagi-

*R*eading to students of all ages is one of the most important classroom activities. A teacher who regularly reads aloud to students helps give them the gift of literature.

nation and provides images and ideas for children to write about . . . enriches their language . . . develops their concepts, knowledge and thinking ability . . . illustrates specific concepts . . . is the surest way to develop a love and appreciation for books . . . establishes a mutual bond among listeners. (Cramer, 1975, pp. 460–461)

In the "old days," perhaps when Kevin's teacher received her training, teachers were often taught to read to their young students for twenty minutes a day. Although twenty minutes a day is more than many students receive, even that much time allows for only a couple of hundred books, short ones at that, to be read in a year. If you read long continuing books like *Charlotte's Web*, you may not even finish a hundred. It helps, but it is not enough. Consider youngsters who, blessed with book-loving families, enter first grade having heard a storybook read aloud every day for most of their lives. They have a background of a *thousand* or more books in their experience (Huck, 1976), which they can apply to make the task of learning to read easier.

Another big plus for children is storytelling. Helen Huus described this aspect of the "good old days," one that many of us never knew. In ". . . the 1920s, schools that followed the platoon system usually had a children's library and a separate period when pupils went to their literature teacher. She was a specialist, just as others were specialists in arithmetic, reading, social studies, or sciences" (Huus, 1973, p. 795). The teaching of literature as a subject included many of the elements in today's language arts, but an important activity in earlier days was storytelling. In fact, in the last century students at the "normal schools" nearly always were required to take a course in storytelling, or oral interpretation, as well as courses in oral reading, elocution, and other skills then thought necessary for all teachers. Today, storytelling is almost a lost art, and the loss is great because, like reading to children, it provides them with a rich store of characters, scenes, and plots. It feeds their desire to read that particular story for themselves. (After you read or tell a story, try displaying the book prominently in the classroom. It won't sit there very long.)

Reading to children and storytelling should not end after the primary grades. Older poor readers or nonreaders have as great a need to hear and enjoy stories as little children do, if they are to improve their reading. In the upper grades, where the range of reading abilities in any class widens rapidly, a listen-and-discuss activity such as a directed listening-thinking activity (Chapters Three and Seven) keeps a group together and allows students of very different reading abilities to work together in a discussion.

An anecdote shared with us by an in-service teacher illustrates this point. During her first year of teaching she struggled hard to get her ninth-grade English students to read selected short stories. The fourth period was a daily trial because Jim, a very poor reader, was constantly disruptive. One day in desperation she read a favorite short story aloud to the class. To her surprise,

Jim listened and even answered several questions. On his way out she commented on his perceptive answers and asked if he particularly liked that story. He glowered at her, leaned forward, and muttered, "It was the first time I finished the story at the same time as everybody else!" As if ashamed of his candor, he stalked out. She never forgot the lesson Jim taught her: that listening can draw a poor reader into a literature activity that reading shuts him out of. Storytelling, too, has its place in the upper grades, especially as a stimulus to writing and acting out scripts (see Moffett and Wagner, 1976).

Having Children Read

Encouraging children themselves to read is another important activity. It is often said that we learn to read by reading, by wading in and making sense of print. That does not mean that we always learn without help, but there is no substitute for reading real text for some purpose, no matter what that purpose may be.

Kevin, compliantly coloring his geometric shapes, was unable to cope with the basals and was not being provided with anything he could read or be helped to read, such as experience stories or pattern books. He was not doing *any* reading. The poor readers in Morris's survey were exposed to text for less than five minutes a day. Nobody ever learned to ride a bike by avoiding any contact with bikes, and nobody ever learned to swim by looking at water for a few moments a day. There are, of course, many different ways to approach reading instruction, but whatever the approach it is best for children to read whatever they can read as soon as possible, and then spend more time reading. In the words of Edmund Henderson, a reading educator and horseman, you learn to ride only by "spending time in the saddle."

Stauffer (1980), Allen (1976), and others who advocate using language experience as a first reading method recommend writing down a group-dictated experience story and choral-reading it on the first day of school. The first graders then go home to report proudly, "What did we do today? We wrote a story and we read it too!"

Language experience is not the only approach that allows an immediate start on real reading, even before children have mastered any skills. Several commercial basal series, such as Holt, Rinehart and Winston's *Sounds of Language* series and Scott Foresman's *Reading Unlimited* program begin with repetitions, patterned stories children can read as easily as a dictated story. The first passage in the first preprimer of *Sounds of Language* is the text of the song, "Happy Birthday." Here are the teacher's manual directions:

> These sentence sounds already are in most children's heads. Support their immediate belief that they can read this page. Here's a chance to connect oral and printed language. Role-playing the act of reading is a child's first step in becoming a successful reader. (Martin and Brogan, *Sounds I Remember*, 1974, p. 11)

Martin and Brogan have also produced the *Instant Readers,* sets of highly patterned children's books. A book like *Brown Bear, Brown Bear* may be the first whole book a child ever reads straight through. Its highly repetitious text and picture clues make it a completely supportive experience ("Brown bear, brown bear, what do you see? I see a *red bird* looking at me. Red bird, red bird, what do you see? I see a yellow duck . . . blue horse . . . grey mouse," etc.). Here is what Martin and Brogan have written about such books:

> Children in our society inherit the need to read. They also inherit the expectancy that they will read a book on the first day of school. When they don't, they go home disappointed — and the first breach between a child and reading success has been created. How much better to invite those "first-dayers" to hear a highly structured book that they immediately can "read back" cover-to-cover. . . . Over the years teachers, lacking surefire beginning books, have been forced to engage children in all sorts of reading readiness materials that have no connection whatsoever with a book, and sometimes even less with language. Consequently, children have been denied for six or more weeks fulfillment of their strong urge to read a book . . . all too many begin their reading careers by losing the urge to read and even by becoming confused about the act of reading. (Martin and Brogan, 1971, pp. 12–13)

Martin and Brogan, Stauffer, Allen, and others contend that children's *belief* that they can read, belief in themselves as readers, is the most basic factor underlying the acquisition of all other skills. In addition, the careful studies of beginning reading carried out by Marie Clay (1979) and others have shown us that there are many concepts about print and reading that beginners need to acquire, but most of them are usually not taught explicitly. They include concepts like the direction of the print, the concept of a word in print as a bound configuration, the idea that the print and not the picture tells the story, and others. Our experience tells us that the early scanning of dictations or books like the *Instant Readers* provides these basic orienting concepts much better than duplicator sheets or other lessons that fragment real reading.

In the case of children who have already begun to read, the need for real text is even stronger. Reading is not simply a matter of decoding words or sentences. It is an elaborate response to large structures of meaning — structures like paragaphs, episodes, arguments, chronologies, hierarchies, and whatever other structures authors may choose to convey their thoughts. We find all too often that reading materials are short and sterile. Since learning to read requires learning to respond to and make predictions about these larger structural elements, texts that do not have these structural elements do not teach children real reading. Teachers may not even realize that the reading that results is artificial, as long as reading test scores are adequate. But most testing procedures in regular use in our classrooms do not test real reading either: they test children on the same sorts of short, sterile passages with which the children are so often taught to read.

Our task is to get each student reading extended prose. The job may entail other types of activity, to be sure, but having children read rich, connected text should predominate over everything else.

Reading to Satisfy Inquiry

It is not enough to have children "just read." *What* they read and *why* they read it are also important. Real reading, the kind that fluent readers do every day, means reading to satisfy a variety of purposes. Sometimes we want to entertain ourselves, so we pick something that is really entertaining (we reject anything that isn't) and we normally read it quickly. Sometimes we have to learn about a subject. If we are preparing an academic paper, we may read from several books and look for ideas these several sources bring to bear on a single topic. We may read six novels, for example, to find out how a certain Victorian author developed female characters. Sometimes we read to find out how to do something. We may want to try a new procedure for improving comprehension, for example, and elect to read up on the directed reading-thinking activity described in Chapter Five. In this case we would read the relevant passages closely. We might read them several times and take notes. Then, after we had tried to carry out the procedure with students, we very likely would return to the passages and read them again, this time to make sure that what we did conformed to what the passage in the book described. We read for other reasons too, but the three just described give examples of the very different purposes we may have in mind.

If school instruction is to lead directly into fluent reading habits, it too must include real purposes. Moreover, the purposes must vary from time to time, which means that the tasks must not be limited to the reading period but extended right across the curriculum. Children have to read extensively for all subjects, such as science, social studies, health, art, and music and not just "reading." For a start, the book reports that children are required to do can be broadened out into research reports in some subject area field. The reading, and the discussion of it, should be carried out in the other textbooks a child is assigned, not just the basal readers. When teachers read to the children, the material should include interesting nonfiction as well as fiction. Listening can be made into a stimulating inquiry exercise if the techniques of the directed listening-thinking activity (see Chapters Three and Seven) are used.

It is important to note here that we are not only concerned with varying the subject areas of the reading materials but also in setting realistic and motivating purposes for doing the reading. Ordinarily, adults read something because they *want* to or because they *need* to. Children usually read something because they are *told* to. The difference in motivation is a big one, and the question is: How can we help children set real purposes for reading? The answer is to create a school situation that will call for reading as natural means to some important ends. Examples of such situations are inquiry units, when open-ended questions are placed before the whole class, and individuals or groups read and investigate the issues. Ultimately the students publish a newspaper, or hold a panel discussion, or make a television show about the questions. Thus reading is done as a natural and important part of the inquiry. Similarly, the teacher can provide equipment for carrying out an experiment or leave open a book passage that describes the steps for carrying it out. Or the class can plan a group play or television production and consult books on television photography, costume and set design, stage directions, and script writing.

Teachers should cultivate the habit of examining every unit they are about to teach and deciding how reading for a purpose can be incorporated in the most interesting way. Whether the subject is health, science, social studies, or something else, teachers should give the unit an activity component in which the children will have to do some creative project on their own rather than just following directions. It is usually the creative projects that give children the latitude to develop their own purposes for reading, to find out what they need to know to achieve some end, and then read to gain that knowledge. The teacher's role is to raise good questions, encourage children to frame the inquiry or set the plans for a project, and then to provide reading material and other resources that they can use.

On the question of how teachers can set up challenging projects that require real reading as a matter of course, John Merritt (1978) came up with the terms "Mickey Mouse" and "gerbil" activities. Merritt, and the British teachers he works with, noted that the closer a project came to some real purposes that real people would have in the real world, the stronger its potential to summon up real communication on the part of the children. With all due respect to the beloved cartoon character, they chose Mickey Mouse to denote activities that were cute and cleverly designed, but unreal. Gerbil activities were those that were essentially unpredictable and messy, yet capable of yielding real and sometimes unanticipated insights. Gerbils mess in their cages, have offspring, and sometimes die. Mickey never gets his white gloves dirty.

How can you tell a gerbil activity from a Mickey Mouse one? Here are two examples.

In some areas, local history is studied by reading histories of the area and doing library research. Such activities often culminate in a written or oral report to the class, a meal of local foods, or an art activity. They are usually fun but of a temporary nature, and the results are of little lasting value: Mickey Mouse.

Loban (1979) describes a project in which elderly people come to the school to record an "oral history." It includes reminiscence of important events as well as the interweaving of events from their personal lives and their personal opinions and values. These recordings are transcribed by the students, illustrated with old or recent photos and other artwork, typed, edited, and bound into books that become a treasured part of the school's and community's heritage. We know one rural area in which this was done, and when some of the elderly participants later died, their recorded accounts and the photographs they donated became a living legacy to those they left behind. The children involved came to know the elderly as real people with fascinating lives the children never guessed they had experienced: gerbil.

In a nearby high school, tenth-grade biology students were dissecting frogs. In one class, students carefully studied the structure of the frog's body, its diet, and life cycle. They completed detailed notes and drawings of their dissections at various stages, and prepared large colored drawings of the various parts of a frog's body, each carefully labeled and displayed around the science room. They painted a large mural of the life cycle of a frog and hung it in the hall. Everyone concerned enjoyed the drawings and the mural: Mickey Mouse.

In another class, after the dissection was completed the teacher proposed two problems. The students chose one that they would investigate and present to the class. The problems were:

1. Would you donate an eye or kidney to an organ bank? Would you donate your body to science? Why or why not? What is involved in doing so? How are the organs taken, stored, and used?
2. Would you eat a frog? Have you ever eaten one? If you were lost in the wilderness and starving, what would you eat? What would you refuse to eat? Why? If you were in a war and starving, where would you draw the line on what animals you would eat? In these situations, what have some people really eaten? Would you?

These studies resulted in such far-flung outcomes as visits to a local organ bank, talks by an undertaker and a surgeon, extended reading about famines, concentration camps, and wilderness survivors, a debate on the relative "value" of different forms of life, and a panel discussion by organ donors and recipients. The unit required weeks of work and took many surprising turns along the way. At times the teacher felt he had lost his grip on the curriculum, but he believed he had brought the students' own values into their study of biology: gerbil.

In order to see how far the normal school day has moved from gerbil activities, observe the practice of *uninterrupted sustained silent reading* (USSR) (McCracken and McCracken, 1972, 1978). This practice calls for shutting down the entire school curriculum for periods ranging from thirty to forty-five minutes a day. Its proponents claim that the children do more reading this way than they would otherwise. Given all the interruptions, the testing, and other nonreading distractions in reading classrooms like those described earlier in this section, it is possible that USSR may lead to more reading than most children are doing now. As Edmund Henderson (1981) has noted, however, USSR stands as a gaunt witness to the poverty of the school curriculum because it implies that we must shut down everything we are doing in order to have children read. What, we wonder with Henderson, *were* we doing? After writing out a day's lesson plans but before putting them into practice, teachers may now ask themselves, would the students be better off if we put all of this aside and simply *read* today? If the answer is yes, do it. If, however, the regular curriculum offers extended reading for real purposes every day, it will not be necessary to resort to such drastic means. The USSR has served one useful purpose, though: it has given reading teachers a fundamental test of their teaching ability.

Integrating the Language Arts

Reading, writing, speaking, and listening are all interrelated communication skills. Speaking and listening are usually thought of as "primary" functions by linguists — that is, language is primarily oral; writing and reading are derived from oral language. This does not mean that written language is of little importance in our world. On the contrary, adults depend on writing for their preeminent mode of communication.

The situation is different, however, in the case of children. Language for them is first a matter of speech, since they generally talk for five or more years before they read and write. Therefore, they must develop language structures in speech before they will be able to respond to them adequately in print (Allen, 1976). Children whose command of English syntax is not well developed, for example, will not make much sense of book language until their syntax matures.

Young children's listening comprehension is usually more fully developed than their speech production. Children can understand complex grammatical forms they hear before they can produce similar constructions (Brown, 1973). They can become sensitive to spoken language structures by listening and be better prepared to respond to similar structures when they encounter them in print. Therefore, listening practice should be developed at the same time that initial reading instruction is going on. Such practice in speaking and listening can help children because it develops their langue base. In time they will be able to transform visual symbols into language structures and thus be able to comprehend what they see in print.

What all this means is that children should listen to and discuss material read aloud to them: books, newspaper articles, songs, and poems. They should listen to one another describing things and be encouraged to press for information. They should summarize and restate what has been said and ask questions when things are not clear. Classroom dramatics activities provide good oral language stimulus, since drama and the physical movement it entails is an early-developing and powerful response to language (Moffett and Wagner, 1976).

What about writing? Writing is sometimes thought of as the "active" counterpart to reading, a "passive" process. We are very unhappy with this view because it takes the position that expression is active but reception is passive, which is of course nonsense. Goodman (1970) suggested that we construct for ourselves what an author is attempting to communicate as we predict what words and ideas may occur next. This is certainly a cognitively active process. Writing and reading trade on the resources of written language. They clearly help each other. We would not have the structures of written language available to us if we had not read them elsewhere. We would not have as fine a sensitivity to words and how they go together if we did not write.

Linguists (Chomsky, 1973; Chomsky and Halle, 1968) have demonstrated that our comprehension of words sometimes depends on our perceiving shared similarities of structure between words of a common origin. Thus, for example, *sign* and *signal* reveal their common origin from the Latin base *signum* and

*W*riting helps beginning readers understand that written language communicates and eases children into reading the words of others.

the meaning they have in common. It is true that fluent readers do not take the time to process all the structural features present in written words. Evidence of this lies in the fact that some people can see certain words numerous times but not be able to spell them.

Writing, however, forces us to concentrate on choosing words that reflect our meaning as precisely as possible and to compare our own output with the words and letters written by others. Do the letters used reflect the sounds heard? Do the letters look like those others have written (Chomsky, 1971)? It is in writing words that we deal with their features in earnest. Writers are often better readers, and one reason is that they deal carefully with word structures. They take more interest in print than people who do little writing. Mature writers have control over grammar, sentence construction, and paragraph organization. They use story structure phrases like "once upon a time," expressions like "therefore," "however," and other structures that reveal the organization of a piece of writing. People who write, children and adults, are more aware of such elements than those who don't write.

As we pointed out in Chapter Six, many young children like to invent their own spellings for words if encouraged to do so. In the process of creating these spellings, they go through a lot of sounding out. After all, in order to invent a spelling for a word, a child has first to examine the word and break it down into its constituent sounds. The next step, of course, is to find a letter that can represent each sound.

Invented spelling is a natural source of practice in *phonemic segmentation,* or the ability to break a word into its phonemic components and count the number of sounds heard.

As we saw in Chapter Six, invented spelling gives us an indication of how far the child's phonemic segmentation ability has advanced. Note, for example, these three spellings for the word *duck:*

Amie	*Burt*	*Larry*
D	DK	DOK

Amie's effort shows that letters spell words on the basis of their sounds, but she is not yet able to break the word down into its parts. Burt indicates that he can separate a word into more than one sound, but he is not yet sufficiently adept at separating the consonant and vowel sounds. Larry, however, is able to represent all three phonemes in *duck.* Note that the word has three phonemes represented by four letters, with *ck* standing for one sound.

It seems likely, as Chomsky (1971) has indicated, that giving children the opportunity to experiment with spelling helps them learn to read. We know of no studies that have subjected this point to rigorous testing, but we do have the accounts from a New Hampshire writing project in which a team of researchers carefully observed the writing development in several primary classrooms where creative writing and invented spelling are encouraged (Graves,

*W*ord sorts are productive group or individual activities for independent practice. Tonya is categorizing words by their initial sounds by sorting picture cards.

1979). According to Graves, the first graders did a tremendous amount of sounding out in the process of writing their early compositions. By videotaping children as they wrote and recording what they said, Graves demonstrated that the children repeated words, syllables, and individual letter sounds over and over to themselves as they spelled. They would decide on a word to write, say it several times, repeat the sounds they heard in sequence over and over and reread the word or a whole phrase as they selected and wrote letters to represent those sounds. These youngsters spontaneously demonstrated a great deal of letter-sound awareness and consciously attempted to choose letters they thought represented those sounds.

To summarize, one of the characteristics we look for in a productive reading classroom is a wise combination of the language arts: a careful development of spoken language and listening and writing as well as reading. These subjects need not all be pursued at the same time, but teachers should make it their responsibility to see that every child works in each of the four areas of the language arts some time during each day.

Displaying Reading Materials

One of the authors of this book needed a certain woodworking tool while traveling in Mexico. He didn't know the Spanish word for "dovetail saw," but he assumed he could browse around the hardware store until he found one. He quickly discovered how wrong he was. All he saw was a counter up front where the salespeople took orders. The storage room was in the back, out of sight. In order to buy something, the customer had to name it or describe it sufficiently well for the clerk to make a successful hunt for it in the jam-packed storage area. In this case, the salesclerk made several trips. He brought out four different saws, one at a time, and two kinds of knives, but no dovetail saw. The author left empty-handed.

There was a time when most stores in this country were like that; the customers knew what they wanted, and if they didn't want something in particular nobody tried to talk them into buying. How different things are now! Most of us go to a store to buy one thing and walk out with several. Stores always succeed in putting fascinating, irresistible things in front of us. Merchants know this, as you can see in any supermarket. In order to enter you must often make your way through a maze of baked goods, soft drinks, potato chips, and beer. Look at the cereal aisle; all the sugary cereals are located at a child's eye level. The checkout aisles are bottlenecks jammed with displays of candy bars, gum, cigarettes, flashlight batteries, small toys, and magazines. *Try* to leave without one of these!

It is useful to compare the way schools sell literacy with the way American supermarkets sell their products. The stores advertise with catchy slogans and tunes, wrap their items in colorful packages, give away free samples, feature well-known people giving testimonials, and lay out the stores so you are stopped by artful displays at every turn. What does your classroom or school library do to sell its contents? Is it possible to get in and out again without being seized with an irresistible desire to pick up something to read?

As part of the countywide reading study referred to earlier, the authors of this book were requested to do a survey of a school district's libraries. These were our findings. Does this sound like your library?

> If there is a serious effort in this county to promote literacy, the action has bypassed most of the school libraries. Too many libraries are stuffy, bland, and uninteresting. If they were grocery stores, nobody would buy anything in them. We looked in vain for eye-stopping displays of reading matter, interesting library activities in progress, or comfortable places to plop down with a book. What we saw again and again were tall shelves looming around the walls with volume after volume of tired old books bearing oppressive titles. We saw children in hard wooden seats at long, bare tables. We saw librarians performing clerical and police functions only. Little use of students' work in any form was seen anywhere. We observed no reading aloud, no book talks,

little unrequested aid in book selection, and little encouragement in talking about books.

Our report was harsh but accurate. Particularly ironic was the fact that the school officials talked freely and often about their commitment to reading. Yet the libraries were set up to handle only highly motivated readers, those who knew just what they wanted and weren't put off by unfriendly treatment or faded books tucked cover-to-cover into high shelves. The trouble was that none of the schools seemed to have any such readers. And the libraries weren't circulating many books either.

How can a school library sell reading successfully? Like a supermarket, it has to be full of lots of wonderful things, displayed in such appealing ways that children can't help but pick them up and read them. Books there must be, of course, of every kind, everywhere. As many as possible should be displayed on table tops and low shelves, standing up with front cover foremost. They must be at a height that invites picking them up. Using the topmost shelves, over the librarian's head, for display of books defeats the purpose. There should be numerous magazines and paperbacks conveniently displayed and located near comfortable chairs or floor pillows to invite readers to begin their reading right there. Traditionally libraries have been furnished as places to study, but to appeal to large numbers of students, they should be furnished as places to read for pleasure. Hence the floor pillows and soft furniture alongside the regular chairs and tables. The library should be gay and appealing with children's art, crafts, and writing everywhere. Mobiles, posters, paper book jackets, poems and stories, jokes and riddles, shoebox dioramas — all can be produced in the classroom and displayed in the library. Students will feel that the library is *theirs* if their work is incorporated in it.

Classroom libraries are another necessary ingredient for a successful reading program. Barbe (1961) suggested a minimum of 100 books at any one time. The school librarian can probably arrange for you to keep a collection of books in your room for several weeks or a month at a time. Building classroom libraries is a good project for PTA groups, and students too can donate books they have purchased through the paperback book club. A great idea is to have stickers that read "Donated through the generosity of ____" to put in these books. Classroom libraries, like school libraries, should be comfortable, inviting places where you can curl up with a book. A few low shelves and a bit of carpet may be enough, with lots of books arranged with their covers facing out to attract browsers (Fader, 1976; Veatch, 1968).

Classroom libraries have a couple of advantages over school libraries. First, the children have greater access to them. There are many times during the day — before school, at lunch, or between activities — when they have time to browse through the classroom library. Also, students in the class are likely to have read some of the books, and by talking about them they may

C *lassrooms that really promote reading and writing feature functional, everyday reading tasks. Here a classroom grocery store of empty packages is a continuing source of words, directions to follow, and dialogues to make up.*

arouse the interests of others. The teacher can help this process along by inviting children to talk informally about good books they have read recently from the classroom library or elsewhere.

After you read a book to the class, it is a good idea to place it in the classroom library. Usually at least one child will want to read the book after hearing it. Whenever a new book comes in, or if a topic comes up that is covered in a book in the classroom library, call it to the children's attention by talking briefly about it and displaying it prominently.

A special source of books for the classroom library is what the children write themselves. Classroom publishing can be a highly motivating activity for students, and the books that result are usually the most popular in the school. Most teachers use book publishing as an occasion to point out the need for editing and writing a final draft. Once students have written the text for a published book, they can create a hard-cover binding so it can be circulated. Allen (1976) described very fully several classroom centers developed for the purpose of publishing children's writing. He goes into much detail because he believes that publishing of their own work is the "peak experience" in early reading and writing. He organized committees to work on the editing, typing or printing, duplicating, illustrating, and binding of books.

Binding sturdy classroom books is easy:

1. Cut two pieces of cardboard for the front and back covers of the book. Make sure they are the same size. Lay the pieces side by side. Leave enough space between for the pages to be inserted. The width of a pencil is enough.

FIGURE 10.1.

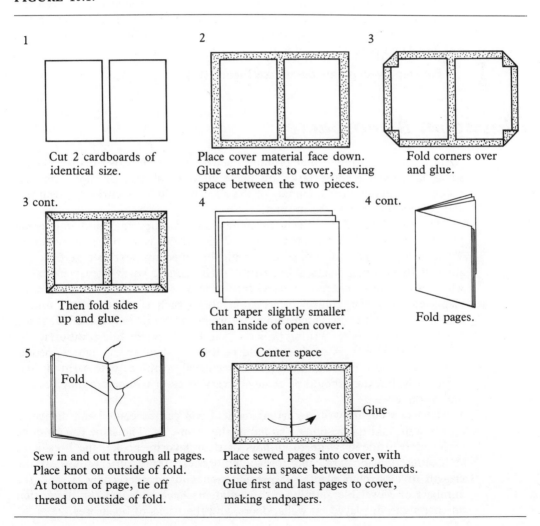

1

Cut 2 cardboards of identical size.

2

Place cover material face down. Glue cardboards to cover, leaving space between the two pieces.

3

Fold corners over and glue.

3 cont.

Then fold sides up and glue.

4

Cut paper slightly smaller than inside of open cover.

4 cont.

Fold pages.

5

Fold

Sew in and out through all pages. Place knot on outside of fold. At bottom of page, tie off thread on outside of fold.

6

Center space

Glue

Place sewed pages into cover, with stitches in space between cardboards. Glue first and last pages to cover, making endpapers.

2. Place the cardboard on top of the cover material which has been cut 1 in. larger than the cardboard on all sides. Use any attractive paper, wallpaper, fabric or contact paper for covers. Bond the cover material to the cardboard with glue, or photographic drymount paper and a warm iron.
3. Fold down the corners of the cover material over the cardboard. Then fold over the edges and glue the corners and edges to the cardboard.
4. While the glue dries, cut sheets of paper for pages. Cut each sheet slightly smaller than the entire opened cover. Don't cut down the middle of the sheet! Instead, fold here and sew the sheets down the fold using white thread. Place stitches about ¼ inch apart.
5. Place sewn pages into cover with stitching against the space between the cardboards. Glue the first page to the inside front cover, covering up the raw edges of the material. Repeat with the last page and back cover. This forms end papers and holds the entire book together.

For step-by-step illustration, see Figure 10.1.

Classroom Atmosphere

A classroom atmosphere that promotes active reading has two main features. First, functional reading tasks are made an integral part of classroom life. Second, the psychological climate of the classroom induces curiosity, security, and respect for people and property.

In classrooms that actively promote literacy, important and interesting messages displayed at students' eye level should be very much in evidence. Written instructions for animal care could be taped up next to a gerbil cage, along with pertinent facts about them: their names, when they were born, what they eat, and where they came from. Pictures of class members could be displayed with biographical information about each student written underneath. For activities in which things are weighed, compared, classified, taken apart, and put together writing projects would be a worthwhile addition to the regular assignments. Wall charts could be used to show sports figures, people in the news, historical automobiles, or medieval costumes with written facts about each, but they should be changed every week or two before they become dull to the eye.

Letters students write to arrange a field trip can be copied and displayed on the wall, and the responses added as they come in. The same can be done with letters students write to authors of their favorite books, the President, astronauts, movie stars, and foreign embassies. Daily observations of the growth of classroom plants, of precipitation and weather changes, and the numbers of recyclable aluminum cans students have collected can be written on charts and displayed on walls, doors, and the backs of bookcases.

In short, reading and writing in the classroom should serve functions for which adults value them: they record important events and facts and offer a means of communication with others across space and time.

The climate of classrooms for reading instruction should encourage curiosity and risk taking but of course within the bounds of respect for others.

Language instruction often creates noise. The activities necessary for developing language ability cannot flourish in a silent classroom, but children need order, too. They need at least enough order to feel secure, to know that their concentration will not be unduly interrupted when they are engaged in a task, and to be assured that the teacher is not silently seething and about to erupt because they are too noisy. One can usually tell when the activity level in the classroom is just right. There is neither an oppressive silence nor a brain-jarring din, and the individuals in that setting look intent on what they are doing, but not tense.

There are several ways to set up such a classroom. One is to make clear to children what is expected of them in the way of behavior and where the limits are. Many teachers have class meetings at the beginning of the year, when they allow children to suggest rules for conduct and discuss each one before the class either accepts it or rejects it. Those that pass the discussion (and which the teacher can live with) are written up on tagboard and posted on the wall. The teacher then reminds the children of these rules from time to time, and occasionally the class will revise one or more of them.

William Glasser's *Schools Without Failure* (1969) program extends the idea of the class meeting throughout the year. It is modeled on the old town meeting, a form of government in rural New England where all the people in the town came together regularly to discuss issues affecting life in the area. Glasser's class meetings are like that: once or more each week all the students sit in a big circle and, under the teacher's direction, discuss issues of importance to them. The classroom atmosphere, problems they are having, things they are excited about or frustrated about, new procedures they are going to try out, all are discussed calmly and openly in a setting where everyone is encouraged to participate.

Another means to a relaxed, but businesslike atmosphere is for the teacher to make sure that all the children know what they are doing, why they are doing it, and how well they are doing it. In Chapter Two we discussed the notion of cognitive clarity. What this means is that children should know what reading is for, how to go about learning it, and what all the "parts" are: words, letters, lines, sounds, and so on. We have visited too many classrooms where children were aimlessly filling out duplicator sheets. "Why are you doing this?" we would ask. "Teacher said to," was the reply. "But what are you trying to learn by doing this?" "*I* dunno" was often the response. Cognitive clarity is best achieved when the teacher tells the students what they are to do and what purpose it serves.

The question of knowing how well they are doing is a tricky one. Many teachers find their children *too* eager to know how they rate in relation to their peers. "Whadja get? Whadja get?" is a disturbing thing to hear children say over and over to their classmates. Yet the other extreme is not really better. If they go for long periods of time without knowing how they are doing, whether or not they are doing what they are "supposed to," or whether they are meeting the expectations of whoever set up the tasks for them, they often get listless and lose interest in the activities. Ideally, we want them to want to do well, although it is not always healthy for them to define success in terms of their peers. One of the best ways to let children know how well they are doing is to compare them against themselves. Keep records and samples of their work (in their work folders). Show them past samples from time to time and get them to compare their previous work with their present production. Point out whether there is a lot of progress, a little, or no progress. Some teachers have lists of goals written out for all their students. When the time comes for a periodic review, they check the progress against the goals; for example, how many words have they added to their word banks? How many trade books have they read? What projects have they done? Realistically, this sort of evaluation will not replace grades in most schools, but it does give children a qualitative idea of what they are doing right and what they can do better.

One final point we should make about the classroom atmosphere is the arrangement of the space. Every elementary classroom should have an area for small group assembly, arranged in a place where the teacher can see the rest of the room. There should also be a quiet area for reading, which is out of the way of traffic patterns through the classroom (i.e., not situated between the seats and the bathrooms). Each class should have an activity area where children can make puppets, sew together books, and so on.

Different teachers will require different sorts of work areas. In a typical class there will be areas for learning centers as well as small group meeting areas, quiet reading areas, louder activity areas, and neutral desk areas. There are three things the teacher should do when planning classroom space to accommodate these different areas:

1. Arrange the space so that you can keep visual contact with all or most of the room.
2. Make sure that the children won't bother one another with their noise; avoid putting a quiet area adjacent to a loud one.
3. Leave room for travel paths so the children won't create a disturbance in getting from one place to another. Plan in advance where most of the movement in the class will be concentrated and leave open space for it, but be prepared to revise your plan if traffic patterns prove to flow elsewhere.

Careful planning of space can eliminate many problems before they arise. Compared with other settings where people spend long periods of time, twenty-plus children in one classroom is a lot of bodies in one space. Teachers must plan carefully to coordinate the space so that all these bodies can carry out their varied activities without disturbing others. If they succeed in this, teachers will have gone a long way toward achieving a relaxed but businesslike atmosphere.

Summary

It is our belief that reading assessment cannot end with the child; we must also look closely at the classroom. In order to have a good reading instruction environment, there are four major guidelines we ought to follow:

1. Instructional goals should be set by informed teachers, not dictated by commercial programs. Under this principle we noted that teachers should have an adequate understanding of how children learn to read, and they should have the responsibility for making day-to-day instructional decisions consistent with their understanding of the reading process and the needs of their students.

2. Children in a reading class should spend their time doing profitable tasks. Careful examination has revealed that in many classes, children spend only a few minutes a day reading real text while most of the time is spent doing nonreading activities. The tasks we believe should occupy the most time are reading aloud to the students, having the students themselves read real text, and seeing to it that they read to satisfy inquiry. Other tasks are undoubtedly worthwhile, but these should be strongly in evidence. Integrating the language arts is also advised, if not during the same period, at least during the same day. Since reading development is interrelated with the development of oral language and with writing, teachers should see that all these communication skills go forward.

3. Interesting materials should be displayed in an eye-catching manner in the classroom library as well as in the school library. We cannot assume that the students will have sufficient interest in reading to go to the library and ask for a book by title, no matter how old or young they may be. The teacher and librarian must use every device they can think of to put interesting materials in the path of children, in such a way that they cannot be ignored. Setting up classroom libraries is most worthwhile, and books written and bound by the children themselves should be part of the collection.

4. The classroom should have a relaxed but businesslike atmosphere: open enough for students to pursue their tasks without undue pressure, yet sufficiently controlled for them to feel secure and free from distraction. Creating such an atmosphere involves the following. First, the teacher should give the guidelines for behavior, although they may also be set by the whole class after discussion. Second, the teacher should make sure all of the students understand the purposes behind the tasks in which they are engaged. Third, they should be given progress reports from time to time on how they are

doing, but these reports should not take the form of comparisons with other children. Fourth, the classroom space should be arranged so that the full range of tasks can be carried out while keeping distractions to a minimum, which requires careful planning of the respective locations of a reading circle, an independent reading area, an activity area, and traffic lanes. The teacher must be able to maintain visual contact with all parts of the room.

Extension Activities

1. If you are not yet teaching, visit a class in grades one through six during the reading instruction period. Pick a child at random and sit somewhere so that you can observe what the student is doing. Keep track of the amount of time spent on reading connected text during the period. If you are in a class, arrange to have three pupils visit one class, each to observe the reading time spent by students designated as good, average, or poor readers, respectively. Compare the results.

2. Locate an elementary reading program that uses a skills management system, one published by the basal system company or one bought to supplement the basal instruction. Look over the teacher's manuals. Without listing every skill, can you state in simple terms what competencies the system suggests students should have? Which seem to you to be readiness skills? Which deal with word recognition and analysis? Which with reading comprehension, especially comprehension beyond the literal level? How do these competencies compare with those we described in Chapters Three, Five, and Six?

3. Identify the work that one child would typically carry out in the management system. Choose any skill level you wish. Try to calculate the total amount of time the student spends doing each of the following activities each week (Table 10.1).

4. Interview five teachers. Ask them to describe:
   a. four activities they feel are most effective for teaching word knowledge (recognition of words and their meanings)
   b. four activities they feel are most effective in developing reading comprehension

   If the teachers mention the use of commercial materials such as SRA kits, ask them to describe what the students *do* in such materials that is effective.

5. Interview four students of different ages. Ask them to describe:
   a. the activities they do in reading or language arts that *help* them the most in learning to read or improving their reading
   b. the activities they *enjoy* the most in reading or language arts

   How do their answers compare? How do they compare with the activities the teachers described as being most helpful?

TABLE 10.1 Student activity time.

ACTIVITY	TIME (IN HOURS OR FRACTIONAL HOURS PER WEEK)
1. Listening to stories	_____
2. Listening to nonfiction material	_____
3. Reading fiction text (more than a paragraph)	_____
4. Reading nonfiction text (more than a paragraph)	_____
5. Workbook activities	_____
6. Duplicator sheet activities	_____
7. Discussions and dramatics	_____
8. Extended writing	_____
9. Watching television	_____
10. Word games, etc.	_____
11. Other	_____

Total time reading (3 + 4)	_____
Total time listening (1 + 2)	_____
Total time discussing (7)	_____
Total time on worksheets (5 + 6)	_____
Total time writing (8)	_____

Suggested Readings

George, Mary Yanaga. **Language Art: An Ideabook.** *Scranton, Pa.: Chandler Publishing Company, 1970.* Reading teachers will find valuable advice in language arts methods books. This one is short, and also especially thoughtful.

Griffin, Peg. **"How and When Does Reading Occur in the Classroom?"** *Theory into Practice XVI, No. 5 (December 1977): 376–383.* A study conducted at the Center for Applied Linguistics that examines the reading occurring in classrooms outside of the reading circle.

Guthrie, John T.; Martaza, Victor, and Seifert, Mary. **"Impacts of Instructional Time in Reading."** *In Lauren B. Resnick and Phyllis A. Weaver, eds. Theory and Practice of Early Reading, Vol. 3. Hillsdale, N.J.: Lawrence Erlbaum Associates, 1979.* Explores the often neglected premise that the time the child spends interacting with print affects achievement more than the instructional method employed.

References

Allen, R. Van. *Language Experiences in Communication.* Boston: Houghton Mifflin, 1976.

Barbe, Walter B. *Educator's Guide to Personalized Reading Instruction.* Englewood Cliffs, N.J.: Prentice-Hall, 1961.

Brown, Roger. *A First Language: The Early Stages.* Cambridge, Mass.: Harvard University Press, 1973.

Chomsky, Carol. "Write First, Read Later." *Childhood Education* (March 1971): 296–299.

Chomsky, Carol. "Reading, Writing, and Phonology." In Frank Smith, ed. *Psycholinguistics and Reading.* N.Y.: Holt, Rhinehart & Winston, 1973.

Chomsky, Noam & Halle, Morris. *The Sound Pattern of English.* N.Y.: Harper & Row, 1968.

Clay, Marie M. *The Early Detection of Reading Difficulties: A Diagnostic Survey with Recovery Procedures,* 2nd ed., Exeter, N.H.: Heinemann, 1979.

Cramer, Ronald L. "Reading to Children: Why and How." *The Reading Teacher* 28, No. 5 (Feb. 1975), 460–463.

Estes, Thomas H. & Johnstone, Julie P. "Twelve Easy Ways to Make Readers Hate Reading (and One Difficult Way to Make Them Love It)." *Language Arts* (Nov.–Dec. 1977): 891–897.

Fader, Daniel. *The New Hooked on Books.* N.Y.: Berkley, 1976.

Glasser, William. *Schools Without Failure.* N.Y.: Harper & Row, 1969.

Goodman, Kenneth S. "Behind the Eye: What Happens in Reading." In Kenneth Goodman & Olive Niles, eds. *Reading: Process and Program.* Urbana, Ill.: National Council of Teachers of English, 1970.

Graves, Donald. "The Growth and Development of First Grade Writers." Paper presented at the annual meeting of the Canadian Council of Teachers of English, Ottawa, May 1979.

Henderson, Edmund H. *Learning to Read and Spell: The Child's Knowledge of Words.* Chicago: Northern Illinois University Press, 1981.

Huck, Charlotte S. *Children's Literature in the Elementary School,* 3rd ed. N.Y.: Holt, Rinehart & Winston, 1976.

Huus, Helen. "Teaching Literature at the Elementary School Level." *The Reading Teacher* 26, No. 8 (May 1973): 795–801.

Loban, Walter. "Relationships Between Language and Literacy." *Language Arts* 56, No. 5 (May 1979), 485–486.

Martin, Bill Jr. & Brogan, Peggy. *Bill Martin's Instant Readers, Teacher's Guide.* N.Y.: Holt, Rinehart & Winston, 1971.

Martin, Bill Jr. & Brogan, Peggy. *Sounds of Language.* N.Y.: Holt, Rinehart & Winston, 1974.

McCracken, R. A. & McCracken, M. J. *Reading Is Only the Tiger's Tail.* San Rafael, Cal.: Leswing Press, 1972.

McCracken, R. A. & McCracken, M. J. "Modeling Is the Key to Sustained Silent Reading." *The Reading Teacher* 31, No. 4 (April 1978): 406–408.

Merritt, John. *Reading, Writing and Relevance.* London: Open University Press, 1978.

Moffett, James & Wagner, Betty. *Student-Centered Language Arts and Reading, K-13: A Handbook for Teachers,* 2nd ed. Boston: Houghton Mifflin, 1976.

Morris, R. Darrell. "Some Aspects of the Instructional Environment and Learning to Read." *Language Arts* 56, No. 5 (May 1979): 497–507.

Sarason, Seymour B. *The Culture of the School and the Problem of Change.* Boston: Allyn and Bacon, 1971.

Stauffer, Russell G. *The Language-Experience Approach to the Teaching of Reading,* rev. ed. N.Y.: Harper & Row, 1980.

Veatch, Jeannette. *How to Teach Reading with Children's Books,* 2nd ed. N.Y.: Citation Press, 1968.

Index